Converging Worlds of Welfare?

with thanks for all
your help

[signature]

Creating Sustainable Growth in Europe Series

Creating sustainable growth in europe (*csge*) was a policy research initiative launched and funded by the Anglo-German Foundation. It was designed to explore how—if at all—we can increase economic growth in Europe without tipping the balance against social justice and the environment. Four linked research programmes took up this challenge through original empirical research and by pooling and comparing data, experience, and ideas from the UK, Germany, and beyond. The initiative culminated in a series of publications, conferences, and seminars in late 2009. For more information see www.agf.org.uk

Series Editors

A. B. Atkinson and Ray Cunningham

Books in the series

Environmental Tax Reform (ETR)
A Policy for Green Growth
Edited by Paul Ekins and Stefan Speck

Converging Worlds of Welfare?
British and German Social Policy in the 21st Century
Edited by Jochen Clasen

Converging Worlds of Welfare?

British and German Social Policy in the 21st Century

Edited by Jochen Clasen

OXFORD
UNIVERSITY PRESS

OXFORD
UNIVERSITY PRESS

Great Clarendon Street, Oxford OX2 6DP

Oxford University Press is a department of the University of Oxford.
It furthers the University's objective of excellence in research, scholarship,
and education by publishing worldwide in

Oxford New York

Auckland Cape Town Dar es Salaam Hong Kong Karachi
Kuala Lumpur Madrid Melbourne Mexico City Nairobi
New Delhi Shanghai Taipei Toronto

With offices in

Argentina Austria Brazil Chile Czech Republic France Greece
Guatemala Hungary Italy Japan Poland Portugal Singapore
South Korea Switzerland Thailand Turkey Ukraine Vietnam

Oxford is a registered trade mark of Oxford University Press
in the UK and in certain other countries

Published in the United States
by Oxford University Press Inc., New York

© Oxford University Press 2011

British Library Cataloguing in Publication Data

Data available

Library of Congress Cataloging in Publication Data

Data available

Typeset by SPI Publisher Services, Pondicherry, India
Printed in Great Britain
on acid-free paper by
MPG Books Group, Bodmin and King's Lynn

ISBN 978–0–19–958449–9

1 3 5 7 9 10 8 6 4 2

Foreword

In 2004, the Trustees of the Anglo-German Foundation made a brave and important decision. They decided that the Foundation had largely fulfilled the objectives for which it was created in 1973 and that it should bring its work to a conclusion in 2009. This was a brave decision since few institutions have the courage to draw an end to their activities when they have served their purpose. It was an important decision, since they decided to spend the Foundation's final resources on a five-year major research project. It is the fruits of this research that are reported in the impressive volumes in this series.

The world has changed greatly since 1973, and so too have the two countries—Germany and the United Kingdom—who established the Foundation. At that time, the United Kingdom was just on the point of becoming a member of the European Communities, joining the six founder Member States. Germany was divided, as was the world, politically and economically. Today is very different. The European Communities have become the European Union, with twenty-seven Member States, and more countries applying to join. China, Brazil, and India have become major economic powers. It is therefore not surprising that the Foundation decided that its founding purpose—in encouraging the exchange of knowledge, ideas, and best practice between the two countries—had been served. These activities have now moved to a global plane. As it was put by Ray Cunningham, final Director, in his history of the Anglo-German Foundation, the two systems should now be seen, not just together, but 'rather as two linked entities within a much larger economic and political whole' (*The Anglo-German Foundation 1973–2009*, AGF, London, 2009).

Concern with the changing world context underlay the Trustees' choice of subject for the final major research initiative: *creating sustainable growth in europe (csge)*. As they recognized, the key issue faced by policy makers, and by individual citizens, is the capacity to adapt to global developments in a way that preserves the essential qualities of our societies. This will involve institutional change—including, as they themselves have demonstrated, that institutions should come and go. Change is inevitably disruptive. It will necessitate major shifts in our future lifestyles, and the burden of adjustment needs to be shared fairly. In achieving the necessary change, a key role will be played by research. All of the four programmes that formed part of the *csge* initiative may be seen as contributing to our understanding of the problem of reconciling the desire for progress with environmental sustainability and social justice.

Indeed, in highlighting environmental and social sustainability several years ago, when the *csge* initiative was launched, the Foundation was ahead of the public debate. Regrettably, it remains, five years later, just as much the case that we need to bring together research on environmental sustainability with the mainstream debate about macroeconomic policy, employment, and growth. We have not really grasped the macroeconomic nettle. Nor is it sufficiently recognized that sustainability at a global level can only be achieved if we address at the same time the longstanding issue of securing more even global development. We need to remember the words of President Heinemann, when announcing the creation of the Foundation: 'all of us, young or old, face the necessity to halt the ravaging of the resources of nature and the poisoning of our environment and food, in order to counter the hunger of millions of people which can lead to world-wide conflict' (quoted in the history of the Anglo-German Foundation referred to above).

How can the research of the *csge* initiative, reported in these volumes, contribute to the policy debate? Here I will highlight just two themes. The first is the integration of economic and social policy. Too often these are treated as unconnected, and today, with government debt dominating policy discussion throughout the industrialized world, there is a serious risk that the positive functions of public spending will be ignored—to our long-term cost. But issues such as pensions have to be seen as an integrated whole. Pensions are not just relevant to macroeconomic stability, but affect the lives of most of us. Moreover, in the debate about future consumption levels, pensions form a key part of any intergenerational compact. As should investment in infrastructure. There are many other examples where research can facilitate joined-up policy-making. As the EU moves slowly towards a common immigration policy, the design of the policy has to take account of the implications for the labour market, for the macroeconomy, for social cohesion, and of the environmental impact. When we discuss the introduction of environmental taxes, we have to consider their distributional burden. Sustainability is a social as well as an environmental concern.

The second theme is the identification of the *key actors*. The mission of the Foundation was to contribute to the policy process and to encourage exchange between researchers and practitioners. Over the past third of a century, the policy process has changed. Evidently, the EU is now a leading world player, and, for all the inherent difficulties in making decisions with so many Member States, is increasingly providing the locus for policy formation. Power has also shifted downwards, with increased responsibilities being assumed by regional or local governments. In this respect, the United

Kingdom today looks more like the Federal Republic of Germany. But policy is not just made by politicians. Research on the *csge* initiative has emphasized the key role of managers, the role of social partners, and the role of families. We need to understand better the mechanisms by which change is determined and facilitated.

The *csge* initiative was steered by an Academic Advisory Board, which I chaired, and I would like to end by thanking the members of the Board for their helpful and constructive participation, and Ray Cunningham and his colleagues at the Foundation, with whom it was a great pleasure to work.

Tony Atkinson

September 2010

Acknowledgements

Most chapters in this book arose from research conducted as part of the initiative 'Sustainable Welfare and Sustainable Growth in Europe' (2006–9), commissioned by the Anglo-German Foundation. We would like to thank the Anglo-German Foundation not only for research funding but also for the always collaborative, helpful, and friendly support received. In particular, we would like to express our thanks to Ray Cunningham, Ann Pfeiffer, Annette Birkholz, and Regina Vogel.

We would also like to thank colleagues who provided invaluable input as members of the programme steering group: Jane Lewis, Kathleen Thelen, Jørgen Goul-Andersen, Claus Offe, and Maurizio Ferrera; as well as those who supported particular projects: Karen Andersen, Thomas Bahle, Giuliano Bonoli, Rosemary Crompton, Linda Hantrais, John Hills, Christina Klenner, Trudie Knijn, Edeltraud Roller, Friedbert Rüb, Adrian Sinfield, Stefan Svallfors, and Wim van Oorschot. Helpful comments and contributions were received from Ute Klammer, Tania Burchardt and Holger Lengfeld, and Patrick Sachweh.

Finally, for research assistance I would like to thank Jannis Johann and Evgeniya Plotnikova.

Jochen Clasen

Edinburgh, July 2010

Contents

Contents

List of Figures

List of Figures

List of Tables

Notes on Contributors

Paul Bridgen is a Senior Lecturer in Social Policy at the University of Southampton. His main interests are in pension policy and the politics of policy making, mainly from a comparative perspective. His work has been published in, amongst others, *Ageing and Society*, *West European Politics*, and *Social Policy and Administration*. Recent book publications include *Private Pensions versus Social Inclusion? Non-state Provision for Citizens at Risk in Europe* (2007, with Traute Meyer and Barbara Riedmüller).

Christoph Burkhardt is Ph.D. fellow at the Bremen International Graduate School of Social Sciences (BIGSSS). His areas of research are migration, comparative welfare state research, and social inequality.

Jochen Clasen is Professor of Comparative Social Policy in the School of Social and Political Science at the University of Edinburgh. He has published on social security policy, comparative welfare state analysis, labour market policy, and unemployment, mainly in a European context.

Mary Daly is Professor of Sociology at the School of Sociology, Social Policy and Social Work at Queen's University Belfast. Among the fields on which she has published are poverty, welfare, gender, family, and the labour market. Much of her work is comparative, in a European and international context, and she is especially interested in matters to do with how policies in different European countries relate to families.

Timo Fleckenstein is a Lecturer in Social Policy at the London School of Economics and Political Science. His main research interest is the politics of social policy, with a focus on labour market and family policies from a comparative perspective. His research has been published, among others, in the *Journal of European Social Policy*, *Social Policy & Administration*, and the *British Journal of Industrial Relations*.

Ann-Kathrin Jüttner studied paedagogy, sociology, and gender studies at the University of Göttingen. She was a research assistant in the project 'The Gateway of Family and Education Policy' at the University of Applied Sciences in Cologne. Presently she is a doctoral candidate in the research project 'Language support for children with migration background at preschool level,' which is based at the University of Braunschweig (Göttingen).

Sigrid Leitner is a political scientist. She holds a professorship in Social Policy at the University of Applied Sciences in Cologne. Her research focuses on comparative social policy analysis, pension and family policy, and gender effects of social policy.

Kathrin Leuze is Assistant Professor for Education Sociology at the Free University of Berlin and directs a research group conducting the German National Education Panel Study in the fields of vocational education and training and lifelong learning at the Social Science Research Center Berlin (WZB).

Rose Martin is a member of the Unemployment and Labour Market Disadvantage team at the Institute for Employment Studies in Brighton, where she contributes to a variety of research and evaluation projects. She was previously employed at the School of Social Policy, Sociology and Social Research, University of Kent, working on a comparison of British and German attitudes to social justice and the welfare state.

Steffen Mau is Professor of Political Sociology and Comparative Social Research at the University of Bremen and Vice Dean of the Bremen International Graduate School of Social Sciences (BIGSSS). His areas of research are comparative welfare state research, inequality, Europeanization, and transnationalization.

Traute Meyer is a Reader in Social Policy, University of Southampton. Most recently she has conducted research projects and published in the fields of European welfare systems, pensions and social inclusion, business interests, and social policy.

Anneli Rüling is a sociologist and political scientist in Berlin. Her research interests include family policy, international comparative welfare state analysis, and reconciliation of work and family. She is co-editor of the journal *Femina Politica*.

Martin Seeleib-Kaiser is Professor of Comparative Social Policy and Politics and Fellow of Green Templeton College, University of Oxford. His research focuses on the politics and political economy of social policy. Recent book publications include *The Dual Transformation of the German Welfare State* (with P. Bleses), *Party Politics and Social Welfare* (with S. v. Dyk and M. Roggenkamp), and *Welfare State Transformations* (ed.). He has published, among other journals, in *American Sociological Review*, the *British Journal of Industrial Relations*, *Comparative Political Studies*, *Social Policy and Administration*, and *West European Politics*.

Peter Taylor-Gooby, FBA, FRSA, AcSS, is Professor of Social Policy at the University of Kent, Director of the ESRC Social Contexts and Responses to Risk Programme, and Co-director of the Risk Research Centre at Beijing Normal University. Recent publications include *Reframing Social Citizenship* (Oxford University Press), *Risk in Social Science*, (with Jens Zinn, Oxford University Press), *Ideas and the Welfare State* (Palgrave), and *New Risks, New Welfare* (Oxford University Press).

Lisa Warth is Associate Expert on Gender at the United Nations Economic Commission for Europe. She holds a Ph.D. from the London School of Economics and Political Science, where her research focused on the importance of time in the work/family interface. The views expressed in her chapter are those of the author and do not necessarily reflect the views of the United Nations.

Michaela Willert is a sociologist and works as a Senior Research Assistant at the Political Science Department of the Freie Universität Berlin. She has participated in several national and international research projects in the area of pensions, with a special focus on pensions and the consequences of pension reforms, privatization, and Europeanization for social inclusion.

1

Introduction

Jochen Clasen

Before the onset of the current financial and economic crisis, the future of advanced welfare states seemed already to be in doubt. During the course of the 1990s it became clear that growing economic internationalization would provide opportunities and create new jobs, but also pose employment problems manifest in registered unemployment and other forms of labour market inactivity. The shift from industrial to post-industrial labour markets and the growing service-sector dominance implied a lower potential for productivity gains. Demographic challenges and lower economic growth than in earlier decades put pressure on welfare state resources (Pierson 1998). However, simply dismantling traditional welfare state structures and shifting social protection from collective to individual responsibility seemed politically, socially, and also economically counterproductive. Welfare states play a vital role in ensuring that growth is economically and socially sustainable. Economic and employment growth can be supported by social protection programmes as these help to ensure social integration and social inclusion in the face of rapid societal change, while keeping costs at a widely acceptable level. Social policies not only contain poverty and reduce inequality, but contribute to a healthier and more educated population and thereby influence life chances and opportunity structures, support socially disadvantaged groups, and help maintain social solidarity in the face of rapid societal change.

Industrialized nations have thus been increasingly faced with a serious challenge: to reconstruct existing welfare state structures in order to adapt to changing socioeconomic conditions while not undermining the role of, and popular support for, collective welfare provision. The particular intensity and manifestation of this challenge, as well as the feasibility of engaging in innovative policy responses, varies across countries partly because of differences in national contexts, including those in welfare state institutions. In this respect, a comparative investigation into ways in which policies have been changing in the United Kingdom and Germany and are shaping up for the twenty-first century seems highly instructive. These two large European countries have often been portrayed as prototypical examples of distinct 'worlds of welfare capitalism' (Esping-Andersen 1990), embedded in different political economies or 'social systems of production' (Hollingsworth and Boyer 1998) with arguably respective 'comparative institutional advantages' (Hall and Soskice 2001). Traditionally, the UK has been characterized as dominated by deregulated and flexible labour markets and a strong reliance on market-based co-ordination. The financial sector and in particular the role London holds as one of the major global locations for international trade and the emphasis on 'shareholder values' has become even more dominant than it was before the 1990s. By contrast, in Germany the stock market plays a much smaller role in corporate finance and the role of 'housebanks' has, at least traditionally, been a more important source of capital for companies (Hall and Soskice 2001). The labour market is more regulated, firms compete but also cooperate, agreeing on industry-wide standards, for example, and benefiting from traditional and broadly supported training systems. In short, labour relations are less market-dominated than in the UK and rely on an institutionalized dialogue and cooperation between employer and employee associations (Wood 2001).

The above is linked to differences in labour law and employment protection legislation in particular (Emmenegger 2009) and social insurance benefits such as unemployment, sickness, or old age pensions. Both of these protect income streams (Bonoli 2003a) for average and better earners more extensively in Germany. In the 1950s and 1960s social insurance benefits were improved and became more earnings-related in character, securing accustomed living standards and thus functioning as deferred or 'social wages' (Rhodes 2000). These elements of the German welfare state are as much elements of social policy as they are part and parcel of industrial relations, and they are more 'status-confirming' instruments than vehicles of redistribution. By contrast, after a relatively brief period of experimentation with the principle of earnings-related benefits between the 1960s and early 1980s, British social protection in case of unemployment, sickness, and also retirement reverted to flat-rate provision aimed at poverty prevention rather than replacing lost earnings and securing living standards (Clasen 2005). Unlike in Germany, better-paid employees are implicitly and at times explicitly referred to non-statutory sources for income protection, such as occupational benefits (pensions, redundancy pay) or private provision (personal pensions, mortgage payment protection).

However, since the 1990s there has been considerable change in the contexts within which social policy operates. Greater economic openness, deregulated financial markets, more intensive tax competition between

2

developed nations, and a general acceptance of the dominance of liberal capitalism seemed to clash with a regulatory role of the state and undermined institutions fostering coordination between key economic actors. The pervasiveness of the 'German model' seemed to decline (Busch 2005), as indicated by dwindling trade union membership, fewer firms participating in employer associations, a declining scope of sector-wide collective wage agreements, a retreat of banks on supervisory boards of major companies, and a growing emphasis on investment banking and shareholder values. Unsurprisingly, until recently many commentators regarded the German political economy model as outdated (see, for example, Streek and Hassel 2003). Others were less pessimistic though (e.g. Busch 2005) and the turmoil on world financial markets in the past two years and the problems created by unregulated investment banking have certainly dented what appeared to be the superiority of liberal capitalism until then.

Rather than the viability or otherwise of models of political economies, this book is concerned with developments in social policy provision in comparative perspective since the 1990s. However, actual and perceived changes in the contexts within which social policy operates have certainly influenced and framed political and public debates about welfare reform. Moreover, as several chapters will demonstrate, some changes already introduced suggest less variation across national respective social policy structures. More specifically, in the light of the perceived superiority of neo-liberal policy orientations towards the end of the twentieth century, it seems reasonable to ask to what extent Germany might have adopted elements which are more akin to British social policy. For example, is the role of social insurance as a distributive mechanism declining and being replaced by targeted means-tested support? Are there signs of a greater role for non-statutory social policy at the expense of publicly provided welfare? Asking such questions seems much more justifiable today than at any time after World War II. Back in the 1980s German social policy was widely regarded as part of a successful societal arrangement, contributing to economic growth, productivity, high employment, low poverty and inequality, and stable industrial relations. By contrast, British reluctance to engage more in publicly provided income protection, preferring instead to focus on basic poverty alleviation programmes, was regarded as reinforcing problems such as social exclusion and labour market marginalization.

This picture changed dramatically during the 1990s. The cost of German unification, sluggish economic and employment growth, low birth rates, economic and social problems, chronic fiscal deficits, mass unemployment, and rising poverty, with apparently little prospect of improvement dominated a period of gloom and search for policy alternatives (Kitschelt and Streeck 2003). In the UK, poverty rates and inequality remained high (Hills et al. 2009), as well as labour market inactivity for some groups such as low-skilled men (Clasen et al. 2006). However, the situation of other groups such as lone parents and families with children, as well as pensioners, improved. Moreover, population ageing was somewhat slower than in Germany and pensions less dependent on public finances due to a stronger reliance on occupational and other non-statutory provision. Moreover, unemployment continued to decline between 1993 and 2005 and new jobs were generated. It thus seems of little surprise that some German policy makers began to see potential in learning from British policies. Particularly the Labour government's welfare reform and 'making work pay' strategy certainly influenced the first 'red–green' coalition under Chancellor Schröder after 1998. In both countries centre-left parties were in power for many years (Labour from 1997 to 2010; the SPD as senior coalition partner from 1998 to 2005) and in the late 1990s there was a clear indication of considerable overlap and common ground within leaderships of the Labour Party and SPD respectively (Jeffery and Handl 1999).

Apart from an apparent exhaustion of the 'German model' of capitalism and some political alignment between centre-left governments, there were other factors contributing to potentially greater rather than diminishing similarity, such as an international consensus on the ways in which social policies should be reformed. For example, in the early 1990s the OECD began to actively advocate the idea of 'multi-pillar' pension schemes, which implied containing the scope of public pay-as-you-go programmes while expanding private and occupational-funded pension provision. In its OECD Jobs Study (OECD 1994) it urged advanced economies to shift resources from 'passive' benefit provision to 'active' labour market programmes. Similarly, the EU promoted the idea of 'activation', making unemployment benefit systems more 'employment-friendly' (European Commission 1997). Moreover, as EU member states, both the UK and Germany were subject to renewed attempts by the European Union to stimulate policy coordination via instruments such as the Open Method of Coordination, with commonly agreed benchmarks affecting social policy domains such as labour market policy (Büchs 2007).

Macro-level indicators suggest that there has already been some convergence between the two countries. Germany still spends more on social policy as a whole, but the gaps in total social expenditure, as well as outlays in particular areas, such as pensions, health, or the family were certainly wider in the 1980s than in the early 2000s (Castles 2009). Differences in the ways of raising revenue for welfare spending, i.e. in the balance between taxation and social security contributions, have also declined somewhat (Starke et al. 2008). During the first decade of the twenty-first century, poverty and inequality rose steadily in Germany, narrowing the gap with the UK to some extent (European Commission 2010) and with the same applying to in-work poverty (Lohmann 2009).

In short, despite the arguably strong path dependence in social policy making (Pierson 2001) and the slowness of change in some domains such as pension provision (Hinrichs 2001) it seems entirely reasonable to ask about the prospect of distinct British and German social policy arrangements. Recent trends of input and outcome indicators suggest a degree of convergence brought about by Germany approaching the UK. Of course, many caveats must apply here since convergence is a complex yardstick which can be conceptualized and measured in several ways (see Starke et al. 2008) and be caused by a multitude of factors which can be difficult to disentangle (Holzinger and Knill 2005). The term can be applied to a multitude of indicators, including policy inputs, institutional configurations, policy goals, outputs, or a combination of these. While observing trends in one of these indicators might suggest convergence, using others might point to divergence or little change.

The chapters in this book do not adopt a single indicator and subsequently delineate the degree of convergence in a quantitative fashion. Our aim was more modest and explorative. The starting point was the notion of distinct principles of social policy embedded in particular ways of delivering social protection manifest in the two countries, as described above. Consolidated between the 1950s and 1970s we ask ourselves whether the distinctiveness can still be detected in the context of change in the economic, social, and political contexts within which social policy has operated since the 1990s. We explore whether and in which ways there is now greater similarity between British and German social policy than there was a few decades ago. Moreover, given the global trends since the 1990s and beyond we expected Germany to have adopted social policy traits associated with the UK, as discussed earlier, although this might be different in different policy domains (see below). Finally, we are less concerned with social policy outcomes such as poverty or inequality, or outputs such as benefit rates (although Chapters 10 and 11 provide projections of pension policy outcomes). Instead, on the whole the emphasis is on changes in the principles and institutions which govern social policy provision.

At the risk of oversimplification these characteristics include the emphasis on social insurance and earnings-related benefit rights, i.e. on income maintenance and status preservation, within the German welfare state. They also refer to a dominance of public provision and crowding out of market-based or occupational social protection. For the UK this involves the embrace of means-testing (certainly since the 1990s), a concomitant decline of the role of contributory benefit rights for people of working age and the fostering of market-based and occupational social protection, especially for persons in retirement. Although often associated with welfare states as a whole, such a depiction does not represent the entire repertoire of British and German social policy. There are policy domains, such as health care or social services, in which these principles do not apply, or much less so, and in which German and British characteristics might be less distinctive. Moreover, even within the same policy domains, e.g. social security, there are programmes in which we find greater similarity rather than characteristic differences (e.g. child benefits).

In other words, our aim was not to generalize and make claims about declining similarities across welfare states as a whole, however defined (Bonoli 2007a), but to concentrate on three policy domains only. This selection was due to three considerations. First, we chose policy areas in which the characteristics commonly associated with the German and British 'welfare regime' (Esping-Andersen 1990) are particularly prominent, such as pension policy but also unemployment protection. Second, we chose family policies as a field with a different dynamic than most other social policy fields, i.e. of public investment rather than retrenchment. Finally, since we were interested in statutory and non-statutory provision, pensions as well as family policy are fields in which we were able to consider trends in both public and company-based policy provision.

Social policy convergence which is enduring rather than temporary requires welfare reform which is supported by broad popular acceptance and somehow aligned with dominant values of fairness, reciprocity, and social justice. On the other hand, the latter themselves might have changed since the 1990s in the context of social, economic, and political transformations, as well as debates about the need for policy adaptation in the light of challenges, such as demographic aging or globalization. This is the reason why we investigate not only policies but similarities and differences in public perceptions of social protection, as well as normative orientations towards welfare provision and greater room for self-responsibility.

The structure and the chapters of this book

The overarching aim of this book is to assess policy trends in Germany and the UK since the 1990s. We analyse the ways in which the German and British welfare states have adapted to common and country-specific challenges and assess the extent to which policy reforms might have brought about greater similarity between the two countries. We concentrate on three policy domains in particular: public policies in support of families, provision of income security in old age, and labour market integration. Departing from much conventional analysis, we investigate not only trends within public policies but include non-state provision and actors, and assess how far policy changes align with traditional or foster new conceptions of social justice and solidarity.

Following on from the introduction the twelve substantive chapters of this book are subdivided into Part I (welfare values) which covers public attitudes and perceptions and Part II, which is devoted to policy analyses. An overarching question for Part I is whether and to what extent traditional ideas of social policy provision have changed in recent years, and to what extent attitudes to social justice correspond to policy changes. How are the new key themes in welfare reform viewed and discussed by ordinary citizens? In Chapter 2 Christoph Burkhardt, Rose Martin, Steffen Mau, and Peter Taylor-Gooby start from the premise of Germany and Great Britain as representing two welfare state regimes which have traditionally relied on different distributional principles: liberalism and corporatism. Against this background the authors ask to what extent principles of social justice embedded in institutional designs of welfare state structures are reflected in differences in public opinion. Making use of data from various quantitative surveys, the chapter analyses how recent changes such as the emphasis on individual responsibility and social investment are viewed by the general public. It shows that attitudes do not differ greatly in relation to overall support for public provision. However, there are differences in particular areas. Much more than in Germany the role of the British government is seen as provider and regulator of welfare provision which should not undermine individual commitment and self-responsibility. A stronger notion of individualism and market freedom is also reflected in the greater social acceptance of purchasing better services in the areas of education and health care for those who have the means to do so.

In Chapter 3, Peter Taylor-Gooby and Rose Martin analyse the results of an original qualitative study which illustrates that concepts such as 'equality of opportunity', 'social contribution', and 'market freedom' are all valued in both countries but often understood differently. This questions the often emphasized contrasts between Germany as a conservative regulated market approach versus the UK as a liberal market regime. On the one hand, the corporatist and liberal frameworks respectively influence ideas ordinary citizens have about social provision. On the other, there is substantial agreement in approaches to employment and social inclusion. Both might be reconcilable since they may mask real differences in the way basic ideas about social provision are understood in different national contexts.

In Chapter 4 Christoph Burkhardt and Steffen Mau explore the potential impact of migration and greater ethnic diversity on attitudes towards the sustainability of existing welfare state structures. As in other European welfare states, the UK and Germany have been confronted with increasing migration, resulting in more diverse populations for some time. In addition, while access to welfare benefits used to be closely tied to citizenship in the past, western welfare states have become more inclusive by making benefit rights increasingly a matter of residency. Based on the analysis of focus group interviews, the chapter finds that, on the whole, German respondents were slightly more positive towards immigration. However, respondents in both countries valued the contributions made by migrants which help to deal with labour shortages and maintain the economic sustainability of social policy provision. On the other hand, ethnic segregation and the dependency on welfare services were highlighted as negative effects.

The subsequent nine chapters of Part II deal with three policy domains, beginning with family policy. As the most expansive and dynamic social policy field in both countries since the 1990s, in Chapter 5 Mary Daly identifies the changes undertaken in family policy in Germany and the UK and presents a framework to understand and analyse such changes. The chapter has two aims. First, it identifies and reflects on the main trends and compares these two influential countries in Europe which historically represented very different policy approaches to the family. In the second part, the author engages in a more general discussion of the risks and tensions inherent in contemporary family policy and how these might be investigated and assessed.

In Chapter 6 Ann Kathrin Jüttner, Sigrid Leitner, and Anneli Rüling analyse how a particular discourse, i.e. the debate about productive or 'investive' social policy which emerged in the late 1990s at a supra-national level, translated into national family policy debates and policy prescriptions in the UK and Germany. In both countries the parallel expansion of early childhood education and care in recent years was justified on economic grounds. However, this convergence in policy output does not mean similarity in policy goals. The British expansion in this field was accompanied by policies aimed at facilitating labour market entry as well as poverty prevention policy. The German discussion focused on securing economic growth through higher employment rates of mothers, higher fertility rates, and the creation of new jobs in the childcare sector. The authors illustrate how the introduction of children's centres in England and 'Familienzentren' in North-Rhine-Westphalia reflect the international economic discourse within family policy as well as national welfare traditions.

Lisa Warth too explores policy choices which appeared to pursue the same objectives in the UK and Germany. In Chapter 7 she shows that the analysis of family-friendly organization of working time provides an excellent illustration of the ways in which governments deal with the challenge of accommodating conflicting interests while pursuing their own particular policy goals. Whereas financial transfers and services to support work-family reconciliation can be directly provided through the welfare state, employee-orientated time flexibility is subject to negotiation between employers and employees and therefore largely beyond direct government control. The chapter explores how the British and German governments addressed this challenge of steering from a distance through a mix of encouragement of good practice and statutory regulation. Differences in policy choices can be explained by situating them within nationally specific preferences, overarching policy goals, government-stakeholder relations and past policy choices.

Finally, Timo Fleckenstein and Martin Seeleib-Kaiser focus directly on the role of companies in family policy. In the wake of a call for less statutory social policy since the 1990s in both countries, politicians have argued that employers could take on greater responsibilities. In Chapter 8 the authors show that companies have indeed expanded their provision of family policies over the past decade. Asking why this should be the case, they show that in the UK and Germany (but also in the United States) the overwhelming majority of employers engaged in firm-level family policies were motivated by the aim of recruiting and retaining (highly) skilled employees. However, there are significant cross-national variations which can be explained with reference to industrial sectors and national political economies.

The subsequent three chapters focus on retirement pensions, which is a major domain of social policy in both countries dominated by governments' attempts to cut back expenditure. At the same time, this is a field which expresses strong cross-national variation. In Chapter 9 Traute Meyer and Paul Bridgen assess the evolution of public as well as occupational pensions in Britain and Germany from 1945 to 2009. They argue that the 'liberal' label has never appropriately captured the nature of British pensions since it neglects the strong role played by the British state both as a regulator and employer. For Germany, the 'conservative' label captures the pension landscape fairly well for the period between 1957 and 2000. However, since then, the retrenchment of the statutory pension scheme and increased public support of voluntary pension savings have undermined the traditional principle of 'status preservation' within German pension policy more than is generally acknowledged. The authors argue that pension systems in the two countries have developed in opposing directions: in Britain towards a social-democratic model and in Germany towards liberalism.

In the subsequent chapter the same authors investigate the effects of recent policy making in German and British pension provision. Chapter 10 makes use of policy simulation to illustrate the scale and nature of reforms introduced during the first decade of the new century. For a range of hypothetical biographies projected outcomes are compared with those had the systems not been reformed. The results show that there is no evidence of institutional convergence on the basis of a 'race to the bottom'. This does not mean that little has changed, however. Instead, confirming the review of policy trends in the previous chapter, the outcomes underline Britain's shift towards a social democratic and pension regime and a growing liberalism in Germany's pension landscape. In the short term these developments might generate some degree of convergence of pensions received as German citizens spend more of their working life under the less generous state system, while British workers gradually gain the benefits of recent reforms.

Finally, in Chapter 11 Michaela Willert asks whether personal pensions are able to bridge what can be considered as savings gaps in both Britain and Germany. The savings gap is defined as the distance between state pension income and a 'social inclusion line' set at a particular income level below which pensioners are at risk of poverty. Willert investigates two crucial factors in this respect: the take-up of voluntary pensions and the performance of pension products. She illustrates that both are influenced by state regulation and by strategies on the part of pension providers such as life insurance companies. The chapter contrasts the regulation of welfare markets in the field (i.e. the purchase of pension products) developed since the late 1980s in the UK and after 2002 in Germany, respectively. Once again making use of micro-simulations, the analysis shows that the savings gap may be closed for middle to higher income earners, but the inclusiveness of pension arrangements as a whole is questionable in both countries.

The final two policy chapters focus on the labour market and policies aimed to facilitate labour market integration. In comparative research on the transition from vocational education and training to work it is well known that the occupational specificity of training systems influences the ways and ease with which young people enter employment. Comparing vocational training systems, Germany depends on a fairly high level of occupational specialization while the UK relies more on general skills. In Chapter 12 Kathrin Leuze investigates whether this can be found at the level of higher education too. She asks whether and how differences in the occupational specialization within the same degree programme influence graduate employment. Results indicate that the higher occupational specialization within higher education in Germany leads to a tighter match between university credentials and occupational outcomes than in Britain. However, there are considerable differences within countries, pointing to the fact that occupational specialization varies both across degrees and across countries.

In Chapter 13 Jochen Clasen concentrates on labour market policy in both countries. Both the 'welfare-to-work' reforms in the UK from 1998 onwards and the changes introduced by the so-called Hartz reforms between 2003 and 2005 in Germany have brought about far-reaching transformation. German legislation was in many respects influenced by British welfare principles and policies introduced by the Labour government. As a result there has been some degree of policy convergence both in the ways in which unemployment protection is structured and in the scope and emphasis within active labour market policies. However, there are also fundamental differences which have prevailed, such as the role of social insurance, including earnings-related benefits, for many unemployed in Germany.

In the concluding chapter Jochen Clasen, Steffen Mau, Traute Meyer, and Martin Seeleib-Kaiser revisit the preceding twelve chapters, summarizing the main findings and addressing the question of policy similarity across the two countries. They also place Germany/UK discussion in a wider European context, asking about the future of social policy both from the perspective of support for collectively provided social protection and more general trends and outlooks in the three policy fields under investigation.

Part I
Welfare Values

2

Differing notions of social welfare?
Britain and Germany compared

Christoph Burkhardt, Rose Martin, Steffen Mau, and Peter Taylor-Gooby

2.1 Introduction

European welfare states face severe pressures from globalization, changing labour markets with high unemployment, demographic change, and shifts in social structure. Policies to address the banking and economic crisis will impose substantial demands on public budgets (OECD 2009a: ch. 4). Under these conditions the traditional ambitions and objectives of welfare state intervention need to be reviewed. This chapter deals with attitudes towards normative principles of state welfare. Popular understanding of social justice contributes to the stability and resilience of the welfare state by defining the acceptable direction of policy. Two factors are important: first, public opinion in this field is changing and the existing societal contract that governs the distribution of burdens and benefits becomes increasingly contested. Second, movement towards a new European welfare settlement requires new conceptions of social justice.

Germany and the UK represent different welfare regimes. The UK is the leading European example of a Beveridgean tax-financed type of welfare state with largely needs-based welfare provision. Germany is the ideal type representative of the Bismarckian approach. The German system of social security relies mainly on contributions by potential benefit recipients. Entitlement is based on the former contributions by the members of the social insurance system. These different kinds of social security imply different levels of benefits, but also different distributional outcomes. However, both countries, Britain and Germany, have introduced reforms in order to enhance the sustainability and adaptability of their welfare systems. We start from the hypothesis that the need for sustainable welfare state intervention has advanced on the agenda. Increasingly *future-orientated criteria* such as the *enhancement of human and social capital, the impact of welfare on work incentives and individual conceptions of responsibility* and *the management of an increasingly diverse population* are important in policy making (Esping-Andersen et al. 2002). Welfare states thus have to face three new themes influencing their future sustainability.

The *first theme* of welfare state intervention is future-orientated social investment. To ensure the sustainability of the welfare state, policy reforms focus on welfare spending that is orientated less towards consumption, and more towards the social and economic development of households, communities, and society as a whole. Such a paradigm shift entails that specific groups and life circumstances are identified as more 'deserving' of help because they have differing potentials for development. On the one hand, policies are developed to support low-waged workers, eliminate 'poverty traps', constrain taxes on earned incomes to enhance work incentives, improve education and training, and promote family-friendly workplaces. On the other, benefits for non-working people of working age are constrained and mechanisms for monitoring unemployed people are intensified.

The *second key theme* of current welfare state development is reciprocity. Current welfare state reforms aim at linking rights to social benefits with obligations. This approach implies that those receiving benefits should do something in return to contribute to the community they live in. This conditionality of the payment of benefits exceeds the usual contributions and tax payments which are made in advance. It requires that people actually engage in the society, actively seek work, and behave according to officially defined standards of responsibility. The *third issue* of future welfare state intervention is the need of welfare states to accommodate increasing ethnic diversity: the higher levels of migration resulting from globalization produce more diverse populations in European countries. Greater ethnic diversity may undermine the solidarity on which the commitment to the welfare state is based. In the last part of the chapter we will thus analyse attitudes towards immigrants.

This chapter takes up these new issues by analysing public social attitudes in the UK and Germany. Public social attitudes have been found to have an impact on social policy reforms in many studies by scholars dealing with welfare state development (see, for example, Pierson 1994). In a study using comparative cross-sectional data on policy preferences of the public, Brooks and Manza (2006) reported that 'cross-national differences in the level of policy preferences help to account for a proportion of the differences among social, Christian, and liberal welfare state regimes'. Their analyses show that mass public opinion has an influence on social policy making with respect to levels of public social expenditure. In line with these findings, our assumption is the following: the future development of the welfare state depends to a large extent on the support it receives from its citizens. The legitimacy of the welfare state is connected to and reflected in overall solidarity among the population, but also in public social attitudes towards welfare state institutions (Gilley 2006). Against the background of different welfare state legacies in Britain and Germany this chapter addresses the following question: 'How are the new themes of social welfare viewed by the ordinary citizen?' To what extent do we find convergent views in the face of similar challenges?

For the first part of this chapter, we will give a broad overview of the key institutional features of both welfare regimes and recent changes. In addition, we strive to identify a link between the institutional architecture of the welfare state and public social attitudes in the UK and Germany. The major part will then consist of an analysis of social attitudes towards the welfare state, placing special emphasis on issues like social investment, reciprocity, and ethnic diversity. We use comparative data from the European Social Survey (2002/2003) and the International Social Survey Programme (2006, Role of Government IV) as well as various identical items from the British Social Attitudes Survey (BSA, 2004 and 2006) for the UK and from the German Justice in the Welfare State Survey (2007). These include a well-established welfarism scale to examine different attitudes on welfare, but also items asking whether an increase or decrease in payments to certain social groups would be supported and whether the government can ask for increasing personal responsibility in relation to social security. Our analyses provide an overview of notions of welfare and reciprocity of the people living in both countries. The results give insight into the evaluation of the welfare state and welfare recipients and how this might be influenced by the social security system itself.

2.2 Institutional architecture and public social attitudes in the UK and Germany

Within the European context, Germany and Britain represent distinct social policy models which are often used as examples of particular regimes in various welfare state typologies. Both systems are characterized by a distinctive set of welfare policies that are not only different in terms of programmes, but also in terms of the normative underpinnings of the welfare institutions. What is represented by different entitlement modes, ranges of coverage, and levels of benefit rests on different normative notions of why and to whom welfare should be delivered. Moreover, the two countries have pursued markedly different historical trajectories that highlight how different ideological concepts have contributed to shaping the welfare state. Both welfare states can be considered as pioneers of welfare developments that have evolved as interlocked competitors observing and responding to each other (Hennock 2007). Finally, both welfare regimes are said to rest on different concepts of legitimacy. The German welfare state represents a comprehensive system with high middle-class legitimacy, whereas the British system targets its resources to the lower sections of the population. Its legitimacy derives mainly from measures that provide a social minimum rather than from providing high income replacements.

For comparing Germany and the UK, one can draw on the distinction between 'Bismarck' and 'Beveridge' styles of welfare state (Hills et al. 1994; Palier and Martin 2008). The Bismarckian tradition relates each wage-earner's rights proportionally to the contribution that he has made, whereas a Beveridgean welfare state stresses the importance of a minimum income floor for the whole population (Chassard and Quintin 1992: 94; Bonoli 1997). This distinction captures not only the different objectives of social policy, such as status or the prevention of poverty, it also considers how welfare is delivered. The first model is based on social insurance and provides earnings-related benefits, mainly for employees according to a contributory record, whereas the second model is characterized by universal flat-rate provision which is tax-financed and based on residence and need (Palier and Martin 2008). The productivist assumption of the liberal welfare regime rallies the slogan 'Work, not welfare' emphasizing that 'people are supposed to earn their living on the labour market, and public welfare programmes are supposed to serve only as a residual fall-back' (Goodin 2001: 13). The corporatist regime, instead, ties entitlements to the contribution of welfare claimants to production, and articulates a 'Welfare through work' ideology (ibid.).

But how are these institutional set-ups actually linked with people's attitudes? Research on welfare attitudes in Europe has repeatedly revealed that most of the European welfare states and their core institutions enjoy widespread support (see e.g., Kaase and Newton 1995; Svallfors and Taylor-Gooby 1999; Bonoli 2000a; see next paragraph for studies dealing with the UK and Germany specifically). One strand of comparative attitude research has focused on the analysis of differences in the level of support for public social welfare drawing on Esping-Andersen's welfare regime typology (1990). However, with regard to the link between the welfare regimes and public social attitudes the findings are not clear-cut. On the one hand, scholars were arguing that there is some influence of the institutional architecture on welfare attitudes (Andreß and Heien 2001; Arts and Gelissen 2001; Brooks and Manza 2006; Dallinger 2008; Jæger 2006, 2009). By looking at the relation between welfare regimes and support for welfare policies Larsen (2006, 2008) was able to show that there is indeed a link between the institutional design of a country and the willingness of the population to support other members of the society. On the other hand, there are scholars arguing that welfare regimes and the design of the social security system have no or only limited impact on attitudes towards the welfare state in general and solidarity in particular (Svallfors 1997; Gelissen 2000; Aalberg 2003; Svallfors 2003). Nevertheless, even though there is comparably little agreement on the specific relation between welfare regimes (as framed within the literature on typologies) and public social attitudes, there seems to be agreement among scholars that a relationship exists between country characteristics and attitudinal patterns (Svallfors 2010a).

If we compare the German and the British welfare state support it becomes clear that differences exist: Mau (2003) finds that the majority of the population of both countries actually supports redistribution, but that support was actually higher in the UK than in Germany, mainly due to the lower level of welfare state intervention in the UK. Also from the perspective of beneficial involvement the German and the British welfare regimes appear to be rather distinct from each other. In conservative welfare regimes many welfare schemes are explicitly designed to institutionalize 'middle-class loyalties' by giving priority to horizontal redistribution and status maintenance. In liberal regimes, where state activity concentrates more on the bottom end of society, the middle classes are less attached to the welfare state, since they purchase a greater share of social security at the market. In the past Germany did not display major distributive conflicts and there was a relative satisfaction with the higher-tier benefits such as pensions. In Britain, in contrast, the attitudinal patterns were less integrated with regard to the principle of income distribution and state schemes were not generally understood to give good returns (see Mau 2003).

In the next section we will analyse recent shifts in welfare state arrangements in Britain and Germany. This will provide a background understanding of the current landscape of public social attitudes in Germany and the UK.

2.3 Recent developments

As we know, welfare arrangements are relatively stable over time and most changes are influenced by path dependence and tend to be incremental. Nevertheless, we also observe remarkable change. In both countries concepts of social justice emphasizing responsibility, activation, and the enhancement of human and social capital have moved up the agenda. As the European Union plans to become the most competitive and knowledge-based economy in the world there is pressure on all member states to recalibrate their welfare systems. Moreover, nearly all welfare states are confronted with severe pressures from globalization, changing labour markets with high unemployment, demographic change, and shifts in social structure. More recently, severe cost constraints interact with growing pressures on employment and unemployment benefits as a result of the crisis.

Indeed, recent reforms of the welfare arrangement challenge the working assumptions about traditional German social policy. We can observe a weakening of the status-preserving character of the German welfare state and a greater emphasis on social investment, individual responsibility, and private provision. Today, individuals themselves have to take over more responsibility if they want to maintain the status they have achieved in their working lives during phases of unemployment or when they retire. Especially in the area of unemployment protection, we observe a gradual shift towards an Anglo-Saxon style of welfare provision, with less emphasis on status preservation and more on basic provision. The most fundamental challenge to the traditional character of the German welfare scheme has been posed by the reforms of unemployment insurance—the so-called 'Hartz IV'-Reform. The new benefit system has a dual aim: it is designed to prevent poverty, not to secure previous living standards (Konle-Seidl et al. 2007). Like many other countries, Germany also started to place more emphasis on activation measures within the frame of unemployment policies. The new legislation tightened eligibility and conditionality criteria, placed more emphasis on job-seeking efforts and training measures, applied more extensive definitions of suitable employment (so that claimers were less able to reject low-paid or undesirable jobs) and put more effective benefit sanctions in place (Clegg 2007; Dingeldey 2007).

Since the 1990s, many European countries have introduced pension reforms which have contributed to a multi-pillarization of the pension systems and a strengthening of the private and occupational sector. These elements already played a significant role in Beveridgean systems, but were not central to many Bismarck systems (Schludi 2005). The Social Democrats, who were in power from 1998 till 2005, have introduced reforms by modifying the pension formula and thereby lowering the replacement rates substantially (for an overview, see Schulze and Jochem 2007). In order to mitigate financial losses and to maintain living standards during retirement, they also introduced provision for a fully funded and tax-subsidized private pension, the so-called *Riester Rente*. For parts of the middle and the upper classes, in turn, the dependency on public pensions has weakened over time (Ebbinghaus 2006). Besides, benefits and services have also been curtailed in German health insurance while supplementary private payments have been increased. Though most of the medical and hospital expenses are covered by the statutory health insurance, German patients are increasingly expected to make co-payments for a larger number of services. As a consequence of these developments, the role of individual responsibility and private provision has been strengthened. Somehow different are the developments in the area of family policy. A new parental leave policy to counter low fertility rates and encourage fathers to take over more responsibility for care work for young children has been introduced. Family policy has moved up the public agenda and become an issue of competition between the major parties.

Recent developments in the UK have two main themes: strengthening the market orientation of the welfare system, and expanding state support for individual citizens to operate as market actors. The Conservative government from 1979 to 1997 vigorously pursued the first approach. Social benefits were cut back and entitlements made stricter, culminating in the abolition of insurance-based unemployment benefits in 1996 and its amalgamation with means-tested assistance in the time-limited and conditional Job Seeker's Allowance. The state contributory pension scheme was also restructured to reduce entitlements over a twenty-year period to about half of what had been originally planned and an ambitious programme to expand private pensions across the workforce was implemented (Taylor-Gooby and Mitton 2008).

The Labour government from 1997 adopted and developed many features of the previous regime. Social investment, private responsibility, and private provision climbed further up the political agenda, as in Germany. The unemployment benefit reforms were carried further with more limitations as to entitlement and a complex system of case management to put more pressure on the individual and to move claimants off benefit. Access to benefits became tightly linked to conditionality and focuses on those who display commitment to work. Pension reforms aimed at an expansion of private pensions and increased private responsibility. However, benefits for pensioners have been improved by a substantial expansion of the means-tested last resort pension and the flat-rate first-tier pension as a Guaranteed Minimum Income. The growing relevance of social investment as an aspect of public policy became more evident when the Labour government increased resources for welfare and pursued a far-reaching and integrated programme of using the welfare system to develop human capital and national competitiveness focused especially on education and training. The education system underwent substantial expansion, culminating in an increase of participation rates. Other reforms expanded training programmes at a number of levels and linked them more closely to benefit entitlement.[1] The attractiveness of work for the low-paid and lower-skilled was improved by establishing a minimum wage and introducing tax credit benefits to raise living standards for workers on low wages, especially those with young children, and to pay for childcare to release more mothers for paid work. Further reforms were designed to

---

[1] E.g. with the 'New Deal' programmes which became compulsory for most groups of claimants unemployed for longer than six months.

improve work–life balance by extending parental leave entitlements and introducing further work-place rights in excess of EU minimum entitlements.

Besides these reforms, a further key theme in popular consciousness of welfare concerns ethnic diversity. Both countries have attracted large numbers of immigrants during the post-war period as a result of the economic opportunities they provide and, in the case of the UK particularly, through the links established in the era of imperialism. As the global economic crisis impacts, migration rates have fallen sharply. However, in recent years immigration has become an important issue in popular discourse in relation to welfare. This can be shown by country-specific figures: although net inflow to Germany fell from 2.8 per thousand of the population in 1995 to 0.9 by 2005, with immigrants mainly coming from post-socialist East European countries, as well as Turkey and Southern Europe, the stock of foreign-born people increased to 12.9 per cent of the total population in 2003 (latest available data). For the UK, net inflow was 2.2 per thousand in 1995, rising to 5.2 by 2005, with immigrants mainly from India, East Asia, Australia, and Eastern Europe. In the period up to 2006 the stock of foreign-born migrants increased to 10.1 per cent of the total population (OECD 2009b).

In Germany the theme of entitlement through social contribution coupled with the tradition of *ius sanguinis* (citizenship through hereditary) led to disquiet about the access of incoming groups to social benefits. In the UK the citizenship tradition has been based more on *ius soli* (citizenship acquired through residence). However, the racism against black minorities evident since the imperial era combined with concerns about incomers taking jobs provokes public concern that centres on the provision of social benefits to those seen to be undeserving and outsiders.

2.4 Empirical findings: welfare state legitimacy and new themes

There is good reason to believe that the success of policy reforms depends to a certain extent on mass policy preferences. Social policy reforms aiming at introducing new themes of welfare intervention into the institutional architecture of established welfare states need to take these public social attitudes seriously in order to sustain the legitimacy of the welfare state. In the following section we will give an overview of more recent attitudes towards the welfare state and popular reactions to the changes laid out in the previous section of this article. First we look at the pattern of support for the welfare state in general in areas such as attitudes towards redistribution and the role of the state. We then turn to more recent developments in the two welfare states which emphasize the themes of social investment, reciprocity, and diversity in their welfare policies. Social investment is to do with a tighter linkage between training, education, and benefit; reciprocity is related to the social contract of contribution for entitlement in German and of individual activity and responsibility in return for opportunity in the UK; and diversity concerns the expansion of ethnic minorities in both countries. For this section we make use of comparable data from the 2006 British Social Attitudes (BSA) Survey and a German dataset, the 2007 German Justice in the Welfare State Survey, with a representative national sample of 1000 respondents. In addition, the 2006 module of the International Social Survey Programme (ISSP) on 'The Role of Government' is used to tap issues of social investment and public spending priorities. To explore the issue of ethnic diversity we make use of the first wave of the European Social Survey (ESS) 2002/2003.

For scrutinizing general views on the welfare state we first make use of the social welfarism scale, a composite index which has been developed by researchers involved in the British Social Attitudes Survey. The welfarism scale is based on a battery of welfare-related items and measures support for state welfare. Our German survey reproduces these questions. At a comparative level, we see that the proportion of respondents which can be classified as either sympathetic or unsympathetic does not differ so much between Germany and the UK (see Table 2.1). However, a greater proportion of Germans can be grouped into those being very unsympathetic or very sympathetic. It seems that German public opinion on welfare state measures is polarized, while Britons tend to be more or less undecided with a slight tendency to being unsympathetic.

Detailed examination of a broader set of items gives a more nuanced picture of public perceptions of the welfare state (Table 2.2). We have three items measuring attitudes towards redistribution, namely 'The government should redistribute from the better-off to those who are less well-off', 'It is the

Table 2.1: Welfare values: Welfarism scale

Welfarism scale (%)	Germany	Great Britain
Very unsympathetic	15	6
Slightly unsympathetic	39	50
Slightly sympathetic	35	39
Very sympathetic	12	4
Cronbach's alpha	0.69	0.76

Notes: The Welfarism scale consists of the following items: (1) The welfare state encourages people to stop helping each other. (2) The government should spend more money on welfare benefits for the poor, even if it leads to higher taxes. (3) Around here, most unemployed people could find a job if they really wanted one. (4) Many people who get social security don't really deserve any help. (5) Most people on the dole are fiddling in one way or another. (6) If welfare benefits weren't so generous, people would learn to stand on their own two feet. All items originally ranged from Agree strongly to Disagree strongly (5 categories). The index for the scale is formed by scoring the most pro-welfarist position with 1 and the most anti-welfarist position with 5 and by dividing the outcome into the categories displayed in the table. The scores to the questions in the scale are added and divided by the number of items of the scale. Reliability scores (as measured by Cronbach's alpha) are reported in the table.

Source: Great Britain: BSA (2006); Germany: German Justice in the Welfare State Survey (2007), weighted data.

Table 2.2: Redistribution and helping those in need

	Germany	Great Britain
	% of respondents agreeing	
Redistribution		
Differences in income in this country are too large	80.5	65.0
The government should redistribute from the better-off to those who are less well-off	43.2	32.3
It is the responsibility of government to reduce income differences	58.2	45.2
Helping those in need		
If we want to live in a healthy, well-educated society, we have to be willing to pay the taxes necessary to fund it	88.1	87.3
It's only right that the taxes paid by the majority help support those in need	81.8	73.2
Cutting welfare benefits would damage too many people's lives	72.4	49.1
The government should spend more on benefits for the poor, even if it leads to higher taxes	38.5	37.1

Notes: Item categories range from Agree strongly (1) to Disagree strongly (5). For the tables, the percentage of agreement was computed by combining the two categories indicating agreement with the statement.

Source: Great Britain: BSA (2004), Germany: German Justice in the Welfare State Survey (2007), weighted data.

responsibility of government to reduce income differences', and 'Differences in income in this country are too large'. Starting with the latter we find that over 80 per cent of the Germans and 65 per cent of the British respondents feel that income differences have grown too large. Though this critical view on inequalities is a recurring finding of attitude research (Svallfors 2006; Mau and Veghte 2007) it may also reflect real changes in the income distribution. In both countries we observe a widening gap between high and low income earners which has become a matter of public concern (for Germany Grabka and Frick 2008; for the UK Hills 2004; see Atkinson 2007 for an overview). Fifty-eight per cent of the Germans and 45 per cent of the British respondents share the view that it is the responsibility of the government to reduce income differences. Support for government intervention in income distribution follows roughly a similar trajectory in both countries, with rather more generosity in Germany. Here again, the Germans are more in favour of governmental responsibility to redistribute or to reduce income differences.

There is stronger support if one asks more directly about the goals of welfare state intervention such as living in a 'healthy society' and helping those in need. These objectives receive markedly more approval than questions related to redistribution as a more abstract principle. Here it seems that the people are willing to support the welfare state if certain socially valued goals are achieved. However, we also note that statements of principle receive majority consent, but as the comments move closer to policy, involving direct state interventions and imposing higher taxes and social contributions on those interviewed, support falls. This is most apparent for the last item in the table which makes explicit that more spending on the poor would eventually lead to higher taxes.

As already pointed out, Germany represents a relatively large welfare state with a strong concern for status maintenance established and supported as a corporatist and consensual system. In comparison, the UK welfare provision is smaller, more targeted, and with an orientation towards individual responsibility. However, in both countries policy makers now place greater emphasis on investment-orientated social policies and the long-term effects of social intervention. This paradigm shift entails a different weighting of social groups who are considered 'deserving'. Those with high potential for future development are especially likely to receive greater support. Education, training, and support for the family moves up the agenda.

With regard to country differences we can observe that social provision is valued in both countries for the obvious reason that it addresses risks people might face in everyday life (row one of Table 2.3). Respondents in the UK are much more likely to think of social welfare as provision targeted on poor minorities (row 6), more likely to express concern about whether recipients deserve the benefits they receive (row 2), and to be tolerant of better-off people buying private services that enable them to secure preferential treatment

Table 2.3: Paying and receiving welfare

	Germany	UK
	% of respondents . . . ... agreeing	
The best reason for paying taxes now is that you never know when you might need benefits and services[a]	84.5	77.1
It's not right that people benefit from services that they haven't helped to pay for[a]	47.7	50.3
It's not fair that some people pay a lot of money in tax and hardly use the services their taxes pay for[a]	41.4	34.2
Is it right or wrong that people with high incomes can buy[b]	. . . saying it is right	
. . . better health care than people with low incomes	17.8	48.2
. . . better education for their children than people with low incomes	12.4	50.2
	. . . saying they benefit more	
Thinking of people on low incomes, how much do you think they benefit from overall government spending on health and education, compared to people on high incomes?[c]	19,1	31,9

Notes: [a] Item categories range from Agree strongly (1) to Disagree strongly (5). For the tables, the percentage of agreement was computed by combining the two categories indicating agreement with the statement; [b] Item categories range from Definitely right (1) to Very wrong (5). For the tables, the percentage of agreement was computed by combining the two categories indicating agreement with the statement; [c] Item categories range from Benefit a lot less (1) to Benefit a lot more (5). For the tables, the percentage of respondents saying that people on low incomes benefit more was computed by combining the two categories indicating that they benefit more.

Source: Great Britain: BSA (2004), Germany: German Justice in the Welfare State Survey (2007), weighted data.

(rows 4 and 5). In Germany, most people do not share the vision that those who can afford better welfare and education should be able simply to buy it. Here we find indeed a stark contrast between the two countries, which relates to the existing institutional arrangements.

It is not surprising that the growing divisions between the statutory health provision and the private health insurance as well as issues of charging students receive a good deal of public attention and are often met with resistance. They seem to contradict the well-entrenched normative principles of the German system. However, in the targeted British system significantly more people think that those on low incomes benefit more from overall government spending on health and education compared to those with higher incomes (Table 2.3, row 6). Indeed, in the Bismarckian system most redistribution takes place within classes and across the individual life-cycle, and does not alter the structure of social inequality fundamentally. Less pronounced are the differences in relation to the items that it is not right that people benefit from services they have not paid for (row 2) or that some people pay a lot of money in tax and hardly use the services their taxes finance. Between one-third and half of the respondents share these views (row 3).

The survey findings also give information on similarities and differences in support for an increase in government spending in specific areas of social welfare provision, as well as for different groups of beneficiaries. When asked whether the respondents would like to see more or less government spending on particular areas of state welfare the following outcomes emerged (see Table 2.4): The desire for an increase in government spending for public health care is more pronounced in Great Britain than in Germany. 82.1 per cent of the Britons favour more spending on the health service, while rather less than two-thirds of the German population share similar views. The result is almost exactly reversed when it comes to education. 82.4 per cent of the German population would like to see an increase in education spending,

Table 2.4: Preferences of spending for different areas

The Government should spend more money on . . .	Germany	Great Britain
	% of respondents agreeing that the government should spend more on . . .	
Health	65.7	82.1
Education	82.4	72.6
Old age pensions	51.5	74.5
Unemployment benefits	32.8	15.7

Notes: Item categories range from (1) Spend much more to (5) Spend much less. For the table, the percentage of people wanting more spending was computed by combining the two categories indicating a preference for an increase in public spending.

Source: ISSP (2006).

which clearly underlines support for social investment, as against 72.6 per cent of the British sample. With regard to old age pensions the outcome is the other way round again. Britons do seem to favour an increase in public spending for the elderly. In turn, only 51.5 per cent of the German population would support an increase in spending for pensions. This could be related to different traditions in financing the system of old age pensions. The German pay-as-you-go public pension system is mainly based on contributions of the working population and pays relatively higher benefits. With regard to the support for an increase in spending on unemployment benefits it becomes obvious that people in both countries do not endorse this approach. Only one-third of the Germans and 15.7 per cent of the Britons support an increase in spending for the unemployed. In both countries almost half of the respondents would like to leave the level of spending untouched.

When the questions turn to groups of beneficiaries rather than types of benefit, a similar pattern emerges (see Table 2.5). In both countries, the unemployed receive low support from the population, whereas at the same time parents on low incomes (both deserving because they work and needy because they have very low incomes) receive high support in terms of a demand for an increase in government spending. Retired people are the most enthusiastically supported group in the UK, probably due to respondents sensing an overall low level of pensions in the UK that leads to disadvantages on the part of pensioners and which needs to be taken care of. Disabled and retired people, both groups outside the labour market, are well supported by public opinion in this country, indicating that factors other than a productivist understanding of desert play a role. On the other hand, single parents are only supported by roughly one-third of the UK population, in marked contrast to Germany. In the latter country judgements about the actual needs and living standards of different groups make a difference, since support for

Table 2.5: Benefits for different groups

	Germany	UK
Would you like to see more or less government spending on . . . ?	% of respondents agreeing that the government should spend more on . . .	
Parents who work on very low incomes	76.7	64.0
Single parents	69.8	36.1
Disabled people who cannot work	69.4	65.3
Retired people	46.3	74.1
Unemployed people	27.6	15.4

Notes: Item categories range from much more (1) to much less (5). For the tables the percentage of people wanting more spending was computed by combining the two categories indicating preference for higher spending.

Source: Great Britain: BSA (2004), Germany: German Justice in the Welfare State Survey (2007), weighted data.

pensioners, who are understood to be receiving relatively high pensions, is at a similar low level.

Central to the organization and the legitimacy of the welfare state are norms of reciprocity. Reciprocity defines certain actions and obligations as 'repayments' for benefits received (on reciprocity see Gouldner 1973: 226ff.). In practical terms it implies that rights to a certain level of welfare (economic security, care, protection against various risks) are granted on condition that the beneficiary fulfils legal duties and normative obligations vis-à-vis the community: contributing to the welfare of society, performing paid work, taking responsibility for and undertaking care for children and other dependants, participating in other socially valuable actions, ensuring that one pursues appropriate training opportunities, and so on. This also matters at the level of individual motivations. We know that people's propensity to engage in a costly collective endeavour is strongly enhanced by reciprocity assumptions. People expect something in return for their efforts, but this 'something' can be different in value and kind. For example, it has been empirically shown that when people assume that the beneficiaries make efforts to be self-sustaining and to re-enter employment they are more in favour of public assistance (Bowles and Gintis 2000; Overbye 2000; Mau 2003). Many welfare state transfers carry the notion that those who benefit should make 'good-faith efforts' (Arneson 1997: 339) to provide something in return.

For these reasons, the question of whether the welfare beneficiaries are viewed as 'deserving' and whether transfers are framed as conforming to the prevailing norms of reciprocity is significant (see Table 2.6). We observe strong

Table 2.6: Deserving and undeserving poor: The reciprocity issue

	Germany	UK
	% of respondents agreeing	
Deservingness		
Most people on the dole are fiddling one way or another	47.5	42.0
Around here, most unemployed people could get a job if they really wanted one	52.3	70.6
Many people who get social security don't really deserve any help	40.0	39.9
Negative benefit effects		
If welfare benefits weren't so generous, people would learn to stand on their own two feet	60.5	47.9
The welfare state makes people nowadays less willing to look after themselves	53.9	51.0
The welfare state encourages people to stop helping each other	51.0	24.6

Notes: All items range from (1) Agree strongly to (5) Disagree strongly (5 categories). To report the agreement in per cent the two categories indicating agreement with the statement were combined.

Source: Great Britain: BSA (2006), Germany: German Justice in the Welfare State Survey (2007), weighted data.

anti-scrounger sentiments and also perceptions of negative benefit effects in both countries, rather more so in Germany, with the exception being responses to the question in the second row, which may be coloured by the actual availability of work. Unemployment stood at 5.3 per cent in the UK, but 9.8 per cent in Germany in 2006 (OECD 2009c). This reflects the commitment in Germany to status maintenance which often sets the established core working class against the more marginal groups in the labour force, who tend to receive means-tested supplementary benefits.

There are similarities and differences in views on welfare and the state in Germany and the UK, as this brief review of evidence indicates. In the UK the welfare state is understood more narrowly, as something that fits round the edge of the market system, and which must accommodate both private provision and ensure the work orientation of the poor. German respondents tend to support a more expansive system. However, as our data shows, they also have real concerns about the extent to which social benefits maintain incomes for core groups in the population when outside the labour market, and how far they enable those at the bottom to encroach on the living standards of the rest. Half of the German respondents, but only one-quarter of the British respondents thinks that the welfare state encourages people to stop helping each other. Welfare disincentive issues, which have always been a prominent theme for the liberal British welfare state, seem to be coming to the fore in the more comprehensive German system, making the welfare arrangements prone to specific criticisms.

Finally, we turn to the issue of diversity and migration, which has a direct impact on the sustainability of the welfare state. Many authors have argued that the legitimacy of the welfare state is influenced by the ethnic composition of the respective country and that greater diversity undermines the solidarity on which the commitment to welfare is based (Alesina and Glaeser 2004; Goodhart 2004; for counter-arguments see Taylor-Gooby 2005). Increasing ethnic diversity might lead to conflicts between the host and the immigrant society, culminating in a loss in overall solidarity. The welfare state, relying greatly on solidaristic support from its citizens, might be damaged by a declining willingness to endorse redistribution across the population. Migration has thus been on the agenda of many European welfare states for some time and has gained even more prominence in the face of the economic crisis. The high levels of migration resulting from globalization produce more diverse populations in European countries, and with that the issue of integration and inclusion becomes more pressing. Indeed, many Europeans have adopted a 'boat is full' attitude, demanding that national governments restrict immigration (Boeri et al. 2002), but it is unlikely that this process can be halted.

Table 2.7: Attitudes towards immigrants in Germany and the UK

	Germany	Great Britain
	% of respondents agreeing	
Average wages/salaries generally brought down by immigrants[a]	35.9	37.6
Immigrants harm economic prospects of the poor more than the rich[a]	53.7	50.4
Immigrants help to fill jobs where there are shortages of workers[a]	56.1	56.7
If immigrants are long-term unemployed they should be made to leave[a]	48.9	52.8
Immigrants should be given same rights as everyone else[a]	58.6	66.8
Government spends too much money assisting immigrants[a]	73.3	67.7
	% of respondents agreeing that immigrants take out more than they put in	
Taxes and services: immigrants take out more than they put in[b]	54.1	57.5

Notes: [a] Item categories range from 'Agree strongly' (1) to 'Disagree strongly' (5). For the tables the percentage of agreement was computed by combining the two categories indicating agreement with the statement. Analysis was restricted to respondents holding the citizenship of the respective country.

[b] The item is measured on a 11-point scale labelled at both extremes, one being 'Generally take out more' (0) and the other being 'Generally put in more' (10). Values for this item represent the percentage of people stating that immigrants take more out of the welfare state than they put in (categories 0–4).

Source: [a]ISSP (2003); [b]European Social Survey (2002/2003), weighted data.

Overall, we find that the attitudes towards immigrants do not differ substantially between the countries (see Table 2.7). For most of the items included in the table the differences between the countries do not exceed 5 percentage points and are thus comparatively small. In both countries about 36 per cent of the population thinks that immigrants tend to bring wages down. The majority of the population does not seem to be afraid of a possible decrease of wages due to migration. A majority of 56 per cent of the population in both countries thinks that immigrants help to fill jobs where there are shortages of workers. Another finding is that only a slightly higher share of the Germans thinks that immigrants harm the economic prospects of the poor more than the rich. German citizens seem to be slightly more sensitive to the negative consequences of migration for the disadvantaged (row 2). More than two-thirds of the population in both countries think that the government spends too much money on programmes to assist immigrants, with 6 percentage points more in Germany than in Great Britain (row 6). With regard to the question whether immigrants take more out of the welfare state than they put in, the majority in both countries believes that this is the case (row 7).

Only with regard to the question of whether immigrants should get the same rights as everyone else there appears a different evaluation of the status of immigrants and equal treatment with regard to social rights and law (row 5). Although majorities in both countries support this view, Germans are not as willing as Britons to grant the same social rights to foreigners as to the native population. The reason for the difference might be located in the different immigration laws and traditions of the countries. Compared to Germany, the British immigration law gives easier access to citizenship for immigrants. In addition, most of the immigrants coming to the UK already hold British citizenship and are thus allowed to claim the same social rights as native citizens from the beginning. We expect this to be the reason for the greater willingness of British respondents to offer common citizenship to immigrants. Although a majority of 58 per cent supports the inclusion of immigrants in Germany, more than 40 per cent of the population does not endorse this item. Obviously, a significant share of the population opposes the equal status of immigrants in Germany.

2.5 Conclusion

Germany and the UK offer contrasting examples of European welfare states. As we have seen this is at least partly reflected in notions of solidarity and in the welfare attitudes of citizens of both countries. Especially when it comes to redistributive measures, the German population is more in favour of government activities and intervention than the Britons, but attitudes also seem to be more polarized in this country. In terms of government spending, people in both countries mostly favour an increase in areas where they see a need for improvement (the NHS in the UK and the education system in Germany). We also observe differences with regard to the issue of whether it is right that people with high incomes can buy better health and education. Germans have much stronger reservations against an unequal distribution of life chances than the British respondents.

By and large, the welfare attitudes seem to be more or less in line with the welfare state arrangement of both countries and pertinent political debates. While Germans are in favour of a strong welfare state and tend to be more solidaristic, Britons rely more on the individual and the power of the market to make a change. However, with regard to many items the differences between the two countries were not striking. Especially, issues of deservingness and investment have become prominent in both countries. With regard to the evaluation of the issue of ethnic diversity as one key theme of future welfare state activity, differences in attitudes between the two countries appear to be rather limited. Although there are differences in terms of the migratory history and the composition of the immigrant community, quantitative results only point to minor differences in attitudes between Germany and the UK. Nevertheless, as we will see in Chapter 4 of this volume, analysis of qualitative data reveals substantial differences in the attitudinal framing of immigration and in responses to increasing ethnic diversity.

With regard to the sustainability of the welfare state, both countries have undertaken measures in response to the pressures of globalization, labour market change, and population ageing by implementing reforms of the social security system. Further reforms are clearly underway, triggered by the economic crisis and cutbacks in public spending. However, despite these pressures common to both countries, the key differences remain. The German welfare state is more solidaristic, status-centred, and comprehensive in its approach to welfare, while the UK treats social provision more from a market perspective, and is concerned more about the impact of the system on incentives and responsibility (the virtues of the market actor), rather than on the social relationships of an established and consensual social order.

With regard to social investment, reciprocity, and ethnic diversity as new themes and challenges in welfare state reform, we have pointed out that these changes in institutional design are at least partially reflected in people's opinions, but are also to some extent contested. To accommodate these new themes welfare states must change, but they do so within the constraints of the national traditions, political economies, and constitutional frameworks that created the existing systems, and the shared understandings of the citizens regarding what the state ought to do. Indeed, when taking up these themes welfare reforms have to take into account the aspirations and expectations of the public. As Esping-Andersen (2002b: 8) pointed out 'We must be certain that any design for a new social contract conforms to prevailing normative definitions of justice. This means specifying the bases of rights and reciprocity, and delineating the claims that citizens can justly make on society.' Future reforms of the welfare state and a sustainable foundation of the social contract upon which it rests will depend heavily on the quest for plausible and appealing concepts of social justice. This means that in their reform attempts, politicians are advised to embrace both considerations of financial sustainability *and* principles of social justice. If policy shifts are not in line with the aspirations of the people, these reforms are highly likely to fail.

3

Fairness and social provision: qualitative evidence from Germany and the UK

Peter Taylor-Gooby and Rose Martin[1]

3.1 Introduction

Germany and the UK are often contrasted as leading European examples of the two main currents in the political economy of state welfare. Germany represents the conservative corporatist regime, dominant across the heartland of the European continent and providing benefits and services linked to occupational status, financed mainly through social insurance. The UK typifies the liberal market approach, with weaker and more highly targeted benefits, mainly financed through direct taxation and concerned with mitigation of poverty and immediate need rather than status maintenance (Esping-Andersen 1990, Allen and Scruggs 2004).

German and UK approaches to welfare are frequently contrasted in political economy as well as in welfare policy (see Chapter 1). Social provision in Germany is set in the context of a semi-sovereign, federal, and consensual polity, while the UK political framework is much more centralized and majoritarian, so that the party of government has more immediate authority and is less constrained by pressures to negotiate with influential industrial or trade union groups (Lijphart 1999). In economic regulation, Germany is the leading exemplar of a coordinated market economy, while the UK is the largest European liberal market economy (Soskice 1999). In the former, government seeks to manage the economy to ensure a strong role for manufacturing industry through management of infrastructure, human capital, trade, and

[1] In collaboration with Steffen Mau and Christoph Burkhardt (University of Bremen).

economic activity, while in the latter these matters are left more to the play of market forces.

A number of commentators (including Pierson 2001, Swank 2002, Taylor-Gooby 2004, and Bonoli 2005) have pointed out that West European welfare states face broadly similar pressures from two developments: globalization and post-industrialism. The chief issues in relation to globalization are the necessity of adapting to more intense international competition and the much higher levels of immigration in both countries (see Chapter 3). Post-industrialism has led to shifts in the labour market (a higher proportion of service-sector jobs), in family structure (women play a more important role in formal employment and family life becomes more flexible, less structured on the lines of a gender division of labour), and in demographic patterns (birth and death rates decline and the population ages). Welfare states have their own distinctive national formations. Similar pressures from the international political economic environment might plausibly lead to convergence in policy development, probably in a more liberal direction, since market considerations dominate in this field. This would have implications for the future of the European welfare state and particularly for the resilience of social provision in the face of the current economic crisis. The pressures on governments in all developed countries is to cut taxes and social spending to restore public finances after the unprecedented spending to ensure the solvency of the banking system. As the OECD delicately puts it, 'substantial consolidation of public finances' will be required (OECD 2009d).

Most analysts of recent developments in German and UK welfare policies identify some superficial indications of similarities in policy development, for example in Schroeder and Blair's discussions of the Neue Mitte in the late 1990s (Busch 1999) or in the interest in activation of the labour market, or in the expansion of the role of private pensions in both countries. However, they conclude that the distinctive differences between regime types remain (Scharpf and Schmidt 2001; Hudson et al. 2008; Leisering 2008).

In this chapter we examine public understanding of fairness and social provision in Germany and the UK in order to investigate whether people's ideas remain linked to the traditions of their national welfare systems or whether they have moved closer together. The structural differences between the two countries in social provision might be expected to correspond to differences in popular values. The German institutional framework links earnings-related contributions and entrenched rights to benefits and services so that moral discourse tends to associate the two (Offe 1991). Respondents in this country whose social rights are embedded within this framework might be more accepting of the status differences implied by the social insurance system. People in the UK, whose welfare rights are more a matter of the outcome of political contest might be more likely to follow a moralism directly expressed in overt political decisions about who should get what in social provision. They may also be more likely to accept individual responsibility to pursue opportunities in a competitive setting rather than expect others to provide for them, so that fairness becomes a matter of equality of opportunity rather than of outcome (Blair and Schröder 1999). Similarly, they might be excepted to display a higher tolerance of the unequal outcomes of the exercise of market freedoms. We analyse evidence from recent surveys to see how far these distinctions remain true in the first decade of the twenty-first century.

The chapter falls into three sections. The first considers attitudes to welfare in different regimes and points to disagreements among previous studies which are mainly quantitative. Our work includes both quantitative and qualitative material and the next section introduces our qualitative work, designed to explore the basic standpoints and conceptions that underlie the responses that people give in attitude surveys. We then go on to examine responses in three areas where the structure of German and UK welfare systems implies differences in attitudes: the role of social contributions, ideas about equality, and privilege, and the legitimacy of inequality. The analysis shows that strong differences remain between popular understandings in the two countries, but that these differences are reflected more clearly in extended discussion than they are in the prestructured responses of quantitative surveys. This is because the conceptions used, most notably what counts as a social contribution (a social insurance payment or commitment to the work ethic) and how equality of opportunity is understood (as the provision of a high level of support especially for disadvantaged groups, or as the availability of opportunities, leaving it up to the individual to take responsibility for grasping them), differ between the two countries. These issues are discussed in the concluding section.

3.2 Attitudes to welfare in Germany and the UK

Most of the work that compares attitudes to welfare in the two countries is based on quantitative studies such as the International Social Survey Project (ISSP), the European Social Survey (ESS), or the Eurobarometer surveys of the EU. A weak relationship between attitudes and the character of different welfare states is a common finding. One of the leading analysts of comparative welfare values points out on the basis of an extensive analysis of ISSP data: 'expectations that attitudes towards welfare policies should differ systematically between different welfare regimes receive little support' (Svallfors 2003: 513). In fact, in his analysis the differences in attitudes between pairs of countries that are typically identified as members of the same regime group are greater than the differences between regime groups. Other researchers find

Table 3.1: Attitudes to welfare: % agreeing + strongly agreeing

	Germany		UK (2006)	
	ESS (2006)		*ESS (2006)*	
Income differences in Germany/ UK are too large	81		76	
Government should reduce income differences	58	61	63	57
Government should spend more on the poor	38		36	
It is important the people are treated equally and have equal opportunities		73		73
Right that people with higher incomes are allowed to buy better health care:				
Yes	18		48 (2004)	
No	75		24	
Right that people with higher incomes are allowed to buy better education for their children:				
Yes	12		50 (2004)	
No	79		24	
N	1000	2786	3748	1877

some relationship between regime type and welfare state attitudes (Arts and Gelissen 2001: 283; Linos and West 2003; Jaeger 2006).

A particular puzzle in welfare values from quantitative surveys is illustrated in Table 3.1, which includes recent data from the European Social Survey for both countries, from British Social Attitudes Survey for the UK, and from our own Attitudes to Welfare survey,[2] which used questions from BSA and ESS, for Germany. Data is for 2006 except where otherwise stated. Despite the different orientations by welfare regime, people in the two countries share remarkably similar attitudes to the problems of inequality and poverty and of the desirability of government action to address them, and to the importance of equal treatment and opportunities. Large majorities see inequality as an issue, smaller majorities think government should address it, and even smaller (but still substantial) groups want government to redistribute to the poor. In these areas citizens in corporatist-conservative Germany do not seem distinctively committed to the principle of maintaining existing status orders, while the market-centred UK seems correspondingly supportive of interventions directed at moderating market outcomes.

In other areas, attitudes correspond more closely to the theoretical regime model. In Germany market freedoms that confer inappropriate advantages in the core areas of social provision are viewed with disapproval. In the UK they

[2] The Attitudes to Welfare Survey included questions taken from the 2006 UK British Social Attitudes and the 1999 International Social Survey Project surveys. It was commissioned from IPSOS-Mori and carried out by telephone between April and May 2007, with a representative sample of 1000 respondents in Germany.

are regarded as perfectly acceptable. This pattern of attitudes in our study corroborates Svallfors's analysis of 1999 International Social Survey Project data which showed that only 12 per cent of those interviewed in West Germany and 10 per cent of those in former East Germany regarded the private purchase of better treatment in health care as acceptable, as against more than 41 per cent for the UK. For education, corresponding statistics were 12 and 9 per cent, as against 44 per cent (Svallfors 2006).

In this chapter we will examine the relationship between attitudes to fairness and social provision and regime in the two countries, using qualitative material to analyse the way in which ordinary people understand these concepts and paying attention to the arguments used among different social groups to justify their viewpoint. We focus on three areas that enable us to contrast a conservative-corporatist and more market-orientated liberal system: rights to welfare, equality, and market freedom. While we do not regard strict hypothesis testing as appropriate in an exploratory study of this kind, and we expect national differences to be matters of degree, we would anticipate on the basis of the above discussion:

- stronger commitment to social rights earned through paid work and insurance contributions in the German context, and a more moralized discourse reflecting judgements on fulfilment of the obligation to pursue paid work and provide for one's own needs so far as possible in the UK;
- acceptance of restriction of state activity to providing a fair starting point for people to compete and achieve unequal outcomes in the UK, with a stronger expectation of intervention to constrain inequalities in life chances in Germany; and
- greater endorsement of restrictions on individual rights to buy privileged services in core areas of social provision in Germany, and a stronger commitment to consumer freedom in the UK.

3.3 The study

The qualitative work is based on analysis of material from six focus groups held in Germany, in the Hamburg and Cologne areas, and eight in the UK in the vicinity of Birmingham and London. We wished to examine how people understood and talked about fairness in social provision in relatively free conversations within peer groups from a similar social background, where the groups allowed us to take into account major differences in class and age group (Stewart et al. 2006: ch.1). Participants were recruited by a sampling agency through random telephone contact using a screening questionnaire to achieve a range of political viewpoints along a left–right spectrum, to ensure that only citizens of the country were included and to produce a balance of ethnic groups corresponding to the national population. They included between eight and twelve participants, aged between 21 and 65, half men and half women. The groups were divided equally between inner city and suburban areas. Half the groups contained older (over 45) and half younger participants. The UK Office of National Statistics Office SOC2000 occupational grouping (ONS 2008a) was used to differentiate occupations and ensure that half of the groups contained workers from routine (semi or unskilled) and half from non-routine (managerial, professional, and skilled) jobs.

The focus group schedule was developed in four preliminary groups in the UK, translated by the German team, tested in both countries, and agreed. It started out with general questions about fairness and social provision and included prompts on reciprocity, different conceptions of equality, social investment, the impact of ethnic diversity, and the kind of society in which the group members would like to live. The groups were facilitated by a professional from a survey organization, recorded and transcribed, and then analysed by theme and by the arguments used by the various participants in their interactions to explain and justify particular positions.

3.3.1 *Contribution and the right to welfare*

The idea that access to social benefits and services should be linked to contribution emerged in both countries, but in rather different ways. The theme of contribution and earned rights to welfare is central to German discussions of fairness and social provision and emerged immediately when the theme of fairness was first introduced. There is a noticeable concern among older groups that continuing reforms in social provision may lead to those who have contributed during much of their working lives, losing out on some of the benefits which they expected to receive from the social insurance system. Many of the younger participants fear that the benefits they eventually claim, especially pensions, will not match the amounts they have contributed. Anxieties about loss of entitlements are strongest among routine groups.

German group 1, routine, 46+
4 Of course, pensioners should receive their pension and of course it should not always become less and less in a way that the people finally don't know how to make ends meet. Everything is becoming more and more expensive and people get less money.
9 It is fair that you can enjoy your old age after a long working career. That you get support when something bad happens, sickness, unemployment. But also that people who have never paid their share and who have never contributed don't take advantage of the system. Instead those who contributed should profit.

German group 3, routine, 46+

5 The problem is that they do not distinguish anymore with regard to unemployment. If you become unemployed, after 40 years of work then this is just bad luck. Nowadays you get 18 or 24 months of money and afterwards you receive as much as someone who was unemployed for 30 years, and this is the problem we have in our society. That we start to treat all people the same way and that those who contributed for years are treated just like those who have never contributed. That's a big problem in our society. That's what we call 'fair society'. That's not the case at all, people are slapped in the face literally. It is really a mess going on here and the government just goes on acting cold as ice... Those politicians who sit there and argue are not connected to the base anymore. They just don't know what the ordinary people encounter in their everyday lives.

It is this concern that is associated with support for equal opportunities in areas like education, as a way of permitting the weaker groups access to social provision if their contributions become devalued. The contribution approach which underpinned the social inclusion of those with access to employment in the traditional German system is seen as under threat. Rather than shifting responsibility to the individual as in the UK case, government retains an important role in sustaining the values of the system. However, individuals bear some responsibility in that there is strong support for the idea that people should contribute through work in return for social benefits. The government should assist by supporting the weakest in gaining access to employment.

German group 3, routine, 20–45

1 I think that the government should encourage the people to take more responsibility because there are a lot who say: 'if I get money from the government why should I go to work?'

The interlinkage between the established logic of a contribution-based entitlement to social provision achieved through social insurance and ideas about individual opportunity and responsibility in Germany is complex. The role of government is seen as both providing a level basis for all to take up opportunities and as ensuring that the opportunities are available. At the same time, individuals need to take some responsibility for contributing to society. The obligation to work and contribute to the finance of social insurance is the clearest example of this.

UK groups did not endorse the idea that contributions (or tax payments) earn proportional rights to welfare benefits. There was a strong emphasis on the work ethic and on the concern that the availability of benefits encouraged laziness. This reinforced the argument for individual responsibility and for the role of government in promoting a sense of responsibility for outcomes on the part of the citizen, rather than damaging it by making benefits available too easily.

UK group 3, routine, 46+

8 [British people]...want to be unemployed. They don't want a minimum wage you see.

6 It's the benefits.

8 They can't live on a minimum wage, so if they go on unemployment and they get...all the benefits. [voices agree]

UK group 1, non-routine, 20–45

8 I would say that people on benefits are on the breadline through choice, because yes they have children and think, 'well I'll get myself a flat', but a lot of them are happy with that: they don't particularly want to move on. It's passed down through the generations... I think ultimately it comes down to a distinct lack of education....I don't think they're educated enough to know that if they put a bit more effort in—and it's not that difficult—they can move up levels, you know, progress.

UK group 3, routine, 46+

Q So what are you going to do tomorrow, what will you do tomorrow if it was your job to, you know, sort out this kind of issue about benefits and work and single parents and...

6 Gradually withdraw, gradually withdraw this benefit system...

5 Shame them into it.

8 That's right.

5 Don't let them, shop at the same shop that has given, give them the tokens so you've got to go and get your food from there.

6 That's what they do in America.

The discourse in the UK also supports extending equality of opportunity, although there is much less discussion of a basic underpinning equality of outcome provided by the government. As in Germany, there is a strong emphasis on people contributing to society through work. However, the contribution is understood in terms of individual moral standing and responsibility for oneself, rather than contribution to a system of inclusion for all contributors. This leads to the idea of designing the benefit system so that it reinforces the work ethic.

UK group 2, non-routine, 20–45

4 Well I am not 100 per cent sure, I mean I quite agree with these two when they say about...the benefits, because that's a big thing....I used to do some accounting and a lady who had two kids, she got three kids and getting more tax credits, so basically the more kids she was popping out the more money she was getting,....[voices agree].

5 almost like what the lady said there, it's like a cycle of deprivation, they are in that cycle and they don't know any different [male voice agrees] I don't think anybody would like sit there and think oh I'll have another child because I'll get an extra £50 a week...But that's their whole expectation. So it's more about education...how to be responsible citizens in any country.

UK group 5, non-routine, 46+

6 I know people with young children and I know people who are unemployed who do better than me who works full time [voice agrees]...

Q Is that financially better?

6 Financially better. They claim this, they claim that, they've got big 42 inch TVs they watch all day because they claim this benefit and that benefit, and I've got a very small television...

Q So should there be less emphasis on supporting sort of families with young children?

[Some agree]

3 Not less emphasis but a different emphasis...More sort of focused on how you are supporting them. Are they going to say well 'I can't be bothered, here's £20...come back next week and I'll give you another £20', or...'What is it that you're capable of doing. What can you do to dignify yourself?'

8 Exactly...But I do think that the idea of evening it out, and maybe—it's giving people their dignity. It's not charity. [...]

5 Exactly, it's the dignity.

In both countries the ideas that individuals should contribute to society and that government should provide the opportunities for them to do so are strong. However in the UK, contribution is contrasted with the laziness of those who are seen to live off benefits. In Germany, contribution is more a matter of working and paying social insurance contributions, in a context in which government values those who do so. In the UK welfare state discourse tends to be directed downwards, and contrasts the self-supporting responsible market actor with the welfare cheat. In Germany the included worker who earns the right to social provision is contrasted with those who are excluded. Unemployed people should be given the opportunity to secure entitlement for themselves through work, but the earned rights of standard workers should be protected.

3.3.2 *Equality of outcome and equality of opportunity*

At the start of the focus group interviews, the participants in both countries were asked what they felt a fair society was and what is unfair about society today. In both countries there was strong support for equality of opportunity. However, the notion of opportunity was often closely linked to equality of outcome, and the discourse about equality differed substantially between the two countries.

The participants in the German groups stressed both equality of opportunity and equality of outcome. In general, the more non-routine groups saw the role of equality of outcome, particularly in areas like education, as providing services to compensate for differences in ability, skill, or background so that opportunities might become more equal for different social groups. There is thus an important role for the government in redistribution. Equality of opportunity is not seen as a justification for state withdrawal from direct intervention.

German group 6, non-routine, 20–45
Q What do you think of when asked about fairness?
2 I like the thought of a society where also the weak are protected, such things. On the other hand it is maybe also important to think about how to reward achievements. . . .
4 I think that there is something like a fair society and that the government is responsible for that. To establish a code of law making the society fair.
Q What do you think characterizes fairness?
4 Equality of opportunity or that people who are sick and those who cannot work get their money through tax redistribution in a way that everybody can simply live here. Everybody needs to have a basic standard that he can launch from.

Among routine respondents, equality of opportunity was again seen as most important, and the role of education and other services in enabling people to gain equal opportunities stressed. There was also some support for equality of outcome.

German group 3, routine, 45+
Q What do you understand by the term 'fair society'?
1 One point is equality of opportunity and the possibility of having a social base or foundation [Fundament]. That the government provides support if someone is in need of help. That you have the possibility to work your way up again. But also to receive help to help yourself, a service that needs to be structured accordingly. And of course a decent system of health care that just needs to be there. . . .
4 What I consider to be a fair society that everything a society produces, and that is always the case in a society, that all the members together produce a GDP, a cake, and that everyone who contributed to this cake gets his fair share.
9 That's a keyword for me, foundation. . . .
2 I see the necessity of equal opportunities with regard to education and this starts with a dilemma. Because children have parents with different backgrounds they also do not have the same educational opportunities and this especially gets more important when you get old. Not only when you grow old but during your whole working career.
German group 1, routine, 45+
Q The government has different possibilities to provide social services. It can ensure it deals with relatively similar income and living conditions by redistributing from the better-off to the less well-off but it can also provide equal opportunities. What do you think is more important?
9 Both. This goes together. You cannot separate this.
5 Both. The government needs to protect, by providing vocational training for example or support, in any way. To make sure that people of all kinds of ages have a chance to move on.

42

3 But the problem is the youth. Most often it is the pupils from lower secondary school [Hauptschule], they just do not want to engage themselves.

Interestingly, among one group of younger routine workers the notion of fairness was related closely to equal opportunities, but also to the importance of linking the benefits and services people get to the contribution they make. This group contained a high proportion of relatively disadvantaged people including those out of work, who would have obvious interests in redistribution and equality of outcome, but this is not the approach they endorsed.

German group 4, routine, 20–45
Q What do you understand by the term, 'fair society'?
9 That you get what you deserve for what you put in and that you can get a job that matches your qualifications. [. . .]
7 To me fairness means equality of opportunity. To me the reward is more or less secondary. Everyone needs to have the same opportunities.
6 Fairness is also if someone becomes sick—something nobody can influence—or if one loses his job, that he still then has a chance in society.
2 I think fairness is provided in Germany. Everyone has the opportunity to do whatever he wants to. You do have the chances with regard to education you do not find in other countries.

In Germany the traditional approach is to link benefits to contributions. This assumption underlies the logic of social insurance and has been seen as central to the conservative assumption of status maintenance and the corporatist idea of social provision as involving the institutional representation of both the employees and employers who are stakeholders in the system by virtue of their contributions. The striking feature of the German responses is that this approach does not come to the fore in discussion of fairness, although it does emerge elsewhere in the interview. The dominant theme across both routine and non-routine and younger and older groups is that fairness is most strongly associated with equality of opportunity. Many participants argue that a substantial measure of equality of outcome is necessary to achieve equality of opportunity.

In the UK case, equality of opportunity is also stressed, but the notion is not a simple acceptance that opportunities should be available. Opportunity and responsibility are seen to go hand-in-hand. People can only take more responsibility for outcomes and not rely on the state if opportunities to do so are available to them, and also if they grasp the opportunities.

Members of the groups attracted most agreement and approval when they stated that 'equality of opportunity' already exists to a large extent in contemporary British society. Especially at the beginning of the conversations, many respondents insisted that opportunities are already equal, since everyone has access to universally provided education and health. However, in some groups, some respondents argued that services were unfairly distributed and better provision was available in some areas, despite the conviction that equal opportunities exist. The rationale behind this apparent contradiction lies in beliefs about individual agency. The responsibility for addressing such challenges rests with individuals. Inequalities of opportunity were seen as the outcome of individual choice, shaped by personality and peer culture. The responsibility of government, even in the limited area of providing equal opportunities for different social groups, is further constrained by the fact that outcomes may depend on the different capacity of people to grasp opportunities.

UK group 1, non-routine, 20–45

8 I grew up in one of these inner-city impoverished areas. We had nothing, poor, I went to a school . . . where they used to sniff glue in the toilets, fight the teachers, drink in the lessons . . . I have not continued that trend with my children, you know, I pay over the odds for my house because I wanted my kids to be in a completely different school.

6 Yes, and I bet there aren't many like you. . . .

8 . . . I bump into people maybe in the supermarket from school and I think god, life hasn't been kind to you—but you know what, it was their choice. [voices agree].

UK group 4, routine, 46+

3 But I think it's like we said, life is too easy for them now, they know they can go and get money, whatever, off the dole or whatever, and then they are not going to work, they don't want it.

1 People make choices in life, whether you choose to have a baby when you're 16, 17, you know you've . . . made that decision . . .

7 When we left school we went straight into a job, we didn't think of going and signing on. [agreement from others in group]

When we asked about the extent to which equal opportunities existed in the UK employment market, focus group members often raised the issue of whether unemployed people should be expected to be proactive in finding work. Most participants strongly emphasized individual responsibility to find appropriate jobs, especially for younger people. However, government should at the same time also support opportunities. Members of all groups agreed that, while unemployed people should display flexibility in their labour market behaviour, re-training and job entry schemes were essential.

UK group 3, routine, 46+

3 Over the years jobs have changed, industries have gone, skills have gone and all the rest of it. You can't expect people to train and that job to be there forever . . . [it] might disappear and something else come in. And then you've got to re-train again.

UK group 6, non-routine, 46+
1 For instance, . . . I think there could be a lot more training for jobs in this country, right, and I think that if people are out of work they should be given the choice to go and . . . be trained but to a certain extent if they're not prepared to do it they should be penalized. . . .
[consensus that there should be more apprenticeships, sponsored or subsidized by government]

Respondents, especially those in the routine working-class groups were aware of the difficulties in grasping opportunities. For example, moving to a different area of the country to find work might involve real costs.

UK group 4, routine, 46+
9 In areas that we've just talked about, say the mining industry up North where the industry has completely gone . . . it is harder for them, but what's stopping them from moving? [. . .]
7 Money. Not everyone can afford to up and go, . . . if you be realistic.
9 But if they haven't got a job somewhere where they are living at the moment and there's a job for them somewhere else.
6 Then you've got to move the kids out of one school to put them in another school, you know there's a lot.
9 Schooling is free. [. . .]
1 It's normally those on big salaries.

They were also conscious of the existing structure of inequalities and the vulnerable position of unskilled workers at the bottom.

UK group 8, routine, 20–45
Q What do you think is unfair in society today?
3 Well just about, the way everything's stacked . . . Everything in society at the moment is shit on everyone at the bottom, blatant, ... you've got Tesco's making £3 billion profit, right, if you work in Tesco's 40 hour a week, you don't have enough money to even pay rent. . . . .
Q How far do others believe this to be true?
1 He's just about said it all, really.
5 Yes.

However, almost all participants endorsed equality of opportunity. They laid little stress on the term 'equal', and argued that it should be up to individuals to take responsibility for grasping available opportunities. The discussion also favoured activation policies with strong pressures to take jobs, but also recognized the importance of providing good opportunities for retraining and support in moving between jobs. The UK participants endorsed the importance of government establishing equal opportunities but stressed the role of individuals in grasping opportunities, and despite some agreements, mostly believed that opportunities were substantially equal at present.

The overall picture is that equality of opportunity predominates in discourse about fairness and welfare in both countries. However, equality of opportunity is understood in rather different ways. In Germany the role of government in redistributing to provide a common foundation and specifically to address the disadvantage of the most vulnerable receives more attention. In the UK, equality of opportunity is understood more as involving roughly equal access to basic services, while imposing a stronger obligation on individuals to take responsibility for taking hold of the opportunities available.

3.3.3 *Privilege and the legitimacy of inequalities*

In Germany, most participants across the different groups would prefer a system in which everybody has access to similar services, at least so far as education and health care, which are seen as the basic elements in social provision, are concerned. The routine working-class groups simply thought that it was unfair that those who have more money can buy themselves and their families superior health care and education. The idea that a basic level of equality in these services was an essential element in a fair society was strongly supported.

German group 4, routine, 20–45
Q Do you think that it is fair that richer people can buy better services than poorer people? For example better health care by private insurance schemes, better education and higher pensions?
1 With regard to health care I don't think that this is fair. Everyone should have the same conditions here.
2 My flatmate has private health insurance and . . . if he is in a hurry he says, 'I am a private patient' and then they say, 'Oh, I have found a free slot, please come immediately'. This really is a mess, but if you know that it works like this then you should do everything you can to become a private patient. [. . .]
7 Health care should be equal, education as well. Old age pensions should refer to the standard of living, which means that this does not necessarily need to be equal.

Among the non-routine groups, most participants believed that a basic level of provision should be provided for everyone in these services.

German group 2, non-routine, 20–45
Q Again, if we think of justice and injustice, do you think it is fair that wealthy people, people with more money, are able to afford more than people who aren't that well-off? Thus, wealthy people are able to get access to things which poorer people cannot afford. By that I don't mean cars or something like that, but health care or education for children.

4 I would think it is upsetting—like it is in England or other European countries nowadays—that you have to take a lot of money in your hands to finance your children's education. I think we don't have this status yet.

8 Generally, I think basic provisions always should be given; whether it is health or education and in principle potentials that are within our society should be fostered. Well, with the tuition fees . . . as already said, schemes could absolutely be better financed.

There was also a strong emphasis that people should work and pay contributions to finance these services and to achieve access to basic equal provision, which should be at a decent level.

German group 6, non-routine, 20–45

Q So you think that you have worked for a long time and should thus receive a lot of support?

7 Yes.

4 But I think that one should create more jobs to let people who receive social benefits do some work in return. I don't like the idea of someone receiving social benefits and not doing something in return.

2 . . . Of course I also think that someone who worked for 30 years should receive a different kind of protection. I think it is shocking that it is not that way. But my clients are drug addicts and are not able to engage in the regular labour market. Sometimes they do have good phases, sometimes not. I am also happy when they do their community service [Sozialstunden]. . . . I just say 'this is something a society just has to pay for'.

The non-routine participants tended to distinguish services like pensions. They felt that the capacity of better-off people to purchase better services privately should be tolerated, while they did not regard it as necessarily desirable.

German group 2, non-routine, 20–45

2 I think it is unfair [that the better-off can buy better services] . . . , it is a fact, that if you have more money you can finance a better education for your children and you can raise them easier. . . . I think that is unfair.

7 But I actually think for the society we live in, a capitalistic society, well, he has honourably achieved, he has lawfully earned his money, that he can afford different things, that is bitter for me . . .

3 Yeah, cars, but not for these fields. It is just about education.

7 Yeah, I actually understood that. You got me wrong here. It actually hurts and it is awful if the one sitting next to me is a private patient and is therefore being treated differently, but unfortunately that is the society we already live in. I don't like that, but we are already there.

There is a strong tendency among those interviewed in the German groups to follow through the idea that the core of social provision should be available equally to all to the idea that better-off groups should not be permitted to purchase superior services. Rather, everyone should be expected to work and contribute and should receive a decent standard of provision.

German group 6, non-routine, 20–45
Q Do you think that it is fair that the better-off can afford better services than the poor?
2 This question sounds almost like a joke. Of course this is not fair. I don't know what to answer here, to be honest.
9 If the base is a good basic social care for everyone then the rich can afford a hospital on the Bahamas if they've got the money for this. If the base level is decent and fair then I wouldn't have a problem with it.
6 If basic social care is provided but there are always grades.

This contrasts with attitudes in the UK, where members of all groups endorsed the idea that those with higher incomes should be free to purchase better services in areas like health care and education if they so choose, although this produces inequalities.

Most people sympathize with the motives of those using private services and aspire to do so themselves. Linked to this is the widely approved justification that elite access to better or faster health care and education is yet another incentive to better oneself:

UK group 4, routine, 46+
7 They've earned it, it's their money, they spend it on what they like.
3 I mean if I'd got money that's the first thing I would do is health care, private health care.
UK group 1, non-routine, 20–45
3 There's got to be an incentive to get there, there's got to be a reason to go for it and at the end of the day that's survival of the fittest, isn't it? That's the law of nature, that's reality.

The concept of completely equal access to the services which are fundamental to equality of opportunity finds little support. Only five respondents, out of seventy-one, voiced doubts about whether such steps might lead to an unjustified inequalities.

UK group 7, routine, 20–45
4 It's your life, it's health, it's different. Like, if you're earning it you have the right to have a better car, a better house, and all these assets. That's like you improve your quality of life. If it's your health, . . . why should you have more of a chance? I don't think that's fair.

These dissenters received little endorsement from other members of the groups and their ideas were largely dismissed. Three of the anti-private respondents were ambivalent in their views, changing their mind in response to others' arguments or remaining in favour of the choice afforded by the existence of private-sector services, despite their doubts. Respondents felt that any unequal opportunities resulting from private-sector use were seen as inevitable and not something that the state is in a position to tackle:

> UK group 5, non-routine, 20–45
> 6 All my socialist tendencies here are screaming... it's not fair that somebody can't afford something and somebody else can... Absolutely, that is so wrong... But let's be realistic about this... things always apportion themselves, the fat and the thin: that will always happen.

However, the UK participants were more cautious about moving to a pure market position under which the wealthy could choose to abandon both rights to services from and the obligation to pay taxes to the state and simply buy what they wanted. A strong discourse across the groups was that the use of private health care was acceptable, but only so long as people continue to pay their taxes.

> UK group 1, non-routine, 20–45
> 8 If you've got the facility, they worked for it, they've earned it, they can do what they like with it.
> 1 Why should they pay twice?
> 3 [No,] they don't pay less tax, they're still putting their money in.
> [agreement from others with M3].

The only respondents to agree with the idea that those who bought private services might be exempted from paying tax for the welfare state came from members of non-routine groups who saw themselves as paying twice, once for private provision for themselves and once through tax for the welfare state for others.

> UK group 5, non-routine, 46+
> 1 ... one of the things that perhaps would make it fairer is if people are having to opt out of it, you know to go for private medicine... then they perhaps ought to get tax relief on that..., having three children in a private school, ... I am having to pay twice.
> Q So what do others think about this idea of sort of getting tax relief because you're not using as much?
> 9 There's a lot in Sweden and also you get it on private medical. [voices agree] If you opt into the private medical side, then that portion of your tax is given back to you. [...]

This was an issue where (unlike Germany) there was some division of class interest. Some of the better-off respondents felt that they were paying in at a high level, yet not receiving a commensurate service in return:

UK group 2, non-routine, 20–45

7 I'm a higher tax payer and have been for a number of years now, and . . . I don't get any better service. In fact I get a less better service because I have to pay additionally to top up how I want something to be done. Whether it's your rubbish, whatever it is . . . schooling, and you end up—if you don't go to private school you end up with tutors because the class sizes are too big. So you end up topping up in every dimension but you don't actually see anything better for your money that you're paying in. You still pay NHS . . .

The German and UK groups offer a contrast in their views on how far richer people should be allowed to use their more favourable market position to buy better services. In the UK, respondents are much more willing to accept class inequalities stemming from the market. The logic is that if someone is better off they have earned the right to do as they choose in their own interest. The German approach is generally less individualist and typically acknowledges limitations on freedom to spend one's money as one chooses. It was understood in the German groups that people have the obligation to work and contribute to society and earn rights to welfare and government should ensure that at the basic level at least provision is equal. In the UK, there is an indication that some better-off people would prefer to opt out of taxes and benefits from the welfare state, while class differences in Germany were less marked.

3.4 Conclusion: social meanings and social welfare in Germany and the UK

In this chapter we have discussed some recent evidence on popular ideas about fairness and social provision in Germany and the UK. A common position contrasts the two countries as at opposite poles, representing corporatist conservative and liberal market-centred welfare systems. Quantitative research shows substantial similarities in attitudes to equality and to state interventions to address such issues issues, but differences in relation to the exercise of market freedoms. Qualitative research indicates that different structures of ideas may underlie similar statements in areas like the value of equality of opportunity.

The similarities between discourse about fairness and social provision in the two countries are that in both there is a strong emphasis on equality of opportunity as a major objective and on contribution to society through work as central to individual citizenship obligations. German participants, however, make a much closer link between equal outcomes in the core areas of social provision and equal opportunity in the sense that genuinely equal opportunities are assumed to lead to much greater equality of outcomes. Those in the UK tend to acknowledge social inequalities in life chances and to regret them, but nevertheless to take a robust view that individuals should be able to overcome such obstacles if they are sufficiently determined, and that the responsibility lies with them to do so.

Social contributions in Germany are much more likely to be understood within the logic of social insurance as guaranteeing social rights. In the UK, the concern is with the extent to which the individual takes full responsibility for maintaining themselves in the market, in just the same way that individual commitment is seen as able to contest inequalities and develop opportunities. Correspondingly, in Germany the assumption that government should support the more vulnerable in access to employment so that they can gain rights through contribution is emphasized. While this is also recognized in the UK, there is a much stronger concern that government should regulate welfare so as not to undermine the individual's commitment to take responsibility for themselves.

The stronger theme of individualism in the UK also emerges in ideas about the legitimacy of buying better services in the core areas of education and health care, which make a substantial difference to people's opportunities in life. While the German participants, even middle-class people, tended to disapprove of this in the core areas of social provision, almost all participants in the UK endorsed the idea of market freedom.

Both German and UK participants stress the theme of equality of opportunity. The differences lie in assumptions about individual responsibility and about the role of government in securing social inclusion that lie behind equality of opportunity policies. In the UK, government is expected to provide a roughly level playing field in basic services and individuals are then free to achieve unequal positions in society and bear chief responsibility for outcomes.

European welfare states face strong pressures from globalization and post-industrial shifts. This leads to concerns about an erosion of traditions of social provision and the encroachment of market values in areas where concerns about fairness and equality had previously been influential. A number of studies indicate that differences between welfare state regimes remain important. This research indicates that key differences between corporatist conservatism and market individualism also remain at the level of welfare discourse, despite indications of similarities from quantitative attitude surveys. These differences appear to exist and to be supported by different understandings of social rights and of the ideas about entitlement, opportunity, responsibility, and privilege that surround them, although both countries have experienced similar pressures from shifts in the international political economic context during the past two decades. The fact that national patterns of welfare values are resilient to shifts in international political economy indicates that commitments to social provision may also be resilient in the face of severe political pressures for retrenchment in response to the international economic crisis.

4

Challenges of ethnic diversity: results from a qualitative study

Christoph Burkhardt and Steffen Mau[1]

4.1 Introduction

In recent decades Western Europe has faced increasing migration, resulting in more diverse populations. Ethnic diversity and, as a direct consequence, the question of adequate inclusion of immigrants into the social security system have put the welfare state under pressure. National welfare systems face a challenge, because as soon as migrants take up permanent residence within their territory, it is in the public interest to include them in the welfare system in order to minimize problems arising from ethnic segregation and marginalization (Guiraudon 2002). At the same time, it is clear that the inclusion of migrants or groups who are not considered as 'belonging' could undermine the legitimacy of a social security system based on solidarity with one's own community. Moreover, in many Western European welfare states immigrants tend to be, proportionally, more reliant on state support than natives (Boeri et al. 2002). Hence, a fundamental problem associated with all policies on immigration and integration is to find a balance between the openness and exclusivity of the welfare system without endangering the universal consensus of the welfare state (Faist 1998: 149; see also Bommes and Halfmann 1998; Banting 2000; and Banting et al. 2006).

In the literature, there is some debate on the possible repercussions of the inclusion of migrants. Taking the US as an example, Alesina and Glaeser (2004) expect that the European welfare states—once based on social and ethnic homogeneity—will have difficulties in accommodating increasing diversity (for the British case, see Goodhart 2004). The link between the level

---

[1] In collaboration with Peter Taylor-Gooby and Rose Martin (University of Kent).

of immigration and solidarity has also been scrutinized by research on prejudice and racism (Pettigrew 1998; Pettigrew and Tropp 2000; Gang et al. 2002). This research reveals that there is a general tendency towards in-group preference because people are more inclined to concede rights and entitlements to their own group than to those regarded as different. Numerous studies confirm that social acceptance of migrants and the extent to which they are granted rights is directly related to the 'perceived ethnic threat' that arises from the presence of ethnic minorities (Scheepers et al. 2002; Raijman et al. 2003). In addition, majority groups tend to evaluate the presence and the characteristics of groups who enter 'their' territory negatively and with reservations (Elias and Scotson 1965). Within the hierarchy of who is considered deserving, migrants are placed beneath native groups (van Oorschot 2006; van Oorschot and Uunk 2007). Nonetheless, a number of authors have also challenged the assumption that increased diversity necessarily undermines welfare state support (cf. e.g. Taylor-Gooby 2005; Banting et al. 2006; van Oorschot 2006; Mau and Burkhardt 2009a, b). Furthermore, qualitative research dealing with the issue of public attitudes towards migrants by Pearce and Stockdale (2009) suggests that opinion polls may exaggerate the negative views held by the population.

Against the background of this research, we will examine attitudes towards migration and the inclusion of migrants into the welfare state in Germany and the United Kingdom. We use qualitative data collected from focus group interviews. Our research focuses on the divergent views on migration arising from differences between the countries with regard to their institutional welfare design and their differing migratory history. After highlighting the differences between the countries from a migration perspective we describe the methods, the data, and the sampling of the qualitative approach used in this study. We will then try to shed light on attitudes towards migration by looking into the qualitative data.

4.2 Different (welfare) regimes—different attitudes?

As a point of departure, we assume that the attitudes are linked to the specific immigration and/or welfare regime. Let us first consider the differences in terms of the welfare regimes. The Beveridge versus Bismarck distinction marks the difference between tax-financed state provision and contributory social insurance provision (Bonoli 1997). The former, for which the UK is the prime example, focuses on the prevention of poverty for all citizens and the latter, epitomized by the German system, on status maintenance policies for employees. Though it is relatively costly, the Bismarck-type welfare regime limits interpersonal redistribution and promises the maintenance of the relative status position of its clientele (Esping-Andersen 1990). Distributional conflicts in the German system should thus be relatively contained, especially when it comes to social insurance benefits. Social assistance benefits, however, might be prone to such conflicts since they might not be framed as 'earned rights'. The Beveridge-type of policy arrangement, in contrast, is financed mainly out of general taxation and characterized by flat-rate benefits at a modest level. In the UK, people are not expected to draw a significant line between contributory and tax-financed benefits. Conflicts might come up across all types of benefits accessible to migrants, but they might not be as fierce due to the relatively low level of benefits available.

The immigration regime, however, might also play a role. Germany experienced an influx of so-called guest workers from the Mediterranean countries between 1955 and 1973, and after the recruitment stopped an ongoing migration inflow due to family migration. The two other major groups are the migrants of German origin (Spätaussiedler), who primarily come from Eastern Europe and receive German citizenship because of their German descent, and asylum seekers and refugees, whose number peaked in the beginning of the 1990s and is decreasing since then due to changes in asylum law. In 2007, 15.4 million people (18.7 per cent of the total population) living in Germany had a migratory background. Out of these, 8.1 million (9.9 per cent of the total population) were Germans with a migratory background and another 7.3 million people (8.9 per cent of the total population) were of foreign nationality (Statistisches Bundesamt 2009). For different immigrant groups different 'inclusion rules' apply: guest workers and their families are included into the welfare schemes mainly through their employment; asylum seekers and refugees are supported by special social assistance schemes which, after public debate in the 1990s, have been lowered and are given mainly as in-kind rather than in-cash benefits; migrants of German origin are automatically included into the different schemes, even into pension schemes by giving credits on the basis of 'fictitious' contributory records in accordance with their employment history before arriving in Germany. EU-foreigners have more or less equal access to most schemes (social assistance benefits are subject to a residence-related waiting period). In terms of welfare reliance we find that the share of social welfare recipients in Germany is higher among immigrants than among German citizens (cf. e.g. Bauer 2002; Riphahn 2004). In 2007, every fifth person with a migratory background in working age was either long-term unemployed or not earning enough and thus dependent on welfare benefits to secure a basic social living standard (payments according to Social Law (SGB II), i.e. Hartz IV).

In the UK, in contrast, the issue of diversity is strongly linked to the colonial past. After WWII many immigrants came from the West Indian islands and took up jobs in key industries. As members of the Commonwealth they enjoyed privileged access to the UK, were entitled to British citizenship, and usually spoke English. There has also been significant migration from South East Asia, especially India and Indonesia, which also matters in terms of family migration. As in Germany, asylum has become significant only after 1990. The annual inflow of asylum seekers rose from 41,500 in 1997 to 103,080 in 2002 and has declined significantly thereafter to 28,320 in 2006 (OECD 2008: 315). Since 1999 the government has introduced measures to restrict the access of asylum seekers to support and health care, assuming that many who claim asylum are not genuinely in need of protection but rather are economic migrants. Also the judgements of what levels of need can be met given the increasing number of asylum seekers changed. For all migrants born in the UK, however, access to citizenship is much easier than in Germany, even though the new citizenship law of the year 2000 made access to German citizenship easier. The UK is currently one of the main destinations for labour migrants from Eastern Europe, especially the enlargement countries. The stock of migrants from the A8 countries increased to 587,000 by 2007 (with an inflow of 218,000 between June 2006 and June 2007), of whom 409,000 were actively participating in the labour market. These workers are mostly young people, filling the gaps in the labour market, particularly in business, administration, hospitality, and the food manufacturing industries. Hence, the number of these migrants claiming income-related benefits has been low (OECD 2008: 286). However, comparing poverty rates of white UK natives with poverty amongst people with a migratory background it becomes clear that the latter are disadvantaged. In the years of 2004 and 2005, almost 40 per cent of people from ethnic minorities were living in income poverty, which was about twice the rate for white people. However, not all ethnic minority groups are suffering equally from poverty. The income poverty rate varies substantially, with the highest rates among Bangladeshis (65 per cent), Pakistanis (55 per cent) and black Africans (45 per cent). In comparison, white non-British (25 per cent) and white British (20 per cent) people have the lowest poverty rates (Kenway and Palmer 2007).

4.3 Research approach

Against the background of country differences we are interested in the way people frame the inclusion of migrants into the welfare state in Germany and the UK. Therefore we will identify views on migration, migrants, and the impact of migration on the sustainability of the welfare state. As we draw on qualitative material, we can provide a close understanding of the arguments used and the reasons given for including or excluding migrants. The theoretical debate we have introduced above lays the ground for the key issues we are interested in:

1. Are there indications for a perceived ethnic threat? Are migrants seen as competitors for scarce resources? Can we identify ethnic hierarchies or hierarchies of deservingness?

2. How do the respondents evaluate the consequences of migration with regard to the welfare state? Do people see migrants and other ethnic groups as net beneficiaries or net payers of the welfare system?

3. On which basis do people justify inclusion into the welfare state? What are the conditions for inclusion (e.g. tax paying, residency)?

For all questions, we will examine whether differences in attitudes between different status groups exist. Are people with lower socioeconomic status more prone to reservations against migrants due to perceived competition? This is likely to be the case, since a significant share of migrants works in labour market sectors offering routine jobs. We should thus expect attitudes towards migrants to come out more negatively among people with lower socioeconomic status and those with routine occupations.

As already pointed out, Germany and the UK experienced different kinds of migration, with different ethnic groups moving into the country. In both countries, perceptions of 'us' and 'them' should play a role, though with emphasis on different groups, for instance less pronounced regarding Commonwealth migrants in the UK or ethnic Germans in Germany and more explicit regarding other groups. However, country differences might also be related to differences in citizenship regimes, with Germans particularly focusing on 'migrants versus Germans' and British respondents emphasising issues of ethnic diversity and multiculturalism. We also assume that people tend to differentiate between migrants coming from other European countries, especially European Union countries, and migrants from outside Europe. For the UK we might also find references to language issues, as some migrants speak English as a mother tongue and others do not. By and large, issues of conditionality and access should be framed in equal terms, emphasizing foregone productive contributions like labour market participation or tax paying on the one hand and long-term residence on the other hand.

4.4 Methods, sampling, and data description

We draw on data from qualitative focus group interviews conducted in both countries. Focus groups are an instrument for grasping attitudes of people towards a certain theme. The group setting helps to get to the core of the world views and arguments of the participants, since positions are often challenged by other discussants. This enables us to get to know not only attitudes but also the arguments participants bring forward to justify their position. One pitfall of this method might be a social desirability bias prompting people to state opinions which are evaluated positively by other group participants. However, in our case this did not seem to be a problem given that participants did not refrain from articulating highly controversial attitudes. The qualitative empirical approach chosen for this study thus helps to reveal attitudes as well as arguments towards migration.

There were six focus groups in Germany and eight in the UK, all held in January 2008, with an average of ten participants ranging between eight and eleven persons. In both countries the groups were recruited and the interview conducted, recorded, and transcribed by a professional survey organization.[2] In Germany the groups were held in Hamburg and Cologne, two large cities in the Western part of Germany.[3] In the UK focus groups were held in London and Birmingham, the two largest cities of the country. In both countries only citizens of the respective country were invited to take part in the group discussion. Each group consisted of an equal share of women and men. Furthermore, half the groups were filled with respondents aged between 20 and 45 years and the other half with respondents aged 46 years and over. There was a quota to ensure that at least one person of different race (for the UK) and a person with migratory background (for Germany) would participate in each of the groups. In addition, the groups were separated by economic status. Selection criteria were participants' occupation and their degree of job autonomy and responsibility. In a first step we classified participants according to the SOC2000 UK National Statistics occupational grouping. We then used a dichotomous scheme to create two groups, with people either being (highly) skilled and having non-routine jobs with relatively high responsibility on the one hand and low-skilled workers having routine jobs on the other. The 'non-routine' groups consisted of participants working, for example, as school teachers or upper or high-ranked public servants. Participants of the 'routine groups' included, for example, sales assistants, porters, and waiters/ waitresses. In both countries half the groups consisted of participants with non-routine jobs and the other half of participants with more routine occupations. These conditions were defined to ensure conversations among peers and people from similar socioeconomic backgrounds.

---

[2] German focus groups were held in German language and transcripts have been translated afterwards.

[3] By choosing Western German cities we strived for comparability with the UK group discussions. This way we could ensure that the debate on differences between Eastern and Western Germany did not dominate the whole session.

4.5 Findings from focus groups

4.5.1 *Ethnic threat and hierarchies of deservingness*

Turning to the question of whether immigration indeed leads to feelings of ethnic threat among the native population, in Germany there was little evidence that the participants see migrants primarily as competitors for scarce resources. Problems were often framed in social and cultural, rather than economic, terms. It was acknowledged that migrants do play an important role in the economy and it was emphasized that the labour market is in need of migrants taking jobs that are rejected by German workers. The participants even welcomed particular initiatives to circumvent shortage of labour in certain areas.[4] In some of the groups, especially with respondents with non-routine occupations, the presence of migrants was even evaluated positively. However, when asked about the impact of migrants on the living situation in Germany, members of the routine groups especially pointed to problems. In several cases the educational system was mentioned: participants reported that schools with high proportions of migrant pupils offer only low-quality education for German children. With regard to ethnic segregation in residential areas one female respondent reported that she felt urged to move to another part of the city in order to stop suffering from disadvantages caused by the presence of other ethnic groups. She stated that she had 'tried everything, to talk to them, everything, but it was impossible. I was part of the minority and I had to leave and I left' (F9, German group 5, non-routine, 46+).[5]

Participants regarded insufficient efforts on the part of migrants to socially integrate to be problematic. The most prominent concern in this regard was the inability to speak the language of the host country. Lacking skills to speak the German language might lead to segregation, it was argued, forcing migrants to interact only with people from the same cultural background. In general, the formation of ethnically homogenous city quarters was seen as problematic. One participant claimed:

German Group 5, non-routine, 46+
M10 We have these very positive results [of migration], but we also have these other things, which, I don't know why, probably are a problem of the cultural background. This causes the formation of ghettos [...]. How can we change this situation, to prevent it negatively influencing the situation of Germans in five generations because of all this? [...] How can we manage not to take

---

[4] For instance, the German Green Card programme inviting computer scientists (2000–4) to work and live in Germany for a restricted period.
[5] Each participant of a focus group was assigned a number from one to ten for reasons of anonymity and to enable separation of the respondents in the transcripts. In addition, a prefix was added to each number indicating whether the respondent was male (prefix M) or female (prefix F).

away foreigners' cultural and religious background and to open them up without forming these really problematic ghettos?

Apart from these opinions on integration, respondents were aware of the fact that both the native and the foreign population are responsible for mutually beneficial coexistence. Lacking knowledge of specific characteristics of the culture and the religion of migrants was mentioned as one major area of possible social conflicts. The threat caused by ethnic minorities could thus be the result of misunderstandings of the habits of unknown social and ethnic groups and not ethnic hostility or xenophobia.

In the British groups, there was very mixed evidence with regard to a perceived ethnic threat. In every group, some sort of migrant threat to British people's job prospects was brought up. The group dynamic to these conversations was mixed. For some it was a straightforward matter of migrants 'stealing' jobs. A discourse like the following one emerged in both routine and non-routine groups:

UK group 8, routine, 20–45
F1 You've got British people that can do jobs fine—but you'll get a Polish person that can do it for £4 [an hour] . . .
F3 Half the price.

The quotation illustrates both the perceived advantages which migrants can bring to the economy, but also the paramount importance attached to the employment of British people. This was a concern voiced in many UK groups. Some feared that, '(a)s a country we are outpricing ourselves on everything because a lot of industries are moving abroad' (Group 4). The solution to this, for some, was not obvious—cheap labour from migrants was seen to be beneficial, especially given a perceived laziness on the part of British unemployed people. However, others felt that there was good reason to close the borders more firmly and focus on training current residents. The uncertainty on the part of many can be illustrated with the following conversation. After some participants agreed that immigration should be stopped, a male participant responded:

UK group 8, routine, 20–45
M2 Well if you do that then the economy collapses because now we rely on everyone, that's the problem.
F1 Exactly, yeah.
M2 They don't just do the trades, the Polish; they come in and do all the jobs we don't want to do as well.

As in the German groups, concerns about the effects of migration on the education system were also at the forefront of many respondents' minds, with an emphasis on the difficulties created by the increase in the number of children whose language skills are not up to the level of their peers.

Language acquisition was certainly seen as an issue, with every group spontaneously bringing this up as a concern. For some, responsibility was placed on the government to provide English classes for the greater good. The rationale behind this was the social and economic desirability of migrants to integrate and for skilled or other working migrants to make a full contribution:

UK group 5, non-routine, 46+

F3 I mean I do think it is very important to learn the language of the country you're working in [male voice agrees]...It is really important to become a citizen...you would stop the ghettoization, hopefully, and all of these things. But you make it possible. Because there are people—doctors and things—who cannot qualify here because they can't get English lessons.

However, for others the onus was placed more on migrants themselves. One male participant (M5, UK group 6, non-routine, 46+) talked about communities of 'people that don't even speak English' who 'have almost isolated themselves'. He thinks that 'if we are going to have ethnic diversity [...] those people have got to want to integrate into our common society'.

Another issue we explored was ethnic hierarchies. German focus group participants seem to make a difference between migrants from within the EU on the one hand and on the other migrants from outside, privileging the former. Participants also drew a line between ethnic groups in terms of their phenotypical appearance and cultural habits. When asked which groups they think of as ethnic minorities, references were made to skin colour, but also to religious differences. One female participant (F7, with migratory background, German group 2, non-routine, 20–45) stated that she felt closer to members of her own religion (in this case Christian). She did not feel close to Turks because 'with their Muslim culture, including the treatment of women, that's what I think of as problematic'. Although often not expressed explicitly, it was possible to identify Turks as the most disadvantaged ethnic group. This appears to be very much in line with other studies, which emphasized that people distinguish between migrants coming form countries such as Italy or France in contrast to Turkey (Ganter 2003). Compared to other ethnic groups in Germany Turks are still the most disadvantaged group in terms of labour market participation and educational attainment, and they are also the group viewed with the most scepticism.

In the UK there was no overt racial element to the discussions about migration, also with regard to ethnic hierarchies or phenotypic appearance. As expected, the impact of migration from the Commonwealth was clear. This phase of immigration was generally evaluated positively in comparison with current migration streams 'because in the 1950s...they needed them to build the railways and the roads and bridges. So they invited them to come and stay, because they couldn't do the jobs themselves' (M4, UK group 8, routine,

20–45). When asked which groups they would term 'ethnic minorities', there were a variety of reactions. Some groups rejected the phrase as outdated and irrelevant. To some respondents (e.g. F5 and M1, UK group 5, non-routine, 46 +) it occurred that one might think of, or might in the past have thought of, non-white people as 'minority'. Therefore one could conclude that phenotypic appearance is something which does come into respondents' minds as a potentially relevant characteristic. However, this was rejected during discussion, either because it was genuinely felt to be an outdated relic of history, or because of social pressure.

Coming up in many of the UK groups in answer to the question about the meaning of 'ethnic minority' and the issue of immigration was a perceived division between British and non-British people—and that subdivisions beyond this were meaningless.[6] As F5 (UK group 5, non-routine, 46+) puts it, 'I just think British or not British'. 'British' tended to be defined in terms of birth in the UK, or in terms of cultural behaviour and migrant tolerance of British ways. The latter seemed to receive a particularly heavy emphasis. There was a perception that migrants were unwilling to integrate: failing to learn English, choosing to live in separate areas, and imposing their value systems on others. Unlike in Germany, homogenous religious identity did not appear to be a foundation of solidarity per se. Nevertheless, perceivably extreme religious views among the non-Christian population were clearly a cause for concern. The Muslim population in particular was mentioned frequently, with concerns emerging about public money going to minority community initiatives such as mosques. The small number of Muslim participants also commented that they felt more vulnerable to racial targeting and held the most extreme Muslim minority, but also the overall increase in numbers of Muslim immigrants, partially responsible for this. This attracted agreement from some of the white British members of the group.

4.5.2 Immigration and the welfare state

As pointed out above, immigrants are more likely to receive welfare benefits than the native population since they are disadvantaged both economically and in terms of educational qualifications. Thus an increasing number of immigrants relying on state benefits and transfer payments could be met with reservations. In fact, the question whether migration might have

---

[6] Interestingly, longitudinal studies using quantitative data show that though immigration to the UK has increased over time, there was a weakening of the prejudice towards ethnic minorities. Moreover, the acceptance of the majority of the population of equality of opportunity for people of different races and minorities has grown stronger (Evans 2006).

negative consequences for the welfare state evoked controversial discussions, with both positive and negative opinions raised in both countries. Starting with Germany, the discussions on the impact on the welfare state were at times highly controversial. The following quote documents that there were varying ideas on the effect of migration among the focus group participants:

German group 4, routine, 20–45

F9 If many people come to Germany who have never contributed [to the welfare state] and claim benefits when they come here, because they have no job and try to integrate themselves, then this is a great burden for the welfare state. The people [i.e. migrants] take advantage of this before these people have achieved anything here in this country. [...]

M4 This is actually wrong. Moreover it is rather the case that especially young Turks, especially because there are young male Turks coming to Germany, the government does not have to pay for their education. [...] These are educated young men, it's perfect, they do not cost anything and they just come here.

Regarding the impact of migration, respondents mentioned economic gains resulting from tax payments and contributions by migrants. On the other hand, respondents also had the impression that migrants, compared to native Germans, tend to overuse the social benefits system, leading to a higher need for social spending and increasing problems for the financial stability of the welfare system. One outcome was that people are aware of the fact that monetary resources of the welfare state are limited. As a result, respondents are willing to accept migration as long as the current level of benefits can be kept constant for both Germans and migrants already living in Germany.

However, these dissimilar perceptions of effects of migration on the sustainability of the welfare state did not overlap much with the perceptions of the actual net contributions of migrants to the welfare state. We asked whether respondents saw migrants as net beneficiaries or net payers of the welfare system, i.e. whether the relation between paying taxes and contributions and receiving social benefits on the part of the migrants is perceived to be in balance or not. In most of the German group discussions the respondents thought that migrants do not take more out of the welfare state than they put in.[7] However, some of the respondents pointed out that the word 'migrant' entails a variety of people, which made it impossible to make a conclusive judgement.

[7] Using quantitative data on Germany Mau and Burkhardt (2008) have shown that many people think that contributions to the welfare state made by foreigners are smaller than benefits received (for a comparative overview on European countries see Mau and Burkhardt 2009a). Different results may be due to the specific characteristics of the qualitative study, where people take a more nuanced view.

German group 1, routine, 46+

M6: There are minorities, that exists everywhere, who take more out than they put in. But I think that this is a minority. This does not hold for everyone. I think we should treat foreigners in a way we would like to be treated when we are abroad.

In the focus groups German respondents seemed to be aware of the fact that migration helps to finance social security. Hardly anyone perceived migrants as freeriders; instead they saw their contributions as essential for the financial sustainability of the welfare state.

In the UK the economic contribution some migrants make was seen as considerable. Some respondents gave examples of prominent successful migrants (e.g. Lakshmi Mittal) who have made massive commercial contributions (UK group 8, routine, 20–45). On a more general scale, migrants were seen (particularly by those in the non-routine groups) as filling gaps in the labour market. Migrants' willingness to work and their high skill levels were praised in this context. However, there were serious concerns too. When asked whether migrants take out or contribute more to society, many British respondents regarded as common knowledge that more was received in benefits. This was seen partly as a problem with migrants' intentions, blaming them for moving to the UK because of the welfare system and benefits they could receive here—the welfare tourism argument. Others were less critical of migrants per se, but felt that there are already enough people living in Britain, so the country should focus its resources on the existing population, both in terms of current benefits and in terms of future training/investment. A major reservation was that migrants, compared to British people, tend to weaken the British economy by sending their money to their families abroad and not spending it in Britain to support the country they live in. In four of the groups participants expressed their acceptance of migrants participating in the labour market, yet were disgruntled by their perception that migrants send money 'home' while benefiting from scarce services. This was an argument which, when it occurred, frequently drowned out more tolerant discourses.

UK group 3, routine, 46+

F2 I work with a girl and she goes home every 2 months with £4,000 cash...a Polish girl...She works but she takes it all back...She doesn't spend a penny over here, she won't...She doesn't go to a supermarket: everything she takes back.

F4 It's like the NHS and nurses, where my sister worked, they import the nurses over and they send the money back to their families.

F3 Apparently they are not spending a penny, the Polish here.

Some participants expressed belief that jobs and contracts too are kept within ethnic groups. Although not all participants saw it as a net loss to the country, there was a broad consensus within each of the British groups that migration has contributed to a strain on limited resources for services. In this respect, migrants are blamed for having a negative impact on services in the British welfare system. Participants raised concerns that immigrants worsen the situation for native Britons. This was particularly marked in relation to health and schooling, but housing too. In fact, housing was raised as an issue most frequently and vociferously in the routine occupation groups, while non-routine groups were concerned about the general housing market and about council accommodation. Some participants stated that, in their view, in terms of housing local governments give priority to migrants (especially asylum seekers). Apart from that, participants blamed migrants' English skills for having a negative impact on the learning environment for pupils in schools. Furthermore, strains on health care were perceived to be the result of migrants entering the country as 'welfare tourists' (i.e. migrants entering the country solely because of the advantages of the welfare system in place). In response to a male participant talking about people feeling more and more uncomfortable with the allocation of the limited resources of the welfare state, another male person stated:

> UK group 6 non-routine, 46+
> M2 I think the problem is ... people get discontented when they feel they're not getting their fair share of social care, social services, because it's inadequate to cope with the volume of people that are coming into the country. It is not the fault of the immigrant in a way and it is not the fault of [Britons]. It's just bad planning ... and there should be more controls.

As discussions of the British welfare system have pointed out, flat-rate, non-contributory schemes can create vulnerability to accusations of fraud and of 'sponging' from the welfare state (e.g. Clasen 2001; Mau 2003). Participants were (for the most part) careful not to say anything too inflammatory which could easily have been interpreted as racist. However, the openness with which certain statements were made reflects the acceptability of certain beliefs, which one commonly overhears in day-to-day conversation and sees in the media. These include the belief that a significant proportion of migrants exploit the welfare system; that there is a migrant culture of working cash-in-hand (so that benefits can be claimed while working); and that people come to the UK especially to benefit from the universal health system. These views were not always accepted—for instance, participants were aware, especially within British non-routine groups, that the media does not always represent issues dispassionately. There was no simple dichotomy between hard-working British versus sponging foreigners either. Complaints about migrants were often countered (if not necessarily denied) with the fact that some British people also exploit the system.

UK group 2, non-routine, 20–45

Q [...] Are there any other groups? Is it just Eastern Europeans taking?

M3 It's our own country as well...Children can go to school now...they come out and get pregnant and they've got a full range of house, TV, Sky, everything...and we have to work for it.

Thus, for those who accepted that migrants should be able to come in for jobs the discourse was more about contribution than about nationality or race. Unlike the German findings, there were few or no reservations expressed about making generalizations or estimating the balance of givers and takers. The discourse of migrants drawing on the welfare state appeared to be strong enough to remove such doubts.

4.5.3 Justifying inclusion into the welfare state

The final research question dealt with the issue of adequate inclusion of migrants into the welfare state. On which basis do people justify the inclusion of migrants into the welfare state and what are the conditions for inclusion? Looking at the German focus groups first, there were only a few reservations of including migrants into the social security schemes. Apparently, in the eyes of German participants, not formal citizenship but making a productive contribution to society constitutes the right to access welfare benefits. We can assume that the strong insurance logic of the German welfare state, especially in the field of pensions and unemployment benefits, shields the system against debates about fraud, scrounging, or unjustified beneficiaries.

We strived to identify whether respondents think that the inclusion of migrants should be linked to specific obligations such as paying taxes, social insurance contributions, or factors such as the residential status or the duration of residency. In one of the German focus groups participants agreed that the German social security system benefits to a large extent from payments made by migrants living in Germany. With reference to the pension system as one pillar of the welfare state based on the social insurance principle, the participants of this particular group stressed that Germany has profited substantially from contributions made by the immigrant community. For this reason, people agreed that migrants should get the same social rights as German citizens.

German group 1, routine, 46+

Q [...] At the beginning there were only Germans and foreigners were not noticed. Now there is maybe greater influence from foreigners...

F9 But they also contribute.

Q ...who maybe receive payments from the welfare state...

M6 This is inseparable. We have to take the responsibility for those living here and we cannot exclude them.

F3 They have worked and always paid their share.

F10 They pay for our pensions.

M4 If they would go home than the German pensioners would get into trouble just as well as social benefit recipients.

Q So would you say that foreigners should receive the same rights as Germans?

M4 Yes. [Agreement from rest of the group.]

However, it was consensual in most of the groups that payments from the social insurance scheme (pensions, unemployment) should be tied to contributions. More generally, granting migrants the same social rights as others is linked to the fulfilment of obligations. If migrants have the same responsibilities as Germans then they should also have the same rights.

On a more general level, participants agreed that migrants should be able or at least be willing to learn the German language. Otherwise, as all groups agreed, integration would fail. Discussants did not so much focus on obligations imposed by the government but on the willingness on the part of the migrants themselves to integrate both economically and culturally (e.g. German group 2, non-routine, 20–45). To enable successful integration, the government should provide the framework to ensure equal opportunities for German citizens as well as for migrants. This includes possibilities for learning the German language in order to participate socially, but also to take part in the labour market and by doing so to financially contribute a fair share to the financing of the welfare state (German group 5, non-routine, 46+).

The overall disadvantaged position of migrants within German society remained unquestioned among the participants of the German focus groups. Participants with a non-routine background (German group 2, non-routine, 20–45) acknowledged that, compared with the native German population, it is not as easy for members of ethnic minority groups and for migrants in general to make a decent living. On the other hand, it was noted that the German welfare state has not been able to prevent social inequalities between the native and the foreign-born population.

Access to benefit schemes for migrants already living in Germany and participating in society appeared to be regarded as less of a problem than issues of immigration and border control. Some participants suggested allowing only those migrants into the country who have their own means of subsistence. The immigration policies of Australia, the United States, and Canada were referred to as examples in favour of a stricter control of migration inflow which might work for Germany too. Liberal migration policies were seen as problematic because of the risk of 'welfare tourism'. In German Group 5 participants mentioned that better regulation of migration inflow might help prevent problems caused by high ethnic heterogeneity. A male person mentioned that:

German group 5, non-routine, 46+

M6 You can move to Australia if you have certain qualifications or if you have a certain number of points. If you want to move to the US you have to fulfil certain criteria as well. Why is it not possible for us in Germany to say 'we do not want everybody' without being racist? If we need foreigners they have to have certain qualifications, they have to be able to make a living and if they then need social assistance then this is a different story.

However, Germany's obligation to keep borders open for asylum seekers was not questioned. While some respondents emphasized the gains arising from migration with regard to an increase in human capital exceeding any negative impacts, others pointed out that society's capability to take care of its citizens has to be given privilege before allowing new immigrants to move in. More generally, it appeared that respondents in groups with non-routine occupations had stronger reservations towards a restriction of migration. However, it could be that respondents did feel uncomfortable about publicly expressing attitudes that might be interpreted as racist or xenophobic.

With regard to the question on which basis people justify the inclusion of migrants into the welfare state, British focus group interviews revealed the following: respondents most frequently suggested that the conditions of entry for immigrants should in general be stricter, but also related to the economic contribution a migrant is likely to make once he/she has entered the country. As found in the German groups, Canada and Australia were often cited as countries with immigration systems whose example the UK should follow. As previously discussed, respondents were aware that there is a substantial number of migrants who made valuable contributions to the economy. However, there was also a strong feeling that a large number had less wholesome intentions and/or lacked the training and skills to add value to the economy. Thus the issue of conditionality emerged strongly, with almost all respondents wanting to place limits upon inclusion of migrants into the welfare system.

The idea of a link to specific obligations was very popular. Respondents tended not to distinguish between general taxation and National Insurance contributions, as has been found in previous research (e.g. Stafford 1998). However, respondents stressed that it is important that migrants at least prove their willingness to pay into the 'common pot' before drawing out of it. This underlines, as suggested by Miller (2006: 332) that 'immigrant minorities are expected to become loyal citizens of the country that receives them, and to play by the prevailing rules of the game'. For some, this was simply a matter of inclusion—as soon as migrants become (working) UK residents they should be entitled to some welfare services, especially emergency needs such as health. However, this generosity very rarely extended to unemployment benefits.

> UK group 5, non-routine, 46+
> Q What about [a migrant] who puts into the system? What should they be... getting back?
> F3 Well, the same as everybody else, because they are earning, they are paying taxes, paying insurance.
> Q What if they suddenly become unemployed?
> F3 ...They have to leave.

However, there was also a strong discourse of proportionality, which perhaps does not fit precisely within the UK benefits system. Several respondents felt that the amount of benefit received should be in close proportion to the amount paid in. Older respondents especially felt that they had worked for several decades and did not see that migrants should have access to the same welfare benefits: 'What's fair for us? I've worked for 30 years' (UK group 3, routine, 46+). In response to this, our participants proposed that migrants should have to pay for their own insurance or a proportion of their NHS treatment according to the time spent here—even if they have been in the UK for several decades—or to go to their country of origin for treatment and other services.

Length of residency was a concern, with many respondents advocating some kind of 'probationary period' in response to the moderator's questions about how soon a migrant should be allowed to draw on the state system. The time limit suggested ranged between a few months and several years—although this did not apply to the most extreme of the proportionality proponents (the latter was a minority view). These results are in line with findings based on the BSA survey (Sefton 2005): British respondents were much more likely to support restrictions of access to welfare benefits for recently arrived labour migrants rather than for those who had already stayed for a period of two years or more. Respondents' views were also less restrictive when it came to asylum seekers. In the UK, groups' attitudes to asylum were not wholly unsympathetic, but even sympathetic respondents tended to demonstrate some scepticism. There was a strong feeling that the UK accepted more than its fair share of asylum seekers.

4.6 Conclusion

The chapter sheds light on peoples' framing of the relationship between migration and the welfare state from a comparative perspective (for a summary, see Table 4.1). Migration is often seen as one of the key issues influencing the sustainability of welfare arrangements, as it is understood as a

Table 4.1: Summary of findings from focus groups

Country dimension	United Kingdom	Germany
Migrants as perceived 'ethnic threat' and ethnic hierarchies	• History of immigration in the respective country plays a role	
	• Some sort of migrant threat in all focus groups, e.g. labour market competition, ghettoization	• No direct evidence for perception of migrants as 'threat', but perceived negative repercussions of larger groups of migrants (esp. among lower socioeconomic classes)
	• Asylum seekers especially are evaluated negatively	• Turks and people with Turkish background are seen as a group causing problems for social cohesion and social peace
	• Citizenship matters	• Boundaries based on cultural traits
Consequences of immigration for the welfare state	• More negative perception of migrant's welfare balance → contribute less (keep or send home money) and overutilize or 'spoil' services (housing, education)	• Mixed perception of migrants' welfare balance → contribute (spend money) and take out (receive benefits)
Conditions for inclusion	• People are willing to grant same rights to migrants as long as immigration is contained • Preference for restriction of immigration • Desire for better regulation of immigration by a redesign of immigration law (more 'needed' people) in both countries	

solution to the fiscal problems stemming from the aging of the population, but at the same time as undermining collective arrangements based on homogeneity. Against this background, we investigated how people viewed both immigration in general and the link between immigration and the welfare state in particular. Overall, we were able to identify differences in people's attitudes between the countries which are in line with particular characteristics of the German and the UK welfare regime and their respective immigration regimes. However, there are also remarkable similarities in people's opinions, especially regarding the question of how to deal with increasing immigration inflows. In the UK there is greater emphasis on issues of deservingness and fraud which fits with the need-based distribution of welfare services in a liberal welfare system. In Germany, distributional conflicts appear to be relatively contained. This seems to be due to the insurance principle of the German welfare state making social transfers appear as 'earned rights'.

Although conditions of migration and the history of immigration are quite different in both countries, we also found similarities in people's evaluation of the issue of migration: people were positive about migration when it came to possible productive contributions to society but also concerned with regard to problems of welfare dependency and segregation. Overall, though people expressed reservations towards an unconditional inclusion of immigrant groups into the welfare state, we find little evidence for a strong preference for an exclusionary welfare state (see also Evans 2006). As such, migration was not specifically welcomed in either country but seen as one important factor in keeping the labour market and the welfare state functioning. However, people do not favour unrestricted migration. There is a clear fear that the welfare state is not able to deal with unrestricted migration. Therefore respondents favoured the implementation of rules limiting immigration to groups who are economically desirable and for whom there is labour demand. There was also a tendency to place culturally and socially distant minority groups lowest in the hierarchy of deservingness. In terms of conditions of inclusion into the welfare system, tax paying and employment are crucial. Hardly anybody would deny access to the benefit system as long as migrants paid their 'dues'. In fact, it seems that the willingness to redistribute in favour of others depends on whether the in-group perceives migrants as playing fair, i.e. 'as showing willingness to reciprocate when it is their turn to make a contribution' (Miller 2006: 334).

Looking at the results in more detail, we found differences between the different status groups represented in our focus groups.[8] In Germany we observed differences in attitudes towards migration and the perception of an ethnic threat between participants with high economic status and those with lower economic status. Especially the routine groups tended to be more sceptical with regard to immigrant integration; respondents, for instance, referred to the negative consequences of living in city districts dominated by ethnic minorities. Disadvantages for the whole society were seen in terms of a loss of opportunities. However, general solidarity towards migrants as a whole did not seem to be affected by this. Also, the inclusion of asylum seekers remained unquestioned.

In the UK some people were blunter in stating their opinions on migration and migrants. Economic inequalities between different parts of the world were acknowledged but not necessarily seen as a legitimate reason for migrants to come to the UK. However, a need for labour migrants was acknowledged by many and seen as a key to the UK's (until recently) thriving economy. Nevertheless, such views were moderated by beliefs about high rates of illegal migration, cultures of benefit fraud, and fears of migrants threatening the UK's welfare system. There was also concern from those in routine and non-routine occupations that Britons at the bottom end of the labour market lose out to migrant labour. As in Germany, there was a strong desire for a stricter

---

[8] However, differences between participants of different age remained negligible in both countries.

points system (which in fact was implemented at the time of our fieldwork, although there was almost no awareness of this among the participants). In almost all UK groups we were able to identify an ethnic threat on the part of the respondents stemming from migration, but this tended to be related to both recent migrants in general and asylum seekers in particular, who were seen as simply overwhelming in number. Although humanitarian arguments for taking asylum seekers were not completely rejected, there was absolutely no reservation, in most of the UK groups, in taking an extremely suspicious stance towards this group.

The findings laid out in this chapter provide insight into people's attitudes in the UK and Germany towards immigration and the impact of increasing ethnic diversity on the sustainability of the welfare state. Despite the differences in attitudes, there is some indication of the likely role of the media and public discourses in shaping attitudes that both countries have in common. Many respondents held views which linked superficial, often second-hand knowledge with stereotyping and stylized views on immigrants. The representation of migrants in the media is an important source of people's ideas about migrants. It also became clear that the terms 'migrant' and 'immigrant' are often too broad for making sensible judgements. When confronted with more differentiated information or counter-arguments, people often qualified their opinions or restricted stronger views to particular groups. Finally, focusing events as key events that cause members of the public to become aware of certain issues seems to play an important role. Here it is decisive to what extent negative events (e.g. fraud, crime) can dominate the public discourse and also lead to 'distorted views' on the lifestyle and social realities of migrant groups. To analyse the link between these publicly conveyed imageries and what people think remains a key challenge of future research.

Part II
Welfare Policies

II. A. Supporting Families

5

Family policy: striving for sustainability

Mary Daly

5.1 Introduction

It is generally accepted that policies to influence the family are a key element of the new welfare architecture in Europe. What is not so widely recognized, however, is the fact that contemporary policy has to engage with family not just as an economic unit but also as a social unit. In a more globalized world, family life is increasingly subject to rapid economic and social changes and a wide range of cultural influences. As a result, social policy has to negotiate a finer balance in regulating individual choices and collective welfare. For this and other reasons, family policy is growing in significance and complexity in most parts of Europe.

This chapter is concerned both with identifying changes that are underway in family policy and establishing the extent to which new models are in train. The chapter is organized into three parts. It opens with a conceptual outline of the implications of globalization and related changes for contemporary family policy. The case is made that these have to be considered in a broad manner. Rather than just affecting the economic situation, globalization is altering the conditions under which families operate and the leeway that individuals and families have for decision making. Hence one must conceptualize globalization—and changes in family policy—as seeking to affect a range of family-related choices and behaviours and to balance these with the goals of public policy. The second part of the chapter subjects family policy changes to critical scrutiny. Taking a comparative perspective, the intent is to give an overview of key developments in Germany and the UK, with particular emphasis on common trends. The centrepiece of the third section is an analysis of the tensions inherent in contemporary family policy and how states in Europe have sought to manage these tensions. The piece concludes with suggestions for a framework for understanding and researching family-related policy.

5.2 Conceptualizing family policy from the perspective of globalization

Looking across Europe, there has always been something special about social policy as it relates to family, especially if compared with other policy domains. There is the timing, for one—it is only in the last decade that family policy measures have assumed what could be called a 'mature identity' (comprising in their most complete form yet: cash benefits, tax allowances, services, employment leaves). Unlike most other social policies, they needed nearly an entire century to evolve. The politics around family policy are also different— not the classic class-rooted contests but a complex mesh of moral, political, social, and economic agendas and interests.

There is no satisfactory theorization of globalization and its impact on family policy. Most widely, globalization theorists call upon economic approaches to explain family policy. Such approaches have been prominent in the literature. Drawing on structural functionalist roots, the central explanatory thrust, at its simplest, is that the prevailing family form is the one that best 'fits' the needs and capacities of capitalist development (in a globalized world). A variety of arguments can be (and have been) marshalled to prosecute this, essentially evolutionary, contention. One is that supporting unemployed and underemployed people is dysfunctional, among other things reducing national competitiveness in a period when states' relative performance in the so-called knowledge economy is of ever greater import. Hence, as many family members should be in employment as possible. A second current in the economic paradigm focuses on the employment-creation potential of the services generated in support of the two-income family household. Such services potentially constitute a source of economic and job growth. While this approach is good in explaining the current movement to 'activation' on the part of welfare states, it has never been more than a very general argument in relation to family policy—it utilizes a kind of 'default equation' whereby family form is treated as epiphenomenal to capitalist development. In any case, to attribute the reform process to policy makers' slavish responses to market needs is both reductionist and simplistic.

Rather than reaching (precipitously) for broad-brush explanations, it is more revealing to probe in more detail the nature of globalization and how it changes the environment within which families function.

Drawing on the work of Begg et al. (2007: 21–2), one can characterize this phase of economic development as marked by the following broad characteristics and trends: growth in international flows of goods, services, and capital; increased propensity for international migration; spread of technologies and of the multinational companies that play a major role in diffusing them; and intensification of communication exemplified by the spread of internet usage. The classic conceptualization of globalization-related change is fashioned around an analysis that centres upon the economy, labour market, and migration. Drawing on Begg et al. (2007) and also the work of Blossfeld et al. (2005), the following are the most widely referred to axes of change that affect family:

- There is a widening of earnings inequality, pressures on the returns to unskilled labour in Europe having led especially to falling wages of unskilled workers. The emergence of the 'knowledge society' has resulted in an increase in the return on human capital and hence greater vulnerability for some sectors of the population, as well as having increased income polarities more generally. Globalization has fostered the belief that flexibility—as a characteristic of individuals, families, and even employment and policy systems—is highly desirable. Hence, individuals and families are much more exposed to unpredictability and risk. That said, the less well-off families and sectors of the population will be more affected by income shortfalls and increasing uncertainty than others.

- Migration is on the increase, spurred by the relocation of jobs and productive activities, growing inequalities across regions, and a general flexibilization of lives and economies. Higher labour turnover means, among other things, a premium on transferability and relocation and so tends to destabilize family arrangements.

- Countries' social provisions, whether income support, social services, or employment-related arrangements, are increasingly put under the spotlight for their impact on relative competitiveness and incentive structures. This has affected both the volume and nature of family-related provisions across states.

The received wisdom is that the nuclear family can be relied upon less and less to help individuals to absorb risks (Begg et al. 2007: 77). This is especially the case in the countries belonging to Esping-Andersen's cluster of 'corporatist' welfare states—the reliance of countries such as Germany and Austria on the male breadwinner model is difficult to sustain in light of both economic pressures (it is a costly model) and social pressures (it flies in the face of trends such as women's desire for greater independence and a meaningful career). However, if one takes a more sociological perspective, it highlights a different set of exigencies and draws attention to the family as an agent (rather than the passive absorber of effects of processes that originate elsewhere).

A more sociological perspective locates the welfare state and family policy in a social context. This approach 'marries' an analysis of social policy with social conditions and especially social change. It suggests a number of rationales/lines of analysis for contemporary family policy. A first such rationale is that the state has to respond to 'new' social problems that do not always derive from economic issues, but result rather from factors like people's commitment to family (values) and how changing cultural norms and lifestyles affect people's wish to pursue a family-based life (Bahle 2008). State policies might therefore be understood as an attempt to effect a change in how people relate to family, and through this and other means to consolidate family. This kind of approach focuses on the challenges facing family policy. Structurally, incomplete households, unofficial cohabitation, single or two-child families, and more than one marriage throughout the life course all change the landscape within which family policy (and public policy more generally) operates. One can sum this up with a reference to a diversification of life-course practices as opposed to fairly uniform patterns observed in the past. In terms of relationships, there is on the one hand a greater emphasis on individual needs, if not individuality (especially as regards children, for example), and on the other hand a continued significance of collective units and categorical identities deriving from family. Globalization is, therefore, not just (or even) an economic phenomenon—as a term it can and should be used to refer also to the profound changes in values and practices around individual behaviour and family lives. This has been the stuff of much sociological theorizing (Giddens 1999; Beck-Gernsheim 2002) and much sociological conjecture.

A second possible rationale for the focus of family-related policies in the era of globalization may be as an effort to modernize the public policy agenda when it comes to family life. Families are changing rapidly. Both partners now have to/want to work to maintain an acceptable standard of income and a preferred way of combining individual and family lifestyles. In sum, the developed countries have seen 'a massive reordering of work, class and gender relationships' (Stacey 1996: 33). In addition, people are altering their family-related behaviours. Fertility is changing to a degree that is revolutionary, rather than evolutionary, in many parts of Europe. People are 'choosing' not only to have fewer children but to change how children and family fit into their life course. In essence, state policies have to find a middle ground between control and freedom, regulation and choice. The insights of a more sociological approach underline the complexity for states in trying to find a balance between supporting family as a social institution and at the same time allowing individuals a degree of choice about how they manage their family lives and how they interpret family commitments.

How are relevant policy profiles changing in Germany and the UK?

5.3 Changes in family policy in Germany and the UK

In both countries, family is a dynamic policy domain and family policy a site of considerable change. In Germany family-orientated policies have expanded in parallel with retrenchment in unemployment and pension policies. This trend, which started in the 1980s, was accelerated by the Red–Green Coalition in the late 1990s and early 2000s and has been further deepened by the comprehensive reforms enacted by the current grand coalition government. In the UK, family-related considerations were at the heart of British social policy since New Labour's accession to power in 1997. The result is a remarkably sustained (if not always consistent) programme orientated both to family behaviour and individual well-being. While there is variation in the nature of reforms being introduced, it is possible to identify a number of cross-national trends. The following discusses what I consider to be the main four such common trends.

One major trend is what can be termed a move towards services for families with children. We are speaking here mainly of childcare-related services. In Germany out-of-home care and education provision has been targeted for major expansion, especially for children under three years of age. In a move away from existing practice, where home care of younger children is preferred, it became a stated aim of policy that parents were not to be prevented from allowing their children to attend a kindergarten and, in fact, they should receive encouragement for this through the provision of financial incentives. In this and other ways, childcare policy moved in Germany from a somewhat marginal issue to a core concern.[1] Based on the Day Care Expansion Act, which entered into force in early 2005, municipalities were at a first stage required to provide day care for all those children under the age of three whose parents are employed or enrolled in education and training. The aim was to provide 230,000 additional places for the under-threes by 2010. One-third of the extra places were to be provided by registered childminders in private households. This programme was estimated to cost €1.5 billion and was to be financed through 'savings' for municipalities achieved by the merger of the unemployment and social assistance programmes for the unemployed. In a second stage, based on a compromise between the political parties of the

---

[1] Clasen (2005: 159) points out that during the 1990s maternity leave, child pension credits, and child transfers were the main family-related concerns in Germany.

Grand Coalition government in spring 2007, the volume of publicly financed or subsidized care for children under the age of 3 years was to be such as to fully meet the demand by 2013, at which time the government will also introduce an individual entitlement to childcare for every child. In late 2007, the Federal government allocated an additional €2.14 billion to support the expansion of childcare facilities by the Länder.

In the case of the UK, a broad range of supportive services for families (orientated to improving family functioning) has been put in place. As well as education and care-specific services, there has been a move to improve and streamline general services for families orientated to enhancing family functioning and bringing stability to family structure and relations. This was effected in the first instance by the Sure Start programme, which began in 1998 and was modelled on the US Head Start. The aims of this programme lay partly in better governance and a desire for neighbourhood renewal, but they related especially to effecting improved family practices and outcomes. The idea was to ensure that families living in the 20 per cent most 'risky' areas had available to them in their locality a range of child- and family-focused services, including health, family support and outreach, and early learning, so as to improve childhood and parenting and promote parental employment. Conceived as a one-stop shop, Sure Start and the Children's Centre programme which replaced it, which was to oversee the establishment of a much larger network of 3500 centres by 2010 (trebling 2006 provision), were firmly anchored in anti-poverty and social inclusion objectives. By 2010 it was planned that all schools would offer a range of parenting support, including information sessions as well as more specialized support for parents whose children have problems with attendance or behaviour (Treasury 2007). Orientated not just to the substitution of parental care but to the performance aspect of parenthood, the measures were strongly interventionist, in comparison both to past family policy in the UK and developments in Germany. Strengthening family relationships was a strong axis/aim of British family policy under New Labour. As well as services focusing on children, there was investment in relationship support (delivered through the third sector) and also support services for conflict resolution for parents whose relationships have broken down. In addition, the 2006 Green Paper—Care Matters—outlined proposals to help local services support families to stay together, such as assessing the impact of intensive parenting support or therapy (Department for Education and Skills 2006). Social order and social control were strong underlying currents in these and other measures. Parenting Orders, for example, compel parents, where required, to attend parenting classes and fulfil other requirements deemed necessary by the court for improving their child's behaviour. In addition, there are parenting contracts, which are two-sided voluntary agreements between parents and the local authority (or other bodies) to address specific behavioural or attendance problems.

This focus was innovative for both countries, although Germany has historically had an infrastructure of service provision for young children (especially the eastern Länder). Diversity in terms of service provider was also a policy preference in both countries. Diversification has mainly taken the form of an increased or continued strong role for the voluntary and not-for-profit sector (and also, although to a lesser extent in both countries, provision by employers).

A move towards considering or creating children as a category of and for social policy was a second identifiable trend in the German and UK family policy portfolio. This centred on improved access for children to services which are orientated towards their development (e.g., pre-school and other educational services, as well as health services) and the granting of some individual rights to children (the right to a childcare place for example). Moves to counter child poverty were another expression of the child-specific orientation. However while this was a general trend in both countries, improving the performance, and more accurately enhancing the academic and other achievements, of children was a stronger motivator of policy reform in the UK. Some scholars have gone so far as to claim this as a new policy paradigm. Jenson (2006), for example, frames her analysis in terms of welfare states responding to new social risks such that a future-orientated policy paradigm is in the process of emerging. This involves a significant level of politicization of childhood, thereby reducing possible long-term and life-course effects of childhood poverty via early childhood education and care services, as well as activation now and in the future in order to foster social inclusion. As it relates to children, she describes it in terms of three characteristic features:

- It views learning as the route to security (which involves inter alia, increased focus on childhood as a period of human capital acquisition, politicization of childcare and early education treated as an investment, providing the foundational skills for a life of continuous learning—Jenson claims that this emphasis crosses regime types, although there is variation in who cares, who pays, and how childcare is provided);
- It has an orientation to the future and in particular to future life chances. This is the investment theme and also anti-child-poverty theme—good habits on the part of children and their families are encouraged;
- It has perceived benefits for society as a whole—employment is the route to maximizing well-being and the well-being of society and social cohesion depend on this.

Jenson explains the move to this paradigm in terms of: a) pressures coming from fundamental transformations in the economy, family, and society, and b) the development of new idea sets shared across policy communities.

A third cross-national commonality was increased emphasis on reconciliation of work and family life. This legitimated some recognition of family-related exigencies as a counter-claim to employment-based rights and responsibilities, especially in the UK, where family-based claims had less legitimacy historically. 'Reconciliation' had two major expressions in policy. On the one hand, employed parents were given more generous but also more carefully targeted incentives and supports to both not care personally for their children and also, on other occasions, to take time off from employment to provide care personally. This involved the extension of leave programmes in the UK and their refocusing (in terms of income replacement and shorter duration) in Germany. Greater flexibility in regard to the times of parental employment was a related policy reform. Both parents were targeted as potential employees and there was increased interest in encouraging fathers to take (short periods of) time off from work to care for their young children. In Germany a major reform of the parental leave was undertaken in 2000 (by the Social Democratic–Green coalition). Reforms continued under the Red–Green coalition government, orientated to incentivizing both employment and a sharing of caring on the part of both parents. In comparison to the past, flexibility was the middle name of the new parental leave system—the reforms made it possible for both parents to take leave at the same time and they made a return to work on the part of the woman more likely by cutting the duration of the leave and increasing the level of replacement vis-à-vis earnings (for the shorter leave duration). In the UK under New Labour, the general thrust was similar (if the details somewhat different). What one saw there was the unfolding of a series, in the historical context of the UK, of more generous and extensive leaves from employment for family (actually child-related) purposes that target both mothers and fathers. The amount of paid maternity leave was extended (to 39 weeks from 14), catapulting the UK into the lead position in Europe in terms of maternity leave duration. The leave was also made more generous (doubling in value in ten years) and part of it was made transferable from mothers to fathers. In addition, paid paternity and adoption leave were introduced and plans were set out to extend both to 26 weeks. Another innovation for the UK was the introduction of a right to request flexible working for parents of young and disabled children. While this is at the discretion of employers, the fact that workers were given a right to request the leave was far from trivial given the otherwise strong voluntarist tradition in UK industrial relations (Lewis and Campbell 2007: 374). Encouraging parental employment was also effected by another major policy reform—the introduction of family-based tax credits, designed to make employment both feasible and attractive for families by topping up wages.

The second approach to work–family reconciliation was towards activating people to be employed. This could be said to have a 'reconciliation' character in that both male and female parents were increasingly encouraged in both Germany and the UK to be economically active. The two-earner household was seen to be the best chance for economic survival/prosperity and a robust set of tax and benefit reforms was put in place, especially in the UK, towards this end. The introduction of tax credits, to top up wages for those in work, was the central element of New Labour's 'make work pay' strategy. Starting in October 1999, they were designed to make employment both feasible and attractive for families by topping up wages. Here too, the familial or collective orientation of the provision was noteworthy—these were not benefits for individuals but were fundamentally premised on the combination of incomes and behaviours on the part of different family members.

A fourth identifiable cross-national commonality was a closer focusing of state support on parenthood and parenting (as against the status and institution of marriage). Parental or biological responsibilities were emphasized over relations associated with partnership and marriage. The reforms involved charted a move away from the male breadwinner family. The father's role and the obligations of fathers were especially reinforced. There was also a move away from a tax privileging of marriage and a tendency to grant non-married couples similar rights and responsibilities as married couples. In their approach to families, these two welfare states became much more concerned about practice (e.g., parenting, caring) and less about status (mirroring a development trajectory in the sociology of the family). Moreover, the 'ing' seemed to get bigger and the list of 'ings' longer. Mirroring somewhat the general activist thrust to contemporary social policy, state benefits and services were increasingly orientated to the support of activities rather than a more passive endorsement of family or employment status. It is not the circumstances under which you have children that matters but, rather, what you do with them in terms of rearing children and setting them up for a responsible and achievement-orientated future.

Summing up and taking an overview, policy reform in both countries has been quite wide-ranging. Looking at how they have come to this point, the two countries were faced with quite different challenges in making reforms. Germany had to recognize individuals—if not to disaggregate the family as a collective unit then to rethink the heretofore 'relational' and collective focus of its policy. In Germany one finds matters of individual biography quite widely in the discourse, e.g., 'individual life planning' is used easily in the most recent Familienbericht (BMFSFJ 2006a). In addition, the German federal state had to face down obstacles such as those posed by subsidiarity and competency limitations to be able to effect an extension of childcare. The 'political/learning curve' in the UK lay in recognizing family as a source and expression of both inequality and social order/disorder (for the family in its own right and also in terms of its interaction with surrounding institutions and policies). Hence, in an effort to target inequality and improve their legitimacy, the tax credits were reformed to reach families further up the income continuum—an interesting countermove to the general tendency operating in the UK of closely targeting financial support. In effect, the British rush to the market (and to family) acted to strengthen the British welfare state's 'offer' to the middle classes. New Labour also interpreted the challenge in terms of framing a (greater) social order role for social policy. Under its watch, employing social policy as a means of social regulation oversaw the introduction and extension of contractual elements in public support and also strong punitive, if not authoritarian, mechanisms in social policy more generally.

To what extent were the changes 'traditional' (i.e., in line with the historical motivators of family policy) in the two countries? In the case of Germany one could say that the move of family policy towards an employment-reconciliation approach was 'non-traditional' (a change which also acted to move family policy closer to the centre of government policy making in Germany according to Clasen (2005: 164)). While this was set alongside (rather than replacing) the more traditional 'family-centred' focus of policy, reforms interfered with the 'classic balance' in certain ways (Bleses and Seeleib-Kaiser 2004). For example, gender divisions of labour and roles are affected by the daddy months; the changes encourage employment on the part of the mother; children are seen more in individual terms. They also indicated that the public authorities increasingly seek to fashion the family's relationship to German society through the labour market. In the UK, the former universal elements were undermined (especially in cash supports) in favour of means-testing. Clasen (2005: 177–8) sums up the first five years of the New Labour government's approach as follows: 'British family policy under the Labour government has become more interventionist, coordinated, and increasingly coherent, with the explicit aims of reducing child poverty and fostering the employment of parents.' There is no doubt but that under New Labour the family became more rather than less important and that the UK came to develop a more directive and explicit family policy as compared with the past.

Set in its context, there is something genuinely new in the British case—under New Labour there was more family in British social policy as compared with heretofore and the British welfare state saw the introduction of a number of new instruments and measures. The strong focus on children was noteworthy, as was the concern with the quality of family relations and the roles of family members and (some) family practices. So, I would say that, of the two, UK policy underwent greater change and innovation. However, in neither case has there been a paradigmatic shift. The philosophy governing the place and role of the family and family life remains in place, even if aspects of family life, including gender and generational relations, have been altered.

How sustainable are the changes?

5.4 Thinking critically about developments

This section casts a critical light on these reforms and attempts to think through the conditions that make for greater sustainability of family as a key element of social life.

5.4.1 *Risks or tensions inherent in the current reforms*

Taking a broad overview of policy changes in the two countries, two primary tendencies seem to be at the root: a closer focusing of family policy around employment; a 'disaggregation' of family into age groups or categories.

Employment considerations loom larger in family policy today than they did in the past. Policy reform is not so much interested in the family-friendliness of labour market practices and norms as the employment-friendliness of family forms and practices. This has led to a narrowing of family policy as compared with the past. Historically these two European countries, as well as others, constructed their family policy around a number of key considerations. Most countries were concerned to financially support families, in order to limit or prevent family poverty and/or to effect greater equality by redistribution towards families with children (Wennemo 1994; Gauthier 1996; Hantrais and Letablier 1996). In addition, population considerations were important, especially in the early phases of family policy (albeit again in some countries more than others). These three sets of concerns—the financial well-being of families, financial equity, and population growth and renewal—continued to influence public authorities' approaches to family but they were joined from the 1970s on by concerns about gender equality. Some of these concerns have been displaced—the financial support of families is increasingly moved to the labour market, and financial equity across different family types is less important than it was. Today, work–family 'reconciliation' towers over the family policy field and as a rationale for family policy it has little resonance with any of the original motivations for family policy, except perhaps gender equality.

The risks or tensions associated with narrowing family policy down can be appreciated from the work of Kaufmann (2002: 426–8) and others[2] on the historical motivators of family policy and the 'settlements' around family policy and their cross-national variations. One can in fact identify a wide-ranging set of actual or possible motives for family policy in contemporary times:

- the natalist motive—the importance of demographic reproduction;
- the economic motive—improvement of the stock of human capital;
- the socioeconomic motive—balancing employment (self-sufficiency) and support for the family;
- the societal motive—the significance of the family as a form of social capital;
- the sociopolitical motive—compensating for the costs of having families;
- the institutional motive—to protect the family as a valued institution;
- the gender equality motive;
- the children's welfare motive.

When set against this backdrop, the motivations of family policy in Germany and the UK in recent times appear not just narrow but also very instrumental.

A second tendency, visible in UK especially, is for family-related policy to become more specialized in the sense of focusing more closely on population categories or sectors. The inherent thrust is towards splitting up the family, in terms of treating it as a collection of related individuals. Hence, 'family policy' as a way of promoting family as a collectivity and maintaining a distance between the family and public life (whether in terms of the state or the market) is losing meaning and significance in the policy makers' repertoire and we see more and more the emergence of policies for specific categories, such as children, parents, lone parents, and so forth. Visible also are efforts to redistribute some family functions outside of the family, especially to the market and the wider 'community'. This serves to individualize family.

Thinking about these two tendencies—of narrowing and disaggregation—leads me to identify a number of potential risks involved in the current policy trajectory, especially from the point of view of sustainability. I want to emphasize three such risks: the downgrading of family as a social collectivity; decontextualization of family life and relations; instrumentalization of family policy.

The first is that the collectivity (of the family) is downgraded. One can only understand the kind of risk involved here when one takes a view of family as a core social institution. Family policy in France (and in Germany, but to a lesser

---

[2] For example, Bahle (2005).

extent) historically offers a model which helps to elucidate the meaning of this. In this perspective the family has value as a political and moral entity and so state policy is imbued with both the legitimacy and obligation to secure the material and moral functioning of the home and society (Lenoir 1991; Leitner et al. 2008). With familialism, an ideology that promoted family as a way of life and as a force for social integration, deeply embedded historically, a key aspect of the state's role was to defend and protect families. While familism is declining in Europe—and probably never held much sway outside of some of the Continental European countries—it is useful first to underline in these seemingly overwhelmingly neo-liberal times the fact of the existence of an alternative approach to the family and secondly, as a point of reference, to pinpoint the challenges involved for policy in finding a balance between the continued functioning of family as a social institution and increasing individual autonomy. For Kaufmann (2002: 431) this is such an important consideration that he integrates it into his consideration of what constitutes 'explicit family policy' (along with the institutionalization of family policy). For him, family policy is explicit insofar as political measures are legitimized by family as against other, say economic, issues. Opening up the matter of family as a social institution allows a space to debate important considerations such as care, for example. Tronto (1993) and Sevenhuijsen (1998) suggest that caring should be at the centre of social policy. One also has to take account of tensions emerging in policy on children—the movement of large tranches of care from the family acts to diminish the family life of children (see especially Lister 2003, 2006).

A second kind of risk associated with an approach that operates in terms of social categories is of decontextualization (that is, removal from social and relational location). The notion of 'defamilization', a term that has evolved especially in the feminist literature on the welfare state but has actually been employed in a variety of ways (Leitner 2003), is useful here. It has to be understood as signifying a process that applies at different levels, however, rather than seen as descriptive of how the welfare state treats individuals and especially women (the main way in which it has been deployed in the literature).[3] Looked at from the perspective of how individuals are treated, the risk in the current reforms is that people will be seen only, or primarily, in terms of their functional utility (either for the family or the market). The critical expression of decontextualization at this level is where family members are divorced from their familial setting, relations, and responsibilities. The literature is littered with criticism of policies that treat people unidimensionally— the lifeblood of the feminist literature, for example (on the welfare state among

---

[3] See, for example, Bambra (2007).

other institutions) is the need to view women not just as workers or mothers but as both, and more.

The risk of instrumentalism is another associated possibility. Looking at social provision in Germany and how it is changing in comparison to how it was in the past, Leitner et al. (2008) speak of a move from a relational logic, whereby provisions in the familialist model of the German welfare state as it existed in West Germany attached benefits to status and relations rather than to individuals, to a more individual-orientated and instrumentalist policy. Instrumentalism is a consideration that is emerging especially from and high-lighted by the literature on the social investment state and the turn to children as future citizens. Lister (2003: 433) suggests that the child is utilized as a 'cipher for future economic prosperity'. 'Children matter instrumentally, not existentially' (ibid. 434). While policy is to some extent always instrumental (especially if one recognizes the state as an actor with interests), it does appear that issues of economic functioning (rather than, for example, any number of goals or objectives in relation to social welfare) are more domi-nant as drivers of policy now than they were in the past. To take another example, when one unpicks the meaning of 'work–family reconciliation', the policies involved are revealed as 'chipping away' the boundaries between work and family life. The goal is not just (and maybe not even) to get more women into employment but to alter the nature of family life such that it is rendered more compatible with the rhythms and exigencies of economy and employment.

In the final section I want to bring the different insights together into a framework which can be used either to conceptualize the challenges facing policy or to analyse family policy itself.

5.4.2 A framework for understanding contemporary family policy

For analytic purposes, contemporary state action in the field of family has to be viewed as operating at different levels, engaging particularly with the welfare and autonomy of individuals, their relationships with family, and the relations between family and other institutions. Rather than treating these as separate, I suggest that analysts as well as policy makers have to see the domains as multi-dimensional and interconnected (Daly 2000).

The first dimension relates to the extent to which individuals, adults and children alike, are encouraged to see themselves as family members and to behave in a certain fashion in that capacity. Individualization is the most common framing of the processes involved here. In my view it is more appropriate to name and conceptualize the processes as defamilization, for two main reasons. First, 'familization' is the original orientation of family policy. That is, although varying in extent and emphasis, the classic post-

Table 5.1: A framework on family policy

Focus	Trend/Line of development
Individuals relating to families	Inscriptions of roles and intergenerational relations encoded in policies Images and symbolic representations of family categories, relations and identities Individual or 'family' as agent of welfare Degree and nature of focus on entitlement for children Promotion of employee role of women Emphasis on intergenerational relations
Role of family and divisions of labour associated with family activities	Functions allocated to family Degree to which obligations of solidarity are encouraged/enforced Provision of services to substitute for family Potential for partnerships (between family and other institutions and also at micro level) Distribution of tasks and resources within families

war welfare state across countries tended to encourage the nuclear family form and to buttress the authority of husband and father and a family-based role for women. Familization is, then, the condition that states are moving from (or indeed shoring up). Second, familization is a more relational concept than individualization and hence better captures the interdependencies that make up social life and the significance and persistence of family-related ties. As Table 5.1 makes clear, there are a number of possible lines of consideration here, stretching across cognitive processes around family and private life and the way in which family statuses and relationships are configured by social policy. What is of interest is how social policies seek to affect people's subjectivities and social identities and the linkages that they construct between identity and action (actors' sense of themselves and their familial (and social) role and positioning).

A second dimension relates to the kind of division of labour and relations that are envisaged in and promoted by policy. There are macro (inter-institutional) applications as well as micro dimensions involved here. At the macro level the key questions centre on family as a domain of activity and functions. Given that the changes are multilayered and speak to the place of the family in society as a whole rather than subdomains, this is not an either/or matter but centres on the relationships that exists between families and other institutions. To what extent are services that substitute for family made available and their use encouraged and incentivized? At micro level, there are issues about task and resource (re)distribution within families and, equally, the extent to which interdependencies are encouraged. The state can be conceived as a third party—Brandth and Kvande (2001: 263) point out that in the context of the Norwegian daddy leave the state there acted as a normative third party and took over from mothers much of the onus for convincing the fathers that they should share in their children's care.

It is worth emphasizing, by way of concluding, that sociological processes have to be considered alongside other factors as considerations for both family policy and its analysis. What we are seeing across countries now is no less than a new way of organizing everyday family life in which states as well as international organizations and markets are more prepared to get involved for the purpose of reconfiguring the family's place in society and aspects of its 'internal' organization. The concerns are sociological as much as they are economic in that they are centrally interested in the family as the guardian of a number of social institutions (marriage, childhood) and as a form of social organization and social integration. In the end, it is important not to view family policy as unidimensional—rather, different motivations and policy intents are layered one on the other so that the processes and reach of change are broad-ranging.

6

Increasing returns: the new economy of family policy in Britain and Germany

Ann-Kathrin Jüttner, Sigrid Leitner, and Anneli Rüling

6.1 Introduction

Since the late 1990s, the emergence and diffusion of a supra-national discourse on the economics of social policy, which in Germany has been coined '*investive Sozialpolitik*' or the 'social investment state', can be observed (Giddens 1998; Blair and Schröder 1999; Merkel 2004). The central and very basic argument of this, is as follows: money that is spent on social policy is to be seen as an investment in the future of society and the economy. A good investment strategy will yield increasing returns, whereas a bad investment strategy will not. Thus, decisions on social investments should be made on the basis of the expected positive or negative economic returns. Based on the assumption that the effects of social policy can be easily quantified, economic reasoning becomes the determining criterion for social policy decisions.

With regards to family policy, the economic discourse claims that investments in the education of children should be made because of increasing returns. Whilst children without high-quality education may fail to become adults with the ability to contribute positively to society, children who have acquired high levels of skills will benefit the future labour market and the economy as a whole. Moreover, the expansion of high-quality childcare will enhance the labour market participation of parents and thus prevent more families from poverty. In the long run, policies which help to support the reconciliation of work and family, together with high employment rates of women, will have positive effects on the birth rate and thus secure the future labour supply. This kind of rationale has been advocated by international organizations as well as experts on comparative social policy.

For example, documenting the development of early childhood education and care (ECEC) across several countries, the OECD has argued that ECEC has an impact on the future educational achievement of children (OECD 2001; 2006). Furthermore, the OECD 'Babies and Bosses' series analysed reconciliation policies across countries and pointed out that good quality childcare is also a precondition for employed parents (OECD 2007a). The EU employment policy increasingly promotes an 'adult worker model family' (Lewis and Giullari 2005), in which both parents participate in the labour market and children attend day care: by 2010 the average employment rate of women should increase to 60 per cent (from 51 per cent in 2000) and institutional childcare coverage should be secured for 90 per cent of all children aged between 3 and 6, and for one-third of all children below the age of 3. In 2005, the European Council stressed the need for investment in young people in its 'European Pact for Youth'.[1] The aim is to tackle child poverty and to prevent the long-term effects of social exclusion in childhood (Marlier et al. 2007). Last but not least, internationally acknowledged social policy experts also promote a 'child-centred social investment strategy'. For example, Gøsta Esping-Andersen (2002a) regards universal and high-quality day care as the core of an inclusive social policy: the attendance of day care forms the foundation for a child's life-long ability to learn, and this is the most important qualification within a knowledge society. Because families with limited resources often fail to provide cognitive stimulation for their children, the welfare state has to invest in the education of children early in order to avoid social exclusion in the future.

The interesting question is how this supra-national discourse on investive family policy translates into a new economy of family policy: does economic reasoning even result in a turnover of national traditions in family policy? In our research project, we began with the empirical observation that the UK and Germany have both expanded early childhood education and care in recent years, although neither the UK as a liberal welfare regime nor Germany as a conservative welfare regime seems to be predestined to push for an expansion of ECEC. How can we explain this seemingly convergent policy development? From a theoretical point of view, both countries changed their traditional paths as well as their dominating 'Leitbild' of childcare policy, which is often brought about by input from innovators from outside the system (cf. Beyer 2005). In a liberal regime, the state refuses to intervene in the private sphere of the family per se. In a conservative regime, the state supports the family with transfer payments rather than institutional childcare for children under the age of three. Therefore, we hypothesize that the more or less

---

[1] Presidency conclusions of the Brussels European Council (22 and 23 March 2005).

simultaneous expansion of childcare in both countries may be driven by the diffusion of the supra-national economic discourse on family policy. We ask whether the expansion of ECEC was caused by an 'economic turn' in British and German childcare policy.

In the following, we will first compare the political debates and discourses around the introduction of two central pieces of legislation introducing childcare for children below the age of 3. It will be analysed whether and, if so, how the aforementioned points on childcare as political investment can be found in the national debates. Our central hypothesis is that the changes in ECEC coincided with a shift in meaning within this policy field, which explains why childcare climbed so high on the political agendas of both countries. Previously considered as 'soft' topics, childcare became reframed as a 'hard' economic issue in both the UK and Germany between 2002 and 2006. In the respective political discourses, the extension of childcare was justified with reference to 'objective' evidence and 'economic' rationality. Nevertheless, it will be interesting to see if the supra-national discourse on the economics of family policy was taken up differently in both countries due to their particular historical legacies with regards to their respective welfare regimes.

Second, we will scrutinize the introduction of integrated services in both countries as a concrete example for a specific policy of investment in children. Again, we started from an empirical observation. Both countries introduced measures which explicitly aimed at investing in children and their parents in order to improve the educational and social development of children, with the English Children's Centres inspiring the introduction of the North Rhine-Westphalian 'Familienzentren'. Both kinds of centres follow the logic of one-stop agencies for the purpose of family matters and represent a change in the mode of governance in local family policy. Our comparative analysis, which we will present in the second part of this chapter, asks to what extent this example of policy transfer leads to a convergence in childcare policies between the UK and Germany. Or to put it differently, is the economic orientation in family policy equalizing welfare traditions?

6.2 The economic turn in early childhood education and care

Until recently, both (West) Germany and Britain had a traditionally low public involvement in early childhood education and care. In conservative, strong male-breadwinner-orientated Germany (Lewis and Ostner 1994), care for young children was considered to be the responsibility of the mothers. Similarly, in the liberal British welfare state, intervention in the family was traditionally low, except in areas of child neglect or abuse. However, both countries have experienced dramatic reforms in the past ten years: a first step was the introduction of public childcare for pre-school children (aged 3 to 6 in Germany and 3 to 5 in England) throughout the 1990s (Evers et al. 2005). A second was the expansion of ECEC for children under 3 years of age.

Between 2004 and 2006, the governments of both countries assumed responsibility for the organization of universal childcare and early-years services for children under the age of 3 for the first time. In both countries, this national responsibility for childcare was laid down in national legislation: the Tagesbetreuungsausbaugesetz (TAG) (BMFSFJ 2004a) in Germany and the Childcare Bill (House of Commons 2005) in England.[2] In the following, we will analyse the political and public debates around the introduction of these central pieces of legislation.[3]

6.3 England

In England, universal childcare for children below the age of 3 was not on the political agenda before 2004. However, there had been a debate on childcare and early-years services for some years previously. In their manifesto for 2001, the Labour Party promised to introduce universal childcare services for children aged 3–4 years, and to extend the model of Early Excellence centres in 500 new Sure Start centres for children aged 0–5 (Labour Party 2001). In 2004, the Labour government presented a ten-year strategy named 'Choice for Parents, the Best Start for Children' (Her Majesty's Treasury 2004a), which set up an extensive policy framework for the development of childcare. Among other aspects, the programme aims to increase the supply of childcare places (with some universal care for children from age 3) and to raise the quality of childcare over a period of ten years, through inspection as well as education and training of the childcare workforce (ibid.). Furthermore, it is intended to increase the number of Children's Centres (Vincent and Ball 2006: 33). Policy objectives of the strategy include the reconciliation of family and gainful employment for parents, and the enhancement of child development.

As one element of the ten-year strategy for childcare, the Childcare Act was passed in the House of Commons in 2005 and came into force in 2006 (House of Commons 2005). In this document, the government assumed the legal

---

[2] We refer to England rather than Britain, since childcare policy as well as the introduction of Children's Centres is a policy limited to England, with separate developments in Wales, Scotland, and Northern Ireland.

[3] We looked at central policy documents, parliamentary debates, and conducted expert interviews with key policy makers and scientific advisors in both countries. For a full description of the methodological set-up of the study, see the preliminary report (Rüling 2008).

responsibility for the provision of childcare places for children of all age groups for the first time. The bill defines the duty of local authorities, in order to ensure sufficient childcare for children below the age of 3, provided parents were in employment, training, or had special needs. Local authorities have been requested to assess and monitor childcare needs and coordinate local childcare services. In order to raise the quality of childcare, the Act established a curriculum ('Birth to 3 Matters'), which has become integrated into a national educational curriculum for children from birth to 18 years of age. Furthermore, the 'Transformation Fund', which subsidizes training of the staff providing childcare, was introduced as an element in the Childcare Act. Finally, the Act regulates the extension of Sure Start Children's Centres, aiming for an expansion to 3500 centres nationwide by 2010—one in every community, starting with the most disadvantaged areas (Linsey and McAuliffe 2006: 405).

Political debates during the passing of the Childcare Act in 2005 particularly addressed the quality of childcare, outcomes for children, and whether parental care or external childcare is better for child development. Generally speaking, all parties favoured the expansion of childcare, albeit with different priorities. However, there was a shift in the political discourse, since family policy as such had not existed in the British welfare state and for the first time the state took over the responsibility of the regulation of this field.

An important argument in favour of the childcare bill was that integrated services would help to improve the situation of children from disadvantaged backgrounds. According to Labour MPs, childcare would be provided in the form of Children's Centres and these would receive subsidies in disadvantaged areas in order to close 'the gaps between the development of wealthy and disadvantaged children'. Through early access to education, it is possible to 'break the link between people's incomes and their opportunities' (House of Commons 2005, 2nd reading of childcare bill, Column 28).

To prove this point, several Labour and Liberal MPs in the House of Commons made references to scientific studies and evaluations of the impact of ECEC on the child's cognitive development. For example, Helen Goodman stated that 'by the age of 3, children of professional families already have vocabularies that are greater than those of adults in the poorest families' (House of Commons, 2nd reading of childcare bill, Column 61). The argument made in support of the ECEC was that every month of high-quality preschool education increases school-readiness of children from the age of 1 onwards. In this context, the question of the quality of childcare was an essential point. In order to increase the quality of childcare, the government set up a special fund ('transformation fund') as a subsidy for education and training of the childcare workforce as an element of the childcare bill.

The high level of concern over the quality of childcare had already been mentioned by all parties in the parliamentary debates on the childcare bill in 2005. However, Conservative speakers stressed the fact that parents worked not because they wanted to, but out of economic necessity, even though home-based care may be better for children. 'Young children are much better off in the care of their mother, father or members of the close family in the early years from birth to 3', said Rob Wilson (Conservative, Column 64). This position was backed by the speaker, with scientific arguments over the 'attachment theory', claiming that in the first years children need a stable relationship. Especially the lack of sustainability of childcare placements, with high staff turnover rates was considered to be problematic.

In England, the main and foremost drive for the expansion of childcare is the aim to fight child poverty and to enable parents to return to employment (Ball and Vincent 2005; Sylva and Pugh 2005; Smith et al. 2007). The political strategy against child poverty works on two dimensions. First, there is a strong attempt to get unemployed parents back to work and to increase female employment rates, especially of single mothers (Clarke 2007). Since employment has been found to be the most effective method of preventing poverty, making parents return to the labour market is regarded as the first step towards the eradication of child poverty. As a consequence, the expansion of childcare constitutes an element of a welfare-to-work policy targeting low-income parents. Second, through socially inclusive programmes targeted at disadvantaged children, the poverty and welfare-dependence cycle can be broken.

It can be argued that the priorities of the Blair government with regards to childcare shifted during its three terms in office. During the first years, the question of maternal employment, especially for single parents, was considered of paramount importance in order to combat child poverty. With the introduction of the childcare strategy in 2004, the quality of childcare entered the political agenda. According to our expert interviews, this shift was due to the fact that a one-sided work-orientated strategy was criticized in the public debate as potentially harmful for children in low-quality childcare settings. Following the criticism of an economically driven welfare-to-work agenda, the Labour government changed its perspective and started to emphasize the quality aspect. From this perspective, childcare should benefit children, rather than serve the parents' interest.

The aim of the childcare strategy was to give 'children the best possible start in life' (Her Majesty's Treasury 2004a). In the context of social inclusion being considered within the English policy paradigm, the connection between education and care was much more apparent than in Germany. By targeting children from disadvantaged backgrounds, there was a need to legitimize the public policy through emphasizing its effectiveness with regards to child development and its outcome on social inclusion. Consequently, research cited in public and scientific debates indicated that children from disadvantaged backgrounds benefit from ECEC, especially from access to high-quality care before the age of 3 (Melhuish 2004; Sylva and Pugh 2005; Lavalle et al. 2007).

The idea followed the logic of childcare policy being a social investment in children and especially of children 'in need'. The naming of the programmes— such as 'Sure Start' or 'Every Child Matters'—is telling, as it evokes the image of the state having to rescue children from socially deprived backgrounds and from the risk of neglect or abuse. The policy is 'pre-emptive', insofar as the idea is to help parents in difficult circumstances, as well as to invest early in today's children in order to prevent low labour market detachment, crime, and antisocial behaviour in the future. One influential summary report on the effectiveness of early-years intervention for disadvantaged children concludes:

> The evidence on childcare in the first three years for disadvantaged children indicates that high quality childcare can produce benefits for cognitive, language and social development. Low quality childcare produces either no benefit or negative effects. (...) Studies into adulthood indicate that this educational success is followed by increased success in employment, social integration and sometimes reduced criminality. (Melhuish 2004: 4f.)

The political and scientific debates relied heavily on a variety of scientific studies that investigated the effect of ECEC on the development of children from disadvantaged backgrounds. In this respect, the expansion of children's services in England remained within the frame of a liberal welfare state, as political activities in childcare were justified through positive effects for children from disadvantaged backgrounds. Financial support was targeted mostly at the population with lower levels of education.

6.4 Germany

The Red–Green coalition treaty of 2002 proclaimed the aim of achieving a 'sufficient childcare coverage rate' of at least 20 per cent for children under 3 years of age by 2010 (SPD and Bündnis 90/Die Grünen 2002: 29). This was during the Red–Green coalition's second term of office.

Whilst the Green Party, with its roots in feminist movements, had for a long time been keen on more publicly provided childcare, the topic had to be established as a principal issue for the second term of office within the SPD (Mackroth and Ristau 2002). Previously, family policy was considered a conservative topic, and was therefore not popular within the Social

Democratic Party, which focused more on education policy. Childcare was framed as an element of family policy and understood primarily as 'care', not as 'education'.

In the Federal election of 2002, family policy and the role of women was made into a major issue in the national campaign and marked a central dividing line between conservatives and social democrats. In the election, the CDU/CSU had promised a generous level of universal care allowance for all parents with children aged 0–3 whilst ignoring the issue of extending childcare or whole-day schooling. The SPD promised to facilitate the reconciliation of work and family life significantly for working parents during the election campaign (Rüling 2003).

Subsequently, the expansion of ECEC became part of the so called 'Agenda 2010', the principal welfare state reform document of 2003, and was finally substantiated in the 'Tagesbetreuungsausbaugesetz' (TAG), which passed parliament in 2004. The government estimated that 230,000 new childcare placements would be required by 2010 in order to fulfil the needs of parents in employment, those searching for employment or in education or apprenticeship, as well as for children with special needs. In order to fulfil these aims, the establishment of a child-placement ratio of 20 per cent nationally, with 17 per cent in the Western states and 39 per cent in the Eastern states, was considered sufficient (BMFSFJ 2007).

The TAG bill required local authorities to supply 'sufficient' childcare for children under the age of 3. The government legislated that the €1.5 billion saved annually due to labour market reforms was to be invested in childcare by local authorities.[4] The act came into force in January 2005. Compliance is documented in an annual report to parliament. The act also stated that childcare for children under the age of 3 should fulfil the aims of increasing the children's education, care, and socialization, and called for an integrative approach (BMFSFJ 2004a: 4). Thus, the TAG can be seen as a breakthrough in childcare policy since the state for the first time assumed responsibility for childcare placements with regard to children below the age of 3. Furthermore, for the first time childcare was also framed as education.[5]

In the parliamentary debate on the TAG, the family minister Renate Schmidt described the extension of childcare as the 'first pillar of a sustainable family policy' which aimed at helping parents to balance work and family and which should benefit children through better quality education (Deutscher

---

[4] This point has been politically contested ever since—many federal states and local authorities in charge of childcare claimed that the money was not really 'saved' in labour market reform or was distributed unevenly (Deutscher Städtetag 2004).

[5] In September 2008 a new childcare act ('Kinderförderungsgesetz—KiFöG') passed through parliament. The KiFöG calls for a childcare coverage rate of 35% and a right to a childcare placement for every child from the age of 1 from 2013 onwards.

Bundestag 2004, 1193B). According to Schmidt, the extension of childcare creates a paradigm shift in German family policy. Previous family policy, consisting of spending money on family benefits, had not been successful, leading to low birth rates in Germany and high levels of childless women (especially higher qualified women) in international comparison.

In the ensuing parliamentary debate, there were some minor disagreements between the parties regarding the question of the best quality of education, as well as quarrels on the financing of the bill and the responsibilities for the federal states and on the national level. However, generally speaking, all parties argued in favour of the extension of childcare placements for children under the age of 3. This is surprising, since the extension of childcare for young children was relatively new on the political agenda and the conservative party had previously argued that young children would be best cared for at home by their mothers. In contrast, during the TAG debate, arguments that childcare enhances the reconciliation of work and family and could lead to increased birth rates, as well as the idea of childcare as an investment which will foster economic growth, were often mentioned in the debate by conservative party members. Investment in ECEC as a preemptive social policy had become consensual across all parties (Deutscher Bundestag 2004).

How can this sudden trans-party consensus be explained? We argue that parliamentary debates prior to the passing of the TAG in 2004 can be seen as the result of a paradigmatic shift in the meaning of childcare. The previous ideological debates on the role of mothers and ideals of a 'good childhood' were replaced by economic arguments which helped to break up the persistent, traditional family models and which enabled a political consensus on the modernization of family policy. Over a period of two to three years, childcare was re-framed in the demographic and economic context of the new paradigm 'sustainable family policy': reconciliation of work and family life and the employment of mothers should be enabled through the extension of childcare— in the hope that this will eventually help raise birth rates in Germany. We agree with previous research, which shows that the main policy driver for family policy reform in Germany is the increased attention to demographic issues (Auth 2007; Leitner 2008).

The latter was fuelled by a dominant public debate on low birth rates, a fear of the 'dying nation', as well as the economic costs caused by the ageing society, which especially affects the pension system (Berger and Kahlert 2006; Auth 2007). In the political sphere, there has been a growing re-thematization of pro-natalist policy in the context of family policy since 2002, with the ministry of family affairs in the forefront of the debate. Previously, the issue of pro-natalist policy had been taboo in post-war family policy, due to the racial pro- and anti-natalist policies during the Nazi period (Willenbacher 2007).

However, Renate Schmidt, minister for family affairs at the time, put the demographic issue on the agenda as the new aim of family policy. This can be documented by a sequence of policy documents from that time.

A central policy document was the Seventh Family Report that stated that the 'old' family policy supporting the male breadwinner model was based on outdated gender roles (Sachverständigenkommission 2005). It argued that qualified women refrain from having children if they have to decide between a career and a family due to insufficient reconciliation policies. Reform was considered necessary since 'family policy on the national, Länder- and local level has ignored for much too long the fundamental changes of economic, social and cultural patterns in Germany' (Bertram 2006: 8; *translation A.R.*). The foremost aim should be to raise the birth rate up to the 'desired level of children'.

This demographic argument allowed a reframing of family policy from a 'soft' issue focusing on equal opportunities and enabling women's labour market participation to a 'hard' issue between the years 2002 and 2005. It was used as an explicit political strategy in order to increase the political weight of family policy (Ristau-Winker 2005). Instead of 'just' enabling mothers' employment, family policy and, specifically, childcare were regarded as fostering economic growth, stabilizing social security systems, and thus making the welfare state 'sustainable' (Sachverständigenkommission 2005).

Sustainable family policy is measured according to several indicators (Ristau-Winkler 2005), such as achieving a birth rate of at least 1.7 children per woman in the medium term, better reconciliation of work and family, lower child poverty rates through the enabling of both parents to engage in paid work, higher levels of education, especially through the improvement of early childhood education and care, as well as strengthening the competence of parents in the upbringing of their children, which ensures good child development. These aims constitute a clear break with the erstwhile conservative breadwinner model (Pfau-Effinger 2004).

The main driver behind this shift was the Ministry for Family Affairs. Several scientific studies were referred to in order to show the economic effectiveness of measures that enhance the reconciliation of work and family life (Rürup and Gruescu 2003; Bertram et al. 2005; Prognos AG 2005). Many of these studies use international comparisons to show that higher economic performance is coupled with higher birth rates and higher labour market participation of mothers—especially, the Nordic countries and France are popular examples in comparative studies.

Other studies calculate the fiscal effects of childcare as well as the short-term public impact on investment in childcare at the local level. The studies argue that childcare creates high rates of return and 'saves' welfare state expenditure in other areas, since it creates new employment opportunities, leading to higher revenue from taxes and social security contributions (Spiess et al. 2002; Bertram et al. 2005).

The argument that spending on family policy should not be regarded as costs but as an investment in the future is also stated in several studies which analyse the 'effectiveness' of family-friendly policies for the economy as a whole, as well as on the business level (Prognos AG 2005). To prove the 'business case' of reconciliation policy, it is frequently argued that the human capital of highly qualified women is 'lost' through long family leave, which leads to future and already existing shortages of highly skilled workers.

In summary, the general argument in the German debate was that family policy should help to enable the reconciliation of work and family life in order to stabilize human capital. On the one hand, highly qualified women should be retained in the labour market; on the other, the highly qualified women who have fewer children in Germany especially should be encouraged to have children *and* stay in the workforce at the same time, through a good reconciliation policy. The issue of safeguarding human capital is therefore twofold: at present, highly qualified women are required as workers, whilst in the future the human capital of the children from highly qualified parents will be needed. Interestingly, in contrast to the English debate, the fertility or the educational achievement of less-educated women was hardly mentioned in the German one. The policy is targeted mainly at middle-class parents.

The analysis of the English and German policy discourses show that whilst both countries rely on economic arguments for the expansion of ECEC, the economic discourse on childcare is shaped according to national contexts. Not only did the pressure result from different problems—child poverty in England, low birth rates in Germany—the historical legacies of the two different welfare cultures also frame the expansion of ECEC in their specific ways. Whereas the English development fits into the focus on poverty prevention by the liberal welfare regime, the German policy is mainly about changing the traditional gender norms encouraged by the conservative welfare regime. Thus, the convergence of policy output does not reflect a convergence of policy goals.

6.5 Investing in children: 'Children's Centres' and 'Familienzentren'

The national policy development filters may be clearest seen if the implementation of similar measures within the two different social policy contexts are compared. Therefore, we chose the most prominent model of investive family policy in the UK and Germany: the English Children's Centres and their German counterparts, the North Rhine-Westphalian 'Familienzentren'. In the second part of this paper we will analyse their similarities and differences and trace the differences back to different welfare traditions.

For many years, German family policy concentrated on transfer payments for families and on child protection. Since the mid-1990s, childcare services have entered the agenda; however, there has been a reluctance to emphasize family support services. Moreover, the social service system is highly segregated and can be characterized as a mix of market and state regulations. There are contractual relations between the public authorities and the various providers, including third-sector organizations (Diller 2006). Accordingly, the horizontal interlinking of agencies and services is currently one of the political efforts in the field of early years' services.

Apart from child protection, English family policy was effectively non-existent. However, multiple disadvantages for young children were increasingly perceived as a growing problem, since disadvantages in early childhood greatly enhance social inequality in later years. Since children and families were not able to have the same opportunities or take up available services, new forms of service provision were required in order to prevent negative long-term effects. Therefore, families with limited resources needed special services to support their children's early development (Whalley 2008).

Integrated services for children and families are a good practice example for investments in children with a positive return rate. They are expected especially to reach families from disadvantaged backgrounds and improve affordable access to children's services, such as health support, as well as parental education for those who need it most. Families experience help and support through a suitable social infrastructure. New provisions in the UK, as well as in North Rhine-Westphalia in Germany, show that both countries have started to invest in integrated services for children and their parents by creating Children's Centres and Familienzentren. Both Children's Centres and Familienzentren act as mediators between parents and public services by organizing and initiating the cooperation of various parties involved in a municipality, through regulations, guidance, and funding.

Children's Centres in the UK were introduced in 1998 under the previous name of Sure Start Local Programmes. The idea was based on experience from the US programme 'Head Start'. The political driving force behind the agenda was to mainstream integrated services for families with children of pre-school age, using the Sure Start Local Programmes, which are designed as models for the most socially deprived areas of England. Sure Start transformed the way services are delivered for young children and their families. In Germany, the Familienzentren project was inspired by the corresponding developments in England and adapted by the new government of North Rhine-Westphalia (NRW) from 2005 onwards. Whereas the Children's Centres programme is a national initiative and an English 'whole system reform' as part of a broader agenda (e.g. Sure Start Local Programmes; Children's Plan 2007), the programme of Familienzentren focuses only on the federal state of NRW, thus underlining centralist policy making in the field of childcare in the UK and the federal competencies in childcare within the German political system.[6]

In the following section we will analyse similarities and differences between the British model of Children's Centres and Familienzentren in North Rhine-Westphalia.[7]

6.6 The universal access to integrated services

In England, the Labour government implemented the Children's Plan 2007, placing children and their families at the centre of integrated services, regardless of traditional institutional and professional structures within different municipalities. Up until today, the main aim of the local authorities has been to focus on the long-term delivery of reliable, consistent childcare services for families and children, from their birth onwards, in order to ensure a self-supporting, cost-effective market which efficiently meets the needs of parents. The Childcare Act 2006 already required local authorities to secure childcare for working parents, with the aim of transforming services by bringing together education, health, and welfare. This reflects the government's reaction to the challenges faced and the initiation of Children's Centres as service centres for children and families.

Local authorities were made the primary person in the implementing and monitoring of these services. They were expected to work with local private-, voluntary-, and independent-sector providers to meet the needs of the local communities, avoid duplicating services, and underline the importance of effective partnership in providing integrated early-years services. As a result, Children's Centres were built on existing successful programmes like the former Early Excellence Centres to provide high-quality integrated early-years services for local communities through a partnership between agencies and professionals in community-based settings (DfCSF: 2007). This initiative first targeted the most disadvantaged areas, where a high proportion of

---

[6] Many other federal states in Germany have also introduced Familienzentren with different models, for example Rheinland-Pfalz, Mecklenburg-Vorpommern, Bavaria, and Baden-Wurttemberg. However, NRW is the only one to establish centres in every community.

[7] Our results are based on selective case studies conducted in North Rhine-Westphalia and in England, including expert interviews (Meuser/Nagel 1991) with central persons, such as key scientific advisors, managers of Children's Centres and Familienzentren, and representatives of local authorities.

children and their families live in poverty. The aim is to get parents back into work, as well as to integrate the various services for children and to extend childcare placements. However, integrated services are also planned for more advantaged areas in order to provide support and information services for parents (Moss 2006: 167).

In 2005, North Rhine-Westphalia developed the pilot project 'Familienzentrum Nordrhein-Westfalen'. The government's pilot project 'Familienzentrum' started as one of the central family policy measures under the leadership of the Federal Ministry of Generations, Family, Women, and Integration. North Rhine-Westphalia was the first federal state in Germany to implement child- and family-support services under one roof in every local community. The policy of Familienzentren is an attempt to establish general guidelines and standards into a system which is by tradition very decentralized and diversified. Familienzentren are intended as models of good practice for integrated early-years services. They also build upon existing childcare facilities, important everyday drop-in centres for parents. Every family with smaller children, young couples considering family planning, and in particular parents with deprived backgrounds, who have so far been hard to reach, are welcome. One of the major objectives is to improve the outcome for young children and reduce inequalities by ensuring that integrated early-years services are accessible by all children. The aim of setting up and intensifying new forms of cooperation between different agencies should allow every Familienzentrum to develop an individual service profile according to the social environment of its community. The specific profile of these centres has emerged on the one hand by linking already existing offers to form a cooperative service network. On the other hand, the needs of families—such is the concept—could lead to new service ideas and synergetic effects. However, the new network is also expected to improve the quality of service provision.

In contrast to the English Children's Centres, the Familienzentren in North Rhine-Westphalia have tried to reach every family, not only families at risk, right from the beginning of the initiative. They are spread all over the federal state, and include lower-, middle-, and upper-class areas. Although the Children's Centres were also meant to spread to more advantaged areas, the idea of universal access to integrated services has different meanings in England and in NRW.

In England, access to integrated services is much more actively facilitated in the disadvantaged areas, whereas in the well-off areas the Children's Centres can simply be a leaflet with addresses from available services in the area, posted in a community centre. Thus, Children's Centres follow the principle of universal access, even if service provision may differ widely in disadvantaged and advantaged areas. In NRW, every Familienzentrum has developed a service profile, which is adapted to the needs of the specific area. Whilst in disadvantaged areas services may include child health services and parental education programmes, the service coordination in upper-class areas may focus on babysitter services, household services, or arts education for children, such as is done in the Familienzentrum 'Südpunkt'[8] in Cologne, in response to a high number of better-off parents in an upper-class area.

To sum up: the British meaning of universal access is still strongly shaped by a liberal welfare state approach that primarily focuses its benefits on those who need it most, whilst the German meaning of universal access follows the traditional middle-class orientation of the conservative welfare state.

6.7 The kinds of services provided—similarities and differences

Generally speaking, integrated services provide the following: child health services, high-quality early education and childcare, parental education programmes, or employment services. On the one hand, they work to improve the social, emotional, and intellectual development of children, whilst on the other hand enhancing the labour market participation of parents and the economic self-reliance of families. For the well-being of children it is important to involve and empower their parents.

The North Rhine-Westphalian Familienzentren as well as the English Children's Centres have installed a network of providers in order to provide a one-stop agency with integrated service provision for all families with young children, with the aim of tackling child poverty and social exclusion. This multifaceted set of services also includes different aspects such as outreach to parents not attending the centre, management, and workforce training, support for parents and children with special needs (e.g. speech therapists or physiotherapists), a base for childminders, and links with child and family health services or local primary schools.

For this reason, local authorities and their partners are required to agree on structures, roles, and responsibilities in order to design and adapt their own centres to the specific needs of local families. In most centres, pre-existing structures have been joined together. For example, the Familienzentrum 'Wasser- und Sonnenkinder' in Dortmund[9] initialized a network for childminders, a support mechanism for them to meet each other and parents in a lower-class area. Similar programmes were realized in the Rose Hill–Littlemore

---

[8] The Familienzentrum provides fully integrated early-years education with care and family support for children and parents in response to the needs of the local community.

[9] The Familienzentrum's aim is to involve parents in their children's early learning and play, and to work in a partnership with local childminders.

Children's Centre[10] that created a childminder network in a deprived area of Oxfordshire for families from local and non-local communities.

Due to the small number of case studies that we were able to undertake, our results are far from being representative. However, we were at least able to formulate some hypotheses. It seems that Familienzentren operate within the traditional structures of the German welfare system. This means that cooperation is predicated by membership within the same welfare service association, the so-called 'Wohlfahrtsverbände', acting as umbrella organizations. In other words, many Familienzentren coordinate services along the guidelines of the 'Wohlfahrtsverband' they belong to. On the one hand, this has the advantage of stable and established cooperations. On the other hand, however, the strength of local partnerships often depends on the history of previous cooperation in the area. Therefore, those structures which already work within an area are important. By contrast, the Children's Centres are faced with market conditions which pose the central challenge for the coordination and structure. The cooperations may be volatile and uncertain. In both cases, pre-existing cooperations are very important. However, in Germany these cooperations are often institutionalized within the 'Wohlfahrtsverbände', whereas in England they are more volatile and uncertain.

In contrast to the NRW Familienzentren, Children's Centres in England are also linked with higher education training opportunities and employment services in order to help parents acquire the confidence and skills that are necessary to seek employment. For example, the Thomas Coram Children's Centre[11] in London also increased their work with training providers and offered a 'Parents Centre', where parents can participate in training courses and use a career service to prepare for job interviews, for example.

The rationale of this policy in the UK is to enable more families with young children to enter employment with the help of publicly funded, accessible, and affordable childcare and family support programmes. There is an emphasis on outreach and support work to reach those families at risk and to improve community development. Moreover, services are targeted primarily at disadvantaged families suffering from poverty, since Children's Centres are linked with employment programmes in order to promote parents' employability, to help parents cope with changing employment conditions, and to support unemployed parents in finding a new job (Meadows 2008: 123ff.). This is different to the Familienzentren, where unemployed parents are not encouraged to participate in the labour market. The Familienzentren have not

---

[10] Until 2007, the Rose Hill–Littlemore Children's Centre in Oxford was funded as a 'Sure Start Local Programme' (http://www.rosehill-littlemore.childrencentre.org/).

[11] The Thomas Coram Early Childhood and Parents Centre in London opened in September 1998. The centre's aim is to provide a range of services for young children and their families and to work in partnership with parents (http://www.coram.org.uk/).

followed a job-centre strategy. These differences point out that the principles of the English tradition of a liberal welfare state which focuses mainly on poverty prevention and workfare have been adopted for family policy.

6.8 Conclusion

Starting from the empirical observations of convergent developments in British and German childcare policies, as well as the simultaneous emergence of a supra-national economic discourse that promoted the expansion of ECEC, we asked about the interconnectedness of these processes. In a first step, we compared the national discourses around two central pieces of childcare legislation, in order to trace the supra-national discourse at national level. Our results show that whilst the development of ECEC has in both countries been legitimized with economic arguments, these arguments differ decisively. In England, the debate was initially strongly connected to activating a labour market policy with the aim of preventing child poverty, and later on shifted its focus onto the quality of childcare. In contrast, the German debate was primarily focused on increasing the fertility rate by improving reconciliation policies in order to secure the future labour force. Thus, the economic turn in childcare policy was filtered by national welfare traditions.

The liberal British welfare regime, with its traditional focus on poverty prevention, first reacted to the problem of child poverty. This strategy aimed at activating the labour market resources of parents, which is in line with the liberal credo of enabling individuals to help themselves. Consequently, the expansion of childcare was mainly targeted at parents and children from disadvantaged communities. From 2004 onwards, the issue of high-quality childcare caused a shift in the economic argumentation in England. All children should be given 'the best possible start in life' in order to break the welfare dependency and poverty cycle. Obviously, the idea of equal opportunities is at the core of the liberal welfare regime. It is important to note that policy change (i.e. state intervention in childcare) brought about with the Labour government was legitimized by referring to the traditions of British social policy. Thus, the supra-national economic discourse may fit better to the liberal rather than the conservative welfare regime. So how did the German welfare state legitimize policy change?

In Germany, the expansion of childcare was promoted in order to secure economic growth through higher employment rates of mothers, higher fertility rates, and the creation of new jobs in childcare. Although this argumentation resembles the interventionist state in a coordinated market economy, it rather challenges the traditional gender norms of the conservative welfare regime and thus needs further explanation. On the one hand, the new

Red–Green government was definitely saying farewell to the male breadwinner model and promoted continuous employment for both parents instead, as well as short periods of childcare leave and fathers' involvement in the care of their children. The expansion of childcare, however, was based on a rather broad political consensus that included the majority of the conservative party. This consensus resulted from a public discourse on the 'sustainability of family policy' that worked to lessen the ideological sting: 'The new policy connotes a politically neutral and economically moderate path that is not exclusively co-opted by either the Right or the Left' (von Wahl 2008: 37). Thus, the economic reframing of childcare policy makes the reform appear reasonable and forward-looking; the more so through its backing by the supra-national economic discourse on family policy. Thus, the legitimacy pressure that usually evolves from the promotion of particular policy models by the OECD and the EU (Turner and Green 2007) was not a constraint for German politics, but rather opened up alternatives. Institutional change was therefore possible due to the special historical constellation, and also because the innovative element of expanding childcare was added to the old conservative system by a process of institutional layering (Thelen 2003). The male breadwinner elements of family policy have not been abandoned but supplemented, and the traditional middle-class orientation of the conservative welfare regime has been reinforced since the expansion of childcare targets mainly middle- and upper-class women.

As a matter of fact, the convergence we observed regarding the policy output (i.e. the expansion of childcare) does not correspond with a convergence of policy contents and policy goals. However, we see a similar pattern to legitimize childcare policy by economic arguments; although the nature of the arguments also differed. This indicates that the pressure for convergence that emanated from the supra-national economic discourse on family policy was 'channelled through the prism of existing institutions' (Turner and Green 2007: 16).

Similarly, whilst the policy transfer that took place in the field of integrated services represents a convergence of policy instruments, we can still see differences with regard to policy content and policy goals. Both the English Children's Centres and the North Rhine-Westphalian Familienzentren follow the logic of one-stop agencies which provide integrated services for children and their parents. However, they also reflect institutionalized welfare cultures. Children's Centres focus more strongly on disadvantaged families and on the labour market participation of parents, both of which goes back to the traditions of the liberal welfare state. Contrarily, Familienzentren follow the conservative welfare tradition of also including the middle and upper classes; they are not driven by an employment agenda so far.

In sum, what we have seen with regard to the expansion of ECEC and the implementation of investive family policy could be called 'path-dependent parallelism', which describes path-dependent policy development in the same direction. Thus, the economic turn in family policy is a path-dependent move of both the German and the British welfare states towards investive social policy.

7

Family-friendly working time policy in Germany and the United Kingdom

Lisa Warth

7.1 Introduction

In both Germany and the United Kingdom, work-family reconciliation has moved from being considered a private problem solved by the family, to being defined as a societal problem, which, if left unaddressed, will incur significant societal costs. These include a growing dependency ratio through falling birth rates, strain on social security systems, social exclusion, and child poverty. The economic dimensions of the reconciliation problem, which have received growing attention since the late 1990s, have helped to push the reconciliation of paid work and family responsibilities to the centre stage of political agendas (Rürup and Gruescu 2003; Stratigaki 2004). The policy goal of increasing the provision of family leave and childcare services, for instance, has been incorporated into European Employment Guidelines and National Action Plans (European Commission 1998).

The reconciliation of paid work and family responsibilities can be at once defined as a policy goal in its own right, and as a means to reaching other societal goals (OECD 2002). In its own right, successful work-family reconciliation enables individuals to 'increase the living standard for their family, fulfil individual aspirations to have both a career and family, and to give their children the care and support they need' (OECD 2002: 3). Its importance to policy makers lies in the fact that the reconciliation of work and family life is instrumental in reaching a number of other policy goals. In the UK, for instance, it was fundamental to New Labour's social inclusion and poverty reduction agendas (HM Treasury 2004b). In Germany, gender equality considerations and later demographic change, in particular growing childlessness among qualified women and the related macro-economic implications, were major policy justifications for government intervention for an improvement of work–family reconciliation (Rürup and Gruescu 2003; Bertram et al. 2005).

Government policies aimed at facilitating the reconciliation of paid work and family life typically modify the resources available to families, and thereby influence the choices individuals make with regard to how much time they allocate to care and to work (Gornick and Meyers 2003). Time as a 'resource' needed for both paid work and unpaid care does not exist independently. It is created by being backed up either by money or by care for individuals within the family unit, enabling reallocation of time from one to the other. Thus, in the context of work–family reconciliation, time can be conceptually divided into 'time to work' and 'time to care' (Knijn and Kremer 1997; Gornick and Meyers 2003). At one extreme of providing 'time to care' stand family leave policies, which imply a temporary withdrawal from work and the reallocation of time from paid work to family care. At the other extreme, 'time to work' is provided through the externalization of care from the parent to someone else, enabling employment on a full-time basis. Family-friendly working time policy can conceptually be located in between those two solutions, as it aims to provide both 'time to care' and 'time to work' for working parents through the reduction of working time and/or flexible working time scheduling, thereby enabling a flexible adjustment of work and care responsibilities.

Family-friendly working time policy refers to government strategies to improve access to family-friendly working time arrangements. The family-friendly organization of working time is a contested policy field: employers want to retain managerial freedom over the organization of work in order to be able to flexibly respond to market fluctuations. Working carers on the other hand wish to have greater flexibility in their working hours in order to be able to adjust their work and family schedules. Family-friendly working time policy therefore provides an interesting platform to analyse the way governments deal with the challenge of accommodating conflicting interests while pursuing their own policy goals.

The state has only limited capacity to directly influence the organization of working time. Unlike financial transfers to families or services, which can be directly provided through the welfare system, flexible working hours are subject to negotiation between employers and employees and are therefore beyond the direct control of government. Governments wanting to increase access to family-friendly working time arrangements thus face the challenge of steering from a distance, by trying to persuade employers to provide flexibility voluntarily (encouragement of good practice) or by imposing the provision of family-friendly working time arrangements through regulation, for example by legally empowering employees to negotiate the flexibility they need with their employer.

Both the German Red–Green Coalition Government (1998–2005) and New Labour in the United Kingdom (1997–2005) pursued a dual strategy of good practice promotion and statutory regulation in order to improve access to family-friendly working time arrangements. A chronological analysis of the development of national policy strategies, however, reveals opposite trajectories in policy choice. In the UK, there was a gradual build-up from encouragement of good practice to statutory regulation over the time period analysed. Policy development in Germany, on the other hand, moved from the introduction of legal rights to working time reduction during the Red–Green Coalition's early years in office to the encouragement of voluntary provision from 2001 onwards, following a radical shift in policy approach that marked the coalition's second term in office.

These differences in policy strategy in the context of a shared policy goal can be explained by situating policy choices within nationally specific differences in policy preferences, government–stakeholder relations, as well as policy and institutional contexts, which are discussed in the next section. The development of family-friendly working time policy in each country will be analysed in sections 7.3 and 7.4 and compared in the last section of the chapter.

7.2 Explaining variation in policy choices over time and across countries

Between 1997 and 2005 family-friendly working time policy was shaped by centre-left governments in both Germany and the UK, following substantive periods of conservative-liberal rule in the 1980s and 1990s. The fact that policy development moved from encouragement of good practice to more proactive state involvement, including the development of regulatory frameworks in both countries, can at least partly be attributed to different party ideas regarding the relative role of the state, employers, and families in the reconciliation of work and family responsibilities, as there was a clear impetus in policy development associated with the change in government in the late 1990s. As government parties remained stable across the time period analysed, variation in policy choice across this period cannot be explained with reference to social-democratic ideas alone.

Sabatier and Jenkins-Smith's (1993) concept of advocacy coalitions sharing a particular belief system is useful to distinguish between proponents of best-practice promotion and advocates of statutory regulation to improve access to family-friendly working time arrangements across political parties, government departments, and interest groups. The former might be called managerial freedom advocates as they push for solutions which leave the balance of power between employers and employees unchallenged, whereas the latter, which might be called employee empowerment, advocates favour policy solutions that empower employees to negotiate the flexibility they need (Warth 2008). This conceptualization enables us to move beyond the structural divisions of government institutions, interest groups, and political parties and focus on the structuring effect of the empowerment potential of policy choices. Family and equality advocates are thus more likely to have a preference for employee empowerment, whereas employers are more likely to prefer managerial freedom.

Policy makers and stakeholders are interdependent in the policy process. Government actors are reliant on the cooperation of employers, trade unions, and their representatives if access to family-friendly working time arrangements is to be increased, particularly on a voluntary basis. Stakeholder acceptance of policy choices not only furthers compliance but also political legitimacy (Hood 1983; Wilson 1990). The nature of government–stakeholder relations can explain certain governing styles and policy choices, as interdependence and consensus-seeking rule out certain policy choices and promote others. These choices are further shaped by the context of policy goals and past policy choices.

At the specific policy level, both governments were pursuing the same goal, namely to increase access to family-friendly working time arrangements. This specific objective was embedded within a wider agenda, in which it served other, overarching, policy goals such as poverty prevention, labour market inclusion, child welfare, and equal opportunities between men and women (OECD 2002). In other words, although both countries wanted the same at the specific policy level, they may have wanted it for different reasons, which can explain different policy choices.

New policy decisions are made against the backdrop of the 'policy inheritance' resulting from previous years, or decades, of past policy choices which represent a 'vast deadweight of accumulated practices and ways of thinking' (Heclo 1974: 46). These influence the approach of policy makers, who follow established ways of doing, or react against them when these are perceived to create policy failure. In the first case, the literature speaks of 'path dependence', in other words, of continuity along a chosen policy path where preceding steps in a particular direction induce further movement in the same direction (Pierson 2000). Where past policy choices are seen to have failed to achieve their intended outcomes, dissatisfaction can provoke policy change (Palier 2005). Policy change can occur through a process of 'learning' from past experience and new knowledge (Heclo 1974; Hall 1993; Sabatier and Jenkins-Smith 1993).

Finally, policy choices are mediated by the institutional context within which actors operate, such as government departments, parliamentary committees, political parties, advisory groups, and interest groups, which shape their interests in policy output as well as the procedures through which they interact with each other. Due to the instrumentality of work–family reconciliation in a wide array of policy objectives, actors across policy fields are interested in its promotion. The policy process involves a number of policy actors operating in different government institutions where they plan and develop reforms under different policy agendas. Indeed, the development of family-friendly working time policy was in both countries organizationally fragmented, spanning across different policy fields for which different government departments were responsible.[1] Under the roof of employment policy, industrial relations, family policy, equal opportunities, or poverty prevention, measures with implications for access to family-friendly working time arrangements might be developed as a by-product of wider reforms. As different departments have different institutionalized priorities and ways of doing policy, the choice of policy instruments can vary as a result (Linder and Peters 1989).

This explanatory framework is in the following applied to provide explanations for policy variation over time and across countries.

7.3 United Kingdom: from best-practice promotion to the regulation of best practice

British family-friendly working time policy during New Labour's first two terms in office moved after a period of agenda setting and consultation from best-practice promotion under the high-profile Work–Life Balance Campaign to the introduction of a statutory right to request flexible working patterns. Table 7.1 provides a chronological overview.

In their choice of policy instruments, New Labour initially continued on the Conservative path of best-practice promotion. The Conservative Government had pursued a largely non-interventionist approach, limiting its activities to the publication of information brochures in the early to mid-1990s (Employment Committee 1995). Accordingly, flexible working patterns to accommodate care responsibilities should be voluntarily negotiated between employers and employees and not statutorily regulated by government. An 'interventionist' family-friendly policy stood in conflict with the dominant neo-liberal policy paradigm of deregulation and the ideal of the free market.

---

[1] In the UK, responsibility for the development of family-friendly working time policy was primarily shared between the Department for Education and Employment (DfEE) and the Department of Trade and Industry (DTI). In Germany, responsibility was shared between the Federal Ministry for Labour and Social Affairs (BMAS) and the Federal Ministry for the Family, Senior Citizens, Women and Youth (BMFSFJ).

Table 7.1: Family-friendly working time policy in the United Kingdom (1997–2005)

Date	Policy document/measure	Family-friendly working time provisions
Nov 1998	Consultation document: *Supporting Families*	Laid out dual strategy of promoting minimum standards in legislation and encouraging firms to provide beyond the statutory minimum of family-friendly employment rights.
May 1998	White paper: *Fairness at Work*	Statutory framework of basic family-friendly employment rights (protection from excessive working hours, minimum rest and vacation periods, expansion of maternity leave, and protection of part-time workers from discrimination).
May 1998	Framework document: *Meeting the Childcare Challenge*	Envisaged effective ways of promoting best practice by employers enabling parents to spend time with their children.
Feb 1999	*Caring about Carers* document	Discussed the role of flexible employment policies and support services in meeting the flexibility needs of carers (National Strategy for Carers).
Jul 1999	Employment Relations Act	Made provisions for a code of practice to implement Clause 5 of European Framework Agreement on Part-Time Work to facilitate mobility between full- and part-time hours of work. This plan was, however, abandoned in the policy process, resulting in mere voluntary guidance issued to employers via a government website.
Mar 2000	Discussion document: *Changing Patterns in a Changing World*	Launch of the Work–Life Balance Campaign which promoted flexible working arrangements, notably through free consultancy services to employers funded through the Work–Life Balance Challenge Fund. The campaign ran until 2005.
Jun 2000	Work and Parents Review	Largescale review of maternity and parental rights to explore ways of helping parents balance work and family life.
Dec 2000	Green Paper *Work and Parents: Competitiveness and Choice*	Discussed for the first time the arguments for and against the introduction of a statutory right for reduced-hours working.
Nov 2001	Work and Parents Taskforce report: *About Time: Flexible Working*	A taskforce of employers, employer organizations, trade unions, equality and family advocates was set up in June 2001 to negotiate a right to request flexible working. Their recommendations were accepted by Government and included in the Employment Bill.
Dec 2002	Flexible Working regulations 2002	Parents of children under the age of six and parents of disabled children up to the age of 18 received the right to request flexible working arrangements and to have their request seriously considered by the employer.
Apr 2003	-	The 'right to request' came into force.
Feb 2005	Consultation document: *Work and Families: Choice and Flexibility*	Discussed the option to extend the right to request to carers of adults and parents of older children (subsequently, the Flexible Working Regulations were extended to carers of adults in April 2007 and to parents of children under 16 in April 2009).

In contrast to the Conservatives, New Labour's strategy to encourage voluntary provision significantly increased the intensity of information provision. A wider array of measures were grouped under its Work–Life Balance Campaign, which ran over a five-year period from March 2000 to March 2005, and firmly established the concept of work–life balance and its benefits to employees and businesses in the media and public discourse. The campaign rested on three pillars: strategic cooperation with a group of 'best-practice' employers (Employers for Work–Life Balance) to disseminate information and guidance to other employers; free-of-charge consultancy services for employers who wanted to introduce family-friendly working time arrangements (funded by the Work–Life Balance Challenge Fund); and widespread publicity to raise awareness about flexible working options and benefits of a better work–life balance.

Despite significantly greater effort in encouraging voluntary provision of family-friendly working time arrangements, New Labour avoided regulatory intervention during their first term in office if it was not required by European Directives or already in place, as in the case of maternity leave. There are several possible explanations for this path-dependent policy development. Against the backdrop of the non-interventionist Conservative policy legacy, an explicit family-friendly working time policy had to be developed from scratch. While New Labour had come to power with a clear strategy to expand childcare provision, a family-friendly employment agenda had not been formulated during opposition years (New Labour 1997). New Labour underwent an extensive information-searching and agenda-setting phase during the first years in government, in which they consulted widely with experts and stakeholders. In the absence of a pre-formulated policy agenda and in the light of later regulatory intervention, it is plausible to suggest that in the late 1990s the Conservative path of best-practice promotion was continued out of a lack of a regulatory reform proposal on the table rather than out of the same ideational commitment to statutory non-intervention. New Labour's willingness to re-regulate the labour market was evidenced through the signing of the European Social Chapter and the Employment Relations Act 1999.

The emphasis on best-practice promotion during the early years can also be interpreted as an attempt to contain the regulatory 'shock' to business initiated by the European policy agenda. The first wave of regulatory reforms promoting 'family-friendly' employment was almost entirely led by external policy requirements (Dean 2002). The UK, following the signing of the European Social Chapter in 1997, had to 'catch up' on a number of EC Directives, notably on Working Time,[2] Parental Leave, and Part-Time Work. These

---

[2] Which was not part of the social chapter, but implementation had been delayed by the Conservative government.

policies required statutory reforms as implementation through collective agreements was not practicable in the UK industrial relations context. Although the Government pursued a strategy of minimal implementation, reforms were perceived as a wave of regulatory 'red tape' by the employer community and fiercely contested (Lea 2003). While no statutory regulations to facilitate family-friendly working hours were introduced in the context of implementing the Working Time, Parental Leave, and Part-Time Work Directives, the issues of the long-hours working culture, part-time working, and family leave were firmly placed on the agenda during these formative, agenda-setting years (e.g. Education and Employment Committee 1999; Social Security Select Committee 1999).

In terms of government–business relations, the cautious, non-regulatory emphasis on best-practice promotion can be interpreted as a strategy of conflict avoidance and trust building. The incoming Labour Government faced the pressure of proving to a suspicious business community that New Labour was indeed more business-friendly than old Labour had been. A central component of this endeavour was the commitment to reducing regulatory burden, especially for small businesses (Conway 2001). The Government attempted to carefully mediate between the different stakeholder groups. On the one hand, expectations for change from women and trade unions were high after eighteen years of Conservative rule. On the other hand, New Labour, having undergone a redefinition of party ideas and policy objectives during opposition years, was anxious to demonstrate to the suspicious business community that they were not heavily biased towards union interests. They wanted to signal that they could be trusted to promote economic growth and competitiveness and not to work against business (Bara and Budge 2001; Blair et al. 2001). It was thus crucial to strike the right balance between polarized interests. This tension, one may argue, had the implication that the Government wanted to demonstrate that it listened to both sides and wanted to find out what support was needed. It pursued a strategy of consensus building through the practice of wide consultation with stakeholders, who were actively involved in the policy-making process through participation in a number of advisory groups. This approach enabled the Government to reduce stakeholder opposition. Wherever possible, conflict potentials were avoided, as exemplified by the implementation of Clause 5 of the Part-Time Work Directive, in which best-practice guidance was preferred over a more intrusive Code of Practice (see Table 7.1).

7.3.1 *Regulating 'best practice'*

Against this backdrop, the decision in 2001 to provide parents of young children with a statutory right to request flexible working represents a surprising shift in direction. How can this be explained? First, it is important to keep in mind that the right to request is not an absolute right but a way of more effectively encouraging the dialogue between employees and employers. The Flexible Working Regulations are a procedural intervention aimed at regulating best practice in working time negotiation rather than substantively providing working time flexibility itself. The use of legislation rather than merely best-practice guidance gave the issue more visibility, maximizing the outreach of information about flexible working to employers who generally pay more attention to changes in the law than to guidance and information published on government websites. The right to request was kept 'light touch' so as to reduce employer resistance from the outset but the decision to legislate meant that flexible working was discussed on a wide and visible platform.

Second, considering the timing of the reform proposals, electoral considerations seem to have played an important role in the decision to legislate. The decision to introduce an employee right to flexible working was announced strategically just days before the general election in June 2001 (New Labour 2001). The extensive consultation period of the Work and Parents Review had highlighted a high level of demand for flexible working hours among parents and carers (Cm 5005 2000). Trade unions, family and equality organizations demanded a statutory right to flexible working. The Government was under increasing pressure to act. The Employment Relations Act 1999 had gone some way to accommodating trade union demands but arguably had not provided much for the substantial segment of female New Labour voters. The pronounced family-friendly agenda for the second term in office was serving this constituency.

Third, the need for tangible policy outcomes was another driver behind the choice of legislation. Best-practice promotion alone was not a sufficiently strong instrument to ensure widespread and needs-orientated access to family-friendly working time arrangements, as voluntary employer policies were unevenly spread across industries and workplaces (Hogarth et al. 2001). In order to ensure equitable access, a statutory framework was needed to underpin voluntary initiative (Cm 3968 1998; Cm 5005 2000). The choice of a legislative approach was very much conceptualized as a way of speeding up the process of best practice as voluntary change occurred too slowly.

Fourth, working families needed support in juggling the time demands of work and care quickly if they were to meet the Government's employment and poverty targets. New Labour had set itself concrete deadlines of enabling 70 per cent of lone mothers into employment by 2010, by which time it also wanted to have halved the occurrence of child poverty. To both policy goals, the ability to combine care with employment was essential. Tony Blair's overarching orientation to welfare reform ran under the credo that all should be given the opportunity to participate in employment, and contribute their skills and productivity to the economy (Lister 1998). Economic independence through employment constituted a central policy goal in the Government's social inclusion strategy (Levitas 1998). Within this wider policy frame guiding New Labour's approach to welfare, help with reconciling employment and family responsibilities was in part motivated by the goal of preventing social exclusion caused by the reduced ability or inability of care givers to participate in employment (Bonoli 2005). The central importance of employment in New Labour's general policy agenda increased both the need for family-orientated working time flexibility, and its instrumentality in reaching policy targets.

Over time there was a clear trend in family-friendly working time policy from good-practice promotion through information and guidance to employers, to good-practice promotion through procedural regulation of working time negotiations between working parents and their employers. New Labour met the challenge of creating a supportive policy framework while keeping regulatory burdens for businesses low by introducing a 'toothless' right to request (Kilpatrick and Freedland 2004). It signalled to parents and carers that Government was acting in their interest, but in its substance did not harm business interests.

7.4 Germany: policy choices over time—via regulation back to encouragement

Through a series of regulatory interventions in the employment relationship around the turn of the century, the 'Red–Green' Coalition Government intended to enable working parents to exert greater individual and collective control over the organization of working hours. After this short and intensive regulatory spell, there was a policy u-turn to information-based policy interventions from 2001 onwards, in which government interventions focused on encouraging voluntary, employer-initiated provision of family-friendly working time arrangements (see Table 7.2 for a chronology of policy development).

State–employer relations shifted from an authoritative top-down relationship, with the Government attempting to steer employer action by statute, to a more horizontal, cooperative relationship, where a change in employer behaviour was sought through persuasion and voluntary commitment rather than statute.

Table 7.2: Family-friendly working time policy in Germany (1998–2005)

Date	Policy measure	Family-friendly working time provisions
Jun 1999	Action Programme: Women and Work	Outlined coalition proposals to strengthen the legal framework for equal opportunities and to revise the parental leave scheme.
Dec 2000	Reform of the Child Raising Benefits Act (Bundeserziehungsgeldgesetz –BerzGG)	The reform made the existing parental leave scheme more flexible. Both parents were entitled to take up their leave entitlement (36 months) at the same time, and to reduce their working hours to between 15 and 30 hours per week, returning to full-time hours after parental leave.
Dec 2000	Part-Time Work and Fixed-Term Contracts Act (Teilzeit-und Befristungsgesetz - TzBfrG)	Implemented Clause 5 of the European Directive on Part-Time Work, which introduced a general right to reduced working hours for employees in firms with more than 5 employees and more than 6 months of service.
Sep 2001	Reform of Works Constitution Act (Betriebsverfassungsgesetz–BetrVG)	Strengthened works councils to negotiate family-friendly working time arrangements on behalf of employees.
Nov 2001	Reform of Equal Rights Act for the Public Sector (Gleichstellungsdurchsetzungsgesetz—DGleiG)	Stipulated the provision of family-friendly working time arrangements, part-time work, and family-related leave for public-sector employees unless compelling reasons oppose it.
Jul 2001	Voluntary Agreement on the Promotion of Equal Opportunities for Women and Men in the Private Sector	The Central Business Associations agreed to recommend company-based measures for the improvement of equal opportunities for women and men, including family-friendly working time arrangements. The agreement replaced the planned Equal Opportunities Act for the private sector.
Jul 2003	Alliance for the Family	An alliance between a wide array of societal partners was set up to promote family-friendliness in the world of work.
Dec 2003	Assessment 2003	First assessment of the impact of the voluntary agreement through which it became clear that there was no longer the political will to introduce equal opportunities legislation for the private sector.
Jan 2004	Local Alliances for the Family	Alliance initiative further strengthened through promotion of cooperation for family-friendliness at the local level.

7.4.1 *The regulatory drive during the Red–Green Coalition's first years in office*

Until the late 1990s, family-friendly working time arrangements had only been regulated for public-sector employees, but not for the private sector,[3] where provision depended on collective agreements and management decisions unsolicited by government prescription. Following the election of the 'Red–Green' Coalition Government, there was a distinctive shift from a deregulating policy approach to labour law that had been pursued by the Conservative/Liberal governments in the 1980s and 1990s to 're-regulation' in line with their traditional policy goal of redressing the work relationship in favour of the employee (Rose 2003: 121).

An important factor influencing the introduction of statutory regulation of family-friendly working time arrangements was that a regulatory framework was already in place through the Works Constitutions Act (since 1972), the Child Raising Benefit Act (since 1986), and the Women's Promotion Act for the Public Sector and the Federal Courts (since 1994). Amendments of existing regulatory interventions are easier to 'push through' than introducing legislation from scratch, especially when the reforms are perceived as an improvement to the existing rules in place (Heclo 1974). The failure to introduce a planned equal opportunities law for the private sector in 2001 in turn illustrates that the lack of previous legislation in the private sector, however weakly formulated, increased the hurdle to its introduction. Although both coalition partners had agreed to it in their Coalition Agreement, the strong mobilization of employers and business organizations against the law, combined with the relatively low priority of equal opportunities in the hierarchy of policy goals, led to it being 'sacrificed' as a concession to employers (Alemann and Sielschott 2007). Following a large number of legislative reforms during the first years in office, Chancellor Schröder did not want to impose additional regulatory burdens on businesses.

The situation was somewhat different in the case of the Part-time Employment and Fixed-term Contracts Act (TzBfG). Although existing regulations of fixed-term work had to be renewed and the European Council Directives on Fixed-Term Contracts and on Part-Time Work needed to be implemented, this does not explain the introduction of the statutory right to request a reduction in working time. The regulations on fixed-term contracts could have simply been continued rather than creating a new legislation incorporating part-time employment. Clause five of the Part-Time Work Directive did not require implementation by legislation. In this case, the choice of statutory regulation is better explained by the long-standing social democratic policy preference

---

[3] The Employment Promotion Act 1985 had introduced the principle of equal treatment of part-time and full-time employees.

for a statutory entitlement to working time reduction, evidenced by earlier parliamentary motions during opposition years. All reform projects undertaken between 1998 and 2001 were attempts to redress earlier policies in line with 'Red–Green' policy preferences, in each case having unsuccessfully attempted to shape policy development through their own reform proposals during opposition years.

There were no significant institutional constraints preventing the choice for regulation. Rather, such a choice was facilitated by the obligation to implement European directives in national law. Thanks to a majority in Parliament, it was possible to pass working time regulation against the votes of the Conservative/Liberal opposition. The Bundesrat was not a significant 'veto player' as it does not have the institutional power to block reforms relating to labour law (Tsebelis 2002). As there were no direct costs to the public purse associated with working time regulations, there was no opposition from the Treasury (Rose 2003:122).

In the late 1990s, the policy agenda of the 'Red–Green' Coalition Government was favourable to union demands. A large proportion of social democratic delegates were union members. This might have played a role in supporting controversial reforms through Parliament against considerable employer opposition. The 'regulatory spell' in working time policy ended in 2001, with the Chancellor's blocking of the equal opportunities law for the private sector in line with the business and employer lobby. Institutional constraints cannot explain the reluctance to regulate from 2001 onwards. Changing policy ideas and government–employer relations are more likely to provide answers for the second shift in policy approach.

7.4.2 No less than a u-turn: the return to best practice

With the move from the first to the second term in office, there was a shift in the overarching policy goals to which work-family reconciliation was instrumental. Policy objectives shifted from furthering equal opportunities and women's advancement in employment, which had been a core social democratic demand, towards a pro-natalist policy orientation aiming to address demographic change, notably by encouraging more women to have children. Work–family reconciliation was reframed from being key to 'gender equality' to being fundamental to a sustainable family policy. This was initiated through an internal redefinition of the social democratic position on family policy. This process was led by Renate Schmidt and translated into government policy when she took office as Family Minister following the general election in 2002 (Ristau-Winker 2005).

Staff turnover and an organizational reshuffle at ministerial level created opportunities for new policy ideas and priorities to change the policy agenda.

This occurred in 1998 when the incoming social democrats took office with Christine Bergmann as family minister. Under her leadership the reconciliation problem and working time flexibility had formed part of the Government's equal opportunities agenda. When Renate Schmidt took over from Christine Bergmann in 2002, these issues were conceptualized as family policy and moved organizationally from the gender equality division to the family division.

Two policy ideas dominated the new approach to work–family reconciliation in general, and affected family-friendly working time policy in particular: the need for a better (service) infrastructure and the preference for a 'societal' rather than 'state-centrist' intervention to create a more family-friendly society. While the policy approach hitherto had had ambitions to directly regulate the employment relationship and facilitate a family-friendly organization of working time by means of legislative intervention, this was no longer the approach pursued under the leadership of Renate Schmidt. Her approach was to set up an Alliance for the Family between a wide array of societal partners (business associations, trade unions, academia, the media, and local government) to enhance family-friendliness in the world of work through convincing economic arguments, the dissemination of best practice, and initiation of concrete changes in businesses and local authorities (BMFSFJ and Bertelsmann Stiftung 2003).

Schmidt's 'societal' approach relied on cooperation and consensual relations with employers. From 2001, when the Government agreed on the voluntary promotion of equal opportunities for women and men in the private sector—distancing itself from its regulatory intentions of introducing an equal opportunities law for the private sector—the Family Ministry retained merely an informing, motivating, and co-ordinating, but non-regulating, role (see also Klammer and Letablier 2007: 688). Relations with employers and business organizations were managed horizontally rather than vertically so as not to jeopardize the spirit of partnership that had been created in (and was fundamental to) the Alliance for the Family.

Three possible explanations for this shift from a marked legislative approach in their first term in office to a preference for voluntary measures in their second term come to mind. One assumes a problem-orientated choice in the sense that information and persuasion were seen as the logical next step, aimed at complementing the statutory regulations already in place by promoting culture and attitude change. The second explanation would be that the Government 'gave in' to powerful employer interests. This appears to have been at least partly the case in the context of the equal opportunities law for the private sector, where legislation had clearly been planned. Determined employer opposition and internal party conflict cumulating in the Chancellor's veto prevented the passing of the law (Alemann and Sielschott 2007).

While this might in part explain the dropping of the equal opportunities law, it does not plausibly explain the shift in policy orientation leading to the set-up of the Alliance for the Family initiative. Here, it seems to be the case that the Government strategically turned adversaries into allies in the quest for pushing family policy from the margins to the core of sociopolitical debate and attention.

The three explanations are not mutually exclusive. There might have been a process of policy learning within the Government, which had, at first, pursued the same policy line as they had pursued during their opposition years, and then, when confronted with the pragmatic problems of government (including a powerful employer lobby), found that 'equal opportunities can only be realized in cooperation with business, not against it' (BT-Pl. 14/176 2001). This realization might have led to a recalibration of problem formulation and solution finding: in order to improve the conditions for successful work–family reconciliation, employers need to be supportive. In this interpretation, it is not a question of passing a law but of maximizing compliance, which might be better achieved by persuasion than by coercion. Indeed, from 2003 onwards, political discourse stressed the macro-economic benefits of a sustainable family policy to persuade employers of the business case for family-friendliness. The opportunity to return to the initial legislative agenda, which presented itself with the first impact assessment of the voluntary agreement on the promotion of equal opportunities for women and men in the private sector in 2003 was not seized. The lack of political will to legislate was more than obvious. Instead, emphasis was placed on dialogue and voluntary cooperation through the Alliance for the Family and an economically grounded 'sustainable family policy' agenda.

7.5 British and German policy strategies compared

Having explored policy strategies in both the United Kingdom and Germany, it is now possible to draw out the key similarities and differences from a cross-national perspective. Both governments introduced statutory regulations for the first time in this policy field, placing their approach in contrast to the encouragement-based, low-profile, interventions of the Conservative/Liberal governments of the 1980s and 1990s. Both governments introduced high-profile information campaigns and sought cooperative relations with business representatives to promote a more family-friendly organization of working time. Neither government employed economic incentives to encourage the provision of family-friendly working time arrangements. There was a parallel development in both countries towards stronger political prioritization of work–family reconciliation and greater state involvement in its facilitation.

With regard to family-friendly working time policy specifically, opposite trajectories in instrument choice were observed. While the British policy development progressively built up from best-practice promotion to statutory regulation between 1997 and 2005, the German policy development moved from the introduction of statutory reforms during the first years in office to best-practice promotion from 2001 onwards via a radical shift in policy approach.

The governing style and management of stakeholder relations of the UK Government was from the outset non-confrontational and consensus-seeking. The German approach was authoritative during the first years in office. This strained government–business relations through a number of interventions in the employment relationship, peaking in the conflict around the equal opportunities legislation for the private sector in 2001. Following the change in leadership at the Federal Ministry for the Family, Senior Citizens, Women and Youth (BMFSFJ) in 2002, the German approach to government–interest group relations became strongly orientated towards consensual cooperation with societal actors and business in particular. While the British approach served incrementally to prepare the ground for increasingly empowering policy interventions, the German approach of extremes led to a policy approach that ruled out further regulation.

The different policy contexts within which family-friendly working time policy strategies in Germany and the United Kingdom were embedded provide a valuable explanatory factor for differences in the policy trajectories over time and cross-national differences at the level of policy design. Both the different policy legacies inherited by the incoming governments and the different overarching policy goals they were pursuing help to account for differences in the choices made.

In the UK, the legacy of relative non-interventionism in the organization of working time and parental reconciliation choices meant that New Labour gradually had to build up business acceptance of government intervention in support of working parents, moving progressively from less to more empowering policy interventions. In Germany, where past governments had already regulated employment relations, policy reforms came in the form of amendments to already existing regulations. Policy change resulted from dissatisfaction with previous policy choices (Palier 2005). Existing regulations influenced choices as policy makers in both Germany and the United Kingdom attempted to integrate new regulations with existing law to avoid unnecessary complexity. With respect to the treatment of small employers in legislation, for example, past policy choices influenced policy design in opposite ways, leading to a small business exemption in Germany, and the decision against it in the UK (Work and Parents Taskforce 2001; Bothfeld 2005).

While both governments aimed to improve access to family-friendly working time arrangements in order to facilitate the reconciliation of work and family life, their motivations were guided by different overarching policy goals. In the UK, the ability to reconcile work and family life was considered instrumental in achieving economic independence and poverty prevention, particularly as New Labour committed to eliminating child poverty by 2020 (HM Treasury 2004b). Labour market inclusion of parents was a central policy goal within the wider welfare reform agenda (Home Office 1998). In Germany, by contrast, family-friendly working time policy was driven by three different policy goals: first, employment creation and protection through the redistribution of work; second, gender equality through the facilitation of maternal employment through men's greater share in parenting; and third, encouragement of families to have more children by improving the compatibility of work and family life to address the problems associated with demographic change.

These different policy goals were associated with different emphases in policy orientation, which partly accounts for differences in policy design. In the UK, where labour market inclusion was of central importance, reconciliation policies were more strongly orientated towards enabling parents to work. The Flexible Working Regulations accordingly provided a wide scope of flexible working arrangements to suit individual time needs. In Germany, by contrast, both goals of employment creation and gender equality through a greater share of fathers in family care were more strongly orientated towards providing 'time to care' through working time reduction. Although different policy goals were pursued by the two government departments in charge of the BErzGG and the TzBfG, both employment creation and gender equality goals were congruent with the facilitation of access to reduced working hours.

As family-friendly working time policy serves different overarching policy goals, its development was spread across different policy agendas and government departments. Actors working within government departments were influenced in their policy decisions by the respective institutionalized policy priorities. These influenced policy makers either in favour of employee empowerment or in favour of managerial freedom. Policy makers at the BMFSFJ, particularly under the leadership of Christine Bergmann (1998–2002), were more strongly in favour of employee empowerment as departmental policy priorities advocated the interests of families and women. The British Department of Trade and Industry's (DTI) institutional commitment, in contrast, was to promote economic growth and competitiveness. It therefore placed greater emphasis on managerial freedom. From the outset, policy initiatives for working parents that were developed at the DTI were designed within the parameters of a business-friendly approach. When the Work–Life Balance Campaign transferred from the Department for Education and Employment to the DTI in 2001, it became more strongly orientated towards employer interests. Managerial freedom in the German context tended to be advocated by the Economy Ministry, leading to policy proposals being blocked or amended at a later stage of policy formation through processes of interdepartmental bargaining and negotiations (Bothfeld 2005; Alemann and Sielschott 2007; Warth 2008). In short, the fact that family-friendly working time policy was developed within differently orientated government departments with regard to employee empowerment and managerial freedom in the two countries appears to have had an influence on policy choices.

However, government–stakeholder relations played an important role too. In Germany, the radical shift in governing style introduced by Family Minister Renate Schmidt initiated a radically different vision of family policy and the respective roles that government and societal actors should play in promoting family-friendliness. Family policy in general, and reconciliation policy in particular, were conceptualized as a societal responsibility, placing more weight on the cooperation of societal actors in implementing government policy.

The establishment of the Alliance for the Family, which implemented this new approach, created a relationship of interdependence with stakeholders. The wish to cooperate with business and employer associations to promote more family-friendliness in the world of work influenced the shift from an authoritative, regulatory approach to a consensual governing style that was associated with a shift in instrument choice from regulation to voluntary cooperation and best-practice promotion. Another example for interdependent relations with stakeholders was the British Government's aim to work in partnership with Employers for Work–Life Balance. This provided opportunities for the employer group to shape policy design. Thus they were able to negotiate that the campaign should promote work–life balance rather than family-friendly employment, leading to a wider breadth of coverage.

The success of family-friendly working time policy strongly depends on the cooperation of actors who control the negotiation of working time in the employment relations system. Due to the limited capacity of the state to steer the organization of work in market-based economies, the desire to maximize compliance by employers was shown to have had a favourable influence on the choice of less empowering instruments and instrument attributes in both Germany and the UK.

7.6 Conclusion

The comparative analysis of the development of family-friendly working time policy in Germany and the UK between 1997 and 2005 does not reveal a clear picture of convergence or divergence between the two countries, rather one of a parallel shift towards expanding policy efforts to facilitate the reconciliation of paid work and family life. While both employed a similar policy mix of encouragement and legislation over the time period analysed, there was variation over time and in policy design which could be explained by situating policy choices within the wider policy and institutional context within which they were made.

One may argue that family-friendly working time policy is still a relatively 'young' policy field. In order to increase employer acceptance, policy makers may start by choosing less empowering instruments first, then moving gradually up the scale when policies do not engender the desired outcomes (Doern and Phidd 1983). This trend is exemplified in the broader European context by the revision of the Framework Agreement on Parental Leave in 2009, which has increased the leave entitlement by one month, which is non-transferrable between parents to encourage uptake by fathers, and has made provisions for parents to request flexible working patterns upon their return from leave.

It may only be a question of time before governments are prepared to subsidize the provision and use of family-friendly working time arrangements financially to improve access (Hood 1983). Germany has gone a step in this direction by introducing an earnings-related parental pay for up to twelve months in 2007. While it is mainly used to compensate for lost earnings during full-time parental leave for a period of up to fourteen months, it can be used to top up part-time earnings if parents decide to reduce their working hours to provide childcare rather than taking full-time leave (BMFSFJ 2009).

Given the contested nature of working time flexibility and the strong conflict potential associated with state interventions in the organization of work, it seems, however, more probable that governments will continue to prefer to channel resources towards policy alternatives, such as childcare services, for which there is a broader political and societal consensus. While, as Bonoli has argued, there is a 'convergence in interests' between women and employers in support of improved public childcare provision (Bonoli 2005: 443), interests are diverging between parents and employers when it comes to control over working time. This tension has so far prevented a more significant expansion of family-friendly working time policy.

8

Cross-national perspectives on firm-level family policies: Britain, Germany, and the US compared

Timo Fleckenstein and Martin Seeleib-Kaiser

8.1 Introduction

Family policies in Britain and Germany have not only expanded within the public sphere in recent years, as shown in the previous chapters, but also at the firm level. Combined with a shift in the political debate towards more market-driven or private social policy approaches during the past decade, politicians in a number of European countries have argued that employers should take on greater responsibilities in the provision of social policy. However, for employer involvement to happen there needs to be a rationale for them to engage. Thus, the puzzle to be addressed in this chapter is: why and under what conditions do employers get involved?

The study is based on a comparison of German and British companies, complemented in the qualitative section by the inclusion of US companies. The choice of countries is largely rooted in the 'varieties of capitalism' (VoC) literature, according to which different employer rationales in coordinated and liberal market economies can be expected (Hall and Soskice 2001). We have not included Scandinavian countries in our study, as these states have developed comprehensive public family policies, and particularly parental leave and childcare, since the 1970s—a result of the strength of social democracy and organized women in politics (Huber and Stephens 2001)—which have largely led to a crowding out of occupational provision (Evans 2001). Within the countries selected here, we focus on private corporations, since public employers usually follow different rationales in the provision of occupational social policies (Dex and Smith, 2001: 11; Wood et al., 2003: 242; Beblo and Wolf, 2004: 566; Nadeem and Metcalf, 2007: 20).

The chapter is structured in the following way: first, we present a brief overview of the extent of firm-level family policy and its interrelationship with public policies.[1] This is followed by a review of the literature with regards to employer family policy engagement at the firm level, before we present our analysis of structural conditions and causal pathways of employer engagement. Methodologically, the chapter is based on three components: a quantitative analysis of a large representative survey among British and German workplaces, a comparative qualitative analysis (QCA) among leading British and German companies, and a case study analysis of fifteen corporations in Britain, Germany, and the US.[2]

8.2 Public family policy and the extent of firm-level provision

Family policy can best be described as a cross-cutting policy area, encompassing benefits, time, and services (Lewis 2006). Our definition of family policy includes three dimensions: transfers to the family as a unit, parents, and children; childcare programmes; and the regulation of employment for parents (various leave policies and flexible work) (cf. Daly and Clavero 2002). We thus focus on a limited array of explicit family policies and exclude many implicit family policies, such as wellness and health policies (cf. Kamerman and Kahn 1997). As is well documented in the previous chapters and in the wider family policy literature, public family policy has been expanding in many OECD countries during the past decade, while significant cross-national differences have remained (cf. Orloff 2006; Lewis 2009). Although we will not address the interrelationship between public and occupational policies in great detail, differences in public provision have to be taken into account when analysing extra-statutory policies, as firm-level policies are very likely to be affected by the public policies available to working parents.

Overall, we have witnessed an increase in the provision of firm-level family policies in Britain and Germany over the past decade, whereas the development in the United States has been one of stagnation and retrenchment, with the exception of flexible working time provision (see Table 8.1).

[1] It is important to note that we are not looking at the implementation of extra-statutory policy, but their institutionalisation, and we thus cannot provide any evidence on the actual availability of occupational family policies among employees.

[2] We are highly indebted to managers, work council members, and trade union representatives, who have opened the doors for our research and provided us with inside knowledge through their participation in our survey, interviews, and access to company documents. Without their generous support, this research project would not have been possible. We are also grateful for the valuable feedback we received from Jochen Clasen and Ian Kessler on an earlier draft of this paper. Finally, we thank Jessica Haase for her research assistance.

Table 8.1: Occupational family policy measures at British, German, and US workplaces (%)

	Germany		Britain		US	
	2003	2006	2000	2007	1998	2008
Flexible working time[a]	76.8	88.9	81	95	68	79
Extra-statutory maternity leave	N/A	N/A	16	53[b]	31	24
Extra-statutory paternity leave	N/A	N/A	14	18	15	13
Childcare (direct provision)	1.9	3.5	1.7	3	9	9

Notes: The data are not fully comparable between countries as it is drawn from national sources, using slightly different categories and concepts. [a] For Britain and Germany the data provides the percentages of workplaces that at least offer some kind of flexible working time arrangements (these can vary from part-time to working time accounts), whereas for the US the data provided reflects the percentage of workplaces 'allowing (at least some) employees to periodically change quitting times within some range of hours'. [b] The significant increase in the percentage of British workplaces offering extra-statutory maternity leave from 2000 to 2007 might have been influenced by statutory changes that became effective in 2007.
Sources: BMFSFJ 2006b,c; Galinsky et al. 2008; Hayward et al. 2007; Hogarth et al. 2000.

Various studies have shown that flexible working time arrangements are an important concern for parents (cf. BMFSFJ 2004b: 8; BMFSFJ 2006b; DTI 2007: 198), and prima facie companies in all three countries seem to have acknowledged this, as the overwhelming majority of workplaces provide at least some kind of flexible working time arrangement. In both Britain and Germany, statutory rights for working parents to access flexible working time have been strengthened. However, while Britain has introduced a right to request flexible working time for parents with children up to the age of 16, Germany has established a universal right to working part-time in enterprises with fifteen or more employees (see Chapter 7 in this volume). These new regulations might very well have contributed to the expansion of flexible working time arrangements within German and British firms; however, flexible working time arrangements have also expanded in the United States without similar statutory regulations.

Both Britain and Germany have also witnessed expansions of statutory leave entitlements. In Britain, parents have been entitled to thirteen weeks of unpaid leave since 1999. Maternity leave was gradually increased from fourteen weeks in the late 1990s to twelve months in 2007, of which currently (2009) nine months are paid (90 per cent of individual average weekly earnings for the first six weeks, and up to a maximum of €136[3] for the remaining thirty-three weeks). Before the new leave entitlement became effective in April 2007, 53 per cent of companies already provided more than twelve months' maternity leave, while almost one-fifth of companies (18 per cent) offered paternity leave in excess of the legislative minimum of two weeks at

---

[3] Based on an exchange rate of £1=€1.11.

90 per cent of individual average weekly earnings up to a maximum of €136 per week.

In Germany, parental leave was successively increased from ten months in 1986 to three years in 1993, of which twenty-four months was paid leave (of €307 monthly; albeit certain means-testing applied). Since 2007, parents have been entitled to twelve months (with an additional two 'daddy months') paid leave with a benefit replacing 67 per cent of previous earnings (but no more than €1,800 monthly). The total maximum duration of (paid and unpaid) leave remained three years. Unfortunately, no comprehensive data is available on extra-statutory leave periods in Germany. Although a number of collective bargaining agreements include arrangements for longer extra-statutory unpaid leave, the actual relevance of such arrangements seems to have declined over the past decade.[4] In the United States, federal legislation has entitled parents who work for companies with more than fifty employees to a total of twelve weeks unpaid leave since 1993. However, a number of states have indirectly established paid maternity leave through disability legislation. In 2004, California introduced the most comprehensive scheme, with a paid six-week leave benefit that includes mothers, fathers, and care-givers for sick relatives (Kelly 2006). In 2008, 24 per cent of all companies nationwide provided maternity leave beyond twelve weeks, while fathers had access to more than twelve weeks in only 13 per cent of all companies.

The availability of formal or informal childcare is a precondition for both parents to engage in employment. Whereas in the United States childcare in the past had been largely provided through the market, childcare provision in particular for children under the age of 3 had been underdeveloped in Britain and Germany until quite recently. All three countries have seen an expansion of public and publicly subsidized childcare during the past decade. In Britain and the US, the expansion was primarily focused on helping poor parents enter the labour market. In Germany provision of childcare is more universal, but until recently often limited to part-time places, while in Britain the affordability of childcare remains a major issue (Kelly 2006; NIEER 2008; Fleckenstein and Seeleib-Kaiser 2011). In parallel to the expansion of public provision, also childcare organized by companies has been increasing in Britain and Germany, in contrast to the US, where levels are considerably higher but have remained stable.

To sum up, in Britain and Germany, extra-statutory company provision has expanded largely in parallel to expansions in the public realm since the late 1990s, whereas in the United States extra-statutory provision was historically was of greater importance. Statutory entitlements and public provision in the

---

[4] This information is based on a number of interviews with representatives from peak labour organizations and representatives at the firm level.

United States, although also expanding since the 1990s, are still much more rudimentary. Against this backdrop, it is important to acknowledge that extra-statutory provision differs qualitatively in the three countries. However, as suggested by the incident and rise of extra-statutory provision, the expansion of public provision did not fully meet the needs of a significant percentage of companies.

8.3 Explaining firm-level social policies

The literature, which addresses explanations for the provision of firm-level family policies, and occupational social policy more generally, can be roughly divided into functionalist accounts and approaches rooted in organizational sociology. The former is predominantly found in the management literature, where 'business case' arguments assume that the introduction of firm-level social policies is a consequence of interests pursued by rational economic actors. Corporations are expected to provide occupational family policy measures, if the benefits exceed their costs. In tight labour markets, firm-level family policies might function as cost-effective tools to recruit or retain highly qualified staff (Dickens 1994: 5, 10; Glass and Fujimoto 1995: 384; Osterman 1995; Evans 2001: 24–6; Wood et al. 2003: 228; Budd and Mumford 2005: 4). Furthermore, the development of new work systems, such as 'high-commitment' and 'high-trust' work systems, which aim at facilitating loyal employees that are highly dedicated to their jobs, are said to have contributed to the expansion of occupational family policies, as these are thought to increase employees' commitment (Osterman 1995: 684–6; Evans 2001: 26 f.; Budd and Mumford 2005: 5). Even though the parsimony of the business case argument appears compelling, the empirical evidence is ambiguous (see, e.g., Goodstein 1994: 1667; Wood et al. 2003: 242; Whitehouse et al. 2007: 34). Another functional argument brought forward in the literature is the size of firms, as larger companies are said to be more likely to provide extra-statutory programmes, based on economies of scale and their administrative capacities, irrespective of the political economy in which they are operating (Morgan and Milliken 1992: 242; Nadeem and Metcalf 2007: 20).

The literature on 'varieties of capitalism' points to the skills composition of the workforce as an important factor determining employers' social policy preferences (Estévez-Abe et al. 2001; Estévez-Abe 2005). Employers in industries who require specific skills are generally considered to be supporters of public social policies which facilitate the formation and retention of these skills, such as unemployment protection and pension policies, but not family policies because of male predominance in specific-skills jobs. By contrast, companies relying predominantly on general, and thus more portable, skills are expected to show little interest in welfare policies. Although this literature investigates employer support for public rather than firm-based social policies, the distinction between specific and general skills might nonetheless be valuable for the analysis of occupational benefits. In recent work, we have proposed to differentiate between high and low general skills, and that the prevalence of either type might affect the preference formation among employers (Fleckenstein et al. 2011). Workers with high general skills are defined as workers with high educational attainment that have acquired highly portable skills, i.e. managers, professionals, associate professionals, and technicians. As their skills are highly portable and sought by competing companies in increasingly knowledge-driven economies, employers requiring such workers are hypothesized to be more likely to develop firm-based family policies than employers in need of workers with either industry-specific or low general skills. We find workers with low general skills in service industries, such as retail, hotels, and restaurants.

However, occupational family policies can also be affected by the welfare regime within which companies are operating (Den Dulk 2001; Evans 2001). In countries with extensive public provision of childcare and leave entitlements, firm-level policies are usually less developed, as there is relatively little added benefit for employers to provide extra-statutory policies. Conversely, in countries with weak or residual public policies, firm-level policies are said to be more prevalent (Esping-Andersen 1999: 176).

Whilst functionalist approaches focus on rationality and efficiency, organizational theory sees greater room for idiosyncratic if not irrational firm behaviour. The early organizational sociology literature emphasized the normative environment in which companies are operating; it is assumed that organizations seek to legitimize their behaviour in a way conducive to their environment (DiMaggio and Powell 1983). Essentially, it is argued that firms adopt family-friendly measures, if they operate in a normative environment and public discourse in which work–life reconciliation enjoys prominence and experience normative pressure to 'conform' with public expectations. The extent to which employers comply with expectations is dependent upon their visibility in the public sphere and therefore the necessity to generate perceivable legitimacy for organizational behaviour (Glass and Fujimoto 1995: 386; Wood et al. 2003: 223).

However, early institutional approaches have been widely criticized for downplaying the importance of agency and interests. Instead of the perception of an 'iron cage' which determines their development, organizations are able to make 'strategic choices'; that is, they have the capacity 'to interpret and select their environments, responding to relatively fixed constraints and actively modifying other environmental elements' (Goldstein 1994: 350).

Accordingly, with the analytical focus shifting towards agency, some research emphasizes the importance of human resources and top-level managers' perceptions with regard to corporate responsibility for work–life balance issues and their perception of a business case for the extent of corporate family policy provisions (Milliken et al. 1990: 92; Goodstein 1994: 373; Nadeem and Metcalf 2007: 24; Whitehouse et al. 2007: 32). Based on a combination of the business case argument and concepts identified in organizational sociology, employers develop corporate family policies once they perceive that such an approach benefits their bottom line. Should this be the case, employers can in principle become 'protagonists' for firm-level family policies.[5]

However, focusing solely on the role of management assumes companies as highly integrated and hierarchical entities with the prerogative clearly situated within a more or less monolithic management. Instead, in many instances the prerogative of management might be limited by other actors such as employees (organized labour, e.g. in the shape of works councils) or female agency.[6] Organized labour might influence management to adopt policies that they would not have introduced merely from a 'business case' perspective. In this case, organized labour would be a 'protagonist' and employers would turn from being 'antagonists' to 'consenters'. According to this argument, (highly) unionized companies are more likely to provide corporate family policies (Budd and Mumford 2004: 206). In addition, trade unions might draw the management's attention to work–life conflicts among employees. Alternatively, management might consult trade unions on the issue of work–life conflicts. Thus, organized labour might influence the management's interpretation of environmental changes, which might have a profound impact on decision-making.

The evidence of organized labour influencing corporate family policy provision is inconclusive. Osterman (1995: 693) and Morgan and Milliken (1992: 245) do not find any significant impact of trade unions within US corporations. By contrast, a number of authors have identified a positive association between employee representation and the provision of family policies at British workplaces (Dex and Smith 2001: 12; Wood et al. 2003: 242; Budd and Mumford 2004), while others confirm US findings of no impact of organized labour (Whitehouse et al. 2007: 33). With regard to German companies, Beblo and Wolf (2004: 566) emphasize the importance of works councils for the provision of occupational family policies. However, these studies have not analysed agency per se; rather, they have assumed that the

---

[5] See Korpi (2006) for the distinction between employers as potential 'protagonist', 'consenters' or 'antagonists' of the introduction of social policy arrangements.

[6] In this paper we use female agency as a comprehensive concept, capturing various different actors, such as female employees, managers, or equal opportunity officers.

statistical relationship between the presence/absence of organized labour at a workplace and the extent of firm-level provision constitutes a causal relationship.

Similarly, some studies have argued that the share of female employees and managers can be conceptualized as explanatory factors for corporate family policies without explicitly focusing on female agency. A higher share of female staff is said to lead to a higher demand for work–life balance policies (Dex and Smith 2001: 12; Wood et al. 2003: 242; Goodstein 1994: 376). With regards to the impact of female managers, the findings are less clear. Whereas Nadeem and Metcalf (2007: 23) find no general association between the availability of flexible working time arrangements and the share of female managers at British companies, their analysis shows that workplaces with a female share among managers of 75 per cent and more have a greater likelihood of providing financial support for childcare and job-sharing opportunities. Analysis based on descriptive statistics also suggests a positive association between the proportion of female managers and corporate family policies at German workplaces (BMFSFJ 2006c: 9). Wood et al. (2003: 246) argue that 'well-educated' female HR managers have a positive impact on corporate family policy provision.

8.4 Explaining firm-level family policies I: structures and agency

In order to capture specific conditions at the firm level, we relied on the data of the Establishment Survey on Working Time and Work–Life Balance commissioned by the European Foundation for the Improvement of Living and Working Conditions (Eurofound),[7] which provides the only publicly available data, collected in 2004, that allows cross-national comparison of firm-level family policies. The representative sample includes 1191 private-sector workplaces in Britain, and 1117 workplaces in Germany. Independent variables included in the analysis are the size of the workplace, the proportion of female employees, the presence of organized labour, skills and managerial attitudes towards the issue of work–life balance, plus control variables.[8] The European Foundation dataset offers five dependent variables for the investigation of occupational family policies: flexible working time (essentially flexi-time,

---

[7] Information about the survey and access to the data is available through the UK Data Archive at http://www.data-archive.ac.uk/findingData/snDescription.asp?sn=5655. A summary of results was published in various reports by the European Foundation, available at http://www.eurofound.europa.eu/areas/worklifebalance/eswt.htm.

[8] We control for the economic situation of the company, increases in the total number of employees over the past three years, and the organizational character of the workplace, i.e. being one of a number of establishments as opposed to a single, independent establishment.

providing employees with some flexibility regarding the daily starting time and end of work); working time accounts,[9] unpaid or paid long-term leave, corporate childcare facilities, and training programmes for employees returning from parental/maternity leave (for details see Seeleib-Kaiser and Fleckenstein 2009).

A logistic regression analysis of corporate family policy at German enterprises identifies 'strong support for work–life balance among managers', 'organized labour', and the 'size of the workplace' as the strongest structural drivers for extra-statutory engagement in family policy (see Table 8.2). We find a greater incidence of 'flexible working time arrangements' and the 'accumulation of hours' at workplaces requiring high general skills, while such workplaces tend to be less likely to provide long-term leave. For the two service measures, i.e. 'childcare support' and 'training programmes for returning parents', no significant finding can be reported with regard to high general skills. However, a second model, only differentiating between general and specific skills, shows an association between general skills and corporate childcare provision and training programmes for parents. In this model, we also find a greater incidence of kindergartens and crèches at large workplaces. Finally, flexible working time arrangements and accounts as well as corporate childcare and training measures are more prominent at workplaces with a great number of female employees, i.e. workplaces that are not dominated by male workers, which is not the case for long-term leave. Also, workplaces requiring high general skills as well as those that are not dominated by male employees are associated with greater support among managers, while the presence of works councils (organized labour) seems to have a negative effect on managerial support.

The analysis of British workplace practices reveals a less clear picture (see Table 8.3). In workplaces that are not male-dominated and where the support for work–life balance policies as a corporate task is strong among managers, the likelihood of corporate engagement in family-friendly policies is significantly higher, with the exception of childcare provision. Only high general skills seem to increase the likelihood of flexible working time arrangements. In our second model, based on the differentiation between specific and general skills, the predominance of general skills leads to a greater likelihood of long-term leave and corporate childcare provision. Our secondary skills measure[10]

---

[9] Working time accounts usually specify the hours to be worked over a longer time period and provide employees with a significant amount of autonomy as when to work.

[10] Based on the VoC literature, differentiate between 'specific' and, 'general' skills and, in addition, between 'high general skills' and other skills (Fleckstein et al. 2011). For our skills categorization, we use industry sectors as proxies. The secondary sector and the mining and quarrying industry are assumed to be dominated by 'specific' skills while 'general' skills are predominant in service industries. For 'high general skills', we use financial intermediation as well as real estate, renting and other business activities as proxies. Priority is ascribed to the model including the high general skills dummy; we report the general skills model only, if it

Table 8.2: Family-friendly extra-statutory workplace practices in Germany

	Flexi-time working time	Accumulation of hours	Long-term leave	Company kindergarten or crèche	Training programmes for returning parents	Support for WLB as task of company
Non-single establishment	0.764[b]	0.707[c]	1.479[c]	1.543	1.924[c]	1.230[a]
Good economic situation	1.124	1.94	0.933	0.817	1.834[c]	0.888
Increase of workforce	1.019	1.126	1.750[c]	1.262	0.734[b]	1.331[a]
Skilled jobs	1.354[c]	1.586[c]	1.061	0.372[b]	1.563[c]	1.051
Large workplaces	2.108[b]	2.626[c]	1.621[a]	3.442[a]	1.467	0.706
Male-dominated workplaces	0.463[c]	0.561[c]	1.074	0.260[c]	0.442[c]	0.797[b]
Organized labour	2.263[c]	1.954[c]	1.566[c]	4.088[c]	1.783[c]	0.731[b]
High general skills	1.785[c]	1.456[c]	0.612[c]	—	—	1.267[a]
General skills	—	—	—	4.274[b]	1.386[b]	—
Strong support for WLB	2.414[c]	2.560[c]	2.724[c]	7.759[c]	1.687[c]	—
Hosmer and Lemeshow test	0.000	0.000	0.000	0.000	0.000	0.000

Note: [a] $p < 0.05$; [b] $p < 0.01$; [c] $p < 0.001$.

Table 8.3: Family-friendly extra-statutory workplace practices in Britain

	Flexible working time	Accumulation of hours	Long-term leave	Company kindergarten or crèche	Training programmes for returning parents	Support for WLB as task of company
Non-single establishment	0.916	0.869	1.067	0.409[c]	1.217	1.547[c]
Good economic situation	1.003	0.654[a]	1.219	0.373[b]	3.182[c]	1.366
Increase of workforce	1.336[b]	1.358[b]	1.374[b]	1.017	0.927	1.372[c]
Skilled jobs	1.010	1.271[b]	1.065	0.372[c]	1.174	1.304[b]
Large workplaces	0.728	0.797	2.058[a]	2.579[a]	1.039	1.154
Male-dominated workplaces	0.780[b]	0.624[c]	0.912	1.538[a]	0.543[c]	0.589[c]
Organized labour	1.089	1.091	2.743[c]	1.562	2.876[c]	1.092
High general skills	1.581[c]	1.113	—	—	0.976	1.104
General skills	—	—	1.393[b]	2.156[b]	—	—
Strong support for WLB	1.853[c]	1.487[c]	1.526[c]	1.025	1.442[c]	—
Hosmer and Lemeshow test	0.018	0.000	0.000	0.036	0.006	0.000

Note: [a] $p < 0.05$; [b] $p < 0.01$; [c] $p < 0.001$.

('skilled jobs', i.e. at least 60 per cent of jobs at a workplace requiring an apprenticeship, university degree, or some other professional training) is positively associated with a higher incidence of working time accounts and the provision of training measures for parents. The presence of trade union representatives is only significant for the provision of long-term leave and training programmes, whereas the size of the workplace is only significant for the provision of long-term leave and corporate childcare.

Comparing the results of the regression analyses, we find some degree of diversity. First, a positive association between employee representation and the provision of firm-level family policies can be identified for German workplaces. By contrast, trade unions are less important in Britain. Second, general skills—high general skills for working time measures—are consistently associated with firm-level family policies in German firms, while findings with regards to skills in British workplaces are not consistent. However, in no instance have specific skills been significant for the greater provision of extra-statutory family policies. In accordance with the literature on other corporate social policies, the size of the workplace is a significant factor for most firm-level family policies in Germany. At British and German workplaces, the absence of male dominance among the workforce consistently appears to be one of the main determining factors. Thus, it might be assumed that there are specific thresholds with regard to the gender composition of the workforce before certain firm-level family policies are provided. In both countries, we find a strong association between management support for WLB policies and the institutionalization of firm-level family policies. To some extent, this variable might be considered as a proxy for management agency, as it seems plausible that managers who support WLB policies are more likely to be proactive.

After having analysed structural conditions, the following section focuses on agency. We conducted an online survey among DAX, M-DAX, S-DAX, and FTSE 100 companies in the spring and summer of 2007. Managers from twenty-one British and twenty-seven German companies completed our survey, providing us with a response rate of about 20 per cent.[11] Assessing actors in firm-level family policies, we investigate the involvement of 'management', 'organized labour', and 'female agency', making use of Qualitative

---

produces a skills finding that is superior to the other model. To complement this analysis, we have included a 'less demanding skills variable' based on whether at least 60 per cent of jobs at a workplace require an apprenticeship, university degree, or some other professional training.

[11] Theoretically, one might argue that our analysis is biased, as managers that participated in our survey have exaggerated their role in corporate decision-making. However, evidence from our case studies of British and German firms, all of which participated in the survey, reported in the next section, confirms our findings presented here.

Comparative Analysis (QCA) as developed by Ragin (2000). QCA starts with generating so-called truth tables, which provide us with an overview of all possible configurations (including the number of cases) for provision (membership=1). Eventually, eighteen British and twenty German companies were included in the Comparative Qualitative Analysis; cases of configurations that did not meet the minimum of membership consistency of 0.75 were excluded.

In order to assess whether employers can be considered 'protagonists' or 'consenters', we have coded the presence of management agency only in those cases where management initiated the policy. In cases where a trade union or works council either initiated the policy or was involved in its design, we have recorded a positive value for 'organized labour'. A positive value for 'female agency' is recorded if those involved in the policy process were primarily female. In addition, we have included the skills profile of companies to evaluate whether we can identify different actors depending on the skills profile. However, due to the small sample size, we were unable to differentiate between high and low general skills (for details see Seeleib-Kaiser and Fleckenstein 2009).

To make our analysis more parsimonious, we constructed a composite measure as our dependent family policy variable, encompassing policies in the domains of time, money, and services. The various policy instruments were weighted to establish a minimum threshold for family-friendliness. The provision of corporate childcare facilities was weighted with the highest factor (4), as this measure involves a very high institutional commitment by a company, as public or publicly financed childcare provision in both countries for children below the age of 3 is still quite limited. Employer subsidies for childcare provision were weighted with the same factor, as they are more or less functionally equivalent. Emergency childcare, i.e. the provision of childcare in case the regular childcare is unavailable, was weighted with the factor 3 due to a lower corporate commitment. Other childcare support measures, which were not further specified, received a single weight. Based on the level of corporate commitment, one-off payments received a single weight, whereas extra-statutory leave pay was weighted with the factor 3. Working time measures were weighted with factors between 1 (e.g. part-time working) and 3 (e.g. working from home), depending on the degree of autonomy for employees associated with individual measures. Companies that scored at least 11 points on this composite measure were defined as family-friendly workplaces in terms of policies provided (membership in QCA terms). The score of 11 points was chosen to ensure that, in addition to the maximum possible extent of low intervention measures, a company would have to provide at least two policy measures scoring 2 or higher or one measure with the maximum score of 4. Table 8.4 provides an overview of the various policy measures and weights.

Table 8.4: Composite measure of extra-statutory family-friendly policies

Family-friendly measure	Weight factor
Service dimension:	
Corporate childcare facilities	4
Childcare support in cases of problems with regular childcare arrangement	3
Other childcare support (e.g. resource and referral services)	1
Special arrangements for employees during family leave	1
Monetary dimension:	
Single payments (for instance at the birth of a child)	1
Allowances for childcare costs	4
Payments in addition to statutory maternity/parental leave benefits	3
Time dimension:	
Part-time employment	1
Flexi-time	2
Working from home	3
Working time accounts	2
Working time arrangements based upon trust	3
Compressed working week	1
Flexible working time arrangements in consultation with supervisor	3
Term-time work	2
Other flexible working (e.g. sabbaticals)	1
Extra-statutory emergency leave for childcare	2
Extra-statutory emergency leave for elder care	2
Extension of job guarantee after the end of maternity/parental leave	1
Total	40

As Table 8.5 shows, at the eighteen British companies which provided family policies, it was the management that initiated such provision. More specifically, management, in conjunction with 'general skills', can be identified as the driver in thirteen companies. In the alternative (but not mutually exclusive) pathway, management operated in the absence of predominant 'female agency' in thirteen companies. However, the reverse, i.e. predominance of 'male agency' in British companies as a driver for family policies, cannot be concluded from this finding (see Table 8.5).

Table 8.5: Truth table, Britain

Management agency	Labour agency	Female agency	General skills	Number of cases	Consistency	Membership
+			+	6	1	1
+	+			2	1	1
+				2	1	1
+		+	+	3	1	1
+	+	+	+	1	1	1
+	+		+	4	0.75	1
+		+		3	0.6666	0

Thus, for British companies the following two pathways to family-friendly corporate policies, which are not mutually exclusive, can be identified using QCA:

MANAGEMENT AGENCY * GENERAL SKILLS
MANAGEMENT AGENCY * female agency

For the German case, the dominant configuration is the presence of management placing the issue of work–life balance on the corporate agenda and a works council that is involved in the development of policies; this pathway applies for twelve companies. Alternatively, in eight companies we find 'labour agency' in combination with the predominance of 'female agency' in the initiation and/or policy design. We have also run the QCA with female agency coded in terms of the presence of equal opportunities officers. In this alternative analysis, ten companies display the pathway of 'labour' and 'female agency'. Table 8.6 indicates that in five companies management did not initiate the engagement in corporate family policy, i.e. managers were 'consenters' only. In five general skills enterprises, management agency was absent in terms of agenda-setting. However, in three of these five companies, equal opportunity officers were involved in the initiation and/or policy design. Finally, in four firms—predominantly relying on specific skills—management agency was complemented by the predominance of female actors either at the initiation stage or in the development of policies. In the sample of twenty German companies with membership, management was the 'protagonist' in fourteen companies.

Table 8.6: Truth table, Germany

Management agency	Labour agency	Female agency	General skills	Number of cases	Consistency	Membership
+	+		+	5	1	1
+		+		1	1	1
+	+			3	1	1
+	+	+		3	1	1
			+	1	1	1
	+	+		2	1	1
	+	+	+	2	1	1
+	+	+	+	1	1	1
		+	+	1	1	1
	+		+	1	1	1
				2	0.5	0
+			+	3	0.3333	0
+				1	0	0
	+			1	0	0

Table 8.7: Reasons to engage in corporate family policies

	Mean score	
	Britain	Germany
To retain and to recruit qualified employees	4.40 (1)	4.19 (1)
To increase job satisfaction of employees	4.25 (2)	3.96 (2)
To reduce personal turnover and absenteeism due to illness	4.20 (3)	3.54 (7)
To improve the reintegration of parents returning from parental leave	4.05 (4)	3.81 (3)
To reduce absenteeism of parents due to childcare issues	3.80 (5)	3.65 (6)
To grant more time autonomy to employees (especially parents)	3.50 (6)	3.69 (5)
Corporate social responsibility	3.30 (7)	3.08 (8)
Insufficient public family policies	2.55 (8)	3.81 (3)

Thus, for German companies the following pathways to family-friendly corporate policies, which are not mutually exclusive, can be identified using QCA:

MANAGEMENT AGENCY * LABOUR AGENCY
LABOUR AGENCY * FEMALE AGENCY
management agency * GENERAL SKILLS
MANAGEMENT AGENCY * FEMALE AGENCY * general skills

In addition to questions relating to which actors were involved in the policy process, we asked managers for their reasons for involvement. The reported reasons for the various family policies were scored on a five-point Likert scale. Mean scores were calculated to assess the weight of individual motives and the hierarchy of the reasons for firms to engage in extra-statutory family policies (see Table 8.7).

The comparison of British and German companies displays some similarities as well as differences. Companies in both countries share the two most important reasons for their engagement in extra-statutory policies, namely to retain and to recruit qualified staff, as well as to increase job satisfaction among employees. Prima facie, the latter might be interpreted as an altruistic approach towards employment practices. However, in the context of the scores for the other items, and in particular the corporate social responsibility item, we are confident that companies pursue this objective primarily for direct business reasons. Insufficient public policies can be assumed to be a key motivation for corporate engagement in family policies in German companies but not in British. Overall, our data suggests that companies are primarily driven by the business case.

8.5 Explaining firm-level policies II: actors and processes

In order to gain a better understanding of the actual causal mechanisms and processes leading to the institutionalization of firm-level family policies, we conducted fifteen case studies of large British, German, and US corporations listed in the top stock market indices during 2007 and 2008.[12] The decision to include US corporations in our qualitative analysis was driven by the consideration to gain a more encompassing picture of the driving forces behind occupational family policies, as in US corporations occupational benefits have historically played a greater role, especially in certain segments of the economy, largely due to the very rudimentary public family policies, lacking for many years (Kelly 2006). Methodologically, this section relies on (confidential) documents provided by the participating companies and forty-seven semi-structured interviews with HR managers, diversity managers, works councillors, and trade union representatives at British, German, and US corporations. The causal mechanisms and processes we uncover with this qualitative research are more detailed and complex than the findings of our quantitative and QCA investigation. Instead of presenting each of the fifteen case studies in detail, we will provide a comparative analysis along the variables identified in our research presented above and highlight additional factors.

8.5.1 *Management agency*

Our qualitative case study analysis provided rich evidence for management as a key actor in the institutionalization of firm-level family policies, as we would have expected from our regression and QCA analyses. For most companies, the perception of a business case has been crucial in their decision-making process in favour of family policies and as highlighted in the analysis of our survey, retention and recruitment of skilled workers are core reasons for firm-level involvement. Our argument of a perceived business case for occupational family policies is reinforced by the observation that none of the British and German companies in our sample relied on systematic evidence, such as cost–benefit analyses, for the establishment of the business case to justify the policy initiation or expansion. Most companies seem to base their management decisions on the results reported in the management literature or even on 'commonsense' arguments, although some of them have started to gather more systematic evidence. American companies seem to be more likely to take employee surveys and exit surveys (conducted among the employees

---

[12] We selected 15 'pioneering' companies in the provision of corporate family policies based upon information derived from our survey among companies listed in the top stock market indices, benchmarkings in the field, and private conservations with experts.

leaving the company) into account in formulating their policies. One US high-tech company based the institutionalization of its family policies on evidence from regular employee surveys, suggesting a relative sound empirical basis for the introduction and expansion of such policies. According to information from the HR department of this company, these surveys provide robust evidence that in particular flexible working time arrangements are crucial for the retention and recruitment of qualified staff.

Nevertheless, companies differ in their reasoning of the business case, partly based on their very specific needs. As companies are faced with different challenges, it is noteworthy that among our British companies headquartered in and around London, none of which was a financial institution, the competition with the extremely high salaries offered in the financial sector was a key factor for their decision to offer firm-level family policies in their efforts to retain and attract highly skilled employees, as they felt ill-equipped to offer similarly high salaries.[13] Particularly in some German and American firms, current and anticipated future skills shortages were important factors in substantiating the business case. For instance, although one of our German companies had been reducing staff for a number of years and will continue to reduce its overall workforce over the coming years, its HR department is convinced that institutionalizing comprehensive family policies now will significantly contribute to its ability to retain and recruit desired employees in future years. We found a similar argumentation at a US utility corporation, where about 50 per cent of the workforce will be entitled to retirement within the next five years. Thus, while the majority of companies seem to be developing policies to deal with current retention and recruitment issues, some companies are planning for the long term and subsequently the business case is very likely to materialize only sometime in the future. Furthermore, some engineering and high-tech companies have developed firm-level family policies in order to become more attractive for so-called 'high potentials', particularly for female employees. The desire to increase the attractiveness for female employees is often connected to the argument that the workforce needs to be more reflective of the firm's diverse customers. It is argued that female engineers provide companies with the necessary insights for developing products catering to female customers. For a substantial number of companies workforce diversity has become a second motivation after 'retention and recruitment' in recent years.[14]

---

[13] For some companies even more down-to-earth considerations, such as high costs for office space and insufficient parking spaces, were part of the business considerations to introduce flexible working time arrangements, such as working from home.

[14] This item was not included in our survey of German and British companies.

Although the business case has been the primary motivational factor for management to get involved in firm-level policies, external factors can play a crucial role in triggering the process. As we will discuss in the next section, female agency was an important trigger in a number of instances. In addition, the policies of market competitors are an important motivational stimulus, particularly at US high-tech corporations best practices and benchmarking with other companies are common features and provide a rationale to follow pioneering companies, as none of the companies wants to 'fall behind the curve'. The degree to which benchmarking and similar techniques are used systematically, however, varies enormously. At one British company in the financial sector, it was openly conceded that one is more or less uncritically following the trendsetters in the industry with some time lag. Yet, this diffusion of policies should not be read in terms of normative pressure, as some of the early sociological literature would suggest. The collected interview data does not give any indication for this; and organized labour that is typically associated with such pressure is negligible at US and British workplaces. At two British companies, the aim to maintain good relations with the Government contributed to new management initiatives, after work–life balance policies had become a priority within the New Labour Government.

At two German companies, 'foreign' influence triggered a greater degree of activity, overcoming the conservative management culture. In one case, the merger of a German company with an American company led to a greater demand in diversity management, which positively affected the initiation of firm-level family policies in German workplaces. At the other German company, a new 'non-German' CEO provided an important push for greater activity in diversity management.

Personal experiences can also be an important factor. Our data shows instances in which the male CEO was fully supportive and personally pushing the agenda of occupational family policies only after he was confronted with work–life balance issues within his immediate family (for instance, through the motherhood of daughters). We do not want to overemphasize this anecdotal evidence, but what it suggests is that personal experiences can be crucial for the perception of work–life conflicts and have an important facilitating function among the executive management.

To summarize, we did not find significant differences of management's role in British, German, and US companies with regards to initiating firm-level policies. The business case is typically not self-evident, as often external factors and conditions trigger or enhance the business case. Corporate family policies are used as core HR management instruments to retain and recruit qualified female employees in particular, and to contribute to higher levels of work satisfaction among employees. As one manager put it very bluntly,

'Everyone knows that a company can exploit employees better, when they are content.'

8.5.2 *Female agency*

Although management was a key actor driving corporate family policies in all our cases, female agency often played a crucial role in companies, especially within the German corporations of our sample. In three German corporations (two companies in the financial services industry and one manufacturer), female employees voiced discontent—via their female works councillors—with the firms' practices, demanding more family-friendly policies, especially a commitment towards corporate childcare facilities, as early as the 1980s. In the two financial-sector companies, the management initially rejected the demands. The issue of work–life reconciliation resurfaced on the management's agenda in one of the companies, when an employee survey indicated a relatively high level of job dissatisfaction among female employees, who felt restricted in their career development opportunities. The Director for Personnel and the HR department viewed this as a major problem with substantive implications for motivation and commitment of female employees, who represented approximately half of the workforce. To address the issue of female discontent, the HR department launched a project facilitating female career development with a clear equal opportunities impetus. Subsequently, many equal opportunities and work–life balance policies were introduced and the company advanced to become a pioneer in the provision of corporate family policies, including childcare.

The other financial services company did not meet the demand for childcare facilities, and has continued to reject any corporate responsibility for such provision. Nevertheless, the issue of family-friendly policies re-entered the corporate agenda in 1991, when female employees undertook another attempt to push the management to engage in such measures. The initiative received support from the executive management and, in particular, from the new CEO. Subsequently, the company abolished core working time and introduced flexi-time as key measures to grant more autonomy to its employees, complemented with other work–life balance measures. At the manufacturing company, dissatisfied female workers, headed by female work councillors, pushed the issue onto the agenda by initially forming a project group. Subsequently, this group was successful in convincing the works council to call for more equal opportunity measures, to which the HR department was quite receptive. It is interesting to note that at all three companies it was not organized labour as such that pushed the issue, despite all three companies having established works councils, but affected female employees with strong support from female work councillors, who had voiced their discontent with the companies' hitherto lacking commitments towards family-friendly working arrangements.

At a German service-sector company, the Representative of Female Employees (and member of the works council), who later moved into senior HR management, was the primary driver of initiating occupational family policies. In this case, it was crucial that she had strong backing from the Executive Director for Personnel (as well as the Executive Board in general), while the role of the works council was largely irrelevant in pursuing the agenda. A similar configuration of Personnel Director and female agency, but this time two female works councillors, led to the initiation of a corporate debate on equal opportunities and work–life reconciliation measures to improve the family-friendliness of one of Germany's largest manufacturing companies. Both these companies differ from the other companies in our sample. At the former company, we were able to identify a legacy of public ownership that was conducive for the witnessed development. The latter had a long history of corporate family policies dating back to the interwar period, which provided an institutional underpinning for the development since the late 1980s.

As these examples demonstrate, female agency can come in different forms. Our findings suggest that the success of female agency at German workplaces immensely depends upon support from the (typically male-dominated) executive management. Direct female agency was of lesser importance at British and US corporations. Nevertheless, we identified instances of significant involvement. Female managers within the HR department of a British service-sector company were important in driving the agenda. At a US company of the same industry, we find a similar pattern. In both corporations, senior management was highly supportive. The legacy of previous public ownership and a monopoly position provided an environment that was conducive to female agency after privatization and the break-up of the monopoly at both of these corporations. Both cases seem to highlight exceptions within the two liberal economies. Finally, surveys articulating the needs and preferences of employees at one of America's largest high-tech companies triggered the development of corporate family policies. It seems that female agency indirectly, i.e. through the surveys, had an impact on this company, which also more generally seems to rely more heavily on evidence-based human resources management.

8.5.3 Organized labour

Similar to our findings in the quantitative and survey analyses, organized labour as such did not play a significant role in the initiation of firm-level family policies. Employee representatives and works councils tend to be rather male-dominated, with little sensitivity for gender issues and at most pursue a strategy of benign neglect, until female actors—as discussed above—are successful in placing the issue onto the corporate agenda. However, works councils played a significant role in the design and governance of these policies at German companies, whereas in the British and US cases involvement of organized labour was negligible. The different role played by organized labour can be explained by the very different systems of industrial relations in the two liberal economies and Germany, which are related to the mechanisms of market coordination, as discussed in the VoC literature (Hall and Soskice 2001).

The coordinated German market economy is generally associated with a strong (institutionalized) social partnership approach in employment relations at the industry and firm level. Despite pursuing different interests, management and works councils typically aim at finding 'win-win-solutions' through consensus, avoiding severe conflicts. For this reason, German works councils have been characterized as 'co-managements' (Müller-Jentsch 1995; Keller 2004). This general pattern of social partnership also seems to be applicable in the domain of family policy, even though councils did not have any legal rights in this domain until a reform of the co-determination law in 2001. At the industry level, numerous collective bargaining agreements addressing the issue of firm-level family policy have been struck in recent years (BMFSFJ 2005; Klenner 2005). Nevertheless, it has to be highlighted that firm-level family policies, at least until recently, have not been high on the agenda of trade union officials and works councils (cf. Dettling 2004).

Works councils, however, were instrumental in formalizing the policy, as a typical example from a German service-sector corporation illustrates. After debating occupational family policies for some time, management and the respective union signed a firm-level collective bargaining agreement (Haustarifvertrag) on equal opportunity among men and women that set the broad parameters for future policies. The social partners stated in their agreement that the promotion of female employment and career opportunities would contribute positively to the success of the corporation. In addition to qualification measures, the agreement explicitly mentioned that the corporation should aim at accommodating the preferences of female and male employees with regard to improving the 'reconciliation of work and family life'. As the Haustarifvertrag only provides a framework, the works council and management subsequently signed a company agreement (Betriebsvereinbarung) on equal opportunity among men and women covering all employees of the corporation and its subsidiaries. In general, this agreement was very much focused on equal opportunity, as it included the establishment of equal opportunity officers in every company belonging to the corporation, called for preferential treatment of women in all areas in which they are underrepresented and to develop training and qualification programmes to achieve equal opportunity. An appendix to the agreement listed specific measures, which were intended to function as guidelines for the various units of the corporation. It was emphasized that the management and the works council supported a variety of measures for flexible working hours in the interest of employees. Full-time jobs could in principle also be divided into part-time jobs. Part-time employment among management was to be promoted. Specific seminars were intended to raise awareness and design custom-made solutions to address problems related to work–life balance. Tele-working (including work from home and 'satellite offices') was to be promoted among working parents. Part-time employees were to be enabled to participate in qualification and training measures. Employees with school-aged children would be given priority in planning for holidays during term breaks. The various entities of the corporation should aim to find short-term solutions with regard to work organization and working hours, if needed. As far as necessary and possible, the companies of the corporation would support measures for childcare. Childcare services at the corporation's headquarters were governed by an agreement between management and the works council. A seven-member commission, three members representing management, three members representing the works council and one non-voting member (the director of the facility), decided which children to admit. All decisions were taken by consensus.

Collective agreements on corporate family policies, in addition to providing 'legal' frameworks for management and works councils in dealing with the various issues, communicate to managers and employees that the issue is taken seriously by the Executive Board and employee representatives. Through this institutionalized commitment those involved believe that it reduces opposition and reluctance to implementation which is often found among mid-level managers.

In the liberal market economies of Britain and the US, we do not find such stakeholder involvement via organized labour. The weakness of trade unions in family-friendly policies is a reflection of their overall weakness at private-sector workplaces. In the 'voluntarist' system of American and British industrial relations, trade unions are in a comparatively weak legal position, which does not encourage the development of social partnership at workplaces. Instead, the relationship between organized labour and management is typically conflictual, based upon the assumption of zero-sum games. With the decline of trade union influence at British and US workplaces, there is little incentive for management to engage in substantive deliberation on family policies with trade unions (see for an overview of British and US industrial relations Katz et al. 2004; Marchington et al. 2004), thus encouraging unilateral management practices.

8.6 Conclusions

The evidence provided in this chapter supports the claim that public provision has an impact on extra-statutory occupational family policy. Due to the limited public provision in the US, occupational family policy has for some time played an important role, whereas British and German companies can be characterized as latecomers. However, it is important to emphasize that the more recent expansion of public employment-orientated family policies in all three countries did not fully meet the needs of a certain set of companies that continue to provide or even expanded their occupational family policies. Nevertheless, the reach of occupational family policy, especially those measures that go beyond flexible working time arrangements, continues to be limited in all three countries.

According to the VoC literature, we would not expect corporations that predominantly rely on general skills to provide policies such as extra-statutory leave or support for childcare. As general skills are highly portable, employers would be able to replace working parents at low cost. However, our research shows that particularly employers who rely on high general skills tend to provide occupational family policies. By offering extra-statutory policies (particularly, flexible working time arrangements), employers increase the transaction costs for employees that are otherwise highly mobile to leave the company. Though occupational social policies are typically not associated with general skills in the VoC literature, this skills argument is in principle compatible with the approach. Whilst the VoC literature is predominantly concerned with skills formation, our findings address the rationale for corporate social policies for skills retention and unlike, to a lesser extent, recruitment. Hence, greater provision of occupational family policies is more likely in workplaces, predominantly relying on highly qualified employees, who are comparatively mobile as their skills are relatively easily transferable to other companies and industries. One might characterize occupational family policy at such workplaces as an instrument to 'lock-in' highly qualified employees.

By contrast, companies that rely to a greater extent on specific skills tend to engage less in occupational family policies. This might plausibly be explained by the more limited portability of skills, which itself might be sufficient to lock in workers, as reflected in longer job tenure. In addition, the lower provision of occupational family policies at companies primarily requiring employees with specific skills is obviously also affected by the low 'feminization' of these workplaces. In high general skills environments, such as the financial services industry, we not only find a significantly larger and over the past two decades significantly increased proportion of

female employees,[15] but also stronger corporate engagement in and commitment to work–life balance policies. As suggested by Nadeem and Metcalf
(2007) and confirmed in our research, the rate of female employment above
a certain threshold in (high) general skills occupations seems to be conducive to occupational family policies. However, even employers that predominantly require staff with specific skills, for instance in manufacturing,
increasingly use occupational family policies as an instrument to recruit
and retain highly qualified (female) engineers and scientists. Based on these
findings, we suggest that further and more comprehensive analysis with
regards to the association between skills and the presence or absence of
occupational family policies is necessary.

Our findings demonstrate that we need to look beyond structural conditions and simple associations, if we want to understand why companies
provide occupational family policies. As demonstrated, an approach rooted
in organizational sociology can provide a much more nuanced understanding
of the conditions, actors, and processes determining the institutionalization
of occupational family policy. First, it has to be highlighted that the perception of the business case by management is crucial. Second, the business case
is not self-evident, but requires agency to be brought to the fore. Third, in our
qualitative analysis we highlighted various processes, often external to the
management, that have eventually triggered management initiative; for
example, in a number of cases the management was receptive to the discontent of (female) employees with current work practices and subsequently
initiated new policies.

Although we find management predominance in all three countries, the
pathways towards the institutionalization and expansion of occupational
family policies show some cross-national diversity. In contrast to some of
the literature (cf. Beblo and Wolf 2004; Budd and Mumford 2004), our findings suggest that the correlation between the presence of organized labour and
the provision of occupational family policies does not constitute a strong
causal relationship explaining the institutionalization of firm-level family
policies. Organized labour was typically a 'consenter' rather than a 'protagonist'. However, the involvement of employee representatives in Germany
exceeded the influence of organized labour at British and US companies. In
accordance with the specific systems of industrial relations, the design in
Germany very much follows the concept of social partnership, with a greater
involvement of stakeholders, in particular work councils but also female
actors. Our findings suggest that the engagement of German works councils

---

[15] In German banking, for instance, women account for half of the workforce, with an
increasing number of female employees in management positions (from 4.5% in 1980 to 27% in
2008; http://www.agvbanken.de).

heavily depends on female works councillors placing family policies onto the corporate agenda. However, female agency was not limited to female works councillors, but often involved female management at German companies. By contrast, in Britain and the US, the design is usually based on unilateral management decisions without any significant involvement of stakeholders. These differences are also reflected in governance structures. Finally, we find a significantly greater degree of codification of occupational family policies in firm-level collective agreements at German corporations compared to the other two cases.

To conclude, our analysis has shown that management is the primary driver of corporate family policies in all three countries. However, we have also seen that the business case for corporate engagement in this policy domain is seldom self-evident. The perception of a business case is highly contextual, raising questions as to whether a functionalist account can capture the complexity of the rise and expansion of occupational family policies. Following organizational sociological approaches, our findings draw attention to agency in this process, especially HR managers, but also female employee representatives. With proactive agency that mobilizes support from key actors in the firm, occupational family policies can thrive under the 'banner' of the business case. To what extent the severe post-2008 economic crisis will impact the future path of occupational family policies is uncertain. However, it seems plausible that the identified structural factors, actors, and processes will continue to drive occupational family policies, even if the rationales and especially the scope for these policies might change.

Part II
Welfare Policies

II. B. Supporting Pensioners

9

Towards German liberalism and British social democracy: the evolution of two public occupational pension regimes from 1945 to 2009

Traute Meyer and Paul Bridgen

9.1 Introduction

Britain and Germany are often seen to represent a liberal and a coordinated type of capitalism, with two different types of welfare states (Clasen 2005: 1–5 for an overview). This means an expectation that the British state will provide low benefits and adopt light regulation; employers and insurers are free to act as individual, competing agents. The German state will provide generous, earnings-related insurance typical also for a conservative welfare regime (Esping-Andersen 1990) and it will support corporatist coordination to reinforce the country's comparative advantage in the global marketplace (Hall and Soskice 2001; Manow 2001a: 156; Schmidt 2002: 108). It is one of the central aims of this book to determine how both regimes have developed over time. Hall and Soskice have argued that facing economic globalization liberal and coordinated market economies would enhance their typical institutional features: increased international competition encourages further deregulation in liberal market economies, while in coordinated ones governments, unions, and employers defend the existing regime (Hall and Soskice 2001: 57–8). Most recently, Palier and Thelen have developed this argument further; they show a 'dualization' of French and German employment: the shrinking number of core employees in export-oriented manufacturing continue to be protected well, but their security no longer determines the conditions for all workers; thus, a secondary labour market has developed, offering inferior conditions (Palier and Thelen 2010: 122).

In this and Chapter 10 of this volume we assess the evolution of public and occupational pension institutions in relation to both models. We argue that the liberal label has never appropriately captured the nature of British regulation and provision and that it describes even less accurately the system in 2010. Regarding Germany, the conservative label characterizes well the situation until the early 2000s. After that it no longer fits, however; institutional changes have undermined status preservation more than expected by theorists of the Varieties of Capitalism approach and more 'core workers' are affected by social risks in retirement than the argument of 'dualization' suggests (see also Chapter 10). Both systems have therefore not converged but developed in opposing directions, Britain towards social democracy and Germany towards liberalism.

9.2 Low public benefits—strong market intervention: The hybridity of British pension policy

Since the Second World War a low level of public pensions combined with a large occupational pensions sector (Bridgen and Meyer 2007a) has embodied the liberal dimension of the British pension regime. However, alongside it there has also been a statist dimension largely overlooked in the literature on the British liberal political economy. This consists first of generous public-sector benefits, protected by trade unions. Second, this corporatist enclave affected private-sector pensions, too; it fostered incremental regulation over time of the whole occupational sector, aimed at improved protection of scheme members. The liberal–statist hybridity split the group of pensioners in two halves; exclusively affected by the liberal dimension were private-sector workers not covered by defined benefit schemes; affected by the statist dimension were public-sector workers and all other members of defined benefits schemes, whose predicted pension levels are generous because of stronger state intervention (see Chapter 10 of this volume).

9.3 Evolution: British public and occupational pensions

9.3.1 1945–74

The foundations for the hybrid nature of British pensions were laid during this period.Between 1945 and 1974 public pensions were very low, while private-sector occupational schemes expanded largely unregulated, but supported by tax incentives (Table 9.1). In 1946 a Labour government reformed through the National Insurance Act the fragmented system of social insurance under which most British citizens over the age of 65 had lived in poverty. In 1948 the Basic State Pension came into effect for all wage earners and their dependants, including the self-employed. To make this new system acceptable to the working and middle-classes alike it was to be broadly and immediately accessible, without means-test, but it was set at a flat-rate level much below that proposed by the Beveridge Report (Baldwin 1990; Bridgen 2006). The Basic State Pension is still in place today, as a core element of the liberal model (Hannah 1986: 54–9; Bridgen and Meyer 2007b). In terms of gender, the public pension was at odds with liberal tradition. The 1946 Act treated married women as dependants and effectively barred them from accruing independent rights even if in paid employment.[1] Moreover, very low earnings-related benefits were introduced in 1959, in response to demands from the left for the improved protection of workers (Ellis 1989: 16; Fawcett 1996; Bridgen 2000).

The occupational sphere was left largely unregulated until 1974 and British governments supported its expansion through generous tax benefits for employees and employers. Employers were free to establish schemes on a company-by-company basis. In addition, in the private sector organized labour exerted little influence over occupational pensions. The Trades Unions Congress focused its attention instead on the Labour Party's campaign for improved state provision (Macnicol 1998). Moreover, the 1921 Finance Act had exempted employee and employer pension contributions and investment income from tax as an exercise in administrative tidying. This policy had only had a minor effect before the Second World War, but it became a 'leading engine' (Hannah 1986: 45) for occupational pension growth when taxes rose steeply during the conflict, remaining at a high level in the post-war period to pay for reconstruction (Hannah 1986: 19–20, 44–5; Seldon 1960, Wiseman 1965, both quoted in Russell 1991: 133). By 1956/7, the cost to the Treasury of these incentives amounted to about one-third of the National Health Service budget (Bridgen and Lowe 1998).

The favourable conditions for employers, typical for a liberal regime, were constrained by the expansion of public-sector employment and by the onset of regulation. The first government after WWII nationalized a significant section of British industry: mining, electricity, air travel, gas, iron, steel, and transport, increasing the share of the public workforce to around one-quarter by 1950 (Middlemas 1979: 396; Hannah 1986: 40; Foreman-Peck and Millward 1994: 274–5). Between 1957 and 1976 public-sector employment reached between 33 per cent and 42 per cent of that in the private sector (Figure 9.1). In these nationalized industries a single centralized employer was established, collective bargaining was arranged (Chick 1998: 82), and more general consultations with unions were statutorily strengthened (Clegg 1978:

---

[1] For details, see Groves 1983: 46; Land 1985: 54, 56; Ginn 2003: 11–13.

190, 388). Thus, nationalization created within the mainly liberal British economy a large corporatist enclave with strong trade unions. These used the long history of occupational provision for civil servants which had been a precedent for all public-sector employees, to push successfully for the extension of such traditional pension rights to the nationalized industries (Hannah 1986: 4–41; Russell 1991: 128–9). Also, during this period state regulation of private-sector pensions commenced. To ensure that the new small extension in state provision introduced in 1959 would not reduce occupational provision, employers were permitted to contract out of the state scheme more easily, but those who did were bound legally to provide benefits at least at the maximum level of the state scheme and they had to preserve these benefits if the employee changed jobs. This reform had little immediate impact but it started an incremental process of state regulation of private-sector provision which by the end of the century had created a complex public-private system (see below).

Under these conditions coverage of occupational schemes increased rapidly, from 28 per cent of all workers in 1953 to 53 per cent in 1967 and in line with typical features of a liberal market economy. First, growth in private-sector schemes varied in relation to firm skill requirements. In 1970, those sectors

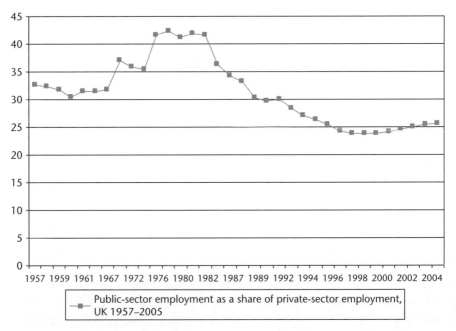

Figure 9.1: Public-sector employment as a share of private-sector employment, UK 1957–2005.

(*Source*: ONS: Economic Trends (various years); ONS 2005).

with lowest coverage for all workers included agriculture, forestry and fishing, retail, and miscellaneous services, where skill requirements might be expected to be lower (Russell 1991). In engineering, relying on high skilled labour, coverage for both manual and non-manual workers was higher. Second, half of the workforce remained uncovered, suggesting that companies were not interested in offering security to a substantial share of workers, many of whom were lower skilled or part-timers. Turning to the evidence for the statist dimension we see that in 1957 the coverage of occupational pensions in the public sector was about three times as high as in the private, and it remained substantially above the private sector until the 2000s (Figure 9.2). Labour's post-war nationalization policies helped to insure manual and non-manual workers alike (Russell 1991). Moreover, female membership increased steadily and long after male numbers declined (Figure 9.2). This is the outcome of welfare state expansion, integrating mainly women into the labour market, who became beneficiaries of the corporatist public-sector enclave as well.

Summing up, until 1974 the system's liberal dimension consisted of low state benefits and the uncontrolled development of occupational pensions in the private sector, supported by a favourable tax regime. The statist dimension was embodied by the generalization of good pension schemes in the national-ized industries and by the beginning of regulation.

9.3.2 *1975–9*

During the second half of the 1970s the state broadened and increased public pensions and tightened private-sector regulation (see Table 9.1). The Social Security Pension Act of 1975 improved the public pensions of blue-collar workers and married women (Barr and Coulter 1990: 281–2, 95). The passing of the Act had been preceded by the political mobilization of private-sector blue-collar workers, who no longer wanted to tolerate the very low level of the Basic State Pension (Baldwin 1990: 241–6; Bridgen 2000). In order to raise benefits for those not covered by occupational schemes, the Basic State Pension was to increase in line with wages and a new second public tier, the State Earnings Related Pension was created (SERPS). These changes guaranteed a pension equivalent to 25 per cent of average earnings in addition to the Basic State Pension. While less generous than the best private schemes, this was a significant improvement on the existing system (Ellis 1989: 50). SERPS was also open to female employees whose pension levels were calculated in the same way as those of men, even though they retired five years earlier and lived longer (Groves 1983: 52; Pascall 1986: 211). In addition, SERPS granted a widow's pension (Baldwin 1990: 241–7). The Act also phased out the Married Woman's Option to relinquish pension rights by not paying contributions

Table 9.1: Evolution of British pension legislation

Pension legislation	Balance of public and private pensions	Private-sector regulation—Private-sector incentives
National Insurance Act 1946 National Insurance Act 1959	Public pension below poverty level, patchy, uncontrolled voluntary occupational sector.	No relevant changes. Contracting-out rules introduced. Perceived as too complicated, thus no incentive (Lynes 1960: 55–6).
Social Security Act 1973		Protection of rights for early leavers of pension schemes increases costs.
Social Security Pension Act 1975	Substantially increased public pension level, incentives and regulation of voluntary occupational pensions strengthened.	Stronger incentives for employers to offer occupational schemes: state compensates employers for declining value of non-indexed occupational db pension payments; reduced national insurance contribution rates; increased state pension offers better foundation. Costs through complexity (Mesher 1976: 321); Guaranteed Minimum Pension (GMP) obligatory for contracted-out occupational benefits, not indexed on payment.
Social Security Act 1980	Public pension curbed through reindexing to prices only (Blake 2003: 14). Increased costs of occupational pensions.	Regulation curbs employers' freedom to select scheme members on basis of age. Early leavers can only transfer rights into contracted-out schemes (Blake 2003: 44).
Finance Act 1981; Health & Social Security Act 1984; Social Security Act 1985	Public pension level constant; occupational pension costs increase through regulation and higher benefit levels for early leavers.	Early leavers have right to transfer rights, and to use greater variety of schemes, their rights on level of GMP indexed to inflation, better information for scheme members. Regulation/costs increased. Employee mobility increased.
Social Security Act 1986	Cuts in public pension. Increased incentives for private-sector voluntarism through contracting-out rules; business costs increase through indexation of occupational pensions. Overall: state costs reduced, private-sector costs and incentives increased.	Contracting-out rules extended to money purchase and personal pension schemes. GMP indexed to inflation on payment for db schemes, increasing scheme costs; early leavers' full pension rights accrual indexed to inflation.
Social Security Act 1989	Role of public pension unchanged. Private-sector costs rise through equality laws.	Access of female employees to occupational schemes made easier.
Social Security Act 1990	Role of public pension unchanged. Private-sector costs rise through extension of early leaver protection and increased regulation.	Indexing of rule for early leavers of occupational schemes backdated to include all (Blake 2003: 146). Introduction of Ombudsman. Winding up of schemes harder. Tighter restrictions on investment; employee rights strengthened in case of employer insolvency.

Pensions Scheme Act 1993	Role of public pension unchanged. Private-sector costs rise through reduced contracting-out rebate.	Reduction of contracting-out rebate for occupational and personal pensions schemes.
Pension Act 1995	Level of public pension reduced. Private-sector costs rise through strongly increased degree of private-sector regulation.	Tightened regulation of pension scheme funding: strict actuarial rules, obligation to appoint professionals to administer schemes, stricter regulation of minimum pension levels; stricter equal rights rules for men and women, strengthening of trustee rights vis-à-vis employers. Pension Compensation Board introduced.
Welfare Reform and Pensions Act 1999	Public means-tested pension level increased for very low paid; private-sector cost rises slightly through regulation of personal pensions for low paid.	Employers must recommend stakeholder personal pension schemes; insurers offering schemes regulated regarding minimum charges, and paying-in mode and scheme funding.
Child Support, Pensions & Social Security Act 2000	Public pension level increased for low earners and carers with employment career. For higher earners low state pensions increase incentive to contract out. Private-sector costs stay constant.	No relevant changes.
State Pension Credit Act 2002	Public, mean-tested pensions for very low paid increased. Private-sector costs stay constant.	No relevant changes.
Pensions Act 2004	Role of public pension unchanged; private-sector costs reduced in some, increased in other areas.	Costs reduced through halving of indexation level for pension payments; costs increased through charge for Pension Protection Fund; more regulation regarding information policies and trustees.
Pensions Act 2007	Public pensions level and scope increased (reindexed to earnings from 2012 at earliest); retirement age to be raised to 68 (2024–46). Private-sector costs increase.	Tax incentives for money purchase schemes and personal pensions reduced. DC schemes and personal pensions can no longer contract out of state scheme.
Pensions Bill (2007–08)	Role of public pensions unchanged; private-sector costs increase.	Employers must enrol all employees in a pension scheme and pay contributions (min. 8% of earnings for dc, guaranteed level for db). Employees can opt out.

Source: OPSI (2010); for a comprehensive overview and analysis of British pensions legislation see Blake (2003)—only most relevant laws, tax legislation excluded.

and ended other restrictions for wives. Moreover, for the first time care times were recognized as equivalent to employment, provided the carer gave up employment and had a contribution record of at least twenty years (Groves 1983: 52; Land 1985: 53–62).

From 1975 state engagement became stronger in the private sector as well, without touching employer voluntarism. To make occupational schemes more attractive for employers a rebate on national insurance contributions for contracted-out employees and employers was established, which remains in place today (Ellis 1989: 48–9; Table 9.1). In return, regulation was tightened: employers offering contracted-out schemes had to include a widows' pension and pay a similar benefit to that received by members in the new state scheme. This Guaranteed Minimum Pension (GMP) increased employer costs, but they did not have to index annual pension payment to inflation, an obligation the state took on.

Between 1975 and 1979 coverage rates were at their highest overall level generally, and reached a peak for men. The decline in the private sector came to a halt, while coverage increased further in the public sector, whose significance for employment was at its highest between 1976 and 1982 (Figure 9.1).

Overall, the reforms of the 1970s would have meant the significant weakening of the liberal dimension and the transition into a statist system. More encompassing, generous public pensions could have lifted above the poverty line many workers and carers who were unprotected previously (cf. Bonoli 2003b: 400). In occupational pensions, the statist side was strengthened through the increase of public-sector coverage and increased regulation of occupational schemes. However, this system did not last long.

9.3.3 *1980–2007*

During the 1980s and beyond pensions were cut. The Conservative government reindexed benefits to prices, and reduced substantially the benefits accruable under SERPS (Pierson 1994: 53–73). Public benefits were cut in successive Conservative reforms (1980, 1986, 1995; for evolution of reforms see Table 9.1). The introduction of the means-tested Pension Credit (1999) by the subsequent Labour government and increased generosity of the second public tier for low income groups and carers (2000), did not lift public pensions above the level of social assistance. That half of employees not covered by occupational schemes therefore faced poverty risks.

In the occupational sector, meanwhile, the statist dimension became stronger for existing providers due to tighter regulation and increased pension coverage in the public sector (Figure 9.2). New incentives for business were limited; in 1986 contracting-out rules were extended to money

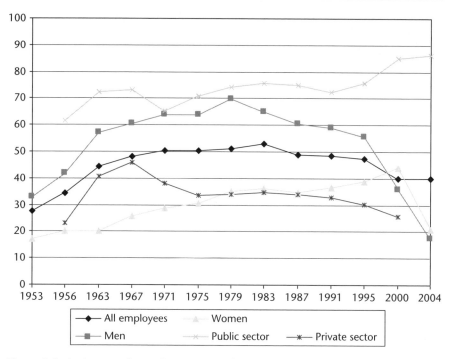

Figure 9.2: Active members of occupational pension schemes as % of employees in employment, UK

Note: figures for all employees for 1963 and 1967 contain armed forces. Coverage for 'all employees' constant between 2000 and 2004 because 5 million members in 2004 not identified by gender.

(*Source*: own calculations based on GAD 2006: 15, *Employment Gazette*, various issues 1955–2001; ONS: 2005).

purchase and personal pension schemes, and in 2004 the Labour government reduced employer costs through allowing pension benefits to rise more slowly. Apart from that, regulation increased costs: particularly during the 1990s, scheme providers had to pay for the indexing of contracted-out money purchase, personal (1986), and contracted-out defined benefit schemes (1995; Blake 2003); gender equality laws restricted their freedom to select scheme members (1989, 1995; Mazey 1998; Cichowski 2004). Employers, pension fund trustees, and insurers also had to observe stricter rules for the actuarial valuation of fund assets, liabilities, and their investment (1990, 1993, 1995). This included the introduction of a Pension Compensation Board (1995) and a Pension Protection Fund to provide compensation in case of insolvency (2004). Regarding coverage, since the mid-1990s pension scheme membership in the public sector increased to unprecedented levels, while private-sector coverage declined strongly, an illustration of the regime's hybrid nature (Figure 9.2). Private employers retreated from a regulatory regime whose costs they found excessive (Bridgen and Meyer 2005), while the Labour government's pro-health and education policies increased employment in the public sector. These trends led to a significant reconfiguration of the regime in 2007/8.

9.3.4 From 2008

The decline from the late 1990s meant that in 2008 for the first time since the 1950s less than one-third of all private-sector employees were covered by occupational pension schemes, while membership in the public sector increased further (Figure 9.2). The statist side of the pension regime drove both developments. In the public sector, high levels of coverage were not questioned and Labour's pro-welfare policies led to higher employment. In the private sector, the mass closure of defined benefit schemes to new members had been caused by a changed view of companies of the role pensions play for the retention of qualified workers, an ageing workforce, changed macro-economic conditions, including economic governance, and the herd dynamics generated by companies watching each other. In addition, costs imposed through state regulation also contributed to the reduced appeal of occupational pensions for business (for an overview, see Bridgen and Meyer 2005: 772–3). As shown above, the light intervention of 1959 which required employers who wanted to enjoy the benefits of contracting out to pay a minimum pension on the level of the state scheme became more and more complex in subsequent decades, and by the late 1990s, when economic conditions further deteriorated, state regulation was one reason why businesses closed schemes to new employees. At the same time, the protection regulation afforded existing scheme members meant that they remained unaffected by the cuts (Bridgen and Meyer 2009). Thus, one long-term effect of the public-sector corporatism which formed after the war, was, paradoxically, the protection of current scheme members, but also the drastic decline of private-sector coverage.

The Labour government responded to this in the customary way: by regulating the private sector even more tightly. In 2002 they instated a Pension Commission which was to consider fundamental reform of occupational and personal pensions, including an introduction of private-sector compulsion, while public benefits were to remain unchanged (Secretary of State for Work and Pensions 2002: 5). This initiative mobilized business and insurers, who resisted further costs and loss of autonomy, while the state pension remained below the poverty line, and who pushed for a significant rise of the state pension. The final report of the Pension Commission recommended a compromise between business and the state: that the state pension level be raised, but also that employer compulsion be introduced for the first time (Pensions Commission 2005). The government accepted these proposals. The Pensions Acts 2007 and 2008 reinforces the statist dimension in both public and private spheres. It strengthens the role of the state as benefit provider, by increasing further the scope and level of the public pension (OPSI 2007; see Chapter 10 in this volume for details). However, it also ends employer voluntarism. In the occupational sphere, from 2012 it will be obligatory for employers to enrol employees in schemes which have to meet minimum statutory criteria, and to which employers have to pay contributions (see Chapter 10); defined benefit schemes have to guarantee a minimum pension level. Employees are free to opt out of schemes (OPSI 2008: and Chapter 10).

9.4 The hybridity of British pension policy

In the second half of the twentieth century the British pension regime appeared consistent with the expectations of theorists of liberal market economies. The state pension was very low, occupational schemes were established voluntarily by employers, and tax incentives fuelled their expansion from the 1950s. Because of this voluntarism, during the 1970s and 1980s only about half of employees—those in the public sector and members of defined benefit schemes in the private sector—had access to occupational retirement benefits, leaving the other half dependent on the insufficient state pension. In the early 2000s coverage declined further, to 40 per cent, caused by the decision of business to close their schemes to new members.

Alongside this liberal dimension, however, has always been a statist one, and this ensured that the 2000s have seen less decline than theorists of liberal market economies might have expected (Hall and Soskice 2001: 57–8). Indeed, it led to the introduction of such unlikely measures as employer compulsion and a return to higher state pension levels. This statist side finds its first expression in nationalization after WWII, supported by the trade unions, which ensured that public-sector employment offered good retirement protection. It was reinforced by the strong growth of welfare employment, induced by the NHS as well as a comprehensive schooling system, offering higher levels of employment than in Germany (Meyer 1997). This growth continued when conditions in private-sector employment deteriorated. From the late 1950s an interventionist state set increasingly tight standards for occupational pensions, at expanding costs for employers, protecting the rights of scheme members, but also, unintentionally, supporting the flight of business from defined benefit schemes from the late 1990s. When business protested strongly against the unfettered continuation of this path from 2002, the Pension Commission brokered a compromise between capital and the state, leading to a reorientation for both, and ensuring that the hybridity of the regime will continue. Regarding the statist dimension, the level of public benefits is set to increase significantly due to the reforms of 2007 and 2008, and all employees will have automatic access to occupational schemes, while existing members of defined benefit schemes remain well protected. The liberal dimension is expressed by the low level of contributions employers have to pay into personal accounts, leading to rather low pension levels overall that those who would accrue rights for their whole careers under the new system can obtain (Chapter 10 in this volume).

Overall the account has shown the role public policy has played in shaping institutional occupational pension arrangements: in important ways policy makers did not take the backseat role expected of them from theorists of liberal market economies (Schmidt 2002: 160). Instead, they expanded and shaped the public sector, and they regulated the relationship between public and private, driven by motives that were more in the spirit of Beveridge than Adam Smith.

9.5 The rise and fall of a conservative pension regime: Germany

Between 1957 and the 1990s West German social insurance emphasized occupational differentiation and class stratification in retirement through income-related social insurance pension benefits with high replacement rates, fitting the model of a conservative welfare state (Esping-Andersen 1990). Companies supported this system and some employers added voluntarily occupational pensions, which were largely consistent with the logic of the conservative model. However, during the 1990s the model's support by German capital and labour weakened (Streeck 2008: 56–65; Palier and Thelen 2010). Business and public-sector employers pushed successfully for public pension retrenchment and cut occupational benefits too. The incentives for occupational benefits introduced since 2001 could not reverse this trend and future benefit levels are thus likely to decline sharply for most of the workforce. For this reason, from 2001 onwards the German pension regime can no longer be regarded as conservative; instead it is now a liberal-conservative hybrid (see also Chapter 10 in this volume).

9.6 Evolution: German public and occupational pensions[2]

9.6.1 *1945–56*

In the aftermath of the war the West-German public pension system, like the British, offered very low benefits, insufficient to protect recipients against poverty (Hentschel 1983: 26–7, 121, 63) and was therefore not conservative in the status-preserving sense. However, occupational benefits did not conform to the expectation that they should be skill-related either (Estévez-Abe et al. 2001): coverage in public and private sectors was much higher and more homogeneous than would be assumed on grounds of qualification (Table 9.2).

Immediately after 1945 social policy makers decided to continue the tradition of Bismarckian, earnings-related pensions (Hentschel 1983: 119–22, 36–42, 45–9). Occupational pensions financed from company revenue, either current or through book reserves, played an important role supplementing public social insurance benefits during this time. Most public- and private-sector workers were covered by them, and especially the large companies were aware of the vital role that their additional benefits played in adding to the low public pensions (Table 9.2; Bischoff 1965: 86; Weiß and Heubeck 1957: 13). Membership in occupational pension schemes was particularly widespread in the high-skill sectors: more than 95 per cent of all workers in large manufacturing businesses were covered, and because large companies invested more for workers' pensions than smaller ones, their benefits were much higher (Weiß 1955: 30–3; Spiegelhalter 1961: 68–74). However, coverage extended well beyond what would be expected purely on the basis of labour requirements, in part because book reserve capital was tax-free (Manow 2001b), but also because employers used occupational benefits to weaken trade union bargaining power in some regions (Trampusch 2004: 233–7). Such pensions were unregulated until 1974 (Hubrich and Tivig 2006: 51). In the public sector social insurance existed for all employed by the federal states and central government whose coverage was granted as part of collective bargaining arrangements; civil servants had a different, tax-financed scheme (Fieberg 2002: 230–1).

---

[2] No comprehensive data set traces the development of occupational pension coverage and levels (compare Infratest Sozialforschung 1990: 21; Schmähl 1997: 115); the IFO-Institute conducted first repeated and systematic surveys (1979, 1981, 1984, 1987), based on a limited sample of private-sector companies (e.g. Flecken 1990: 109). The first survey of occupational pensions for the population above 55 years was done in 1986, 1992, 1995, 1999, 2003, and 2007 (www.alterssicherung-in-deutschland.de/LITERATUR/index.html). This focused on pensioner income, and therefore reflects rights acquired during rules stretching back to the 1920s. The first representative overview of occupational coverage in public and private sectors over time was conducted in 2001 (TNS Infratest 2005a). Our account therefore reflects broad trends only (Table 9.2). See DRV (2009a) for details of the evolution of public pension legislation.

Table 9.2: German occupational pensions, 1951–99

Year	Coverage	Replacement rate of last wage upon retirement	Dominant type of provision
1951	ca 90% of manufacturing	up to 20%	book reserve, db in large manufacturing companies
1945–56	public sector; all employees covered by collective bargaining agreements of federal states and central government; civil servants covered separately	20–25%	db, financed through employer/employee contributions; based on public-sector wide collective bargaining contracts. From 1951 administered by 'Versorgungsanstalt des Bundes und der Länder'
1957	ca 90% of manufacturing, trade, and finance	up to 20%	book reserve, db, in large manufacturing companies
1973	ca 60.5% of all private-sector full-time employees (66% manufacturing, 48% retail/wholesale & banking/insurance, 41% transport & services); public administration, building: 100%		book reserve, db, in large companies and public administration
1975	ca 65% of all private-sector full-time workers; public admin, building: 100%	15—more than 20% in all companies, excl. services, for white- and blue-collar workers	book reserve, db, in large companies and public administration
1976	70% manufacturing; 53% retail/wholesale & banking/insurance; 46% transport & services	Replacement last monthly wage after 35 years— white-collar employees: 55% above 20% replacement; 27% between 15 and 20%. Blue-collar employees: 36% above 20% replacement, 35% between 15 and 20%.	book reserve, db, in large companies and public administration
1979	66% of manufacturing; 23% of retail and wholesale employees		
1981	70% of all manufacturing employees, incl. part-time workers and apprentices; 28% of retail and wholesale employees		book reserve, db, in large companies
1984	72% of all manufacturing, 26% of retail and wholesale employees		
1993	66% of all manufacturing employees and 34% retail and wholesale, West Germany		
1996	65% of all manufacturing employees and 31% retail and wholesale, West Germany		
1999	64% of all manufacturing employees and just below 30% in retail and wholesale, West Germany		book reserve, db dominant (83–90%) in manufacturing companies and in wholesale and retail (64–88%)

Sources: 1951: Weiß (1955: 30); 1945–56: public sector: Schneider (1983: 214–16); 1957: Spiegelhalter (1961: 70); 1973, 1976: Berié (1978: 202–3); 1973, 1975, 1981: van Maydell (1983:

Table 9.3: Germany—occupational benefit coverage of retirees (from 65) by sector

		Private-sector retirees		Public-sector retirees		Civil service retirees	
		Men	Women	Men	Women	Men	Women
1986		40	7	85	52		
1995	West	50	10	89	46	98	79
	East						
2003	West	46	9	88	56	98	76
	East	2	1	6	4	...	...
2007	West	44	10	80	55	99	84
	East	2	1	18	12	...	...

Note: The table refers to entitlements of pensioners; figures are different for coverage rates of employees.
Source: Infratest Sozialforschung (1990: 29–31, 55; 1995: 28–31); TNS Infratest (2005b: 65–8, 93; 2008b: 32, 34, 36)

Regarding benefit levels, before 1957 large private-sector employers aimed to replace 20 per cent of last wages for long-term employees and in the public sector replacement was between 20 and 25 per cent (Weiß and Heubeck 1957: 18; Table 9.2). However, because of the low public pension overall benefits for many retired German citizens remained below the social assistance level, despite the contribution of occupational pensions (Hentschel 1983: 26–7, 121, 63).

9.6.2 1957–2001

From 1957 until 2001 the social insurance pension system was status-preserving and generous, i.e. it turned into the conservative model for which it has become well known.

During the 1950s policy makers became aware that the existing system excluded from participation in the *Wirtschaftswunder*, the post-war rapid creation of wealth, large parts of pensioners who had helped create it, to leave them living in poverty (Hockerts 1980: 16, 422; Berner 2009: 104). After a long conflict with interest groups, and just in time for the federal election in 1957, the Christian Democratic government increased earnings-related entitlements considerably and ensured that pensions would rise in line with wages, with significant effect. From 1957 pensions rose like no other income so that the majority of public pensions paid were well above the social assistance level (Hockerts 1980: 320–425; Hentschel 1983: 165–6). From the mid-1970s a lifelong, full-time worker could expect a replacement rate of about 70 per cent of previous net earnings. In line with the system's conservative nature, there was no minimum pension and wives' dependency on husbands was supported through generous widows' pensions and an absence of care-related rights. However, status differentiation was weakened for higher earners: their contributions and benefits were capped, making them more reliant on a second pension pillar (Berner 2009: 117–19).

Over the subsequent decades the scope of the social insurance pension scheme was broadened, alleviating somewhat class and gender differences helped by favourable economic conditions (Clasen 2005: 104): the dependent status of wives and carers was reduced from the 1970s (Meyer 1998: 822; Veil 2003: 125) and low earners could accrue higher benefits (Hentschel 1983: 171–2; Schmidt 1998: 96).

However, retrenchment pressures started to mount in the late 1970s (Clasen 2005: 104–9) and during the 1990s the system's reserves fell below the required levels on repeated occasions (Anderson and Meyer 2006). The relationship between contributory revenue and pension benefit expenses became unhinged because the West German system was transferred to the new *Länder*. In addition, companies had responded to changing economic conditions by using early retirement on a large scale (Clasen 2005: 107–8; Streeck 2008: 58–61). Moreover, unemployment increased to unprecedented levels in post-war history.[3] In these circumstances policy makers raised social insurance contributions and increased significantly the scale of tax subsidies transferred to public pensions.[4] At the same time governments cut benefits too: early retirement without penalties was phased out, the retirement age for women increased, and the highest possible pension level declined (Meyer 1998: 822; DRV 2009a: 280–4). However, in comparison with the major change that was to come in 2001 and excepting the inclusion of the New *Länder*, the reforms of the 1990s appear only as gradual.

After the increase of social insurance pensions in 1957 occupational pension coverage declined and never returned to pre-1957 levels (Tables 9.2 and 9.3). Retrenchment was not necessarily in the interest of employers, who benefited from the tax-free capital in their book reserve schemes,[5] but businesses realized that the drastic increase in state pension levels would regularly lead to combined pension entitlements in excess of the last wage (BetrAV 1958: 118; Schneider 1983: 214).[6] Adjustment took place by excluding workers from benefits altogether; coverage in occupational pension schemes in manufacturing declined from 90 per cent in the 1950s to about 65 per cent twenty years later (Table 9.2). Benefit levels for those still covered remained

---

[3] West German unemployment rose from 5.5% (1981) to 9.3% (1985); reduced to 6.2% (1991; West), when unification boosted demand. Rates increased to a peak of 13% (incl. East) in 2005 (Bundesagentur für Arbeit 2010a).

[4] Between 1992 and 1999 statutory pension contributions rose from 17.7 to 20.3%; the state subsidy increased by 127% between 1990 and 1999, to 33.3 billion, its strongest increase since 1957 (DRV 2009a: 282–3, 2009c: 239, 2009b: 221).

[5] Between 1953 and 1956 book reserves comprised around 11% of company finance in listed companies (BetrAV 1957: 113–15), but up to two-thirds of company capital in the large companies of the coal and steel industry. After 1957, some of these book reserve schemes were 'overflowing' (BetrAV 1958: 118, also: BetrAV 1967: 155).

[6] This was true for 6.5% of white-collar workers (Heubeck 1958: 109).

Table 9.4: The role of occupational pensions for overall benefits. West Germany, average gross occupational benefits as % of gross pension income by sector, retirees from 65

	Men private sector	Men public sector	Women private sector	Women public sector
1986	25	27	25	44
1992	23	28	29	43
1995	22	26	28	41
1999	27	24	26	39
2003	28	28	27	39
2007	29	26	29	34

Source: Own calculations based on TNS Infratest (2008b: 94, 98, 100).

high (Table 9.4).[7] Despite new legislation introducing more expensive vesting and indexing rules in 1974 there was a brief increase in coverage in the late 1970s (Heubeck 1974; Maydell 1983: 265–73). However, the deteriorating economic climate led to renewed decline. At the beginning of the 1980s unemployment soared (Bundesagentur für Arbeit 2010a), employers reduced benefits and closed schemes to new members.[8] In 1996 occupational pension coverage of manufacturing workers was back to 65 per cent (Ruppert 1997, 2000a: 27–8, 2000b: 686).

Despite this decline, some contrasting developments are noteworthy. First, since 1957 in construction (1957), baking (1970), agriculture (1973), the public sector (1967, see below), and telecommunication (1996) occupational pension schemes existed into which all employees working in the industry were enrolled automatically on the basis of collective bargaining contracts (Bispinck 2001: I-III). Second, during the 1970s, more and more small and medium companies took out life insurance for one or a group of employees, financed either by the employee, some through salary sacrifice (Forsbach 1982: 158), or the employer, or both (Berié 1978; Kessel 1983; Stegmann 1986). Slowing in the 1980s, this trend picked up again thereafter (Kessel 1987; Berner 2006: 10). Third, the Christian Democratic government had tried to stop the decline in occupational pension coverage in 1999, by granting employees who set aside parts of their salary for a retirement

[7] Companies providing occupational schemes agreed that the new system should replace 75% of last wages, customary in the civil service (e.g. Weiß and Heubeck 1957: 18; Heubeck 1958: 105, 15). Therefore, the contribution of occupational schemes to overall pensioner income never dropped below 22% for retirees after1986, and was higher for most others (Table 9.4).

[8] Between 1981 and 1984 13% of all manufacturing, and 8% of retail and wholesale companies cut occupational benefits, affecting 5 and 4% of all workers, respectively (Flecken 1990: 108; Ruppert 1985: 13–14). Coverage numbers only remained stable because between the mid-1980s and mid-1990s overall industrial employment declined, reducing the pool of workers that was the basis for the calculation of coverage. After 1993, 11% of all private-sector companies with occupational schemes reduced benefits, most commonly (72%) by closing schemes to new members (Ruppert 1997: 11; 1985: 13).

pension a reduction in social insurance contributions (Niemeyer 1997). The trade unions used this law and from the late 1990s salary sacrifice schemes became part of collective bargaining agreements in several sectors, such as the chemical industry, wholesale, insurance and banking, iron and steel. Employers were free to offer such schemes and contributions were typically converted from existing benefits such as holiday payments or other savings schemes (Bispinck 2001: III-VIII). Salary sacrifice also became central for the expansion of occupational provision after 2001 (see below and Chapter 10 in this volume).

For public-sector workers, i.e. for all blue- and white-collar public employees and for church-related organizations, the broad coverage of occupational schemes and generous benefits continued after 1957, even though here, too, many pensions were now above replacement level. To address this issue, in 1967, the social partners agreed on a reform which linked public-sector occupational benefits to the state pension. Both benefits taken together would give public-sector employees the same high replacement rate that civil servants were entitled to, at least 75 per cent of last wages after thirty-five years (Fieberg 2002: 231). The link made the level of public sector occupational pensions dynamic and dependent on changes in that of statutory pensions (Schneider 1983: 214–21; Puskás 2002a: 22–3).

Like their British equivalent, public-sector pensions kept their high coverage rates during the 1990s (Table 9.3) and scope increased with their introduction in the New *Länder* in 1997 (Puskás 2002a: 23). However, because they were linked to a statutory social insurance scheme that underwent many changes during the 1990s, as we have shown above, they had also become more expensive and complex to run. These mounting costs prepared the ground for the landmark reform of 2001, which we will summarize below (Wein 2002: 525).

In sum, there is strong evidence that from 1957 onwards an increasingly dominant social insurance pension system crowded out occupational pensions, provided by employers who would otherwise have been interested in keeping the latter as finance vehicles. Less favourable economic conditions after 1980 reduced company interests in occupational welfare further. Nevertheless, occupational pension benefits remained significant. The 1957 reform ushered in an era in which the new function of occupational pensions was to top up social insurance pensions and thus protect employees' standard of living rather than ensuring subsistence (Bischoff 1965: 86). This remained true during the 1980s and 1990s and it was especially so for higher wage earners in the private sector whom businesses helped to achieve the high social wage so essential for the German political economy (Krupp 1983: 127–30; Infratest Sozialforschung 1990: 14, 17, 79; 1992: 47).

9.6.3 *2000–8*

In 1998, the government of Social Democrats and Greens faced strong pressure to address the financial problems that had plagued the social insurance pension system since the early 1990s. Despite a convoluted political process and the incremental nature of change (Clasen 2005: 117–18) successive reforms after 2001 shifted the traditional German pension paradigm (Anderson and Meyer 2003; Hinrichs 2003: 21–2; Schmähl 2004, 2007; Berner 2009: 134). As a whole these reforms aimed to create a multi-pillar pension system, to be achieved through substantial cuts in the public social insurance pillar; most importantly, the benefit level would drop from 70 per cent but not below 64 per cent of previous net wages (Altersvermögensgesetz 2000). Retrenchment was supposed to keep contributions to the public pension insurance fund below 20 per cent of wages until 2020 and at 22 per cent by 2030 (DRV 2009a: 239, 93). However, contribution levels were mainly contained for employers. In order to preserve previous levels of security, employees are expected to save substantially more after the reform, by making additional voluntary contributions (see Chapter 10, this volume; Schmähl 2002: 3; Trampusch 2005).

To enable such voluntary savings, the government provided incentives for employees to join subsidized and licensed occupational and private-funded pension schemes. Since 2002 employees have been able to require their employer to transfer up to 4 per cent of their wage into a licensed occupational or personal pension scheme of their choice (BetrAV 2007: 561).[9] However, where an individual's employment is covered by a collective agreement, this can stipulate how salary sacrifice must be used (Altersvermögensgesetz 2000; BetrAVG 2005). Licensed schemes receive state support. The most broadly used salary sacrifice payments from *gross* wages to occupational schemes receive tax and social insurance rebates (*Eichel-Rente*). The other type of savings are salary sacrifice from employees' *net* wages into fully funded pension schemes (*Riester Rente*) (Berner 2009: 136–46). These receive flat-rate allowances or tax rebates, whichever is more favourable, and contributions for children (AltEinkG 2004). Riester pensions are rarely used as occupational schemes but predominantly as personal savings vehicles (TNS Infratest 2008a: 69, 81; see Chapter 11 in this volume).

Public-sector pensions for blue- and white-collar employees were also changed substantially (Furtmayr and Wagner 2007). Triggered by rising costs (Seiter 2002: 511), a new collective bargaining contract came into effect in 2002 which broke the link between occupational benefits and the statutory

---

[9] Up to an upper earnings limit of 2520 Euro (2006), for occupational schemes a lump sum (1800 Euro, 2007) was added (Bundesministerium für Arbeit und Soziales 2007).

pension we described above and no longer aims to achieve an overall replacement level (Puskás 2001: 309; Hügelschäffer 2002: 237–8). Instead, pensions are now payable in relation to annual individual and overall collective contributions. It is assumed that the reforms have cut occupational benefits by about 20 per cent (Puskás 2002b: 516). As compensation, the trade unions ensured that public-sector workers wanting to save for additional pensions would be entitled to the tax and social insurance rebate enjoyed by private-sector workers.

The turn towards multi-pillarism reversed the decline in occupational coverage. The option to embed salary sacrifice schemes for pensions in collective agreements gave social partners a new sphere of influence and most collective agreements have used it; in 2004 about 81 per cent of all workers covered by agreements had access to such schemes, and thus the freedom to use them (Bundesministerium für Wirtschaft und Arbeit 2004: 57). However, the new legislation did not change greatly the reluctance of business, apparent since the 1980s, to be more involved in company pensions. Indeed, the wide adoption of pension savings in collective agreements was only possible because most employers only committed themselves to cost-neutral solutions, i.e. employees can use for salary sacrifice existing fringe benefits such as holiday pay and an existing savings scheme (*vermögenswirksame Leistung*) and most additional employer contributions did not exceed the amount they saved through the tax and social insurance rebate (Ruppert 2000a: 32; Bundesministerium für Wirtschaft und Arbeit 2003: 636). The possible contributions specified in these agreements were thus very low,[10] and as we show in Chapter 10 of this volume, they are projected to be a long way away from compensating for the retrenchment in public pensions.

In sum, the new incentives supported growth on a low level, particularly where engagement had been less pronounced previously: in East Germany and in smaller companies. Between December 2001 and 2007 the number of private-sector employees who were members in occupational schemes rose from 38 per cent to 52 per cent (TNS Infratest 2008a: 9, 21–2).[11] In line with our argument above, there is strong evidence for a trade-off between contribution levels and pace of growth: average monthly contribution levels amounted to 106 Euro only for the fastest growing type of coverage: the number of legally independent funds (Pensionskassen) more than doubled between 2001 and 2007 to one-third of all private-sector schemes. The traditional book reserve schemes also grew considerably, by 18 per cent; some of

[10] E.g., in 2004 the collective bargaining arrangement in the retail sector in Rheinland-Pfalz stipulated that employers and employees together could pay Euro 300 annually into the pension scheme (Kerschbaumer 2004: 101).

[11] There are differences in coverage levels provided by IFO for the late 1990s and Infratest for 2001 because Infratest included very small businesses as well, and had a larger sample.

this increase is explained by the new vesting legislation (TNS Infratest 2008a: 76, 78, 82–3). The share of employer-only financed schemes declined from 54 per cent to 38 per cent of all between 2001 and 2007, while those financed by employees and employers increased from 27 per cent to 42 per cent; one-third of all are funded by employees only (TNS Infratest 2008a: 50). Thus, funded, individualized schemes, offering low benefits, grew fastest.

In the public sector, coverage rates in the compulsory part of the system declined slightly, but remained very high. The voluntary additional insurance was only taken up by around 6 per cent of employees in 2007 (Thiel 2005: 346; TNS Infratest 2008a: 97).

9.7 The end of status protection

During the period after 1957 and before 2001 the German pension regime fitted well the description of a conservative type. Mandatory social insurance pensions protected full-time workers, and confirmed status differentials, crowding out to some extent occupational pensions that had existed before 1957 (Bonoli 2003b). However, large businesses continued to have a strong interest in occupational pension provision. Supported by a favourable tax regime and a public pension cap for higher earners they carried on providing book reserve schemes, particularly for qualified employees. In smaller companies, individualized personal insurance provision expanded. In the public sector, a defined benefit scheme with levels linked to social insurance pensions also benefited higher earners most. Thus, even though occupational schemes did not play the significant role for protection as in the UK, they were important for status preservation.

From the 1980s onwards business interest in occupational pensions declined and public policy makers were under pressure to retrench the public social insurance pension system. Substantial changes introduced from 2001 onwards lowered the level of statutory pensions and reversed the decline in occupational schemes, thus ending the conservative regime. However, the non-state sector has not yet compensated for public cuts. As shown, in 2007 about half of all private sector employees were without compensation for the losses in public benefits. Moreover, the majority of private scheme members are paying low contributions and most employers contribute little. These changes constitute some evidence that German pension policy no longer conforms with the conservative regime type: retrenchment seems to be significant enough to threaten the status even of the core workforce (see Chapter 10 in this volume).

9.8 Conclusion. Neither convergence nor divergence: reforms in two exhausted regimes

One of the central questions of this book is how two types of political economy have developed in relation to each other since the 1990s; above we have explored this question in relation to pension policies.

First, both systems had reached political limits. Around the turn of the millennium British and German policy makers had arrived at the conclusion that their particular regime needed fundamental change. In Britain, the dramatic retrenchment in the occupational sector convinced reluctant policy makers to *increase* the role of the state and introduce quasi-compulsory occupational contributions in order to address growing poverty risks. In Germany policy makers' main aim was to *reduce* compulsory pension insurance contributions, which came to be regarded as stifling economic growth and employment. As a result, both countries embarked on new courses, each breaking with main principles of their traditional regimes. In Britain, the public pension is set to increase incrementally to higher levels while employer voluntarism has ended. In Germany, the aim of status preservation through generous earnings-related social insurance pensions has been abandoned, while the protection against poverty will now depend much more on voluntary savings. In terms of projected outcomes (see Chapter 10 in this volume), Britain is moving towards higher levels of social inclusion at the bottom end of the income scale and retrenchment for higher earners, and thus has chosen a more social democratic direction. Germany is facing increased poverty risks for many more future retirees; it has moved in the direction of a liberal regime.

Thus, each system reached perceived limits, and was therefore moved into new territory; the British turn is shaped by the failure of long-standing attempts to increase voluntary savings, and to avoid the risk that poverty and dependency on means-tested benefits spreads further, affecting the middle classes as well. The German turn is the outcome of failed attempts during the 1990s to control the costs of the German social insurance pension scheme. The direction of each system differs from the expectations of the Varieties of Capitalism framework (Hall and Soskice 2001: 57–8). The liberal regime has not become more deregulated in the face of globalization and deindustrialization pressures. In fact, it has always been more active than assumed by this framework, and in the 2000s it increased minimum public and private thresholds to protect workers against poverty. Since the 1990s the German drift towards a liberal regime has been possible because employers and the state proved less sympathetic towards maintaining high levels of benefits than would be expected in a conservative regime type.

While national institutions and legacies help to explain the different direction of change, the analysis also shows that business was no longer prepared to pay the increasing contributions necessary to maintain the systems customary during the 1970s, 1980s, and 1990s. British governments have overhauled their regime because private-sector-defined benefit schemes had closed in large numbers, and contributions to new schemes were significantly lower. This trend increased the extent of undersaving and of social risk. In Germany, business pressure to reduce high social insurance contribution had mounted during the 1990s. The government's ultimate motive in 2000 was to contain their level in the interests of employers. Similar circumstances are evident across Europe. Despite the ideological dominance of multi-pillarism business interest in occupational pension benefits is more limited than necessary to compensate for state retrenchment; in countries like Italy and Poland, where occupational schemes had not existed until the early 2000s, they did not expand substantially thereafter, despite favourable reforms (Benio and Ratajczak-Tuchołka 2007; Raitano 2007); in the Netherlands and Switzerland, countries with mature occupational benefits, these have been cut since the mid-1990s (Bannink and de Vroom 2007; Bertozzi and Bonoli 2007; Bridgen and Meyer 2009). This chapter did not aim to explore the general reasons for such decline in employer interest, but the analysis suggests that occupational provision in Germany will not enjoy substantial voluntary support from business in the medium term. Regarding Britain, the policy change strengthens benefit guarantees, which appears to be appropriate considering voluntarism is even less feasible than it was. However, in the aftermath of a financial crisis and facing high budget deficits, it is uncertain to what extent the next government will allow for the new legislation to mature.

10

The impact of the new public and private pension settlements in Britain and Germany on citizens' income in old age

Paul Bridgen and Traute Meyer

10.1 Introduction

In this chapter we use policy simulation to illustrate the scale and nature of the institutional changes made to the German and British pension systems by reforms undertaken in the first decade of the new century—in 2001 and 2004 in Germany and in 2007 and 2008 in Britain. We compare the projected outcomes of the new systems for a range of hypothetical biographies in both countries with those of the systems they replaced and show that the impact of the reforms is consistent neither with the predictions of the globalization thesis (Przeworski and Wallerstein 1988) nor regime theory (eg Esping Andersen 1990; Hall and Soskice 2001). Forecasts associated with the former approach suggest that national pension systems will engage in a 'race to the bottom' in the face of severe exogenous and endogenous pressures (e.g. population ageing, financial globalization etc.), but in fact recent reforms reveal strong national variations. However, this variation is not consistent with regime theory expectations (see also Bridgen and Meyer 2009). If it had been, the British system would have become more liberal on the basis of a generally uniform and extensive retrenchment, while in Germany any retrenchment would be expected to be less uniform, with protection maintained for the privileged core workforce, necessary for the German conservative, coordinated model (Hall and Soskice 2001: 57–8). We argue instead that the British reform will push pension institutions in a markedly social democratic direction, while the changes in Germany will move its system strongly in a liberal direction such that only some small elements of the traditional German model survive.

Given the long-term nature of pension policy, the impact of these institutional developments on the pension received by individuals will only become evident gradually (Hinrichs and Kangas 2003). In the short term there might even be some convergence of outcomes as German workers begin to experience more of their working life under the new less generous state system, while in Britain state provision becomes more generous and occupational provision more uniform. However, our results suggest that if we focus purely on current public/private pension institutions, the German system is now more consistent with an ideal typical liberal regime (Esping-Andersen 1990) than Britain's.

The chapter will be organized in the following way. After a brief summary of our methods, we first compare the performance of the pre-reform and post-reform British systems. We then do the same for the German case, before comparing the performance of post-reform systems in the two countries.

10.2 Methods

To illustrate and compare the impact of recent reforms in Britain's (2007/8) and Germany's (2001 and 2004) pension systems we simulate the pensions on retirement of a range of constructed biographies under the pre- and post-reform systems (see Table 10.17) in both countries. This methodology allows an assessment of the future impact of today's pension policies and thus provides a way of comparing existing pension institutions. At the national level, it isolates the pension system at a particular point in time, providing outcome data on *current* pension system performance which, unlike current pensioner poverty rates, for example, is untainted by the effects of earlier pension policies. It also makes more transparent the long-term impact of reforms whose effects in the short term might appear negligible (Hinrichs and Kangas 2003). In comparative work it illustrates directly the interaction between system features and a person's employment history, making it possible for researchers to bridge the differences in national socioeconomic backgrounds (Johnson and Rake 1998). However, in interpreting the data produced by policy simulation, it is important to be aware that the outcomes it signals are illustrative rather than representative, given the practical impossibility of undertaking simulations for a representative sample; and that in many cases these outcomes can only possibly be fully experienced by individuals entering the workforce today.

Policy simulation has sometimes been criticized for its focus on too narrow a range of work histories (Meyer et al. 2007; PPI 2006), particularly its emphasis on standard 'male' biographies with a full working life (OECD 2005; Social

Table 10.1: Working life details of the illustrative biographies used in pension simulations

	Working time wage as % of gender average[a]	Age when working starts	Age at retirement	Ages when out of workforce
Women	50	18	65	24–5, 27–8
	100	20	65	28–9, 31–2
	150	24	65	32–3
Men	50	18	65	None
	100	20	65	None
	150	24	65	None

Notes: [a] During periods of part-time work wages are pro-rata.

Protection Committee 2006). We seek to avoid this pitfall while still providing a broad illustration of projected outcomes in each country, so have chosen six relatively simple biographies with average work-time incomes between 50 per cent and 150 per cent of average gross wages. Three of these biographies are female and thus experience longer periods of care-related employment gaps and part-time work, in line with current social trends (see Table 10.1).

For each of these biographies we calculate the future public pension entitlements in both countries both before and after recent reforms under various assumptions, as set out in Table 10.17. We also assess the projected level of occupational provision on the basis of a range of scenarios for each biography. For both countries we collected information on a wide range of pension schemes from manufacturing, finance, retail, and the public sector, details of which can be found in Tables 10.18 and 10.19. Once calculated in this way the pension entitlements of all biographies in their various employments have been examined in relation to a social exclusion threshold set at 40 per cent of average gross full-time wages (see Table 10.17). On this basis, median pensions have been calculated both for all variants of each biography and by sector. These medians are used to compare the performance of the pre-reform and post-reform pension systems in the two countries and to compare cross-nationally the performance of the new systems.

10.3 The performance of the pre-reform system in Britain

In Chapter 9 of this volume we argued that the British pension system in 2005 should be understood institutionally as a hybrid between a liberal and/or more statist type, in which a small basic state pension (BSP) was supplemented by a medium-sized public earnings-related scheme and a large regulated occupational pension sector which provided particularly good coverage for public-sector employees. In this section we show that these features are clearly evident in the projected outcomes of the pre-reform system for our six biographies and their variants. An important consequence of this hybrid system in terms of outcome, we argue, was that while protection for lower-paid individuals could be quite precarious, some citizens in this group were protected quite well because they had access to the large and regulated occupational sector. However, the determinants of protection in these cases were largely arbitrary, a product of chance (Meyer and Bridgen 2008).

Starting with the state system as it operated before the reforms of 2007 and 2008, the influence of the liberal strand of British pension policy development is strongly evident: public pension provision on its own in 2005 was both very low and increasingly flat-rate, making means-testing more important. This situation was set to be maintained over the longer term, as can be seen by the projected outcomes for those of our biographies entirely reliant on public pensions (see Table 10.2). Despite the fact that most of this group is fully covered for state pensions while in work, all would still secure benefits significantly below the social exclusion threshold. However, notwithstanding the essentially liberal nature of the public system, the statist strand is also evident in these simulations, particularly in the form of the State Second Pension (S2P), the successor of SERPs, which had been introduced in 1975 with the aim of enabling more workers to gain access to additional provision above the BSP level (see Chapter 9). The introduction of S2P from 2000 made this additional provision much more redistributive towards the lower-paid biographies (Agulnik 1999; Bridgen and Meyer 2007a). As Table 10.2 shows, S2P provides a significant supplement for all biographies, although its impact is insufficient to lift state provision close to the social exclusion line for any of them.

Reforms to entitlement conditions over the past two decades are also the product of the statist strand of British policy development. The simulations show that the introduction of Home Responsibilities Protection (HRP) in 1975

Table 10.2: Projected gross outcomes on retirement of pre-reform[a] UK pension system for biographies without voluntary occupational provision, as % of social exclusion line

	State		Non-state	Overall
	BSP	S2P		
Woman, 50%	16	22	0	38
Woman, 100%	16	27	0	43
Woman, 150%	16	41	0	57
Man, 50%	16	26	0	42
Man, 100%	16	34	0	50
Man, 150%	16	43	0	60

Notes: [a] Rules and stipulations as operating immediately prior to 2007 Pension Act.

Source: Own calculations, based on biographies used in the simulations see Tables 10.17–10.19.

and other protective mechanisms as part of the social democratic phase in Britain's pension policy significantly improved the outlook for women. Thus, while the pensions of all of our female biographies are lower than those of the males on the same working time wage, this is not due to periods of caring, which were fully covered, but the fact that they work part-time for longer. Over time, and in combination with increased labour market attachment among women, the protective mechanisms in place by 2005 were projected to increase the number of women fully entitled to the BSP and the S2P on retirement to 50 per cent by 2010 (DWP 2006: 107). However, entitlement conditions were still drawn quite tightly. Thus, women undertaking care for less than thirty-six hours were not entitled to HRP and protection could only be claimed on a yearly basis, meaning that women were often not protected for years during which they mixed care and work (Hollis 2006). The impact on the pensions of individuals who fell between these still quite considerable gaps could be stark (see Bridgen and Meyer 2007a: 54–7), a situation which those who had retired with state pension records based on pre-HRP arrangements also faced (see also PPI 2006).

Thus, overall, while the state system continued up to 2005 to show the influence of some the social democratic reformism of the 1970s, its projected outcomes remained largely consistent with those which would be expected in a liberal system. Perhaps paradoxically it is only with the inclusion of outcomes from occupational provision that the full extent of the British pension systems' hybridity is evident. Here the hand of the state is also evident. First, the state has provided public-sector workers with quite generous, often final salary schemes, to which they are all automatically enrolled on employment. Second, political regulation of the occupational sector has forced companies which provide a pension to extend availability to all workers, regardless of their age and working time (Blake 2003). As a result, employee coverage by the end of the twentieth century in the public sector was near-universal, while in finance it was 80 per cent and in manufacturing it was 58 per cent (Pensions Commission 2004: figure 3.7). Overall by this date just under 30 per cent of the private-sector workforce were covered (Pensions Commission 2004: figures 3.26 and 3.29). Until recently many of these workers had defined benefit pensions, the impact of which on their retirement income was substantial. Table 10.3 compares the pre-reform projected pension levels of our biographies on the basis of (i) access to state provision only; (ii) access to state provision and also a defined contribution pension; and (iii) access to state provision and also a defined benefit pension.[1] As can be seen, access to state and defined benefit provision during all their working life raises pension levels

---

[1] The level of defined benefit and defined contribution occupational provision for each biography is the median of a selection of schemes available in various employment sectors.

Table 10.3: Comparison of projected gross median outcomes on retirement of pre-reform[a] UK pension system for biographies with and without voluntary occupational provision[b], as % of social exclusion line

	State	State/DC	Difference	State/DB	Difference
Woman, 50%	38	59	21	60	22
Woman, 100%	43	78	35	79	36
Woman, 150%	57	119	62	248	191
Man, 50%	42	83	41	133	91
Man, 100%	50	124	74	220	170
Man, 150%	60	151	91	288	228

Notes: [a] Rules and stipulations as operating immediately prior to 2007 Pension Act; [b] Median state/occupational outcomes are based on schemes detailed in Table 10.18.
Source: Own calculations, based on biographies used in the simulations see Tables 10.17–10.19.

for all biographies by a significant amount and lifts four out of six of them above the social exclusion line. The impact of access to defined contribution provision is not quite so dramatic but it nevertheless lifts three out of six above this threshold.

As Figures 10.1 and 10.2 show, the relative availability of defined benefit and defined contribution pensions has varied by sector of employment. These figures detail the median pension for each of the biographies by sector on the basis of a selection of schemes from each sector. In the public sector, defined benefit pensions are predominant, which means that covered workers in this sector have benefited from some of the most generous occupational provision. In manufacturing, defined benefit pensions have also been the norm among covered workers, although over the past fifteen years they have been in steady decline, especially for new workers. In the retail and financial sector, in contrast, defined contribution schemes with quite low levels of employer contribution have been the norm, meaning that median projected outcomes in these sectors are significantly lower than in the other two sectors. Because defined benefit pensions are particularly advantageous to higher-paid workers it is among this group that the variation in pensions is greatest.

In summary, the overall effect of the combination of liberalism and statism in British pension development up to the middle of the noughties has been the existence of quite substantial, and often arbitrary, variations in projected pensions between individuals (see also Meyer and Bridgen 2008). Some of this variation—between higher and lower earners—would be expected in a liberal system because of the emphasis in such regimes on low public provision and a large role for the market. Variation on the basis of gender (Ginn 2003; Ginn and Arber 1993, 1999), which is evident when the highest and lowest pensions in the two graphs are compared, is a consequence of the gendered nature of the labour market (Bridgen and Meyer 2007b: 20). However, public-sector pensions and state intervention in the private sector have made this variation

185

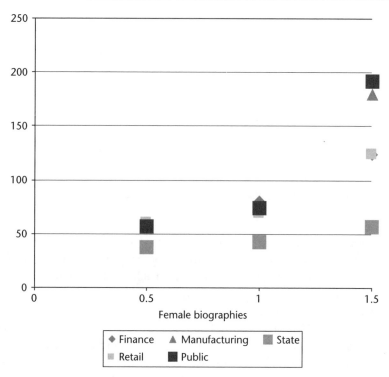

Figure 10.1: Projected gross median outcomes on retirement for pre-reform[a] UK pension system for female biographies by sector of employment,[b] as % of social inclusion line

Notes: [a] Rules and stipulations as operating immediately prior to 2007 Pension Act; [b] Sector medians are based on occupational schemes detailed in Table 10.18.
(*Source*: Own calculations).

more complex: biographies with identical working-life biographies are projected to end up with very different pensions, depending on their sector or company of employment. Moreover, while women are generally disadvantaged, particularly in the occupational sphere, it is they who have benefited most from the almost universal coverage of occupational provision in the public sector, given their disproportionate employment in this sector.

Under the pre-reformed system, these projected variations were set to fall in coming years, as the number of people benefiting from the more generous forms of occupational provision diminished with the retrenchment of defined benefit occupational provision. However, as we will see in the next section, the improvements of the state system and quasi-compulsory extension of the non-state sphere has raised the prospect that they will fall to a significantly greater extent.

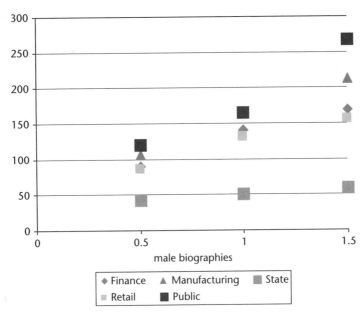

Figure 10.2: Projected gross median outcomes on retirement of pre-reform[a] UK pension system for male biographies by sector of employment,[b] as % of social exclusion line

Notes: [a] Rules and stipulations as operating immediately prior to 2007 Pension Act; [b] Sector medians are based on occupational schemes detailed in Table 10.18.

(*Source:* Own calculations).

10.4 Reform of the British system: the 2007 and 2008 Pension Acts

The 2007 Pensions Act commits the government to reindexing the basic state pension to earnings from 2012 at the earliest,[2] but no later than 2015. In turn, the pension age will be raised to 68, to be phased in between 2024 and 2046. The Act broadens the scope for the BSP and the S2P, by reducing qualifying years to 30 for the former (from 44 for men and 39 for women) and granting more generous credit arrangements to carers and very low earners. This change applied to all pensioners retiring after April 2010 and means according to the DWP that 70 per cent of women will receive the full basic state pension in that year, as opposed to the expected 50 per cent who would have been entitled before the reform (DWP 2006).[3] However, the gap between men and women's state pension is nevertheless likely to be maintained for some time to

---

[2] The Conservative/Liberal Democrat government elected in May 2010 has indicated that it will implement this change from April 2011 (see Conservative Party 2010b).

[3] These figures are disputed by the Fawcett Society (2006), an independent lobby group for women's interests, but most commentators accept that the changes will significantly improve the situation for women.

come not least because entitlement to the state second pension remains more restrictive than that of the basic state pension (PPI 2006; see also Hollis 2006).

In the realm of private pensions, the 2008 Pension Act makes it obligatory for employers to enrol employees in a pension scheme of their choice, which has to meet minimum statutory criteria. Employer contributions have to amount to at least 3 per cent of employee earnings, but the overall amount contributed must not be lower than 8 per cent of earnings. The state contributes 1 per cent. Employer compulsion will become effective in 2012, with a transitional phase of three years. Where no alternative scheme is chosen, contributions will automatically be paid to a new independent pension trust—the National Employment Savings Trust (NEST). Employees are free to opt out of schemes.

10.5 Performance of the British system after the 2007 and 2008 Pensions Acts

In the previous chapter we argued that these latest reforms mark a significant step in a more social democratic direction for British pension policy because they remove employer voluntarism and strengthen the public pension (see also Bridgen 2010). Below we show that for individuals like our biographies that started work in 2007 the improvements in the state system and the introduction of quasi-compulsion in the occupational sector offer the prospect of significantly higher pensions on retirement. However, change will be gradual: for pensioners and many older workers the change in their pensions over the next few years will only be small,[4] although women retiring after April 2010 will benefit immediately from the relaxation of entitlement conditions based on paid work.

It is in the longer term that greater change is evident. The greatest potential improvements are for those individuals who are currently without occupational provision, as is illustrated in Tables 10.4 and 10.5. These show the pre-reform and post-reform outcomes for the group of biographies reliant entirely on state provision under the old system but with the opportunity of access to NEST pensions under the new one. On the assumption (see Table 10.17) that these biographies remain opted in to NEST pensions at the minimum level of contribution (i.e. 8 per cent of banded earnings) and that real rates of return of 3.9 per cent (after charges) are secured, pensions rise for this group by between 32 and 80 percentage points in relation to the social exclusion line for the female biographies, and between 48 and 85 percentage points for the men.

[4] Indeed, changes to means-tested benefits mean that some poorer pensioners will actually be worse off after the reforms than before them (PPI 2006).

Table 10.4: Projected gross outcomes for female biographies without voluntary occupational provision under the pre-reform[a] and post-reform[b] UK pension system, as % of social exclusion line

Biography	Pre-reform			Post-reform				
	BSP	S2P	Total	BSP	S2P	Personal accounts	Total	Difference in total pension
0.5	16	22	38	34	28	8	70	32
1	16	27	43	34	31	29	94	51
1.5	16	41	57	34	31	72	137	80

Notes: [a] Rules and stipulations as operating immediately prior to 2007 Pension Act; [b] Rules and stipulations as operating after full implementation of 2007 and 2008 Pension Acts. See Table 10.17.

Sources: Own calculations, based on biographies used in the simulations detailed in the text.

These increases are a product of both the changes in the state system and the impact of NEST pensions, although the changes to the state system are significantly more generous for the lower-paid individuals than the higher-paid ones. Overall, they are sufficient to pull three biographies, the best-paid woman and the two best-paid men, well above the social inclusion line, with the women on average wages only 6 percentage points short.

Improvements in pensions are also evident for those biographies who had occupational provision before the reforms (Tables 10.6 and 10.7). These biographies also benefit from the improvements in state provision. This is especially the case for those biographies which had contracted-out defined contribution occupational provision under the old system. This cannot occur under the new arrangements, so all of these individuals now receive S2P. This new access together with the re-establishment of the earnings link for the basic state pension boosts their pensions in relation to the social

Table 10.5: Projected gross outcomes for male biographies without voluntary occupational provision under the pre-reform[a] and post-reform[b] UK pension system, as % of social exclusion line

Biography	Pre-reform			Post-reform				
	BSP	S2P	Total	BSP	S2P	Personal accounts	Total	Difference in total pension
0.5	16	26	42	34	29	27	90	48
1	16	34	50	34	32	63	129	79
1.5	16	43	59	34	32	78	144	85

Notes: [a] Rules and stipulations as operating immediately prior to 2007 Pension Act; [b] Rules and stipulations as operating after full implementation of 2007 and 2008 Pension Acts. See Table 10.17.

Sources: Own calculations, based on biographies used in the simulations detailed in the text.

Table 10.6: Projected median outcomes for female biographies with voluntary occupational provision[a] under the pre-reform[b] and post-reform[c] UK pension system, as % of social exclusion line

Biography	Pre-reform		Post-reform		Difference	
	State/DC	State/DB	State/DC	State/DB	State/DC	State/DB
0.5	59	60	87	78	28	18
1	78	79	114	92	36	13
1.5	119	248	169	266	50	18

Notes: [a] Median state/occupational outcomes are based on schemes detailed in Table 10.18; [b] Rules and stipulations as operating immediately prior to 2007 Pension Act; [c] Rules and stipulations as operating after full implementation of 2007 and 2008 Pension Acts. See Table 10.17.

Sources: Own calculations, based on biographies used in the simulations detailed in the text.

exclusion line by between 28 and 50 percentage points for women, and by between 37 and 55 percentage points for men.[5] This lifts two additional biographies above the social exclusion line in comparison with the pre-reform situation, meaning that five out of our six biographies with state and defined contribution pensions are above this threshold. This is important because with the decline of defined benefit pensions this is a group whose size is set to grow. Those with defined benefit pensions remain contracted out of State Second Pension under the new system and thus see their projected incomes rise by a smaller amount, between 13 and 36 percentage points as a result of the improvements in the basic state pension.

Table 10.7: Projected gross median outcomes for male biographies with voluntary occupational provision[a] under the pre-reform[b] and post-reform[c] UK pension system, as % of social exclusion line

Biography	Pre-reform		Post-reform		Difference	
	State/DC	State/DB	State/DC	State/DB	State/DC	State/DB
0.5	81	130	118	146	37	16
1	121	205	170	233	49	28
1.5	146	270	201	306	55	36

Notes: [a] Median state/occupational outcomes are based on schemes detailed in Table 10.18; [b] Rules and stipulations as operating immediately prior to 2007 Pension Act; [c] Rules and stipulations as operating after full implementation of 2007 and 2008 Pension Acts. See Table 10.17.

Sources: Own calculations, based on biographies used in the simulations detailed in the text.

[5] It is possible that the increase in the income of this group will not be as great. At present, their employers receive a contracted-out rebate on their national insurance contributions. With the end of contracting out for defined contribution pensions this rebate will be withdrawn, which might mean that employers will reduce their contributions by the amount of rebate.

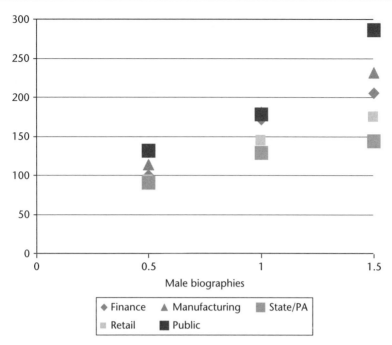

Figure 10.3: Projected gross median outcomes on retirement of post-reform[a] UK pension system for male biographies by sector of employment,[b] as % of social exclusion line

Notes: [a] Rules and stipulations as operating immediately prior to 2007 Pension Act; [b] Sector medians are based on occupational schemes detailed in Table 10.18.

(*Source*: Own calculations).

The overall effect of these changes to state and non-state provision is likely to be a reduction in the levels of inequality seen in the old system. Certainly, the new arrangements look set to significantly close the gap between those who had occupational provision under the old system and those who did not. Thus, the range of median projected outcomes by sector for the males on half average wages has fallen by 33 percentage points (see Figure 10.4) in comparison with the results for the pre-reformed system (see Figure 10.2), while for the man on average wages it has reduced by 54 percentage points and for the man on one-and-a half times average wages by 68. For women, the respective reductions in range are 19 (half average wages), 29 (average) and 48 (1.5 average) (see Figure 10.3).

Two further factors might reinforce this equalizing trend. First, retrenchment in the occupational sphere is ongoing, with the beginnings of a movement amongst companies to close or significantly amend schemes to future accruals from existing as well as new members (Jones 2006). This retrenchment is also likely to extend to the public sector given the budget deficit

191

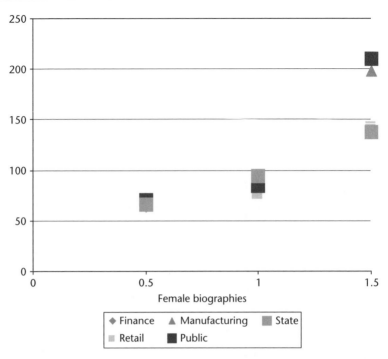

Figure 10.4: Projected gross median outcomes on retirement for post-reform[a] UK system for female biographies by sector of employment,[b] as % of social inclusion line

Notes: [a] Rules and stipulations as operating immediately prior to 2007 Pension Act; [b] Sector medians are based on occupational schemes detailed in Table 10.18.

(*Source:* Own calculations).

problems currently being encountered by the British government. Second, there are some indications that companies who offer voluntary schemes might reduce their contributions or close their schemes altogether in light of the NEST pension system (ACA 2009).

In summary, therefore, Britain's hybrid system has significantly changed track in recent years, with state provision and access to occupational provision set to grow over coming years. The full effects of this change will only be felt over the long term and are, of course, to some extent reliant on the performance of pension investments, but as has been seen above, the potential impact on the pensions of new entrants to the reformed British system is significant. In Germany, in contrast, most recent movement in pension policy has been in a very different direction.

10.6 The pre-reform pension system in Germany

The German pension system has been traditionally dominated by the contributory earnings-related public pension initiated by the 'Bismarckian' social insurance reforms more than a century ago and extended most significantly in the post-war period by the 1957 reform (see Chapter 9 of this volume). This pay-as-you-go system has always been based firmly on the principle of status-maintenance, with contributions calculated as a percentage of gross income and the value of pension benefits strongly linked to contributions paid during the individual's whole employment (Riedmüller and Willert 2007: 141). Almost uniquely among European pension systems, there has been no guaranteed minimum pension within the pension system (Kaufmann 2003: 284). As was seen in Chapter 9, this approach is strongly consistent with the conservative, coordinated market economy model. Nevertheless, the relationship between gross earnings and benefits has never been entirely pure. First, an upper income limit of double the average wage has generated in effect a maximum pension, with reduced replacement rate for high earners. Second, as was seen in Chapter 9, credits for certain caring activities have been introduced incrementally since the 1970s. The cap on contributions for higher-paid earners is one reason occupational provision has played a greater role in the German system than has sometimes been appreciated (see Chapter 9).

10.7 Pre-reform performance of the German system

The outcomes of the pre-reform German state system for our six biographies are clearly in line with those which would be expected in a large conservative social insurance pension system (see Table 10.8). Projected pensions rise broadly in line with the lifetime wages of the biographies, although there is some flattening at the top end due to the contribution cap which reduces the

Table 10.8: Projected gross performance of pre-reform[a] German state system for all biographies, replacement rates, and as % of social exclusion line

Biography	Female		Male	
	Replacement rate	Social inclusion	Replacement rate	Social inclusion
0.5	91	45	61	79
1	80	79	59	153
1.5	54	160	49	190

Notes: [a] Rules and stipulations as in operation immediately before 2001 reform.

Sources: Own calculations, based on biographies used in the simulations detailed in the text.

replacement rates for the best-paid male and female worker. Even so, the pensions of the lower-paid workers are reasonably generous, particularly in terms of replacement rates, due to the high level of individual contributions and the introduction of protection for unpaid caring work.

As would be expected, the public pensions for each of the German biographies are significantly higher than the state pensions for the equivalent British biographies. This is particularly the case for the higher paid biographies which, despite the contribution cap, still benefit most from the close link between contributions and earnings within the German state system. For example, the pensions of the male average earner and the male earner on 1.5 times average earnings are respectively 103 and 130 percentage points higher in relation to the national social inclusion line under the pre-2001 German public pension system than they were under the pre-reformed British state system (see Table 10.2 and Table 10.8). For the female biographies on these wages the differences in pension are 36 and 103 percentage points, respectively. By comparison, the pensions of the female workers on lower wages are comparatively much closer, although the German biographies still do best. Here the generosity of the German earnings-related system causes it to perform better than the much more redistributive but less generous British system (see Myles 1998).

Notwithstanding the comparative generosity of the German state system many German workers, and particularly those in some privileged industrial sectors, were also covered in occupational pensions mainly financed on a 'book reserve' basis and of a defined benefit type (see also Chapter 9 of this volume).[6] On the basis of a selection of these 'traditional' German schemes (Berner 2006: 5) as they operated in 2001, Table 10.9 shows the pre-reform pension of our biographies with and without occupational provision. While not as generous as the British schemes, it demonstrates that this provision was capable of providing a significant supplement to state pensions for a range of different workers. Nevertheless, the work-based nature of these entitlements means that once again it is the best-paid men who benefit most. Thus, when a typical occupational pension is added to the pensions of the best-paid male and female workers they achieve projected outcomes in excess of 200 per cent of the social inclusion threshold, with replacement rates for both above 60 per cent. The male average earner is not far behind this level in terms of the social exclusion threshold and has a higher replacement rate. However, even for lower-paid workers occupational pensions were capable of providing a significant supplementary income. For example, the male worker on half-average

---

[6] Even where defined contribution pensions existed they were not 'pure' forms because they were legally required to guarantee a pay-out consistent at least with a real replacement rate of zero.

Table 10.9: Comparison of projected gross median outcomes on retirement of pre-reform[a] German pension system for biographies with and without voluntary occupational provision[b], replacement rates, and as % of social exclusion line

	State		State/occupational		Difference	
	Replacement rate	Social inclusion	Replacement rate	Social inclusion	Replacement rate	Social inclusion
Woman, 50%	91	45	109	52	18	7
Woman, 100%	80	79	96	93	16	14
Woman, 150%	54	160	67	201	13	41
Man, 50%	61	79	76	98	15	19
Man, 100%	59	153	73	190	14	37
Man, 150%	49	190	62	240	13	50

Notes: [a] Rules and stipulations as in operation immediately before 2001 reform; [b] Median state/occupational outcomes are based on schemes detailed in Table 10.18.

Sources: Own calculations, based on biographies used in the simulations detailed in the text.

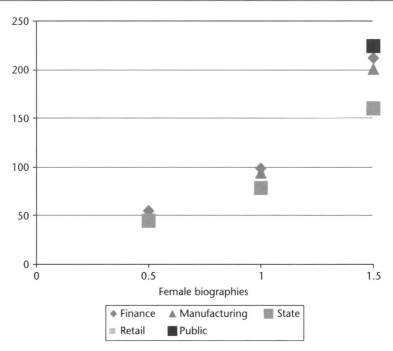

Figure 10.5: Projected gross median pensions under pre-reform[a] German pension system for female biographies by sector,[b] as % of social exclusion line

Notes: [a] Rules and stipulations as in operation immediately before 2001 reform; [b] Sector medians are based on occupational schemes detailed in Table 10.19.

(*Source*: Own calculations).

wages moves close to the social inclusion threshold and the lowest-paid women is above a 100 per cent replacement rate.

As discussed in Chapter 9 of this volume, the coverage and generosity (see Figures 10.5 and 10.6) of German occupational provision by sector has been broadly in line with that which would be expected in a conservative, coordinated market economy. Thus, coverage has been highest in the public sector and manufacturing sector, whereas pensions before 2001 (as illustrated in Figures 10.5 and 10.6) were very generous, especially for those on mid-to-high incomes. In contrast, coverage in the retail sector has been much lower and those pensions that have been provided have lifted individuals only slightly above the state pension level. The somewhat anomalous sector is finance. Here coverage (see Chapter 9) and, as our results suggest, pension generosity too have been higher than in manufacturing, the product mainly of the BVV multi-employer pension scheme for finance companies, which included 680 companies in 2009 (http://www.bvv.de/cms/de/int/startseite/index.jsp).

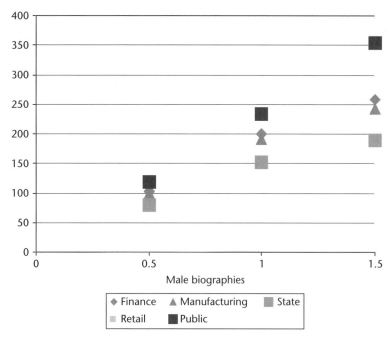

Figure 10.6: Projected gross median pensions under pre-reform[a] German pension system for male biographies by sector,[b] as % of social exclusion line

Notes: [a] Rules and stipulations as in operation immediately before 2001 reform; [b] Sector medians are based on occupational schemes detailed in Table 10.19.

(*Source:* Own calculations).

10.8 Reform of the German system

Change to the German public/private pension mix since 2001 has had three essential elements. First, the public social insurance pension has been significantly retrenched, with changes in the adjustment formula for pensions in 2001 and 2004 leading to pension rates rising more slowly (Schmähl 2004; Schulze and Jochem 2007). Second, various attempts have been made by the state to encourage the growth of non-state provision as a means of compensating individuals for their losses in the state sphere. Finally, companies have accelerated the alteration of their 'traditional' occupational provision (Berner 2006: 5), reinforcing a process that had been ongoing throughout the last quarter of the twentieth century. Thus, while all workers are witnessing a decline in the generosity of their public provision, there is a range of scenarios in the non-state sphere. Those working in companies which had occupational provision before the reforms have either seen this provision maintained unchanged or retrenched. Individuals working for employers without occupational provision before the reform, will now all have access to occupational provision on the basis of collective agreements reached in all industrial sectors; whether they will take up this opportunity will be a matter for them.

In the previous section, we saw that the outcomes of the pre-reform system were largely consistent with those that would be expected in a conservative, coordinated market economy. Is this still true under the reformed system? The varieties of capitalism framework would predict this. This would expect the privileged protection of core workers to continue, with the new pension system encouraging and rewarding skill acquisition among this group on the basis of higher earnings-related pensions. Thus while the balance between public and private sector might have been altered, the reformed system would be expected ultimately to reproduce in different form the old German pensions' model. In the analysis that follows, we argue that while some trace features of the old system are evident in the projected outcomes of the new one, overall the new system will be unable to fulfil some of the basic requirements of a conservative, coordinated pension system. The new system will cause a decline in pension outcomes for all workers, even those in core sectors.

10.9 Post-reform performance of the German system

10.9.1 *The public pension system*

The scale of the retrenchment to the German state system is well illustrated by the results from our simulations in Tables 10.10 and 10.11. These compare the pensions gained by the biographies under the pre-2001 state system with those that would be gained if they experienced their whole working life under the system as it operated in 2007. It thus illustrates the long-term impact of the reforms undertaken in 2001 and 2004 (see Hinrichs and Kangas 2003; Hinrichs 2009). Results show that while the reform has largely preserved the main Bismarckian principle of the state system (i.e. earnings relation), it has done this on the basis of a much less generous pension system overall. Thus, there is a marked and generally consistent decline in public benefit outcomes of all biographies, with, for example, the highest-paid male, on one-and-a-half times average earnings, seeing their public pension benefit decline to about 61 per cent of their pre-reform pension and the lowest-paid male seeing theirs diminish to 68 per cent. This small degree of flattening is due to the shorter length of time the higher-paid individual spends in the workforce due to participation in higher education, for which credits are no longer received under the new system.[7] It also occurs because unlike the other

[7] The woman on one-and-a-half times average wages loses out even more from this change because the previous credit was flat-rate.

Table 10.10: Comparison of projected gross performance of pre-reform[a] and post-reform[b] German state system for all biographies, as % of social exclusion line

Biographies	Pre-reform		Post-reform		Difference	
	Female	Male	Female	Male	Female	Male
0.5	45	79	28	54	−17	−25
1	79	153	48	105	−31	−48
1.5	160	188	85	115	−75	−73

Notes: [a] Rules and stipulations as in operation immediately before 2001 reform; [b] Rules and stipulations as in operation in 2007.
Sources: Own calculations, based on biographies used in the simulations detailed in the text.

biographies the higher-paid individuals are penalized for retiring before the new retirement age (67) due to the fact than in total they have worked for less than forty-five years.[8]

However, while the principle of earnings relation has largely been preserved under the new state system, lower contributions mean that many more workers than before are vulnerable to social exclusion in retirement. Significantly, our results suggest that among this newly vulnerable group is the type of skilled middle-income worker on which the German model is said to have relied. The simulations show that the higher-paid biographies, all of whom were well above the social exclusion line under the old system, either dip below it or are precariously close to it under the new one. The highest-paid woman is the worst off: she moves from a position of relative security to a situation where she is 15 percentage points below the social exclusion threshold. The pensions of the two better-paid male workers remain above the social inclusion line (although for the average paid worker it is likely to fall below it after a few years of retirement), but the replacement rates of both of them fall

Table 10.11: Comparison of projected gross replacement rates under pre-reform[a] and post-reform[b] German state system for all biographies, as % of social exclusion line

Biographies	Pre-reform		Post-reform		Difference	
	Female	Male	Female	Male	Female	Male
0.5	91	61	58	44	−33	−17
1	80	59	50	43	−30	−16
1.5	54	49	30	31	−24	−18

Notes: [a] Rules and stipulations as in operation immediately before 2001 reform; [b] Rules and stipulations as in operation in 2007.
Sources: Own calculations, based on biographies used in the simulations detailed in the text.

[8] The pension is reduced by 3.6% for every year before the legal retirement age. But this reduction only takes place, if the employment record is less than 45 years.

substantially. Thus, even when the new system protects skilled middle-income earners against social exclusion, it does so at a level of income substantially below that which they earned while at work.

As would be expected given reforms of this type, the situation for the lower-paid workers is grimmer still. While the old system was never designed primarily to counteract poverty, its large contribution base meant that it nevertheless offered a substantial degree of protection for the lowest paid despite the earnings relation principle. The maintenance of this principle in a system of much smaller size inevitably means that the pensions of the low paid fall to very low levels indeed. Thus the pension of our lowest paid biography, the woman on half-average wages (when in full-time work), falls to 28 per cent of the national inclusion line, a level 10 percentage points below that received in relation to the British social exclusion line by the same biography under the pre-reformed British system (see Table 10.2). This type of result is the product of the rejection in the pre-reform debate and subsequently of the case for a minimum universal state pension, similar to the BSP in Britain (Riedmuller and Willert 2007).

10.10 The new public/private mix in Germany

Thus when analysis is focused entirely on long-term developments in the public pension system the consequences of recent reforms in Germany are clear: change has been introduced not on the basis of the logic of the previous system but has involved a clear and extensive step towards a more liberal type of system, with lower public benefits and thus more reliance on the market. However, pension system change in Germany has not been this simple. First, many of today's workers will retire before the full effects of the reform process have worked through, which will mean that their public pensions will be higher than those who retire later (see Hinrichs and Kangas 2003). Second, as has been seen, the German system has always included a significant occupational sphere, the growth of which was encouraged by the 2001 reform. It is on this second issue that the analysis of our simulations in this section will concentrate. Does occupational provision now help preserve the fundamental logic of the previous model, albeit on the basis of a very different balance between the public and private sectors?

Our analysis starts with those individuals covered by traditional occupational provision under the previous system. As has been seen, for many in this group pension change has involved not only reform of the public system but also changes to occupational provision. The overall effect of these changes for a new entrant under the new public/private mix is illustrated in Tables 10.12 and 10.13. These tables show the impact for each biography of the addition of

Table 10.12: Projected gross median outcomes for female biographies with voluntary occupational provision[a] under the pre-reform[b] and post-reform[c] German pension system, as % of social exclusion line

Biography	Pre-reform		Post-reform		Difference	
	State	State/ Occupational provision	State	State/ Occupational provision	State	State/ Occupational provision
0.5	45	54	28	35	−17	−19
1	79	95	48	59	−31	−36
1.5	160	201	85	111	−75	−90

Notes: [a] Median state/occupational outcomes are based on schemes detailed in Table 10.19; [b] Rules and stipulations as in operation immediately before 2001 reform; [c] Rules and stipulations as in operation in 2007.

Sources: Own calculations, based on biographies used in the simulations detailed in the text.

a median occupational pension. This median is calculated using the same schemes which provided the pre-reform occupational median above and takes into account recent reforms in the 'traditional' non-state sphere (see Table 10.9). As can be seen, overall projected pension levels for individuals with 'traditional' occupational provision has fallen by a significant amount over and beyond that caused by state retrenchment. This is particularly true for the men, who because they retire on a full-time income benefited significantly from traditional defined benefit provision. For them, retrenchment of this provision adds between 9 and 31 percentage points to their state pension loss in relation to the social exclusion threshold. In contrast, the two lower-paid women who both retire on part-time incomes did less well under the old system and consequently their additional losses are not as great. Not all new employees in companies with 'traditional' provision have been affected by these developments: some larger companies, particularly in manufacturing,

Table 10.13: Projected gross median outcomes for male biographies with voluntary occupational provision[a] under the pre-reform[b] and post-reform[c] German pension system, as % of the social exclusion line

Biography	Pre-reform		Post-reform		Difference	
	State	State/ occupational provision	State	State/ occupational provision	State	State/ occupational provision
0.5	79	98	54	64	−25	−34
1	153	189	105	112	−48	−77
1.5	190	239	115	133	−75	−106

Notes: [a] Median state/occupational outcomes are based on schemes detailed in Table 10.19; [b] Rules and stipulations as in operation immediately before 2001 reform; [c] Rules and stipulations as in operation in 2007.

Sources: Own calculations, based on biographies used in the simulations detailed in the text.

such as Daimler, Fresenius, and Ford, have so far kept their existing schemes open and unchanged, but as will be seen below, in the financial and public sector significant retrenchment over and above that in the state sector is clearly evident.

Moving on to individuals who were previously without occupational provision, the 2001 reform opened up the possibility to mitigate the losses suffered by the decline of state pension benefit on the basis of tax-subsidized contributions set by industry-wide collective agreements. However, our results suggest that the scale of this mitigation is very small. Increased new coverage has in many cases merely taken the form of new contributions from employees, subsidized by the state (TNS Infratest 2008a: 50). By contrast, employer contributions remain very low or non-existent. Thus, as can be seen from Table 10.14, the pension levels that can be expected on the basis of the type of contributions agreed under a typical collective agreement, such as that concluded by the metal industry, have only a marginal impact on the losses incurred due to state retrenchment.

In short, there can be little doubt that the overall situation for *all* workers who contribute to the new system for any length of time will be one of substantial retrenchment, regardless of their wage and sector of employment. Consequently, and to offer an answer to the question with which we began this section, only a very limited degree of consistency with the old conservative, coordinated German pension model is maintained under the new one. Differentials continue to exist between income groups, albeit at a much lower level of income for all and, as can be seen in Figures 10.7 and 10.8, some degree of sectoral variation also remains. However, these sectoral differentials have significantly diminished. Thus, as would be expected in a conservative, coordinated system, the public and manufacturing sectors remain comparatively privileged. However, the degree to which the median pensions in these sectors outstrip those in less privileged sectors has declined markedly. Whereas under the old system the range of sectoral median outcomes for those with occupational provision varied for male workers from between 39 percentage points for the lowest-paid workers and 164 percentage points for

Table 10.14: Projected gross pension for all biographies from the metalworkers' collective agreement,[a] as % of social exclusion line

	Female			Male		
	0.5	1	1.5	0.5	1	1.5
Pension	1	2	4	2	4	6

Notes: [a] For details of the scheme see http://www.metallrente.de/

Sources: Own calculations, based on biographies used in the simulations detailed in the text.

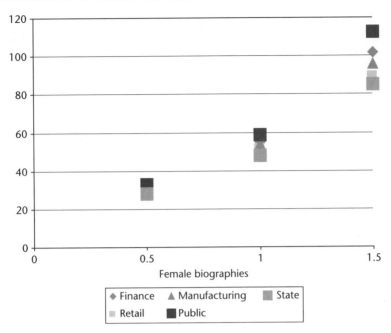

Figure 10.7: Projected gross median pensions under post-reform[a] German system for female biographies by sector,[b] as % of social exclusion threshold

Notes: [a] Rules and stipulations as in operation immediately before 2001 reform; [b] Sector medians are based on occupational schemes detailed in Table 10.19.

(*Source:* Own calculations).

the highest-paid workers, under the new system these ranges are now 12 and 44 percentage points, respectively. In all cases the median pension in the retail sector remains the lowest but it is now much closer to that of the other sectors. The financial sector remains anomalous: pensions in this sector remain closer to manufacturing and the public sector as a legacy of the early development of occupational provision in this area.

This decline in sectoral differentials is in part indicative of the fact that the privileged group of workers has shrunk in size. Thus, while some manufacturing companies such as Fresenius (Fresenius Medical Care 2008) and Daimler (Daimler 2008) have so far maintained their existing occupational provision, others which might have been expected to resist retrenchment, such as BASF (BASF 2007) and Bayer (Bayer 2008) have not done so. As a consequence, the projected pensions of their workers are closer now to those projected for workers in the retail industry rather than those of other workers in the manufacturing sector. Moreover, in absolute terms even this smaller group of privileged workers are projected to experience levels of protection much lower than that provided under the old system. Given the substantial decline in public social insurance pensions, occupational provision will

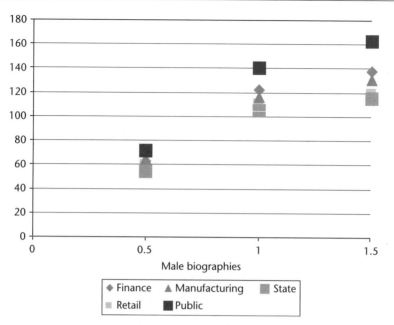

Figure 10.8: Projected gross median pensions under post-reform[a] German system for male biography by sector[b] as % of social exclusion threshold

Notes: [a] Rules and stipulations as in operation immediately before 2001 reform; [b] Sector medians are based on occupational schemes detailed in Table 10.19.

(*Source:* Own calculations).

become a much more important component of their overall retirement income—a means for protection against social exclusion. Among the growing group of less privileged workers the prospects look grimmer still. Those individuals reliant solely on public pensions and collective-agreement-based occupational provision, like the retail workers in Figures 10.7 and 10.8, are extremely vulnerable to social exclusion at or soon after retirement. This is particularly the case for the female biographies, all of whom fail to secure a pension above this threshold on retirement, and even the best-paid male biography surmounts this hurdle by only 19 percentage points.

10.11 British/German comparison

Where does the analysis undertaken above leave us with regard to the question of convergence? Have the British liberal, hybrid system and the German conservative, coordinated system become more similar, as the globalization thesis would predict (e.g. Przeworski and Wallerstein 1988), or have the differences between the two systems been maintained in line with the logics of their particular regime type (eg Hall and Soskice 2001)? What has been the predominant nature of the change that has occurred and how should we now characterize the two systems in relation to regime typologies? In addressing these questions it is important to be clear about the different forms convergence might take. Convergence might be considered in relation to the institutional architecture of the current, post-reform pension systems in Britain and Germany and the respective development of these systems compared to the ones they replaced. Alternatively it might relate to recent changes in pension levels in the two systems in comparison with pension levels before the respective reforms. As was explained in the methods section above, our analysis has used projected future outcomes to assess and compare the nature of the pre-reform and post-reform pension institutions in the two countries. It is thus on this question of convergence between the pension institutions in the two countries that we mainly focus here.

Viewed from this perspective, the answers to the questions about convergence are clear: recent institutional changes have not amounted to a process of convergence. While both systems have changed substantially, or are in the process of doing so, they remain significantly different. Indeed, as will be seen below, in terms of projected outcomes they are more different now than they were previously. This absence of convergence is consistent with the general predictions of the varieties of capitalism framework. However, contrary to the predictions of this approach, the absence of convergence is not due to the maintenance of the dominant logic of the conservative, coordinated type in the reformed German system; neither is it because of faster liberalization in the British system. Rather, our results show that the German system has moved markedly in a liberal direction, allowing us to categorize it as a liberal/conservative hybrid system. By contrast, British pension institutions are in the process of becoming significantly more social democratic in nature, making it plausible to regard it as a more clear-cut social democratic/liberal hybrid than it was before.

To complicate this picture a little, these institutional changes are likely in the short-to-medium term to lead to some degree of convergence of pension levels between the two systems. This is because many of the changes implemented in recent years will have their full effect in terms of outcomes only in fifty or so years, given the long time pension systems take to mature. Thus we will see a transitional period over coming decades with pensions resembling less and less their pre-reformed types and more and more the post-reform ones. In the early stages of this process we would expect there to be a convergence of outcomes for comparable individuals in the two systems as the generosity of German public pensions gradually decline while the British one increases. But so long as current arrangements remain in place this process will eventually lead to the type of differences outlined above.

Table 10.15: Projected gross median pension and range of outcomes for all biographies by gender in pre-reform Britain[a] and Germany,[b] as % of social exclusion line

	UK		Germany		Difference UK/Germany	
	Median	Range	Median	Range	Median	Range
Female						
0.5	53	30	52	14	1	16
1	74	57	93	24	−19	33
1.5	128	179	200	64	−72	115
Male				0		
0.5	82	90	97	39	−15	51
1	125	177	188	82	−63	95
1.5	151	243	237	166	−86	77

Notes: [a] Rules and stipulations as operating immediately prior to 2007 Pension Act; [b] Rules and stipulations as in operation immediately before 2001 reform.

Sources: Own calculations, based on biographies used in the simulations detailed in the text.

This conclusion can be illustrated by considering again our projections of future outcomes.

Tables 10.15 and 10.16 show the median projected overall pension income (i.e. state and non-state) for each biography as a percentage of the social exclusion line on the basis of the pre-reformed and post-reformed systems in Britain and Germany. Thus the median for each biography is calculated on the basis of the range of employer scenarios for each country detailed in Tables 10.17 and 10.19, with an additional scenario for an employee entitled only to state provision.[9] To be consistent with the notion of institutional convergence

Table 10.16: Projected gross median pension and range of outcomes for all biographies by gender in post-reform Britain[a] and Germany[b] as % of social exclusion line

	UK		Germany		Difference UK/Germany	
	Median	Range	Median	Range	Median	Range
Female						
0.5	83	33	33	13	50	20
1	106	54	53	23	52	31
1.5	178	147	96	48	82	99
Male						
0.5	121	61	65	26	56	34
1	175	115	117	43	58	72
1.5	210	176	132	74	78	103

Notes: [a] Rules and stipulations as operating after full implementation of 2007 and 2008 Pension Acts; [b] Rules and stipulations as in operation in 2007.

Sources: Own calculations, based on biographies used in the simulations detailed in the text.

[9] It could be argued that by including only one employment scenario for state provision, the median for each country is inflated, given the coverage limitations of non-state provision in both

we would expect the pensions of each biography to be more similar now than they were in the past. This is not the case. Instead, in most cases the pre-reform differences in outcomes between the British and German system have been more than completely reversed under the post-reform system. Thus whereas under the pre-reform systems almost all biographies would have been significantly better off under the German system, they are all now better off to an even greater extent under the reformed British system. The one exception to this general trend is the lowest-paid woman, who always fared slightly better in Britain than in Germany because of the gender sensitivity of the former system and earnings-related nature of the latter one. Thus, under the post-reform system in Britain five out of six individuals are lifted above the social exclusion line; in German only three out of six are similarly protected. The reasons for these quite dramatic reversals are clear. First, at the bottom end, the British system is now founded on a considerably more generous, redistributive and inclusive state system which is projected to provide all of the lower income biographies with a pension of around 60 per cent of the national social exclusion line. In contrast, the still quite strict adherence to earnings relation in a less generous German system means that the three lowest-paid individuals receive state pensions of only 28 per cent (Woman, half average), 48 per cent (Woman, average), and 54 per cent (Man, average) of the social exclusion line. Second, while projected German state provision still outstrips British at the top end of the income scale (see Tables 10.5 and 10.13), the low level of German occupational provision means that overall the projected British median is higher than the German (see Figures 10.3, 10.4, 10.7, and 10.8). The British performance would be less good should voluntary occupational provision decline further, for example, by levelling down to the level of NEST pensions. However, this situation currently looks unlikely and even if it were to occur, the pensions of all our biographies would still be significantly higher than the German medians (see Tables 10.4 and 10.5). This mix in the new British system of earnings relation at the top end and quite substantial redistribution at the bottom end is similar to social democratic systems such as the Netherlands, Denmark, and Sweden. However, in each of these cases the projected state pension would be somewhat higher and citizenship-based, and non-state provision would be more collectivized and less generous at the top end (Bannink and de Vroom 2007). In the meantime, the German system has become more similar to the type of less generous Bismarckian system seen in the USA.

countries. However, the main purpose of this table is to illustrate the significantly more generous projected outcomes in post-reform Britain than post-reform Germany. If anything, the methodology chosen is likely to inflate the German medians more than it inflates the British ones, given that overall coverage in the latter is likely to rise with the introduction of NEST pensions.

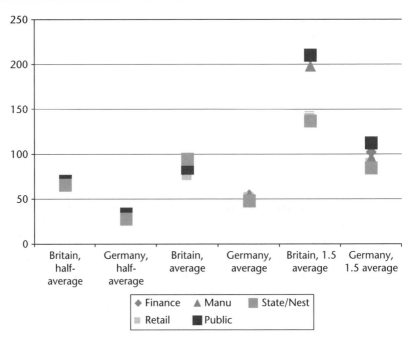

Figure 10.9: Comparison of projected gross median pensions on retirement for female biographies by sector in British and German post-reform pensions systems, as % of social exclusion line

(*Source*: Own calculations).

The better performance in Britain in terms of overall median pension is also evident if the results are broken down by sector (Figures 10.9, 10.10). Thus, while the new German system still privileges workers in some sectors, even the projected pensions of this privileged group are invariably below those projected for NEST pensions in Britain. The only exceptions in this regard are the two better-paid men working in the German public sector.

Thus, in terms of the relationship between the current pension institutions in the two countries and those they have replaced there has been no convergence between the British and German systems. The only caveat that needs to be added to this overall conclusion concerns the durability of the British reform given Britain's large fiscal deficit and the fact that the implementation of the 2007 and 2008 Pension Acts was delayed until 2012 and now seems likely to be overseen by a governing coalition made up of the Conservative Party and the centrist Liberal Democrats. Should this government decide to rein in the changes (Timmins 2009), either by making smaller the improvements in state provision or by reducing employer's contributions to NEST pensions, the liberal features of the British system will remain stronger and the similarities between it and the new German system will grow.

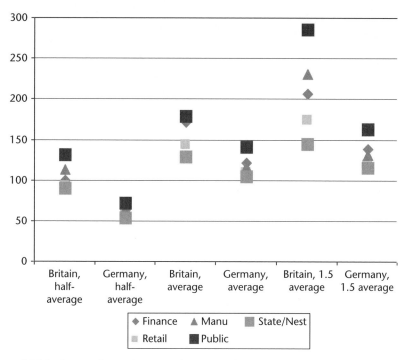

Figure 10.10: Comparison of projected gross median pensions on retirement for male biographies by sector in British and German post-reform pension systems, as % of social exclusion line

(*Source*: Own calculations).

Table 10.17: Details of the assumptions made in simulations in Britain and Germany

	Assumption	Comments
General economic		
Inflation	1.90%	The European Central Bank's inflation target – see http://www.ecb.int/mopo/html/index.en.html
Gross earnings	Gross earnings are remuneration (wages and salaries) in cash paid directly to the employee, before any deductions for income tax and social security contributions paid by the employee. Data is presented by gender for full-time employees in 'industry and services'	See Eurostat – http://epp.eurostat.ec.europa.eu/
Earnings growth	Annual rise of 2% above inflation	Gross disposable income rose by a nominal average of 3.9% in the five years up to 2003 (European Central Bank 2004)
Pension system assumptions		
Britain		
Pre-reform state pension system	Rules and stipulations of public regime as it operated immediately prior to the 2007 and 2008 Pension Acts	
Post-reform state pension system	Rules and stipulations of public regime as it operated after the 2007 and 2008 Pension Acts, with increases in state provision assumed to start in 2012	
Occupational provision	Rules and stipulations of schemes as they operated in 2007. See Table 10.18 for more details. Personal Accounts (NEST) pensions assumed to be phased in from 2012	The occupational schemes included in the pre- and post-reform stage are the same because the main waves of retrenchment to occupational provision had occurred before the 2007 and 2008 reforms were passed
Germany		
Pre-reform state pension system	Rules and stipulations of public regime as it operated immediately prior to the 2001 reform	
Post-reform state pension system	Rules and stipulations of public regime as it operated in 2007	
Occupational provision		

Other assumptions

Post-reform calculations include any reform to occupational provison made after 2001. See Table 10.18 for more details

Replacement rates and early retirement

In circumstances where a biography retires early, their last wage has been projected forward to the date on which they receive their state pension on the basis of the price index

Tax

Tax and social insurance contributions are excluded. We use gross earnings to calculate pension entitlement, and pension outcomes are gross figures

Recent research undertaken by the OECD suggests that the effect of tax on pension outcomes is similar between Britain and Germany. It concluded that the differential between gross and net replacement rates is 17% on average, with little significant variaton between countries (OECD 2005:17)

Rates of return and annuity rates

Where a rate of return and/or annuity rate is not specified in a scheme, a real rate of return of 3.9% after charges has been assumed with an annuity rate of 5%. It is assumed that an annuity is purchased on retirement

On annuity rates, see http://www.fsa.gov.uk/tables/table/ results_frameset.jsp; on real rates of return, the 20-year average annual return was 5.5% for gilts and 4.6% for the FTSE All Share, although figures for the past ten years have been significantly lower (see Barclays Capital 2009)

Table 10.18: United Kingdom occupational schemes used in the simulations

	Type	Contributions	Accrual rate	Source	Year of change if applicable
Manufacturing					
BOC	Defined contribution	Employee pays 3, 4, or 5%; employer pays approximately double employee rate	Not applicable	IDS (2004)	2003
ICI	Defined contribution	Vary by age: under 35, employees 3%; employers 5%; 35–50, 5% and 9%; over 50, 7% and 12%	Not applicable	IDS (2004)	2000
Johnson Mathey	Defined benefit	Employees pay 4% of pensionable earnings; employer contributions as required	1/57th of annual pay on retirement multiplied by years of membership	Union Pension Service (2003)	Not applicable
Reckitt Benckiser	Defined benefit	Employees pay 4% of earnings up to three times the lower earnings limit and 5% above this; employer contributions as required	1/60th of best salary in last ten years of employment multiplied by years of membership	IDS (2006)	Not applicable
Finance					
Alliance and Leicester	Defined contribution	Employees and employer pays 5% of pensionable earnings	Not applicable	Annual report 2003 - http://www.alliance-leicester-group.co.uk/	1998
Barclays	Defined contribution	Age-related: below 35—employee 4%, employer 9.5%; from 35—employee 4%, employer 11.5%; from 45— employee 4%, employer 13.5%	Not applicable	Annual report 1999 – http://group.barclays.com/Investor-Relations	1997

	Type	Contributions	Benefit formula	IDS (2004)	Defined benefit schemes closed in 1996 and 1998
Lloyds TSB	Defined contribution	Age-related: from 25 to 29—employee 2%, employer 2%; 25–9—employee 6.5%; 30–44: 8.5%, 45–60: 10.5%	Not applicable		Defined benefit schemes closed in 1996 and 1998
Prudential	Defined benefit	No employee contributions; employer contributions as required	1/60th of final salary multiplied by years of membership	Union Pension Service (2003); Annual report 2007, http://www.prudential.co.uk/prudential-plc/investors/	Not applicable
Public Sector					
Civil Service (Partnership)	Defined contribution	Age-related: under 21: 3%; 21–5: 4.5%; 26–30: 6.5%; 31–5: 8%; 36–40: 10%; 41–5: 11.5%; 46+: 12.5%	Not applicable	http://www.civilservice.gov.uk/my-civil-service/pensions/	Not applicable
Civil Service (Nuvos)	Defined benefit	Employee, 3.5%; employer, as required	1.3% of pensionable earnings per year increased in line with inflation	http://www.civilservice.gov.uk/my-civil-service/pensions/	Not applicable
NHS	Defined benefit	No employee contributions; employer contributions as required	1/80th of final salary multiplied by years of membership	http://www.nhsbsa.nhs.uk/pensions	Not applicable
Teachers	Defined benefit	Employee, 6.4%; employer, as required	1/60th of final salary multiplied by years of membership	http://www.teacherspensions.co.uk/	Not applicable
Retail					
DSG International	Defined contribution	Employee, 3–5%; matched and doubled by employer	Not applicable	http://www.dsgi-pensionbuilder.co.uk/home	2002
Next	Defined contribution	Employee, 3–5%; matched by employer	Not applicable	http://www.usdaw.org.uk/adviceresources/pensions.aspx/	2000
Sainsburys	Defined contribution	Employee, 4–6%; matched by employer	Not applicable	http://www.jspensions.com/index.htm	2002
Tescos	Defined benefit	Employee, 5%; employer as required	1.5% of average pay revalued in line with earnings	http://www.usdaw.org.uk/pensions/pensions_finder/1145635615_1735.html	Not applicable

Table 10.19: German occupational schemes used in the simulations

	Pre-reform				Post-reform				
	Type	Contributions	Accrual rate	Source	Year of change if applicable	Type	Contributions	Accrual rate	Source
Manufacturing									
Nestlé	Defined contribution and defined benefit	Flat-rate lump sum equivalent to 607 Euro (2007) adjusted in relation to working time; sum increased in line with wages every five years	15% of final salary	Company information	Not applicable	No change	No change	No change	Same
Südzucker	Defined contribution and defined benefit	Flat-rate lump sum equivalent to 607 Euro (2007) adjusted in relation to working time; sum increased in line with wages every five years	15% of final salary	Company information	Not applicable	No change	No change	No change	Same
Bakery	Defined contribution	3.8% employer	Not applicable	WSI 2001	2002	Collective agreement	Flat-rate lump sum equivalent to 607 Euro (2007) adjusted in relation to working time; sum increased in line with wages every five years	Not applicable	http://www.ihre-vorsorge.de/ Betriebliche- Altersversorgung-Service-Tarifvertraege.html
Milk industry Bavaria—Mueller and Zott	Defined contribution	Flat-rate lump sum equivalent to 700 Euro (2007) adjusted in relation to working time; sum increased in line with wages every five years	Not applicable	Company information	Not applicable	No change	No change	No change	Same
Daimler	Defined benefit	Not applicable	1/294th of last salary multiplied by years worked	Company information	Not applicable	No change	No change	No change	Same

Company	Type	Employer contribution	Benefit formula	Source	Year				Website
Ford	Defined benefit	Not applicable	1/250th of last salary multiplied by years worked	*Frankfurter Allgemeine Zeitung*	Not applicable	No change	No change	No change	Same
VW	Defined benefit	Not known—average defined benefit scheme used	Not known—average defined benefit scheme used		2001	Defined contribution	1% of salary and flat-rate contribution of 324 Euro (2007), latter increased in line with wages every five years	Not applicable	http://autogramm.volkswagen.de/04_11/titel/home.html
Bayer	Defined benefit	2%—employer	40% of cons	Company information		Not known—chemiefonds collective agreement used	Not known—chemiefonds collective agreement used	Not known—chemiefonds collective agreement used	http://www.ihre-vorsorge.de/Betriebliche-Altersversorgung-Service-Tarifvertraege.html
BASF	Defined benefit	2% – employer	44% of cons	Company information	2004	Not known—chemiefonds collective agreement used	Not known—chemiefonds collective agreement used	Not known—chemiefonds collective agreement used	http://www.ihre-vorsorge.de/Betriebliche-Altersversorgung-Service-Tarifvertraege.html
Fresenius	Defined benefit	Not applicable	Two-part scheme. Part A: a minimum pension of 153,39 Euro per month uprated by inflation. Part B: Final monthly salary minus fixed amount (613,55 Euro in 2007 adjusted to inflation) divided by 300, multiplied by years worked	Company information	2004	No change	No change	No change	

(continued)

Table 10.19: *(Continued)*

	Pre-reform				Year of change if applicable	Post-reform			
	Type	Contributions	Accrual rate	Source		Type	Contributions	Accrual rate	Source
Finance									
BVV	Defined benefit	6.5%—employer	Conversion rate—11.5%. BVV 2007: for every employee 3.5% of the income is contributed to the scheme. The annual contribution is directly converted into an annuity by age-related factors which were prescribed by the scheme rules.	Scheme information—see http://www.bvv.de/cms/de/int/startseite/index.jsp	2003 and 2007. 2007 scheme is used for post-reform simulations	Defined benefit	3.5%—employer	Conversion rate varies by age and gender	
BVV/Hypo-Vereins bank 2007	Not applicable	Not applicable	Not applicable	Not applicable	2007	Defined benefit	5.5%—employer	Sum of annual contributions	Company information
Public Sector									
Versor gungskasse des Bundes und der Länder	Defined benefit, PAYG	Not applicable	Guarantee of 75% gross replacement rate for state and public-sector pension	See Chapter 9	2001	Defined contribution	Earnings points scheme—points equal ratio between monthly income and reference income of 1,000 Euro multiplied by an age factor	Each point equals 4 Euro of pension	http://www.vbl.de/
Retail									
Retail	Not applicable	Not applicable	Not applicable	Not applicable	2002	Collective agreement	Flat-rate contribution of 300 Euro (2007) increased in line with wages every five years	Not applicable	http://www.ihre-vorsorge.de/Betriebliche- Altersversorgung-Service-Tarifvertraege.html

Wholesale	Not applicable	Not applicable	Not applicable	Not applicable	2002	Collective agreement	Flat-rate contribution of 159.52 Euro (2007) increased in line with wages every five years	Not applicable	http://www.ihre-vorsorge.de/Betriebliche-Altersversorgung-Service-Tarifvertraege.html
Metro	Defined benefit	Not known—average defined benefit scheme used	Not known—average defined benefit scheme used	http://www.metrogroup.de/servlet/PB/menu/-1_l1/index.html	2006	Defined contribution	Flat-rate contribution of 342.76 Euro (2007) increased in line with wages every five years	Not applicable	http://www.metrogroup.de/servlet/PB/menu/-1_l1/index.html

11

Can personal pensions bridge the savings gap? Regulation and performance of personal pensions in Great Britain and Germany

Michaela Willert

11.1 Introduction

Personal pension schemes are independently purchased by individuals who select the material aspects of the arrangements. Access to such plans does not have to be linked to an employment relationship. Such schemes are established and administered by financial institutions like life insurers, banks, or investment funds. Benefits in personal pension schemes are determined by the amount of contributions, the rate of return on assets, and the price of converting assets into monthly pension benefits (annuity rates). Pension outcomes, thus, are highly influenced by the way the capital is invested and the costs of administrating individual accounts. Personal pension schemes therefore differ from state pensions, where membership is mandatory and the material conditions are defined by pension politics. They also differ from occupational pension arrangements which are set up by an employer and linked to an employment relationship. This differentiation becomes increasingly blurred, however, when employers contribute to personal pension schemes. The virtues of personal pension schemes are seen in that they permit individual choice and responsibility in selecting fund managers, good service and performance through competition between fund managers, and limited risks through competition and investment regulation (Srinivas et al. 2000: 5–6).

The UK and Germany both introduced personal pension arrangements aimed at making their state pensions more financially sustainable. While the UK rearranged the pension regime as early as 1988, reforms came into force in Germany in 2002. Both implemented systems which are voluntary in character and thus differ from legal stipulations such as the Obligatorium in Switzerland or the superannuation scheme in Australia, where membership for most employees is compulsory and contribution rates are defined.

This chapter analyses the effects of personal pensions on the material well-being of future retirees in the UK and Germany. More concretely, it asks whether such pension arrangements are able to close the savings gap between state pensions and a social inclusion threshold set at 40 per cent of the national average gross income (see also Chapter 10). In both countries this line is above the threshold for means-tested benefits. The analysis allows for two factors which determine whether the savings gap will be closed by voluntary arrangements: the take-up of pensions and the performance of the pension products which citizens purchase.

The chapter argues that both factors are influenced by state regulation and its interaction with strategies on the part of pension providers as profit-making institutions (Mayntz 1997). Such interaction between state regulation and markets is also suggested in literature on 'welfare markets', where the term 'welfare markets' describes the introduction of 'market means for welfare ends' (Hippe 2007; Leisering 2007; Nullmeier 2001; Taylor-Gooby et al. 2004). Governments may regulate product providers with the aim of creating socially acceptable outcomes or to try to encourage citizens to enter said markets via incentives such as rebates or tax breaks. It is not clear, however, how such 'welfare markets' might work for retirement provision or how they will perform in the long run.

First, this chapter illustrates how regulatory frameworks have developed in both countries. Since broader societal and regulatory frameworks differ, the implementation processes for personal pensions have varied, too. Second, the financial impact of pension regimes for citizens will be assessed by micro-simulating pension benefits. The chapter concludes with a discussion about the ability of voluntary pension arrangements to close the savings gap.

The empirical data for this section are derived from various sources, including legal regulations, a range of official statistics, as well as interviews with actors within the personal pension business in both countries, and an extended newspaper analysis, reviewing particularly the Financial Times, Financial Times Deutschland, and the Börsenzeitung. Table 11.1 indicates the type of personal pensions covered in the analysis.

11.2 Creating personal pension markets

11.2.1 Development in the UK

In 1983 Norman Fowler, then Secretary of the Department of Health and Social Security (DHSS), launched a pension review process. Its main aim was

Table 11.1: Overview of the considered pension schemes

UK	Germany
Personal pensions:	*Riester-pensions:*
Money purchase scheme for employees, based on contracts between individuals and insurers, banks, building societies, or investment funds; may be used to contract out of the State Second Pension (S2P)	Money purchase scheme for employees, based on contracts between individuals and insurers, banks, building societies, or investment funds; may also be facilitated by employers
Stakeholder pensions:	*Money purchase schemes for wage deferral (e.g. Pensionskassen)*
Personal pensions with a price cap, employers with more than 5 employees and without company schemes are legally required to offer them to their employees	Administrated by insurers; employers are compelled to offer them to their employees
Group personal pensions:	
As personal pensions but facilitated by employers	

to 'study the future development, adequacy and costs of state, occupational and private provisions for retirement in the United Kingdom, including the portability of pensions rights' (DHSS 1983 cited by Bonoli 2000b: 65–6). At the time, the broader public was increasingly regarding the well-established salary-related company pension schemes as unfair, because they provided insufficient benefits to employees who left their company before retirement. The government therefore decided to introduce regulation for transferring company pension-fund assets from one employer to the next, i.e. to make pension assets more portable (Nesbitt 1995: 74–9). In addition to this 'objective' problem pressure, the Thatcher government considered occupational schemes—particularly those which were not administrated by life assurances but self-administrated by large companies—as too 'corporatist' (*Financial Times*, 19 July 1984; Nesbitt 1995: 106). The solution for both problems was seen in personal pension schemes. It was argued that personal pensions would give the employee the advantage of '...an identifiable sum of personal savings which belongs directly to him' (DHSS 1985, cf. Nesbitt 1995: 113) and a 'new dimension of choice' (DHSS 1985, cf. Bonoli 2000b: 70). Indeed, 'freedom of choice' as well as 'share-owning society' were prominent phrases used by the government (see, for instance, *Financial Times*, 19 July 1984, 1 February 1986, 13 September 1986; *The Economist*, 21 July 1984).

The first output of the pension inquiry was a proposal to abolish the State Earnings Related Pension (SERPS). Instead, employees were to be obliged to contribute at least 4 per cent of their earnings to occupational or personal pension schemes (Nesbitt 1995). This proposal was met with fierce resistance from the Treasury as well as from life insurers, although the latter would have been the potential providers of personal pensions. The Exchequer was afraid of lost revenues from SERPS contributions. The life insurers argued that the planned contributions of 4 per cent would provide inadequate old-age pensions for most people and

> ...that individual saving against old age by millions of low paid, itinerant workers moving in and out of work would be grossly inefficient. In many cases, contributions [...] would average less than £7 a week. The expense of investing such small sums in long-term securities would be prohibitive—perhaps a third of the value of the contributions. (*Financial Times*, 20 September 1985)

Eventually, the Social Security Act 1986 did not abolish but rather curbed the benefits of the state scheme SERPS and introduced voluntary personal pension schemes.

A particular feature of the UK pension system is that employees are permitted to pass a share of their social insurance contributions to salary-related company pension schemes. Employers and employees get a contribution rebate of the pay roll (5.8 per cent at the time). In return, employees waive their SERPS pension ('opting or contracting out'). In order to qualify for opting out, the company schemes had to guarantee pension benefits at least as high as the foregone SERPS benefits. From 1988 personal pension schemes were also permitted for opting out. In contrast to company schemes, personal pension plans qualified for opting out simply when they received the social insurance rebate. The risk of accumulating assets which are high enough to replace the abandoned SERPS benefits was left entirely to employees. It was also permitted to pool personal pension plans for a number of employees as group pension schemes, which promised to produce lower administration costs due to economies of scale.

In order to boost pension sales from the start, employees who were not members of a company scheme received a temporary incentive of 2 per cent of an employee's payroll, which was contributed to personal plans until 1993. Additional tax breaks were also introduced to encourage personal pensions take-up. For instance, the employees' part of the national insurance contribution rebate (2 per cent) for opting out became tax-exempt, and the tax saved added to the individual contract. Employees received higher tax breaks for contributions to personal pensions than for company schemes (Agulnik et al. 1999: 64). In sum, in the initial phase contributions and incentives to personal pension funds added up to 8.46 per cent of eligible earnings (Disney and Whitehouse 1992: 3). In this way, personal pension schemes were not only intended to attract employees without any access to company schemes, but also the members of such schemes who could be encouraged to leave their occupational schemes or make additional contributions to personal plans.

The Thatcher government intended to create a highly competitive market and therefore personal pensions were to be sold by a range of providers such as insurance companies, building societies, and banks. Moreover, there were no regulations concerning how the assets of such personal schemes should be accumulated until retirement. At retirement, personal pension plans had to provide a lump sum of which one-quarter could be drawn tax-free. The remainder had to be converted into an annuity. In order to make the benefits equivalent to the foregone SERPS pension, annuities, which were derived from contracted-out contributions, were required to be equal for women and men (Disney and Whitehouse 1992: 12). If the retiree was married, the annuity had to provide survivor's benefits. Finally, annuities had to be able to buy a pension-worth which was indexed to inflation and guaranteed at least 3 per cent price growth. Assets which accumulated trough contributions in excess of the contracted-out rebate could be converted by open-market annuities, which differed by sex, reflecting the higher life expectancy of women.

At the time, the regulatory environment of personal pension providers was very weak (Black and Nobles 1998). The *Financial Times* cites the chief executive of the life offices' regulatory body: 'When I joined, the brief I got from the then chief executive was that the industry consisted of good guys with a great deal of integrity—all we need to do is to produce a set of rules' (*Financial Times*, 1 March 1994). The investment of assets followed and still follows the 'prudent person principle' (Davis 2001: 19). That means that assets have to be invested in a diversified way, balancing risk and returns and covering all insured risks. To protect against the bankruptcy of the pension providers they established some mutual compensation schemes. In sum, the government introduced regulations for personal pensions which were primarily aimed at creating a competitive market.

11.2.2 *The German development*

The new private pension landscape in Germany developed out of reforms which were aimed primarily at containing the costs of the state pension scheme in order to stabilize contributions levied on earnings and to reduce labour costs for employers (Schmähl 2003a; Lamping and Rüb 2004), but also to modernize the pension system (Clasen 2005: 114). In 1999 the social democratic Minister of Work and Pensions, Walter Riester, proposed a mandatory private pension with contributions rising to 2.5 per cent of earnings to make up for the reduced state pension benefits (for detailed descriptions of the reform process, see Lamping and Rüb 2004; Trampusch 2005; Schulze and

Jochem 2007). After the tabloid press published the plans, public outcry and fierce criticism followed by the Green Party (the governing coalition partner), the conservative and liberal opposition parties, and trade unions alike. To create consensus with the conservative opposition party, a new political solution emerged which entailed a state-subsidized voluntary private pension arrangement complementing the state pension scheme, the so-called Riester-Pension. It was assumed that 4 per cent of earnings would replace the reduced state pension benefits.

Because the consensus failed and the Social Democrats still needed votes to approve the law in parliament and the upper house (Bundesrat), however, they had to accommodate their own left-wing party members and labour representatives (Clasen 2005). They did so by guaranteeing collectively agreed occupational pension schemes the same tax advantages as privately managed plans, hence increasing the trade unions' power in the emerging new pension landscape. Those types of pension received additional state support in that the contributions were exempt from social security contributions. Moreover, employees in the private sector received the right to transfer part of their payroll into a workplace-related pension scheme (Entgeltumwandlung). Finally, the new saving schemes could also be used for purchasing private property. As in the UK, a broad range of providers were allowed to offer such plans in order to foster competition.

To encourage take-up of the voluntary plans, employees could claim flat-rate subsidies which started at €38 annually and increased to €154 in 2008. Parents received extra allowances of €46 in 2002 and €185 per child from 2008. In addition, contributions to Riester-plans up to €525 annually in 2002 (escalating to €2100 in 2008) received tax breaks. The incentives permitted lower earners to receive flat-rate subsidies which might contribute to private pension assets or tax breaks for middle-to-higher earners. Claimants of unemployment benefits as well as non-working spouses of eligible employees were also eligible to receive state subsidies. The latter was aimed at establishing individual private pension assets for full-time carers. Full state subsidies were paid when employees contributed 1 per cent of their earnings to Riester-plans in the first two years after their introduction. This amount was increased gradually until 4 per cent was reached by 2008.

In order to qualify for state support, plans were required to accumulate funds until the consumer reached the age of 60. The accumulated pension capital had to be paid out in the form of a monthly lifelong benefit (annuity) or instead, by keeping the money invested and taking an income each year until the age of 85 (income drawdown) and annuities thereafter. Lump-sum payments were prohibited. Annuities which ignored differential life expectancies of women and men were explicitly rejected by the government (Leisering and Vitić 2009: 98).

Very early on, the government wanted to tackle cost problems of individual accounts. As a consequence, it was stipulated that fees were to be spread over the first ten years of contributions made in order to reduce the burden levied by up-front costs. Most importantly for the security of pension benefits, at least the nominal value of the contributions had to be available when the contract was due for annuitization (zero nominal minimum rate of return).

Among providers, insurance companies in particular were strongly regulated (Schradin and Reichenbach 2003).[1] Their investments were restricted by quantitative provisions which were at 35 per cent for equities, for instance. Life insurance contracts had to guarantee a rate of return, which was linked to long-term government bonds.[2] In case of insolvency of their provider, consumers were protected by a mutual insolvency fund (the so-called Protektor).

For employees who wanted old-age investments to be provided by their employer, several other types of investments apart from life insurance were recognized. Those investments were less regulated as employers were assumed (and indeed legally obliged) to protect the interest of their employees. Such products, however, also had to guarantee at least a zero rate of return.

To sum up, the degree of regulation of the private pension market in Germany was fairly strong from the start. It also included measures which were primarily aimed at protecting customers, for instance, by preventing high up-front costs of insurance products and guaranteeing the invested capital. Hence, the development was slightly different from that in Great Britain, where regulation was initially rather light and focused on creating a private pensions market. Governments in both countries introduced tax incentives in order to encourage the purchase of new pension products. But whereas the German government increased the tax incentives over time, the UK reduced the initially very high incentives after five years.

11.3 Shaping the personal pension market and its social inclusiveness

In both countries the pension industry was challenged by new types of products in the same way. Their range of products focused on tax-free cash sums, which were particularly attractive for higher earners. The new pension

---

[1] Since 1994 regulation has become weaker. Previously, every new product had to be approved by the watchdog (*Bundesaufsichtsamt für das Versicherungswesen*).

[2] Contracts provided a guaranteed minimum return and a variable surplus. The guaranteed return is fixed at the beginning of the contract. The maximum amount of this guarantee is defined by the Federal Ministry of Finance (Maurer 2003: 9–14) Since 2004 this has been 2.75%.

products, in contrast, were also to be purchased by low-to-middle earners. However, personal pension markets developed markedly differently in both countries (see Figure 11.1).

In 1988 when personal pensions became first available in the UK, more than 3 million contracts were sold, which represents more than one-quarter of the eligible population.[3] Despite a slower pace in the second year, sales grew steadily until they peaked at 5.7 million contracts or 39 per cent of the eligible population by 1994. After that, numbers remained stable, with around 5.5 million contracts in force. Since the mid-1990s, however, personal pensions have been used less for contracting-out, i.e. people paid full contributions to the National Insurance Fund—thereby maintaining their additional state pension benefits—and invested additionally in personal pension plans.

Although the government favoured competition among several types of providers, the bulk of personal pension plans are administered by insurance companies. Initially, consumers preferred pension contracts where policy holders participate in profits that a life insurance company gains as surplus (with-profit policies). These products keep back some of the return from the investment in good years and add back to top up returns in years of poor performance. Although this makes the products rather intransparent, it could be beneficial for long-term investments like old-age savings, because the strategy produces more stable returns over the long run. Customers only benefit from this strategy, however, if they are able to hold the policy until retirement,[4] since otherwise they pay high charges and penalty fees. Another popular product links the policy holders' investments directly to equities (unit-linked products). For consumers who purchase unit-linked products, the status of their investment is more transparent, and in times of high returns such products promise higher benefits in old age. But in times of poor financial market performance the consumers bear the investment risk individually.

Since the mid-1990s, unit-linked products have gained in importance. In 2006 more than two-thirds of assets were held in such unit-linked products (ABI 2008: 3). The insurance sector also became increasingly involved in company pension funds. By 2006 46 per cent of all pension fund assets were managed by insurance companies, compared with 21 per cent in 1987 (ABI 2008: 5).

---

[3] Only people who were covered by the additional state pension scheme (SERPS) but had no occupational pension were eligible to opt out into a personal pension. All UK figures are derived from statistics of the DWP on Second Tier Pension Provision, (ABI 1998: HMRC pension tables 7.4 and 7.5, several years).

[4] Also, insurance companies must be able to keep their payout promises until retirement. Several UK companies did not keep their promises and therefore caused reservations in consumers about this type of product.

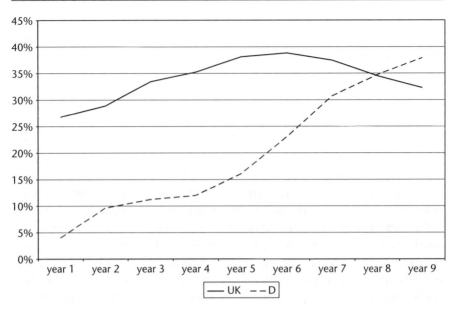

Figure 11.1: Share of the eligible population with personal pension contracts (by year after introduction).

(*Sources*: DWP—*SERPS Statistics*; BMAS 2009 Statistics of Riester-contracts; own calculations).

This was largely the result of increased sales of group personal pension schemes from 1996 onwards, i.e. personal pension products which pooled the investments of a number of employees.

In Germany the initial take up of Riester-pensions was much lower than the growth of personal pensions in the UK. In the second half of 2001—the first time Riester-contracts became available—1.5 million contracts were sold, which equals a proportion of less than 5 per cent of the eligible population. In 2002 the number of contracts more than doubled for a total of 3.4 million, representing only 10 per cent of people who were allowed to receive state subsidies (Stolz and Rieckhoff 2005; Sommer 2007). In the following two years, virtually no new contracts were sold. However, influenced by new regulations (see below), sales figures increased again from 2005, and by the end of 2009 more than 13 million people had entered contracts, representing around 38 per cent of the eligible population (BMAS 2009). Three-quarters of all contracts were signed with life insurers, mainly as with-profit policies. But unit-linked products and contracts with investment funds have expanded strongly since 2005. Additionally, from 2001 to 2006 more than 4.5 million people became members of wage deferral schemes, most of which are administered by insurance companies (GDV 2007; TNS Infratest 2007).

The following section shows how market development in both countries was shaped by government-set regulations, to which personal pensions providers reacted very quickly in order to achieve their company objectives. Moreover, providers adjusted their marketing campaigns to governments' incentives to citizens for purchasing these products.

11.3.1 Development in the UK

Initially the high incentives in the UK as well as their structure 'were a salesman's dream' (*Financial Times*, 20 January 1990). The Department of Health and Social Security passed on contributions from opted-out pensions to providers once a year. For employees, the contributions remained the same as before but were paid (indirectly) to personal pension providers. The National Insurance rebate for contracting-out was equal for all age groups. When passed over to personal pension contracts, this consequentially resulted in higher benefits for younger people with longer contribution records to such plans. In contrast, when entering such contracts in later life, the returns on these opted-out contributions would become too low to replace the foregone state pension. This was compounded by the fact that the rebate for opting out of the National Insurance was reduced from 5.8 per cent to 4.8 per cent in 1993. In addition, the initial incentive of 2 per cent dropped in the same year. Therefore, from 1993 many insurance companies advised customers at certain ages to contract back into the state pension scheme (women at the beginning and men from mid to late forties (*The Independent*, 12 March 1994)). Because this contradicted the government's objective to decrease the role of the state pension in favour of voluntary pensions, a new 1 per cent incentive payment for people aged 30 and over was introduced. In 1997 the opting-out rebate became differentiated by age. This stopped (but did not reverse) the downward trend in the take-up of personal pensions.

After years of stagnation in personal pension take-up, the Labour government introduced new tax incentives in 2001 and 2006. The reforms aimed at simplifying the diverse tax regimes for personal and company pensions. They also removed Inland Revenue restrictions up to which contributions could receive tax relief. Pension providers used these reforms to create new marketing campaigns, and they were able to increase the inflow of personal pension contributions (ABI 2007). Much of this inflow, however, was produced by transfers from one insurance company to another, instead of by greater efforts by customers to save for old age.

The initially rather weak regulatory framework of the British personal pensions market promised high returns to providers even for small individual accounts. Therefore, in those early years, sales forces encouraged below-average earners to enter the personal pensions market (ABI 1998; Ginn and

Arber 2000). Weak regulation, however, resulted in market failure and the so-called mis-selling scandal (Black and Nobles 1998). Around 500,000 employees were advised by sales forces to transfer their pension assets from company pensions to less beneficial personal pension schemes. Another three million low earners and older people were persuaded to opt out of the state scheme into personal pensions, although they would have been better off with state benefits (Clasen 2005: 123).

Subsequently, the government attempted to better protect consumers through higher market transparency and information requirements for pension providers. It also limited the charges and commissions providers could levy, thereby increasing market pressures. Moreover, the advisory process itself became much more expensive because of new information and documentation duties. As a consequence, sales forces became increasingly pushed to sell high-value pension funds in particular in order to recoup costs. This reduced incentives to sell personal pensions to low-to-middle earners (FSA 2000: 19), and consequently, sales became more targeted towards higher earners or more profitable group pension schemes linked to the workplace.

To counteract this, the Labour government introduced the highly regulated Stakeholder pensions in 2001. This new type of personal pension was designed to encourage middle earners to save for old age. For lower earners, however, the state pension became more generous and inclusive through the introduction of the State Second Pension (see Chapter 9). For the new Stakeholder pension plans, the government prescribed that fees must not exceed 1 per cent of the pension fund's value, and they had to be levied over the whole contract instead of the first contribution years (Disney et al. 2007). Consumers could start savings with very low contributions, and they could stop contributing or change the pension provider at any time and without penalty fees. Employers with more than five employees and without a company scheme had to offer Stakeholder pensions to their employees. However, workers were not obliged to enter such contracts and the employer must not contribute to the schemes.

As our expert interview showed, the life insurance companies were reluctant to offer Stakeholder pensions because they were afraid that they could not recoup their costs through the price cap of 1 per cent of the fund value and the prohibition to front-load costs. It was only after the government increased the price cap to 1.5 per cent for the first five contribution years and a new insurance company used Stakeholder schemes as a means to enter the UK insurance market that such pension plans became available for customers. Through the price cap, Stakeholder pensions increased cost pressure on the more expensive personal pensions, because pension providers could not legitimize their higher prices for traditional products. As a consequence, prices for personal pension plans adjusted downwards, and pension products became less profitable than pension providers thought by the end of the 1980s (Caza-let Consulting 2006; Deloitte 2006). It is argued that since 2001 almost no new savings were generated in the personal pension market. Instead, the reported annual growth of new premiums for private pensions by a huge amount resulted from commission-driven intermediaries, who transferred existing pension funds to new providers which paid commission again ('churning the market') (Cazalet Consulting 2006).

These developments had a negative impact on the inclusiveness of the UK pension market. The interplay between lower financial incentives for employ-ees, an increasingly demanding regulatory framework resulting in higher costs pressure for providers, and a more inclusive state pension shaped a personal pension market which now mainly serves higher earners and better-paid employees in big companies. The increasing benefits of the state pension (see Chapter 9) and a financial market which provides lower returns made opting out of the state scheme less attractive over the years. Between 2001 and 2006 the number of contracted-out pensions fell by 3.6 million to 11.8 million (see Figure 11.2). UK employees, however, were still required to save a propor-tion of earnings for old age to avoid heavy drops in their living standards or even poverty after retirement. But the number of such pension plans in addition to the state scheme (contracted in contracts) grew only by 1.2 millions to 7.1 million contracts. Among the latter, group personal pensions and Stakeholder schemes particularly contributed to the growth.

The decrease of non-state pension coverage affected men more than women, who had traditionally been less included in this market (ONS 2008c). Among men, private pension coverage declined particularly for low-to-middle earners. In 2006 both women and men under the age of 29 were less covered than during the previous ten years. Contributions to personal pen-sions were actually too low to create an old-age income to which people aspire (Disney et al. 2001; Pensions Commission 2004), although employers increas-ingly contribute to such schemes (ONS 2008b). In sum, the UK personal pension market has become increasingly socially exclusive.

The UK government has reacted to this trend with 'radical' reforms to private pensions (Emmerson and Wakefield 2009: 4) implemented by the Pensions Act 2008. From 2012 the act obliges all employers to automatically enrol employees from the first day of work in a pension scheme to which employers have to contribute at least 3 per cent of the employees' payroll. Employees have to contribute a minimum of 4 per cent, although they are allowed to opt out of the employers' scheme. The Treasury will add another 1 per cent of the employee's earnings in the form of tax relief to the contract (Jones 2009). A state authority (Personal Accounts Delivery Authority) was created to tackle the problem which employers might face when they look for portable and low-cost workplace pension products to meet the needs of low

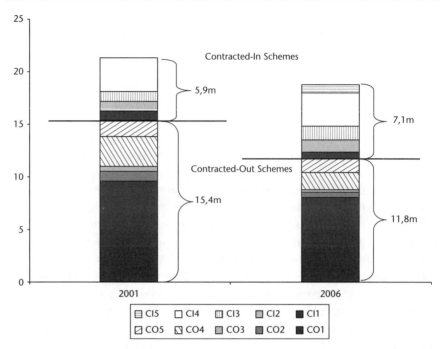

Figure 11.2: Members of additional pensions by type 2001 and 2006 (millions).

Note: CO1—Contracted-Out DB-Scheme; CO2—Contracted-Out DC-Scheme; CO3—Contracted-Out Group Personal Pension; CO4—Contracted-Out Personal Pensions with minimum contributions; CO5—Contracted-Out Personal Pensions with minimum and additional contributions; CI1—Contracted-In DB-Scheme; CI2—Contracted-In DC-Scheme, CI3—Contracted-In Group Personal Pension; CI4—Contracted-In Personal Pension; CI5—Contracted-In Stakeholder Pension

(*Source*: ONS Ashe Survey 2001 and 2006 and HMRC Pension Statistic, Table 7.4).

earners and employees with frequent job changes. In 2010 this authority will introduce an independent pension scheme run by a not-for-profit trustee corporation called 'National Employment Savings Trust (Nest)'. This will serve as one provider of the new schemes among the established providers for occupational pensions products (see National Employment Savings Trust Order 2010, in force from 5 July 2010). The government expects the scheme to draw between two and eight million members (DWP 2009: 9).

11.3.2 *Development in Germany*

In contrast to the UK, the German government phased in Riester-pensions rather slowly, reaching the maximum required savings amount and incentives as late as in 2008, i.e. eight years after their introduction. Low incentives in the first years might have contributed to the lower initial take-up rates. Moreover, in contrast to the UK, where personal pension providers collected contributions from the state pension authority and the Treasury, claiming incentives in Germany was more complicated. Contributions to Riester-pensions were paid by employees out of their net income minus the amount of flat-rate subsidies. The latter had to be applied annually by a newly established federal authority, the central allowance authority for pension assets (*Zentrale Zulagenstelle für Altersvermögen*). Relevant tax breaks, on the other hand, were refunded via the annual tax assessment and did not contribute to the contract.

Due to the procedure for claiming the flat allowances, many people's contracts received subsidies late or were even foregone. The market leader for life insurances, Allianz, stated that 550.000 people—or one-third of those who had entered a Riester-contract in 2002—did not claim their allowance until the end of 2004, when the two-year period for claiming state subsidies expired (*Versicherungsjournal*, 12 November 2004). Therefore, the government simplified the procedure for claiming subsidies in 2005, making the schemes more attractive for customers and providers alike. The products' attractiveness was also enhanced by permitting consumers to take out 30 per cent of the pension fund as a lump sum at the start of retirement. In 2008 the flat allowance for parents of newborn children was increased to €300 per child from €185, and an extra contribution of €100 to Riester-contracts of young employees under the age of 21 was introduced.

A main obstacle to the distribution of Riester-contracts was the stipulation to levy the costs of remunerating sales forces within the first ten contribution years. Indeed, sales forces were paid upfront for other investment products like endowment policies (*Kapitallebensversicherungen*), which also qualified for tax breaks at the time. As interviews and newspaper analysis showed, this and the complexity of advising the new Riester-products initially demotivated sales forces from selling. The number of contracts increased only after the government reduced the spread of commission payments to five years and abandoned tax subsidies for endowment policies in 2005. Moreover, life insurance companies started to pre-fund commission payments, and the sales forces received their full commissions directly after consumers entered the contract. Further regulatory measures stipulated that women and men entering Riester-contracts from 2006 onwards must receive the same pension benefits, in spite of the longer life expectancy of women.

For Germany, an assessment of the level of inclusiveness has to remain tentative for the time being. Although low earners are less likely to enter Riester-contracts than higher earners, Börsch-Supan et al. (2007) showed for the year 2005, that Riester-schemes fared better in including low earners than company pensions (see Figure 11.3). This also applies for blue-collar workers

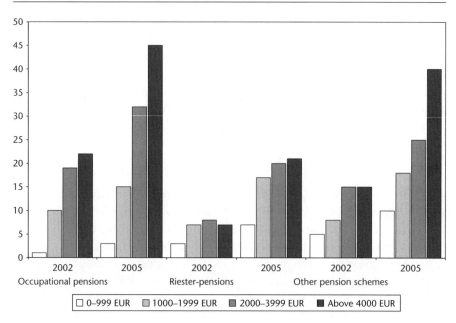

Figure 11.3: Old-age provision by disposable monthly household income in Germany 2002 to 2005 (% of households).

(*Source*: Börsch-Supan et al. 2007: table 6).

and people under the age of 39. Moreover, women are equally as likely to participate in Riester-schemes as men. After 2004 low-to-middle earners were increasingly included in the market (Coppola 2007). People with lower educational level, however, or those who lacked vocational training bought fewer Riester-plans.

In 2008 the government aimed to raise professional standards for sales forces and the advisory process. This might increase the quality but also the costs of advice. The UK's experience and the tightening regulatory framework suggest that the profitability of Riester-products, which has been positively assessed, might be too optimistic. An international rating agency commented on German life insurers as one of the least profitable markets in Europe (Fitch Ratings 2008). Less profitable Riester-products with very low margins and low premium payments have increasingly crowded out traditional products at a time when regulation is likely to increase cost pressure. Moreover, the hope to attract new money with products in addition to Riester-plans (Schmähl 2003b)—that is, using those plans as a door opener for further sales—might not be fulfilled. This could potentially lead to a similar trend as in the UK, i.e. exclusion of lower earners from the pension market.

11.4 Bridging the savings gap?

11.4.1 *Comparing pension products in the UK and Germany*

Private pension plans differ by the investment risks related to different products, the amount of costs charged and the price to pay for an annuity at the time of retirement (Barr 1999). This section analyses the range of pension products available in both countries and illustrates the differences in pension outcomes in two distinct phases:

- In the saving phase during an individual's active years, the amount of fees and charges determines the amount of assets accumulated with different pension products;
- In the dissaving phase after retirement, the costs for converting the pension assets into monthly income become crucial.

The comparison of pension outcomes pertains to typical products of the respective country.[5] As mentioned above, the type of the most popular products differ. Consumers in the UK prefer unit-linked pensions, which invest heavily in shares and equities and have to be converted into pensions by purchasing an annuity. Most German contract holders purchase with-profit policies that include annuitization from the outset.[6] In order to avoid biased results due to outliers, only products with costs between 10 per cent and 90 per cent of the market range have been included. Thus, the range of reported products represents 80 per cent of available pension plans, thereby referring to low-cost and high-cost products when the lower or higher end of this range is considered, respectively. However, the products of the market leaders, i.e. the most successful insurance companies (in terms of sales), are included too.

Figure 11.4 shows accumulated pension assets after contributing €100 or £100 per month over a period of forty-five years. The rate of return is assumed to be 5.9% per year before costs. The assumption regarding contributions represents a best-case scenario, given that only a minority of citizens make contributions over such an extended period (Smith 2006). The shorter the contribution record, the lower the outcome, which is further reduced by even higher fees and charges.[7]

---

[5] The figures are derived from the following sources: for Germany the database 'AV Win Morgen & Morgen' was used, a tool for insurance brokers offering products to their consumers. Thirty-three products have been included in the analysis. The UK figures are calculated with information received from comparative tables of the Financial Service Authority under http://www.fsa.gov.uk/tables/bespoke/Pensions and http://www.fsa.gov.uk/tables/bespoke/Annuities, accessed March 2009. Forty-eight products have been included here.

[6] In Germany, annuities constitute a market niche (von Gaudecker and Weber 2003).

[7] Moreover, this exercise neglects that people might change their pension product and transfer their assets to other providers. For the consequences regarding costs see Murthi et al. (2001).

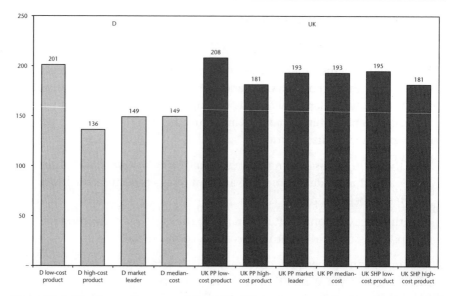

Figure 11.4: Pension assets accumulated with different products (in € for Germany, in £ for UK).

Notes: Assumptions: 100 €/£ per month over 45 years, rate of return = 5.9% before costs.

(*Source*: Own calculations with data provided by 'AV Win Morgen & Morgen' (for Germany) and comparative tables of the Financial Service Authority (for UK)).

In the UK differences between high- and low-cost products are smaller, and plans are cheaper than in Germany. This is caused by stronger market competition, and higher regulatory cost pressure in the UK through Stakeholder pensions, but also due to higher investment guarantees which German insurers have to provide.[8] It seems that the UK governments' interventions in controlling charges have been more successful than in Germany. The charges of the German high-cost product decrease assets by nearly 30 per cent compared to the low-cost product. In the UK, the distance between assets is only 13 per cent. Interestingly, in both countries the products of the market leader represent the median cost load within the available range of products. Apparently consumers' choice of pension plans has been driven by considerations of the cost merely to some extent.

In the dissaving phase, the assets are converted into pension payments. Actually, the range of products available for consumers is rather narrow,[9] in contrast to the broad range of outcomes. For reasons of comparability (see

---

[8] For the development of different types of personal contract related expenses of costs over the years see ABI (2007: Graph 6) and Whitehouse (2000: 40).

[9] The FSA comparative tables include eight providers. Two more are mentioned without comparative results, among which one of the market leaders (see http://www.moneymadeclear.fsa. gov.uk/home.html).

below), we illustrate the impact of annuities on personal pension benefits with income paid to a woman. For median personal pension assets of £193,200 shown in Figure 11.4, a woman would receive a monthly pension between £588 and £751. Figure 11.5 shows outcomes based on a combination of assets accumulated by different pension products within the range of annuities. Whereas the low-cost pension product and the best available annuity results in a pension of £809 per month, the high-cost pension product and the worst annuity pays £552. The latter represents only 68 per cent of the best available product combination.

As of 2006 annuities have to be calculated equally for women and men in Germany despite different mortality rates.[10] Overall, the regulation of annuity calculation is rather tight in Germany (von Gaudecker and Weber 2006: 2). With a low-cost pension contract, Germans achieve a pension of €648

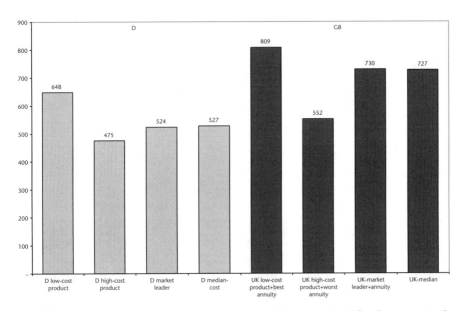

Figure 11.5: Range of monthly pensions in UK and Germany (in € for Germany, in £ for UK).

Notes: Assumptions: Accumulated assets as stated in Figure 11.2. For UK: female buying a single annuity and retiring at age 65. For Germany: Riester-pensions have to provide the same annuities for women and men. For both countries, the pension is guaranteed for 10 years and increases by 3% annually.

(*Source*: Own calculations with data provided by 'AV Win Morgen & Morgen' (for Germany) and comparative tables of the Financial Service Authority (for UK)).

[10] Von Gaudecker and Weber (2006) have shown that since then prices for annuities have been calculated based on female mortality rates. As a result, men receive a lower pension than before, while women are hardly better off.

compared to €475 with a high-cost product. The latter product pays a pension which is roughly equal to three-quarters of the low-cost product—a ratio which is better than in the UK (see Figure 11.6). In Germany, we found no systematic relationship between annuity prices and charges of pension products. That means that insurance companies which are expensive during the accumulation phase might offer more favourable terms for asset conversion. In both Germany and the UK, the market leader's pension is close to the median value.

Results are, however, highly sensitive to the investment risks associated with personal pensions. British pension funds are highly exposed to volatility due to strong investments in the equity markets (Tapia 2008). During the period from 1982 to 2005, Tapia (2008: table 9) reports a real rate of return for private pension funds of 8.7 per cent and a standard deviation of 12.5 per cent. For 2000 to 2005 the real rate of return was only 1.9 per cent and the standard deviation 16.5 per cent. During the financial crisis in 2008, personal pensions lost around one-third of their value (*The Independent*, 27 October 2008).

The consequences of the financial crisis for German pensioners have been less severe since Riester-plans have to guarantee at least the nominal value of the contributions at retirement. Moreover, during the developmental phase of the personal pensions market in Germany, the majority of consumers

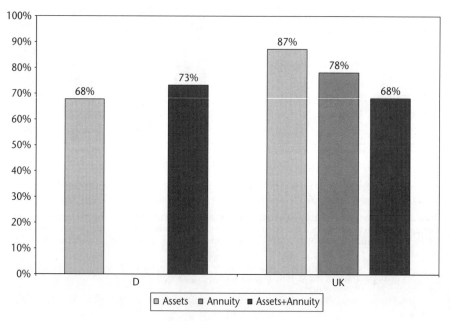

Figure 11.6: Ratios of high-cost to low-cost products (%).
(*Source*: Own calculations according to specifications of Figures 11.4 and 11.5)

purchased with-profit plans instead of equity-linked products, making assets less dependent on market values. The watchdog of the life insurers, the Bundesanstalt für Finanzdienstleistungsaufsicht, reported a rate of return of 3.4 per cent for 2008 (BaFin 2009: 98). Schradin and Reichenbach (2003: table 3) calculate that life insurances achieved nominal rates of return of about 7.7 per cent between 1980 and 2001. The volatility was low, with only 0.43%. Moreover, the authors show that life insurers differed only slightly in their investment performances—with annual returns ranging between 7.26 and 7.99 per cent (ibid; table 4).[11] German insurance providers, however, have invested heavily in bonds (*FAZ*, 1 February 2009), for which the long-term implications are still open. In sum, German insurers provide more security through more foreseeable investment returns than UK insurers, and German personal pension purchasers are more protected against investment losses than their British counterparts.

11.4.2 Closing the savings gap?

Hypothetical biographies of three men and three women illustrate the effects of individual pension provision on old-age income. In order to simulate pension outcomes, the same six work biographies with three different earnings levels as in Chapter 10 of this volume have been constructed and a range of supplemental pension products assumed (see Table 11.2).

For German biographies, the range of individual Riester-contracts has been considered, with contributions to such plans of 4 per cent of income up to the maximum amount which is subsidized by the government.[12] For the state pension scheme, the status of the year 2007 provides the basis for our calculations.

For the UK a broader range of pension products has been considered, including Personal and Stakeholder plans as well as personal pension schemes which are connected to an individual's working place (Group Personal Pensions—GPP, or Money Purchase Schemes).[13] The workplace-related schemes have the same characteristics as individually purchased pension plans but charge lower fees, because providers save administration and marketing costs, for instance, by collecting contributions of a number of members via one employer.[14] We assume a contribution rate of 10 per cent, which is used by

---

[11] See also Maurer (2003: 12), who reports slightly different figures, but also states a high degree of homogeneity of life insurers performance.

[12] In 2008 this was €2,100 annually. For the simulation this amount was adjusted for price inflation.

[13] From the Annual Survey of Hours and Earnings (ASHE) we chose the most common type of schemes per sector of economy; see ONS (2008b: Table 2.1).

[14] For an estimation of the charges see Cazalet Consulting (2006: 31).

the Association of British Insurers to assess the adequacy of pension savings (ABI 2005: 11, see also subsequent surveys) and which is also the most common contribution rate of employers to workplace-related personal schemes (ONS 2008c: tables 6.1 and 10.1).[15] In addition, old-age incomes are simulated for both cases of additional pensions, topping up state benefits (contracted-in) or replacing the earnings-related state pensions (contracted-out), thereby investing the rebate for the National Insurance Fund into personal pensions.[16]

The simulated pension outcomes from state and personal pensions are assessed as a fraction of the social inclusion threshold set at 40 per cent of the national average gross earnings in 2054. Figures 11.7 and 11.8 show the range of the British and German pension outcomes, where the lower black lines represent the level of means-tested social assistance in Germany and the sum of the Basic and S2P (State Second Pension) for the UK. In each case, the bars indicate the range of pensions which can be received when purchasing the low-cost and high-cost products, as discussed earlier.

In the UK, the range of outcomes for the individual biographies is very broad, which indicates a high uncertainty regarding future living standards.

Table 11.2: Overview of assumed supplementary personal pensions

Sector	Scheme type	Employee	Employer
		Contribution	Contribution
Germany			
All	Riester-Contract	4%	–
UK			
All	Opted-Out Approved Personal Pension	National Insurance Opting-Out Rebate + 10%	–
All	Opted-In Individual Personal Pension	10%	–
All	Opted-In Stakeholder Pension	10%	
Manufacturing	Opted-In Group Personal Pension	4%	6%
Retail	Opted-In Group Personal Pension	4%	4.50%
Finance	Opted-In Money Purchase	4%	6%
Public Adm., Education, Health	Opted-In Group Personal Pension	4%	6%

[15] This rate also represents the middle range between 1 and 18%, which the DWP proposed to provide adequate retirement income, depending on the actual income and the desired pension level (DWP 2002: 28). See also the discussion of the Pensions Commission (2004: Chapter 4).

[16] For the different cases the relevant regulations regarding the conversion from assets to monthly pensions were applied, i.e. the same mortality rates for both sexes for opted-out personal pensions and different mortality rates in case of opting in.

Personal pensions for both low and middle female earners fail to close the savings gap to the social inclusion threshold, meaning that respective retirement incomes will expose these women to the risk of poverty. Moreover, low-paid women receive the lowest income when they opt out, irrespective of the personal pension products they might choose. The female biography with 1.5 times average remuneration might be able to bridge the savings gap, but this depends on her choice of personal pension scheme. With individually purchased, high-cost products, whether contracted-in or contracted-out, her income will fall below the social inclusion line. In contrast, the workplace-related group pension plans and low-cost products lift her above the threshold. The male low earner's pension income also approaches the social inclusion line only if a low-cost contracted-out personal pension product has been chosen and additional contributions of 10 per cent made. Only male average and high earners bridge the savings gap with the help of personal pensions. Both benefit from opting out of the State Second Pension and topping up their contracting-out rebate. Individual pension contracts, however, are clearly performing less well than occupational schemes (see also

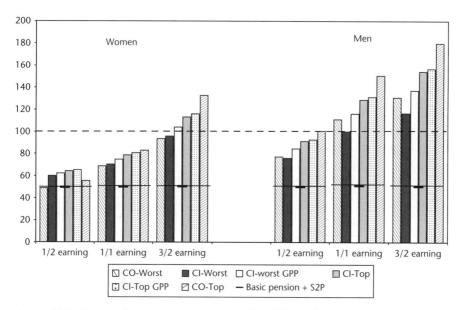

Figure 11.7: Range of pension outcomes in the UK (total pensions as % of social inclusion threshold).

Note: CO-Worst = worst contracted-out product; CI-Worst = worst contracted-in product; CI-Worst GPP = worst contracted-in Group Personal Pension; CI-Top = best contracted-in product; CI-Top GPP = best contracted-in Group Personal Pension; CO-Top = best contracted-out product.

(*Source*: Own calculations of public pensions and private pensions (based on Figure 11.5); Assumptions: inflation 1.9%; earnings growth 2% above inflation; rate of return before costs 5.9%).

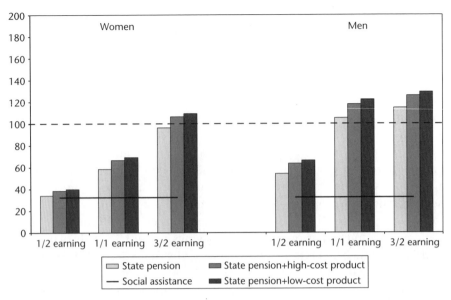

Figure 11.8: Range of pension outcomes in Germany (total pensions as % of social inclusion threshold).

(*Source:* Own calculations of public pensions and private pensions (based on Figure 11.5); Assumptions: inflation 1.9%; earnings growth 2% above inflation; rate of return before costs 5.9%).

Chapter 9 on this) and are creating a large gap between low and high outcomes, thus rendering retirement incomes highly uncertain.

In contrast to the UK, Germany sees a larger savings gap to the social inclusion line for lower earners, but no gap for average and higher-earning males. The state pension plays a major role for retirement income and provides more income-related benefits, thereby creating a much larger savings gap for low earners to the inclusion threshold than the UK state pension. Consequentially for lower-paid women with very low state pension benefits, a Riester-contract might merely help prevent them from having to claim social assistance. The range of pension outcomes from individual contracts is narrower than in the UK. Riester-contracts play a decisive role in surpassing the inclusion line only in the case of the highly remunerated female biography. Riester-pensions, however, increase old-age income for male average earners in particular. For high earners, the pension outcomes seem surprisingly low compared to the average earner. Indeed, the state pension and the subsidies to personal pensions are subject to contribution limits, leaving part of his income without insurance coverage. Particularly the restrictions up to which contributions to Riester-contracts could receive tax relief produce a lower portion of personal pensions in the overall income package compared to the average earner.

11.5 Conclusions

The aim of this chapter was to show whether personal pensions in Germany and the UK are able to close the savings gap between state pension benefits and social inclusion lines set at 40 per cent of the average national gross income. It was assumed that incentives provided for citizens and the interaction of market regulation with the profit-making interest of financial market intermediaries will shape the take-up and performance of personal pension products. Our analyses of the creation of the personal pensions market, the development of regulations as well as the simulations of old-age income from a range of pension products confirmed this assumption and showed that it is hard to balance objectives of social inclusion and profit-making interests in welfare markets. Moreover, it seems that governments need to deliver large incentives to encourage citizens to enter voluntary pension contracts.

Providing for old age by individual contracts seems to be appropriate for higher earners. For lower earners, additional social regulation is required to protect them from high charges, misguided investment decisions, and investment loss. In the UK, such regulation was introduced but proved to be incompatible with the profit-making interests of pension providers. As a result, lower earners became largely excluded from pension markets. For Germany, it is still too early to draw similar conclusions. However, as we have seen yet, the take-up rates differ between income groups, age, and gender in both countries.

Regulation of the welfare market proved to have an impact on the performance of personal pension products used for both the saving and dissaving phases. In the UK, strong regulations of the old-age savings products which were introduced in 2001 decreased the costs of such products for customers and reduced their risk of choosing a too-expensive product. In contrast, low regulation of the dissaving products which turn retirement funds into monthly income (annuities) results in a large variety of pension outcomes. In Germany, it is rather the opposite: lower regulation regarding the amount of charges and their transparency increases the range of outcomes from different saving products and thus the consumer's risk of choosing a high-cost product. Moreover, high protection against investment loss increases the costs of personal pension products compared to the UK. Higher regulation on how life insurances have to calculate annuities in the dissaving phase, however, decreases the range of outcomes compared to the German investment outcomes and also to the UK results.

Our simulations show that the social inclusiveness of pension systems as a whole, i.e. including personal pension contracts, must be questioned. Indeed, neither the British nor the German pension regime is able to prevent low-to-middle earners from the risk of living in poverty after retirement. Particularly for German low earners, the small state pension benefits leave too large a gap to the social inclusion threshold. For middle earners in both countries the choice of the 'right' pension product has a strong impact on their income levels in retirement. Particularly the UK pension regime is characterized by a high level of uncertainty. Since the pension market has increasingly excluded lower earners, social inequality must be expected to increase in the future. Although the German pension regime provides a higher level of predictability with respect to personal retirement income, it also incorporates more social inequality from the outset.

Part II
Welfare Policies

II. C. Employment and Unemployment

12

Higher education and graduate employment: the importance of occupational specificity in Germany and Britain

Kathrin Leuze

12.1 Introduction

European higher education is in transition. Ever since the launch of the so-called Bologna Process in 1999, almost all European countries have started to introduce major reforms within their higher education systems. In Bologna, twenty-nine European governments signed a declaration which aims at har-monizing the structures of higher education systems across Europe by the end of 2010. Among other things, participating countries have agreed to reform their degree structure by introducing short- and long-cycle degrees, such as BA and MA. This should facilitate the mobility of people, enhance the transpar-ency and the recognition of qualification and quality, and establish a Euro-pean dimension in higher education (CRE 2000; Keller 2003). The dynamic of this process is still ongoing, and its consequences for graduate careers are only starting to emerge. Scholars and politicians alike expect a convergence of graduate career prospects, since in the course of this process higher education credentials are supposed to be easily transferable across countries. Yet such a perspective fails to take into account the curricular content taught, for exam-ple, in various fields of study or types of degree courses. Higher education systems are likely to vary in the extent to which they offer curricula designed to prepare students for particular occupations or professions and to award occupation-specific credentials. Just like country-specific degree structures, the occupational specificity of higher education should influence how stu-dents are matched to jobs. Since the content of study is not in the scope of the Bologna Process, national path dependencies might prevail.

This chapter looks at the content of study as imparted by higher education institutions in general as well as by particular fields of study and types of degrees. It investigates cross-national variations of occupational specificity and their possible influence on the transition from higher education to work. Research on vocational education and training (VET) has already widely acknowledged that the transition process from VET to work is influenced by the existence of occupation-specific training systems. In particular, occupational specificity influences the extent to which young people who enter the labour market are subject to spells of unemployment, employment in specific entry-level occupations and industries, or prolonged periods of precarious employment (Shavit and Müller 1998; Kogan and Müller 2003; Müller and Gangl 2003). Germany and Britain differ strongly in their amount of occupational specialization conferred by VET systems and corresponding transition processes: the highly occupation-specific German system leads to rather smooth trajectories into the labour market, while the less occupation-specific British system results in more protracted transition phases (Hillmert 2001; Scherer 2001, 2005).

The importance of occupational specificity should matter for transition processes from higher education to work, too. There are already some empirical studies that point in this direction (see Kivinen and Nurmi 2003; Leuze 2007). For example, Kivinen and Nurmi (2003) illustrate that in some countries, various fields of study hardly differ from each other in terms of their professional orientation, while in others, the level of professionalism is clearly dependent on the field of study. These cross-national differences should have clear implications on graduate employment prospects. Therefore, this chapter discusses as a first step the concept of occupational specificity and its applicability to the analysis of the transition from higher education to work. Its main hypothesis states that a high degree of occupational specialization should lead to a close correspondence between higher education credentials and initial occupation. In order to generate more precise hypotheses about country-specific transition processes, the next section reviews the institutional organization of occupational specialization related to higher education institutions in general as well as to particular fields of study and types of degrees in Germany and Britain. These hypotheses are then tested empirically by estimating event history models on the basis of the German Socio-Economic Panel study (SOEP) and two British cohort studies (NCDS, BCS70).

12.2 Occupational specificity and the match between skills and jobs

The general theoretical problem of successfully assigning job seekers to jobs and thus of analysing the transition from higher education to work can be referred to as a matching problem. The economic job-matching theory (Jovanovic 1979; Sattinger 1993) stresses that a good labour market match is not only the result of an employee's adequate education and experience, but also depends on job characteristics and employer preferences. For a successful assignment, employer and job applicant have to make a positive decision: the employer to hire the applicant, the applicant to accept the job conditions. This microeconomic approach, however, cannot explain why in some countries, the assignment process works 'better' than in others. It neglects that decision-making processes not only depend on specific job requirements, preferences, and recourses of the actors involved, but also on the institutional environment, which affects the range and sequence of alternatives of the choice agenda (North 1990). Country-specific variations of the institutional settings will, accordingly, give rise to different matching processes.

For vocational education and training, a great deal of literature has already investigated the impact of various forms of education and labour market institutions on the matching process. Two basic types of institutional contexts can be distinguished (Maurice et al. 1986; Allmendinger 1989; Marsden 1990; Müller and Shavit 1998; Kerckhoff 2001): a more occupationalized one, where young people are predominantly trained within a standardized apprenticeship system and from thereon experience rather smooth trajectories into the labour market, and a more organization-based system, where universal and comprehensive education without an institutionalized vocational training leads to a more protracted labour-market integration marked by a sequence of stop-gap jobs and higher risks of unemployment. These institutionalized transition patterns are deemed to result from the occupational specificity of training systems, which is defined as the number of credentials designed for a specific occupation and the orientation of curricula towards the teaching of specific occupational knowledge (Müller and Shavit 1998; Kerckhoff 2001).

A close match between vocational training and occupation immediately after leaving education is only achieved in systems with a high degree of occupational specificity. In contrast, in systems with a stronger focus on general skills, the training for specific occupations does not take place within the education system itself but after entering the labour market. The theoretical argument holds that educational resources are not beneficial for individual career outcomes per se. Rather, the structure of education systems provides either general training, or, alternatively, more specific occupational training, which has an effect on the individual labour market entry via the different linkages established between educational and employment systems (Hannan et al. 1999; Gangl 2001, 2002; Rubery and Grimshaw 2003). The micro-mechanism associated with occupation-specific training is related to employers' relative reliance on formal qualifications vs labour market experience as reliable signals of individual skills during recruitment and allocation processes (Spence 1973). To the extent that educational credentials do little to convey job applicants' potential capabilities for a particular occupation, employers will be more likely to assess individual skills either from their past work records or from training on the job. In turn, if training systems provide qualifications that are meaningful indicators of skills for particular occupations, employers should be more likely to use this inexpensive signal of individual capabilities and hire job applicants on the basis of their credentials.

On the societal level, this dichotomy of institutional arrangements can be argued to stem from specific institutional complementarities between training systems and labour markets of different political economies. The notion of institutional complementarities is central to the 'Varieties of Capitalism' approach (Hall and Soskice 2001), according to which two institutions are said to be complementary if the presence (or efficiency) of one institutional sphere increases the returns from (or efficiency of) another (Hall and Soskice 2001: 17). Two different types of political economies with specific institutional complementarities between vocational training and labour market can be differentiated. Coordinated market economies (CMEs) arguably employ production strategies that are based on cooperation and trust, rely on a highly skilled labour force with substantial work autonomy, and consequently depend on a training system that provides workers with such skills. In CMEs, the matching problem is solved by a publicly subsidized vocational training system that is supervised and coordinated by industry-wide employer associations and trade unions, which ensure both that the training fits the firms' skill requirements and that freeriding on the training of others is limited. Countries typically described as CMEs include Austria, Belgium, Denmark, Finland, Germany, Japan, the Netherlands, Switzerland, and Sweden. By contrast, liberal market economies (LMEs) are largely shaped by market competition. Due to highly fluid labour markets with high job turnover, firms are reluctant to invest in apprenticeship schemes training them with occupation-specific skills where they have no guarantee that other firms will not simply poach their apprentices without training any themselves. No standardized vocational training system exists; rather, individuals are encouraged to invest in general skills transferable across firms and industries. Examples of LMEs include Australia, Britain, Canada, New Zealand, and the United States.

Even though Hall and Soskice do not consider individual transition from education to work and their relation to Varieties of Capitalism, it can be hypothesized that country-specific transition regimes are the result of institutional complementarities between education and work. When applying this argument to higher education, it leads to the conclusion that different political economies should vary in the degree to which they offer more or less occupation-specific higher education, too.[1] However, conceptualizing occupational specificity at higher education level requires some adaptation, since no clear-cut occupation-specific entity such as apprenticeship exists. Probably the most important factor for determining the occupational specificity of a country's higher education system is the analysis of different fields of study, which can be directly examined in relation to the occupation-specific content taught and the applicability of knowledge for the labour market. Occupational specificity can also be indicated by the incorporation of practical training phases in particular fields of study or types of degrees or by the extent to which they are the necessary prerequisites for work in particular occupations. In addition, the institutional ideas underpinning higher education in general can be considered important empirical indicators of occupational specificity.

In the following, these dimensions are analysed for Germany and Britain. As a starting point, the historical ideas of higher education in both countries are described, already indicating how different the links between higher education and labour markets are in these two countries. After that, the importance given today to occupational specialization in the German and British higher education system is analysed. Special attention is paid to the applicability of knowledge taught, the incorporation of practical training in particular fields of study or types of degrees courses, and the extent to which they are necessary prerequisites for work in particular occupations.

12.2.1 *Historical roots of higher education in Germany and Britain*

German and British higher education systems follow very different historical traditions regarding the applicability of knowledge for labour market purposes and the training of occupation-specific skills. The ideas associated with higher education in both countries can be traced back to the very beginnings of university establishment in Europe in the twelfth and thirteenth century. At this time the first two universities in Europe were founded in Bologna and Paris. These new types of education institutions offered certificates and credentials and thus offered the first form of organized higher education. However, the focus of both universities could not have been more diverse: while the University of Bologna specialized in the education of law and to a lesser extent in medicine and, as such, in professional knowledge, the University of Paris had a focus on general education by specializing in courses of theology and the artes liberales, such as philosophy, logic, or astronomy (Leff 1993;

---

[1] This assumption is discussed controversially in the literature. When compared directly to vocational training, higher education is often perceived as conferring only general skills and therefore national variations of occupational specificity are considered low (see Estevez-Abe et al. 2001; Estevez-Abe 2005, 2006). However, it is also very likely that on the level of higher education, countries place different emphases on particular types of skills.

Verger 1993; Moraw 2005). After the foundation of these first two universities, other regions in Europe started to adopt this principle of formal higher education through universities. In England, the first universities, Oxford and Cambridge, were founded soon after Paris and Bologna. Both universities evolved as private bodies during the thirteenth century and followed the French tradition of liberal education by focusing on theology, philosophy, and arts to prepare students for careers in either the Church or, to a much lower extent, in public administration (Moraw 1993; Verger 1993). Rather than preparing their students for particular professions, the general education of clergy and gentry was the most prominent idea behind these early forms of higher education in Britain (Moraw 1993). The predominance of such a liberal education at the undergraduate level and the importance of personal development rather than professional education remains a distinct feature of higher education in Britain today. Professional training has remained outside of the British university system for a long time, even though a small minority of institutions, such as the Inns of Court (law) and Royal Colleges of Medicine and Surgery, became increasingly important as providers of professional training and regulation of competence already in medieval times. Over the centuries, governments promoted the teaching of science, technology, and advanced vocational training at universities, and occasionally even offered financial aid for their development. Nevertheless professional training remained mainly a private enterprise. It was not until the nineteenth century that major public universities were founded in England, Wales, and Northern Ireland, which included the more applied disciplines in their curricula (Smith 1999).[2]

Later than in Britain, the foundation of university institutions in Germany started during the fourteenth century. Erfurt was the first university to be founded on what is today German territory, in 1379 (Verger 1993). Different to the established traditions, the principle combined both types of university which existed at the time, the more professionally orientated and the more liberal one in a single higher education institution (Moraw 2005). For the subsequent centuries, four faculties prevailed at German universities: theology, law, medicine, and the liberal arts. Due to the incorporation of both traditions, the aim of higher education was twofold: to educate administrative

---

[2] University education in Scotland also has a long, but nevertheless different history. Four universities—St Andrews, Glasgow, Aberdeen, and Edinburgh—were founded in the 15th and 16th centuries. From the beginning, all placed more emphasis on applied subjects than their English counterparts and stressed the importance of professional training, mainly to offer an alternative to the traditional universities of Oxford and Cambridge. Most of today's Scottish higher education institutions tend to specialize in particular areas, for example in teacher training, art and architecture, or health care. In addition, they offer a broad range of vocationally orientated fields of study at all levels.

personnel for the state and society, and to foster students' personal development. Based on this dualism, the student body at German universities consisted of two separate groups, each of which exhibited specific preferences for subject areas and thus labour market outcomes. Students born in nobility predominantly concentrated on professionally orientated subjects such as law or medicine and thereafter pursued careers either in the upper levels of public administration or as doctors. Students from the lower or middle strata of the middle classes (Bürgertum) tended to study liberal arts and, after completing university, generally returned to their home region without any explicit career prospects. Consequently, many worked in their fathers' crafts, as clergy for the Church, or as writers in regional administrations (Moraw 1993).

Comparing the university development in Britain and Germany from its very beginning, history shows that both countries (or the regions that later became those countries) followed quite distinct paths of higher education. For centuries, professional training in England was not at all connected to university education, while it formed an integral part of German universities from the very beginning. Both traditions of university education still exist today, and both influence the incorporation of occupation-specific training in higher education, as will be shown in the next section.

12.2.2 *Occupational specificity of higher education institutions in Germany and Britain*

Comparing contemporary versions of higher education, German institutions place a much stronger emphasis on professional education and applied knowledge, while their British counterparts continue to advocate the principle of a liberal education with a focus on more general skills, particularly at the undergraduate level. According to the German Framework Act for Higher Education, a degree course at both universities and technical colleges (the so-called Fachhochschulen) has to 'prepare for occupational tasks that require the application of scientific and methodological knowledge or the ability of artistic practice' (BMBF 2002: §1, own translation). In addition, the legislative framework requires that 'teaching and studying trains students for a particular field of occupation and teaches specific knowledge, skills and methods of the respective degree course, in order to enable students to perform scientific or artistic work and to act responsibly in a free, democratic and social state governed by the rule of law' (BMBF 2002: §7, own translation).[3] Thus, training

---

[3] 'Sie [Die Hochschulen] bereiten auf berufliche Tätigkeiten vor, die die Anwendung wissenschaftlicher Erkenntnisse und wissenschaftlicher Methoden oder die Fähigkeit zu künstlerischer Gestaltung erfordern' (BMBF 2002 §1). 'Lehre und Studium sollen die Studierenden auf ein berufliches Tätigkeitsfeld vorbereiten und ihnen die dafür erforderlichen fachlichen Kenntnisse, Fähigkeiten und Methoden dem jeweiligen Studiengang entsprechend so vermitteln,

for particular occupations or professions is an integral element at any German higher education institution.

Universities and Fachhochschulen confer professional qualifications based on examinations, even though the former are traditionally more closely linked to basic and theoretical research than to teaching applied knowledge. At universities, professional training for public-sector employment is closely connected with a specific degree, the state examination (Staatsexamen), as well as with particular fields of study. The term 'state examination' implies a preparation of students for professions of public importance, such as medicine, dentistry, veterinary medicine, pharmaceutics, food chemistry, law, and the teaching profession (Eurydice 2006). An essential difference between the state examination and other academic degrees taught at universities is the incorporation of practical training. Passing the first state examination (Erstes Staatsexamen), which takes place after the theoretical part of a degree course, entitles students to work in the private sector only. Prospective public professionals, however, undergo an additional phase of practical training called preparatory service (Vorbereitungsdienst), which is concluded by a second state examination (Zweites Staatsexamen). Only this second examination entitles graduates to practise a particular profession within the public service.

However, academic university degrees (the so-called Diplom and Magister) also provide several options for occupation-specific training. For example, a number of qualifications, especially in natural and engineering sciences, require proof of work experience (from four to six months, in some cases even up to a year) acquired prior to or during participation in higher education. Many universities offer measures designed to prepare for self-employment and encourage students to set up their own businesses. For humanities students, whose field of study is considered less a preparation for a specific occupation and is more general in nature, many universities have set up programmes in collaboration with employment offices, equipping students with key skills in order to improve their employment prospects (for example, in computing or elementary business skills) and to place them in industry jobs thereafter (Eurydice 2006).

The importance of occupational specificity is even more pronounced at Fachhochschulen. Emphasis on the practical applicability of knowledge as well as specific reference to labour market requirements are characteristic features of the design of degree courses as well as the organization of teaching and studying at this type of higher education. The purpose of occupation-specific training is served chiefly by incorporating one or two semesters of practical training within a business enterprise into every degree course

dass sie zu wissenschaftlicher oder künstlerischer Arbeit und zu verantwortlichem Handeln in einem freiheitlichen, demokratischen und sozialen Rechtsstaat befähigt werden' (BMBF 2002 §7).

(Praxissemester). Furthermore, it is common for students to select dissertation topics based on problems that have been encountered during these training semesters. Some dissertations are even prepared in collaboration with industry and trade. All these measures help students to gain applied knowledge and insights into their field of specialization and to establish contacts with prospective employers before graduating. Taken together, measures offered at universities and Fachhochschulen indicate a high importance of occupation-specific training within German higher education. Although there are differences between universities and Fachhochschulen as to their extent and scope, the overall focus of both institutions points in the direction of the applicability of knowledge and close links to the labour market. As a consequence, German higher education can be characterized by a high degree of occupational specificity.

In Britain, by contrast, the concept of an education that provides training in abstract thought and values knowledge for its own sake has always formed part of the rationale for higher education. In the 1960s, the Robbins Report (1963) specified four aims for higher education: the instruction in skills suitable for the general division of labour; the promotion of general powers of the mind; the advancement of learning; and the transmission of a common culture and common standards of citizenship. Only the first aim was directly geared towards labour market requirements, while the other three emphasized general benefits both for personal development and for participation in society. Interestingly, hardly any of the White Papers and higher education acts over the past decades mentioned the need to train British students for particular occupations. Instead, they tended to respond to problems of mass higher education in relation to the organization of universities, the funding of students, or quality control.

The fact that liberal education and personal development have remained important principles up until today can also be seen in the Dearing Report (Dearing Report 1997) and in the Green Paper 'The Learning Age' (DfEE 1998), in which the British Government sets out its strategy for lifelong learning. The Dearing Report again stressed the intellectual and cultural purposes of higher education and stated that higher education should aim to sustain a learning society through the intellectual development of individuals. Higher education should increase individuals' knowledge and understanding both for their own sake and for the benefit of the economy and society. The Government's Green Paper (1998) argued in a similar fashion, advocating as a major principle that anyone who has the capability of participating in higher education should have the opportunity to benefit from it. Current objectives for higher education stress increasing and widening participation and improving standards and quality of teaching and learning (DfEE 1998).

However, despite the continuing emphasis on general knowledge and personal development rather than occupation-specific skills, labour market requirements have gained more relevance within British higher education in recent decades. A first step in the 1960s was the introduction of polytechnics with the aim of advancing industrial skills and of connecting higher education to industry and businesses (DES 1966). But particularly since the 1980s, occupational aspects have become more relevant in higher education policy making. A Government Green Paper from 1985 stated that the design and content of courses should become more occupation-orientated by means of advice sought from employers (DfE 1985). Many higher education institutions and polytechnics in particular responded by redesigning courses to take into account employers' needs. More occupational courses were introduced and the curriculum for more general courses was adapted to cover key skills such as information and communication technology. Statistics show that in 1994, occupation-specific training was the fastest growing area within British higher education (DfE 1994). The Dearing Report also recognized the part played by higher education in preparing students for work and recommended that institutions should seek to increase work experience for students (Dearing Report 1997).

Nowadays, universities generally provide a range of professionally accredited degree courses including engineering, accountancy, teacher training, librarianship and information science, and medical studies. In particular, some postgraduate degrees teach applied knowledge for professional life (for example, LLM programmes for lawyers or MSc programmes for engineers). However, qualifications specific to a profession and required for practising as a chartered member of a professional association still have to be obtained after completion of a postgraduate degree, often through successfully passing further examinations set or accredited by professional bodies, such as the Chartered Institute of Public Finance and Accountancy and the Council of Legal Education. Today, sandwich courses, which incorporate periods of practical work in organizations outside the university or college into their study programme, are a main means for students for combining coursework with work experience, but many higher education institutions also offer opportunities to gain work experience as part of a degree course. In addition, many employers regularly visit higher education institutions to give students the opportunity to discuss possibilities for employment. The 'new' universities, most of which are previous polytechnics, generally offer a wider range of courses leading to qualifications recognized by professional institutions.

Funding for research and development projects in order to improve graduate employability has been provided by the Higher Education Quality and Employability Division of the Department for Education and Employment (DfEE). Particularly, the reforms introduced by the Labour government signalled a significant shift in the aims and functions of higher education. In the 2003 White Paper and the resulting Higher Education Bill (2004), the Blair Government repeatedly stressed the need to improve national economic competitiveness by tightening the connection between higher education, employment, productivity, and trade, and to enhance student acquisition in employment-related skills and competencies (DfES 2003, 2004). In short, the British development is twofold. Even though legislation on higher education continues to stress the importance of general skills and personal development, the necessity to respond to labour market needs has become more apparent, particularly during the 1990s. Nevertheless, the long historical tradition of liberal higher education is still in place, resulting in a less occupationally specific system than in Germany.

12.2.3 Hypotheses

Higher education in Germany shows a clear occupational orientation which is prevalent not only at Fachhochschulen, aimed explicitly at the preparation for occupations, but also at universities, where courses tend to be linked to future professions, and the connection between fields of study and occupations are generally strong. The British higher education system historically lacks such a tight coupling between specific degree courses and occupations and focuses more strongly on general skills without a clear orientation towards the needs of the labour market. Even though connections between higher education and work have become tighter in recent years in Britain, the occupational specificity of the British system in general is still lower than in the German system. Therefore, the match between higher education credentials and occupations should be higher in Germany than in Britain (H1).

Regarding the occupational specialization of fields of study, it has been shown that in both countries, professional fields of study such as health, teaching, or law, and also engineering, exhibit a high degree of occupational specialization, be it due to the incorporation of practical training phases into the respective degree courses or because these courses form the necessary prerequisite for entry into particular professions. Other fields of study such as humanities or arts lack such practical preparations for particular occupations. As a consequence, the practically orientated fields of study like medicine, teaching, law, or engineering should be more closely associated with matching employment positions than humanities or arts in both countries (H2.1). However, the historical divide between occupation-specific and more general higher education at German institutions might still be relevant today and, if so, is likely to result in stronger within-country variation by fields of study than in Britain (H2.2).

The analysis of different types of higher education degrees in both countries has demonstrated that in Germany, the degrees Staatsexamen and Fachhochschul-Diplom are designed as a preparation for specific occupations, which is less the case for the university degrees Diplom or Magister. This should result in better matches between credentials and occupations for the former two types of degrees when compared to the latter (H3.1). Also in Britain, some postgraduate degrees such as the Masters degree (MA) and postgraduate certificates are designed to prepare for specific occupations. Therefore, obtaining a job in an occupation matching the higher education credential should be more common with postgraduate than with undergraduate degrees (H3.2).

12.3 Data, method, and variables

The empirical analysis of the transition from higher education to work is carried out with the German Socioeconomic Panel (SOEP) and two British cohort studies, the National Child Development Study (NCDS) and the 1970 British Cohort Study (BCS70). The SOEP is a longitudinal survey of private households in Germany (for details, see Haisken-DeNew and Frick 2005). It is conducted as a panel survey and includes a large variety of information on labour market positions, educational attainment, attitudes, and family status. This analysis takes account of all respondents with a higher education degree who graduated in the years 1984–2000 while surveyed by the SOEP. A total number of 878 graduates were included in the empirical investigations.

Data for Britain are drawn from the cohort studies NCDS and BCS70, both of which are providing contemporaneous information on educational achievement and family circumstances during childhood and adolescence, as well as detailed information on early labour market careers and mobility developments (for details, see Bynner et al. 2001). The NCDS is a panel study of all children born in the first week of March 1958. For the analysis at hand, data from sweep 3 to 5 are being used. The BCS70 began in 1970, when data were collected about children born the week 5–11 April of the same year. For the current analysis, sweeps 4 and 5 are employed. In order to achieve a period of labour market entry that is comparable with the German data-set, both cohort studies were pooled. The final data-set covers 3540 graduates completing higher education between 1979 and 1997. (A description of the variable distribution in both data-sets can be found in Table 12.3 at the end of the chapter.)

The transition from higher education to work is a process that does not take place at a specific point of time but develops over a time period. Therefore, the first five years after graduation are examined in both countries. The modelling

Table 12.1 Matching fields of study and occupations

Field of study	Matching ISCO-88 codes
Education	230, 231–5, 330, 331–4
Humanities/Arts	230, 231, 232, 243, 245, 246, 347, 348
Social Sciences (Soc. Sc.) Business, Law	110, 111, 121–3, 130, 131, 230–2, 241, 242, 244, 247, 341–4, 346
Sciences, Agriculture	211, 212, 221, 230–2, 315, 321
Engineering	213, 214, 311–15
Health/Welfare	222, 223, 322, 323

of matching students to jobs mainly focuses on the relationship between fields of study and occupations obtained after graduation. To determine the fit between field of study and occupation, fields of study are matched to three-digit ISCO 88 coded occupations (see Table 12.1). An occupation-specific job match is defined as congruence between field of study and the first occupation held after graduation (see Dekker et al. 2002; Maarten 2003 for similar operationalizations). In this way, it is possible to construct a measure for how well education and labour market structures correspond with each other on the basis of educational and professional classifications. The basic criterion for assigning occupational codes to a field of study is the assumed congruence of skills acquired through the field of study and those needed in the occupation. For example: the field of study 'Sciences' matches the occupations of physicists, chemists, mathematicians, and statisticians (ISCO codes 211 and 212); the field of study 'Health/Welfare' matches the occupations health professionals (ISCO code 222), but also nursing and midwifery professionals (ISCO code 223), since both are taught at British universities. Table 12.1 summarizes the ISCO 88 occupations that match a particular fields of study.

To investigate how higher education systems in both countries influence the match between higher education credentials and occupation, the influence of fields of study and types of higher education degrees are analysed as main explanatory variables. Fields of study are coded in six categories of the higher education subject in both countries, closely representing the classification used in OECD publications (OECD 2004): Education; Humanities and Arts (including Services); Social Sciences, Business, and Law; Sciences (including Agriculture); Engineering, Manufacturing, and Construction; Health and Welfare. To measure the higher education degrees, the CASMIN educational classification is applied. For the British case, the more refined CASMIN levels of general lower-level tertiary degrees (3a_gen = Diploma, Certificate of Higher Education), first degree qualifications (3b_low = BA, BSc) and postgraduate degree qualifications (3b_high = MA, MSc, MBA, Postgraduate Certificate) are used. Since the German higher education system was less differentiated during the period of observation, the basic CASMIN levels of lower tertiary education

(3a = Fachhochschul-degree) and upper tertiary education (3b = Diplom, Magister, Staatsexamen) are taken into account. A further differentiation between different types of university degrees, which cannot be captured by the CASMIN scheme, was implemented as well: the difference between academic (Diplom, Magister) and state (Staatsexamen) examinations.

Control variables on the micro-level consist of general demographic indicators such as gender, having children aged 6 years and younger, socio-economic status of the father, and nationality/ethnicity.[4] Furthermore, additional vocational training and the age of graduation are taken into account. To differentiate between different types of higher education institutions, university institutions are contrasted with non-university institutions, namely Fachhochschulen and polytechnics.[5] To control for changing labour market situations, the yearly unemployment rate and the yearly rate of the GDP of each country is included. Also, an indicator measuring varying degrees of higher education expansion, the so-called age participation rate (APR),[6] as well as the size of the birth cohort are included.

The analysis of the transition from higher education to work is carried out by means of event history analysis (Allison 1984; Blossfeld and Rohwer 1995; Jenkins 2004).[7] With this modelling strategy, all relevant changes of the condition during a time period as well as the timing of events can be considered. This is particularly important for analysing career trajectories, since not only the quality of the matching process matters, but also the time it takes to obtain such a matching job. The central concept for describing the timing and duration of transition processes with event history analysis is the hazard rate. According to Allison (1984), the hazard rate describes 'the probability that an event will occur at a particular time to a particular individual, given that the

[4] Due to data restrictions and missing values, the parental socioeconomic background as well as ethnicity had to be coded differently for both countries. While in Germany the parental socioeconomic status is measured by parental educational attainment, namely whether the father possesses a higher degree or not at age 15 of the respondent, in Britain the parental background measures whether the father is occupied in EGP class I or II at age 16 of the respondent. Ethnicity in Germany is coded as German vs Non-German, while ethnicity in Britain is coded as White vs Non-white. Although these variables measure different socio-structural aspects in both countries and are thus of limited use for direct comparison, they have been included in order to account for within-country variation.

[5] The British data-sets allow the identification of former polytechnics even after the reforms of 1992, when most became officially recognized as universities.

[6] Again, due to data restrictions, this indicator is not strictly comparable across the two countries. The British APR is defined as the number of home-domiciled initial entrants to full-time and sandwich undergraduate higher education aged under 21, expressed as a percentage of the average number of 18- and 19-year-olds in the population. For Germany, the number of higher education students enrolled in German higher education institutions is reported as a percentage of all Germans who are 20 to 30 years old.

[7] By means of event history analysis (also referred to as survival analysis), it can be examined how the probability that an event occurs progresses longitudinally, i.e. over time, and furthermore, how this probability varies according to relevant covariates.

individual is at risk at that time' (Allison 1984: 16). In the following analysis, the hazard rate refers to the probability of obtaining a first occupation matching the field of study within a particular month after graduation for those who have not yet obtained a matching occupation.

As there is no single shape for the hazard function that is appropriate in all contexts, the analysis of event history data requires some model assumptions on how hazard rates vary over time. A model that does not impose too many restrictions on the shape of the hazard function and that furthermore has already proven its validity for studying education to work transitions is the piecewise constant exponential (PCE) model (Falk et al. 2000; Hillmert 2001). Its flexibility stems from the possibility of allowing hazard rates to vary between different time intervals (Allison 1984; Blossfeld and Rohwer 1995; Jenkins 2004). The bands of these time intervals are derived from the descriptive analysis of the survivor function. Estimations are based on logistic regression using STATA Version 10.0, which is a straightforward way to analyse discrete time data with piecewise duration dependence.

12.4 The match between field of study and occupation in Germany and Britain

In order to examine the importance of occupation-specific higher education for graduate employment, the transition to a first occupation matching the field of study is analysed. A rather straightforward representation of the time it takes to enter the labour market after graduation is provided by the survivor function, which indicates the share of persons that have not yet made the transition to a first matching job at any given point of time (Allison 1984; Blossfeld and Rohwer 1995; Jenkins 2004). The so-called failure function is the inverse of the survivor function, referring to the share of individuals that already have made a particular transition (or failure) at any time of observation. Since the analysis of the transition from higher education to work is more interested in the latter group, the failure function for various labour market outcomes is presented next. Figure 12.1 displays the Kaplan-Meier failure functions for obtaining an occupation matching the field of study in Germany and Britain.

As expected in hypothesis 1, the share of graduates obtaining a matching occupational is much higher in Germany than in Britain at any observation month. During the first year after graduation, almost 50 per cent of German graduates find a matching occupation, while only 30 per cent of their British counterparts manage to do so. Thereafter, transitions to matching employment level off in both countries. By the end of five years, almost 60 per cent of German graduates work in matching occupations, but only about one-third of

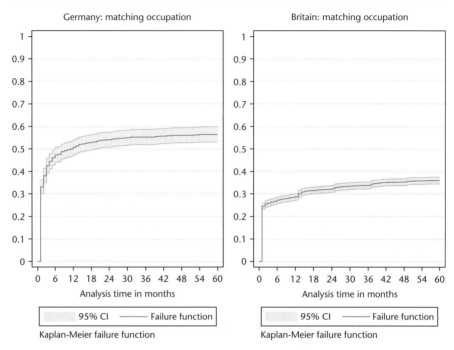

Figure 12.1: Transition to a first occupation matching the field of study.
(*Source*: SOEP and NCDS/BCS70).

graduates in Britain do so. These results indicate that higher education is more occupation-specific in Germany than in Britain, but they also show that intra-national variations exist, since a substantive share does not find matching employment during the first five years after graduation in both countries.

For a multivariate analysis of the transition to a first occupation matching the field of study, different fields of study and types of higher education degrees were taken into account in order to evaluate their impact on the matching process. Presented as odds ratios, with values larger than 1 indicating a positive relationship and values between 0 and 1 a negative relationship (see Table 12.2), some results were as expected beforehand, but others were somewhat surprising. Regarding fields of study, results indicate that graduates who studied professionally orientated fields of study, such as health, engineering, or social sciences, business, and law, have higher chances of obtaining a matching occupation immediately after graduation than humanities and arts graduates in both countries, which confirms hypothesis 2.1. In Germany, this is not surprising since these fields place a stronger emphasis on professional training already during higher education, include practical training more often into their degree courses, and are closely linked to particular occupations. Also in Britain, professional fields of study such as health and education, or engineering, are nowadays predominantly taught at higher education institutions, which obviously results in close matches between credentials and occupations. This interpretation is supported by the positive coefficient of the age participation rate, which signals that in the course of higher education expansion over the past two decades closer links with the labour market have been established in Britain.

However, contrary to the expectations of hypothesis 2.2, the larger variation of odds ratios between fields of study in Britain indicates that transition rates vary more strongly between fields of study than in Germany. Obviously, the German historical division between general and occupation-specific fields of study is less important nowadays for differentiating occupation-specific career prospects than the division in Britain, where recently, only some routes to employment have been established for particular fields of study, while others still lack such a connection to the labour market. This implies that the German system places more emphasis on occupation-specific training in general, while within-country differences are more strongly dependent on particular fields of study in Britain.

The results for graduates of science subjects in both countries, who have the lowest chances of obtaining occupations matching the field of study, are quite surprising. An explanation might be that scientists do not necessarily work in their occupational domain, but rather in managerial or administrative jobs. Studies on the transition from higher education to employment in managerial or professional occupations have shown that scientists in both countries have a relatively good chance of obtaining these types of jobs (Kim and Kim 2003; Leuze 2007).

Looking at the impact of different types of degrees, the results of Table 12.2 mainly display the predicted pattern. In Germany, students with a Staatsexamen have better chances, since their education involves a considerable degree of training for specific professions in the public service, which confirms hypothesis 3.1. Yet in contrast to this assumption, the finding that graduates holding Fachhochschul diplomas by no means have better chances than those with academic university degrees, even though Fachhochschulen place an even higher emphasis on occupational specialization than universities do, is quite surprising. The reason for this finding might lie in the fact that only some fields of study at universities offer bad chances for obtaining a matching job, not academic university degrees in general. In Britain, it is postgraduate degrees in particular which increase the chances of finding matching employment compared to holders of diplomas and certificates, which confirms hypothesis 3.2. This finding is in line with the earlier institutional analysis, where it was shown that most Masters degrees and also postgraduate certificates are strongly specialized and connected to particular occupations (see section 12.2.2). Interestingly, also British polytechnics do

Table 12.2: Obtaining an occupation matching the field of study after graduation

Transition to a first job in a matching occupation	Germany	Britain
Base line (Ref.: Entry in 1st month)		
Entry > 1 month	0.164 (0.023)[b]	0.030 (0.004)[b]
Entry > 3 months	0.074 (0.013)[b]	0.018 (0.003)[b]
Entry > 6 months	0.026 (0.005)[b]	0.011 (0.002)[b]
Entry > 12 months	0.015 (0.003)[b]	0.014 (0.001)[b]
Entry > 24 months	0.004 (0.001)[b]	0.005 (0.001)[b]
Field of study (Ref.: Science, Agriculture)		
Humanities, Arts	2.214 (0.563)[b]	1.632 (0.216)[b]
Engineering, Construction	3.169 (0.664)[b]	2.978 (0.410)[b]
Soc. Sc., Business, Law	3.047 (0.613)[b]	3.275 (0.389)[b]
Health, Welfare	4.072 (1.033)[b]	5.159 (0.741)[b]
Education	1.857 (0.502)[a]	7.006 (1.001)[b]
Type of degree (Ref.: Casmin 3b Diploma/Cert., *FH-Diplom*)		
Casmin 3a *(Diplom, Magister)*	1.114 (0.143)	
Casmin 3a *(Staatsexamen)*	1.479 (0.241)[a]	
Casmin 3a low (BA, BSc)		1.737 (0.206)[b]
Casmin 3a high (MA, postgrad. cert.)		3.218 (0.453)[b]
Control variables		
Female	0.859 (0.102)	0.941 (0.063)
Female with child 〈 6 years old	1.570 (0.421)	0.500 (0.094)[b]
Non-German/Non-white	0.394 (0.094)[b]	0.670 (0.115)[a]
Father with higher degree/upper class	0.942 (0.114)	1.071 (0.068)
Vocational education	0.918 (0.135)	0.861 (0.073)
Age of graduation (Ref.: 24–9 years)		
Younger than 24 years	0.899 (0.206)	1.198 (0.111)
Older than 29 years	0.809 (0.111)	0.528 (0.086)[b]
Graduation in East Germany	1.054 (0.151)	
University institution (Ref.: *FH*, polytechnic)	*1.197 (0.148)*[c]	1.024 (0.070)
Yearly unemployment rate (in %)	1.031 (0.052)	1.040 (0.017)[a]
Yearly GDP (in 1.000)	1.000 (0.000)	1.000 (0.001)
Size of birth cohort (in 1.000)	1.000 (0.000)	0.979 (0.007)[b]
Age participation rate (in %)	0.989 (0.095)	1.058 (0.016)[b]
No. of observations	20614	141944
No. of failures	455	1380
Log-likelihood null model	−1468.5101	−4851.3008
Log-likelihood end model	−1421.0827	−4704.6207
Likelihood ratio text Chi^2	94.85[b]	293.36[b]

Notes: Logistic regression odds ratios, standard errors in parentheses, [a] significant at 5%; [b] significant at 1%; [c] Coefficient stems from a separate model since those students hold *FH* diplomas graduated from *FH* institutions and therefore constitute the same group.

(Source: SOEP, NCDS/BCS70).

not improve the chances of finding matching employment compared with universities, even though they focus more strongly on transferring occupation-specific skills.

It is worth noticing that control variables do not play a major role in finding a matching occupation in either country. Most interestingly, no gender differences exist. This implies that the matching of credentials to jobs is a more gender-neutral process compared with acquiring high-status positions, for example. However, graduates from ethnic minorities have significantly lower transition rates in both countries. In Britain, females with young children and mature graduates are particularly disadvantaged. But apart from these findings, the transition to matching employment seems to depend mainly on variables related to the higher education system.

The descriptive and multivariate results together demonstrate that German graduates are more successful in finding an occupation matching their field of study after graduation than their British counterparts. German higher education institutions seem to prepare their students better for particular occupations and professions. This indicates that the overall idea of German higher education, namely to 'prepare for occupational tasks that require the application of scientific and methodological knowledge or the ability of artistic practice' (BMBF 2002: §1, own translation) is effective for students of all different kinds of higher education. In Britain, the legacy of the notion of higher education providing training in abstract thought and valuing knowledge for its own sake still appears to make it more difficult for graduates to obtain occupations which match their field of study, relative to Germany. However, variations between different fields of study are substantial in both countries, albeit more pronounced in Britain, where only some occupation-specific routes into employment have been established.

12.5 Conclusions

At the start of this chapter, it was assumed that higher education systems and, consequently, graduates' career prospects might converge within Europe as a consequence of the introduction of similar degree structures in the wake of the Bologna process. However, it was also noted that the content of study, which is not within the scope of the Bologna reforms, varies across European countries due to different values attached to occupation-specific training provided by higher education institutions. Comparative studies on vocational education and training systems have shown that only systems with a high degree of occupational specificity offer a close match between vocational training and occupation. By contrast, in countries which put more emphasis on general skills, the training for specific occupations tends to take place after entering the labour market, rather than in the education system. It was assumed that higher education systems might also vary in the extent to which they offer curricula that are designed to prepare students for particular occupations and award credentials that are occupationally specific. Such variation should lead to better or worse matches between higher education credentials and occupations entered after graduation.

On the whole, these assumptions were confirmed. Occupation-specific higher education has always been a prerequisite for entering particular occupations and professions in Germany. In Britain, occupational specialization has to a large extent always been organized outside higher education institutions. Different values attached to occupation-specific training and to applied knowledge lead, as expected, to a tighter match between higher education credentials and occupational outcomes in Germany. British graduates experience lower matches at the start of their careers. This suggests that the degree of occupational specificity related to higher education institutions follows a similar pattern as it does in the field of vocational education and training. There, the Varieties of Capitalism approach (Hall and Soskice 2001) has shown that coordinated market economies are rich in institutions that lock economic actors into long-term relationships, which make it possible for workers and employers to invest in specific skills. Liberal market economies lack such institutions and depend more strongly on market relations. The absence of such cooperative structures makes the acquisition of general skills more important and investment in specific skills more risky.

The analysis of this chapter points to the fact that the connection between higher education and labour markets might follow a similar logic. Germany, as an example of a coordinated market economy, relies more strongly on the supply of specific skills. In cooperation with professional associations and bodies, the state safeguards the provision of specific skills through the higher education system, mainly through particular fields of study and types of degrees. This is complemented by a graduate labour market strongly segmented along occupational lines, which results in a good match between higher education credentials and jobs. Britain, as an example of a liberal market economy, has a higher education system which more strongly focuses on the provision of general skills and on personal development rather than corresponding to labour market demands. The less occupation-specific training acquired by higher education graduates goes hand in hand with a graduate labour market that is less segmented along occupational lines. This makes the matching processes a more individual endeavour, less reliant on specific credentials and more dependent on discretionary employer recruitment and market processes. By and large, the observed occupational specificity of higher education corresponds to the overall logic of the respective 'variety of capitalism' in Germany and Britain. Just like in the area of vocational training, the German higher education system prepares graduates more effectively for particular occupations than is the case in Britain. Whether these cross-national variations in occupational specificity also have consequences for career outcomes other than the match between higher education credential and type of occupation, such as unemployment risks, job duration, or occupational mobility, could not be tackled in this chapter and is therefore left for further research.

Table 12.3: Description of German and British data-sets

	SOEP	NCDS/BSC70
Number of graduates	878	3805
Years of graduation	1984–2001	1979–97
Years of labour market careers	1984–2005	1979–2000
Sample NCDS	n.a.	43.44%
Females	40.66%	50.09%
Females with children under 6 years	2.05%	3.89%
Non-German (Ger)/Non-white (GB)	8.20%	4.26%
Father with higher education (Ger)/employment in EGP class I or II (GB)	26.65%	46.02%
Vocational training	19.93%	26.41%
Mean age of graduation (Std dev.)	28 (4.102)	24 (3.160)
Graduation in East Germany	17%	n.a.
University graduates	65.49%	55.77%
Casmin 3b (Dearing Report)	65.49%	17.08%
Diplom, Magister	46.36%	n.a.
Staatsexamen	19.13%	n.a.
Casmin 3b (low) (BA, BSc)	n.a.	71.67%
Casmin 3a (FH-Diplom, Diploma, Certificate)	34.51%	11.25%
Engineering	26.88%	11.14%
Science	14.46%	16.95%
Soc. Sc., Business, Law	34.05%	32.27%
Health, Welfare	7.86%	9.67%
Humanities, Arts	9.57%	20.05%
Education	7.18%	9.91%

In the end, cross-national differences in the relationship between higher education and labour markets will have to be closely monitored against the background of the Bologna Process, which aims to harmonize the structures of higher education systems across Europe. Such a perspective neglects, however, the existence of path dependencies in the relevance of occupation-specific skills and knowledge transferred by higher education systems. It indicates that national higher education reform projects initiated by the Bologna Process are likely to follow a tortuous route to convergence. This chapter has tried to gain a better understanding of some of the obstacles that stand in its way.

13

From unemployment programmes to 'work first': is German labour market policy becoming British?

Jochen Clasen

13.1 Introduction

Labour market policy is currently fairly high on the public policy agenda in most European countries. This has less to do with the rise in unemployment after 2008 and more with the steady growth of employment after the last but one economic crisis in the early 1990s and the turn towards 'activation' in some EU member states. Looking back further in the post-WWII history reveals that labour market policy, which often implies 'active' schemes such as training, work experience, or job creation programmes, has been pursued more vigorously at some times and much less at others. With Sweden as a forerunner in the 1950s, many other countries turned to training and other schemes in order to facilitate labour market restructuring and responding to labour supply shortages in the 1960s and early 1970s. In the wake of the first oil crisis in the early 1970s, politicians turned to employment programmes as a routine response to periodic employment problems and some so-called 'active' programmes became de-facto instruments of 'parking' people who, at least temporarily, seemed difficult to be reintegrated into jobs.

During the 1990s this trend slowly came to an end and the focus of labour market policy shifted once again, perhaps influenced by the OECD's Jobs Study (OECD 1994), and the organization's call for shifting resources from benefit provision to the 'active' use such as training and intensive job search support. It was noted that in countries in which unemployment declined gradually but steadily during the 1990s, labour market policies had been reformed considerably, making the right to unemployment support more conditional on job search efforts or willingness to participate in employment programmes, for example. Denmark, the Netherlands, but also the UK certainly belong to these countries which turned towards 'activation' earlier than many other EU member states (Clasen 2000). Not surprisingly, the idea of 'activation' became rather prominent also within the EU, which has promoted making benefit systems in member states more 'employment friendly' (European Commission 1997).

Thus, while there are fairly stable differences between countries with relatively high spending on labour market policies and those which devote much fewer resources, there have been shifts in the relative prevalence between different types of labour market policies over time, with certain programmes becoming more and then less prominent across many countries in a parallel fashion (see Bonoli 2011). Irrespective of these changes over time, British and German legacies in labour market policy more generally, i.e. comprising of unemployment benefit provision as well as active programmes, are certainly very different. Nevertheless, as the chapter will show, in some respects the gulf between the two countries was more pronounced two decades ago than it is now. Moreover, it was Germany which recently implemented some labour market programmes which were first introduced in the UK in the 1990s, while many German unemployed persons now receive social security provision which is more akin to 'British' transfer policies. In short, it might plausibly be argued that Germany followed the UK through a process of 'creeping convergence' (Mohr 2008). However, for persons with better-paid jobs who are out of the labour force for relatively short periods of time, crucial cross-national differences remain. The chapter concentrates on developments particularly during the past ten years, as this is the period during which the contours of current British labour market policy have become increasingly clear, while German labour market policy has been subjected to the most far-reaching reform since the late 1960s.[1]

13.2 Signs of convergence—problems of data?

Aggregate statistics on labour market policy in Germany and the UK suggest very different country profiles. Internationally comparable data going back to the 1980s indicate that Germany has always spent more than the UK on labour market policy as a whole, i.e. on benefits for the unemployed as well as active labour market programmes such as training, job creation, start-up grants, and

[1] For legislative change and policy developments during the 1980s and 1990s see Clasen (2005).

employment support services (Grubb and Puymoyen 2008; OECD 2010a). In fact, measured as a share of GDP, in the mid-1990s German spending was about seven times as high as British spending and this ratio was roughly the same in 2007 (OECD 2010a). However, during that period German unemployment was considerably higher than British, explaining part of the difference. Controlling for annual unemployment rates, British expenditure on unemployment benefits varied between a half and a third of German spending between the early 1990s and 2007 (Eurostat 2010), without any sign of convergence during the period. Similarly, spending on 'active' measures has always been higher in Germany than in the UK. Even after adjustment by unemployment, broad statistics indicate that in most years British spending was roughly half of that in Germany. Since the mid-2000s, however, there seems to have been some convergence, due to a decline in overall German and increase in British spending.

International databases indicate clear differences in benefit generosity too. The OECD's (OECD 2010b) 'summary' indicator of gross benefit rates in relation to average earnings (covering different earning levels, family situations, and lengths of unemployment) suggests a decline in the generosity of benefits received by both German and British unemployed persons between the mid-1980s and 2007. After a fairly stable rate for most of this period, the decline in Germany occurred only after 2003, when the 'replacement rate' dropped from 28 per cent to 24 per cent. The decrease in the UK, from 22 per cent to 14 per cent, was a more gradual one.

International data on both expenditure and benefit generosity should be treated with caution though and cannot be more than a starting point for a more careful and nuanced cross-national investigation. There are numerous problems of comparability in both broad categories. For example, the administrative definitions of 'unemployment' and 'employability', which are crucial for benefit entitlement, vary over time and across countries. As Erlinghagen and Knuth (2010) have shown, jobless persons of the same socioeconomic status are more likely to be drawing unemployment benefit in Germany than in the UK, where much of the problem of 'unemployment' has become manifest as labour market inactivity of persons drawing incapacity benefits (see also Konle-Seidl 2009). In other words, unemployment, as well as the receipt of unemployment benefit, should be seen in a wider context of labour market inactivity of working-age persons, supported by a range of other benefit programmes which differ in their prevalence across countries, such as sickness benefits, incapacity support, lone parent transfers, early retirement programmes, or social assistance. The OECD provides a useful overview of the profile and change over time of 'recipiency rates' in a number of western countries since the 1980s (OECD 2003), although these data themselves need to be treated with caution too (see De Deken and Clasen 2011).

A second methodological problem in respect of expenditure is the need to delineate what exactly 'unemployment benefits' entail. Clearly, including only unemployment insurance would be unduly narrow, since the majority of British unemployed benefit claimants are not in receipt of contributory-based but means-tested support. After recent reforms, the same applies to German job seekers (see below). This is why the OECD includes dedicated 'secondary' schemes such as unemployment assistance. However, if a comparison aims to value the level of cash support provided for unemployed persons, it could be argued that further benefits should be included. For example, largely because of the low level of unemployment transfers (Jobseekers Allowance, JSA) granted by the British government (currently equal to just above 10 per cent of average weekly earnings) most people out of work qualify for other means-tested benefits. Housing benefit in particular has become a source of income which is more important than JSA for many unemployed persons. In terms of public expenditure housing benefit transferred to persons of working age was almost twice as high as total JSA spending in the mid-2000s (Clasen 2009). In other words, if the aim is to assess overall public efforts in support of unemployed people, it might be more appropriate to compare 'benefit packages' across countries rather than unemployment benefits in a narrow sense.

Also the concept of 'active' labour market policy and its empirical manifestation in expenditure and participant numbers at international level needs to be treated with caution for several reasons. First, the term covers a range of very diverse programmes, ranging from job search assistance, training schemes, work experience, monetary incentives to enter employment, grants for setting up a business, to direct job creation. All of these and other programmes might involve choices or are mandatory for job seekers in order to maintain benefit eligibility. Depending on their quality and fit with individual as well as labour market needs, they might enhance human capital development or act as 'work test'.

Second, there are programmes which act as functional equivalents but are unlikely to be captured in this way in international data. For example, particularly as a response to the recent economic crisis (Möller 2010), many German employees receive a wage as well as a 'short-term working allowance', which is treated as an active labour market programme since it helps to keep people in work. Other persons claim unemployment assistance even though they are actually in paid employment (see Clasen and Goerne 2011a), combining income from part-time work with the receipt of unemployment benefit. Whereas the former are not counted as unemployed, most of the latter are. In the United Kingdom, persons in the same position, i.e. working in low pay or part-time employment, would not be claiming unemployment benefit but many would receive tax credits as a form of wage subsidy. They would not be counted as unemployed but as employed, and tax credits received would not be part of British spending on labour market policy. In short, aggregate expenditure data on active labour market programmes do not provide the full picture of the actual efforts countries make in order to facilitate people remaining in or entering paid employment.

Irrespective of these concerns, international data suggest that there has been some change within national profiles of labour market policy (see also Bonoli 2011). For example, OECD (2010a) statistics underline the growing emphasis on spending on 'public employment services and administration' for both countries. This category includes job placement support and other activities aimed at labour market integration during the early phase of unemployment, such as work-orientated interviews and short courses. As a share of total spending, this 'work first' component had become the dominant category within British active labour market already during the 1990s (Lindsay 2007), clearly outstripping training and job creation measures (Clasen 2005). In Germany, the latter policies are still much more prominent than in the UK, but a similar decline set in at the start of the 2000s and continued in subsequent years. Recent OECD (2010a) data reflect the erosion of job creation and the decline of training within German labour market policy (see also Ebbinghaus and Eichhorst 2009; Oschmiansky and Ebach 2009).

In short, broad international data on labour market policy need to be treated with caution for cross-national comparisons since they can be less easily applicable than they might appear. Nevertheless, if anything they indicate two trends since the 1990s. First, differences in terms of overall spending on labour market policy between the UK and Germany have remained marked, despite a recent decline in Germany. Second, looking into the composition of active programmes, there has been a shift towards a 'work first' orientation within the repertoire of labour market policy in both countries, with Germany following a trend which started earlier in the UK.

13.3 Institutional convergence?

Assessing the question of convergence from a more nuanced perspective involves a closer look at the institutional setting of labour market policy. This section thus provides a brief characterization of the structure of benefit and employment support as they existed in the late 1990s and contrasts those structures with current arrangements. In order words, the aim here is to capture change both within as well as across the two countries in a somewhat broad approach. Elsewhere I have contrasted the structures of unemployment support in both countries in more detail (Clasen 2005) and more recent publications (e.g. Eichhorst et al. 2008; Finn and Schulte 2008; Clasen 2009; Ebbinghaus and Eichhorst 2009) have covered developments and structures since the early 2000s, thus allowing a merely cursory discussion at this point with a view to emphasizing key differences as well as similarities between the two countries.

13.3.1 *The United Kingdom*

The provision of benefits for unemployed people in the UK has not changed dramatically since the 1990s. Ever since 1996 it has consisted of two separate benefit types: contributory-based Jobseekers Allowance (CB JSA) and means-tested (officially 'income-based') JSA. As an insurance benefit, contributory JSA is technically separate from non-contributory transfers. It is paid out of the National Insurance Fund (NIF), which is the common source for all contributory benefits, with state pensions representing by far the greatest single item. The NIF is financed by mandatory payroll contributions levied on employees and employers. Central government has full control over the Fund which effectively serves, and is generally perceived as, another form of revenue and expenditure alongside general taxation. The British government is not impeded by institutional obstacles which would prevent raising contributions to the fund for purposes other than insurance-based spending.

Contributions to the NIF are proportional to earnings, and benefits were partially wage-related between the mid-1960s and the early 1980s, but have since reverted to modest flat-rate support. Nevertheless, contributed support was still fairly prevalent in the early 1980s, with up to half of all unemployed persons claiming insurance-based benefits. Since then there has been a growing emphasis on targeted (means-tested) support, particularly for working-age claimants. Unlike in Germany, the benefit levels provided by the first (CB JSA) and the second tier (IB JSA) have never diverged much. In fact, they have been identical for many years now. Indexed in line with inflation, its relative value in relation to average full-time adult earnings dropped from about 14 per cent in 1990 to 11 per cent of average earnings in 2009.

Policies during the 1990s made eligibility requirements stricter and reduced the maximum benefit entitlement, thereby accelerating the ongoing decline of contributory benefit support during unemployment (Clasen 2009). Today, only about 20 per cent of all unemployed benefit claimants are in receipt of this type of transfer. Due to the modest rates it is common for recipients of unemployment benefits, and particularly those with a non-working partner or dependants, to be claiming additional benefits. Indeed, the receipt of income-based JSA automatically qualifies for a range of other means-tested transfers, such as free school meals for children, free prescriptions, and exemptions from other health costs and from paying a local tax (council tax benefit). It also entitles JSA claimants to the receipt of the maximum level of housing benefit.

Under the JSA regime benefit claimants are to sign Jobseekers agreements and JSA officials are permitted to issue 'Jobseekers Directions', i.e. requiring individuals to take certain steps to 'improve their employability'. The definition of 'actively seeking work' was also tightened under the JSA regime and more frequent compulsory interviews introduced (Clasen 2009: 76). At different stages different labour market schemes may become compulsory and different types of help available under the 'New Deal' programmes which were introduced by the Labour government after 1998. Thus, after a certain period of unemployment, claimants are transferred to a number of alternatives to benefit receipt, such as training, education, or temporary employment. Having undergone a number of revisions since the late 1990s, the so-called 'Flexible New Deal' was introduced in 2009, which replaced the differential treatments for under-and over-25-year-olds with a more standardized but also 'personalized' support. It involves the transfer of the responsibility for unemployed job seekers from the public employment service (Jobcentre Plus) to public, voluntary, or private providers who are paid by results with bonuses for early labour market integration of claimants. Claimants enter contracts with their providers (personal action plans). Aimed at securing employment, these plans include mandatory work-related activities. Since 2010, long-term JSA claimants (over twenty-four months, or earlier in some pilot areas at the discretion of advisers) have been required to enter a 'work for your benefit' phase of up to six months of full-time employment aimed at improving skills and 'work habits' in return for benefit (DWP 2008a, 2008b).

As far as labour market policy is concerned, the change of government in May 2010 is unlikely to lead to a change in general policy direction due to an implicit consensus between the major political parties, which had become increasingly apparent since the early 2000s. There is common ground in many aspects, such as the acceptance of targeted (means-tested) benefits as the appropriate way to support claimants, as well as a 'work first' orientation within labour market assistance, i.e. a focus on personalized and intensive job search help and short-term courses rather than longer training or job creation. Similarly, both Labour and the Conservative Party favour the contracting-out and marketization of employment services. The British trend towards the commercialization of this sector with profit as well as non-profit organizations paid on a basis of results, i.e. the labour market integration of benefit claimants, has influenced recent German debates and policy proposals (Finn and Lange 2010).

One of the characteristics of British labour market policy under the Labour government was to replace the notion of unemployment in a narrow sense with a broader notion of worklessness (Clasen 2005). In other words, policies have widened the target group for employment-related programmes and blurred the boundaries between unemployment and other causes for working-age benefit receipt. This policy had two components. First, it included groups who previously remained outside the regulation of the risk of unemployment, such as partners and lone parents. Since 2001 unemployed couples without children have been required to jointly claim JSA, i.e. both partners have to register as job seeking and fulfilling benefit conditions. Another example refers to lone parents who used be entitled to benefit support without work conditionality attached as long as their youngest child was no older than 16. On the basis of the expansion of financial support for and availability of childcare (Millar 2008) lone parents whose youngest child was 12 or older were transferred from Income Support (which is not based on job search in return for benefit eligibility) to JSA in 2008. Current plans are that from October 2010 the same will apply to lone parents whose youngest child is 7 or older (for details see Finn and Gloster 2010).

Second, short of a full transfer to JSA, voluntary New Deal programmes have gradually become more employment-orientated. In 2001 so-called 'work-focused interviews' were introduced for lone parents and incapacity benefit claimants. Since 2005 most claimants have had to agree to an action plan which might include referral to a non-mandatory employment programme (Finn and Schulte 2008: 313). In 2008 the Employment and Support Allowance (ESA) replaced Incapacity Benefits (and Income Support paid on grounds of incapacity) for new claimants and by 2013 all claimants with a disability are supposed to be transferred to ESA. Responding to a persistently high number of benefit claims on the grounds of long-term sickness and disability even at a time of declining unemployment (see Clasen et al. 2006), the government implemented a more employment-focused 'capability' test as condition for ESA receipt, and introduced a wage subsidy ('return to work credit') for a maximum of twelve months for ESA claimants who enter employment. Moreover, modelled on JSA the ESA amalgamated contributory and means-tested benefits and aligned incapacity benefit levels with JSA rates thereby inflicting significant reductions in rates for all but a few claimants with a sufficient contributory record (Williams 2009). For the regulation of social security as a whole, the ESA is yet another indication of the increasing irrelevance of the contributory principle and the overriding focus on work conditionality as the only criterion determining social rights for working-age citizens in the modern British welfare state. The previous Labour government justified such a stance with reference to two reports which proposed that social rights for working-age persons should not be determined by benefit received but by personal circumstances and individual need for help with employment support. Indicating a broad cross-party consensus on this issue, one of these reports was published by a centre-left research institute (Sainsbury and Stanley

2007), and the other by David Freud (Freud 2007), who was a shadow minister of welfare reform for the conservative party before the general election in May 2010.

It is thus no surprise that current plans by the new conservative/liberal coalition government broadly indicate policy continuation. In their general election manifesto the Conservative Party (2010b) put emphasis on the notion of long-term benefit claimants having to 'work for the dole', i.e. becoming required to maintain eligibility to benefit support based on participation in community work programmes. Moreover, the prospective aim is to integrate currently schemes for people of working age into a single separate transfer benefit programme, including claimants currently in receipt of incapacity benefit (Conservative Party 2010b). Similarly, the government coalition agreement envisages a single 'welfare to work' programme for all and, presumably as a first step, the transfer of most incapacity benefit claimants to the JSA (HM Government 2010).

In sum, although nominally maintaining a distinction between contributory and means-tested support, contemporary British labour market policy already consists of a single unemployment benefit system not only by name. From the perspective of individual unemployed persons, 'active' and 'passive' support has become much more closely connected than in the past, not least since both services are now coordinated and integrated within the same agency (Jobcentre Plus). In addition, the boundaries of unemployment protection have been extended to previously exempt groups and, at least prospectively, further integration and the creation of a single working-age benefit structure is a distinct possibility (Clasen 2011). As will be shown below, this characterization bears some similarities with policies implemented in Germany since the 1990s.

13.3.2 *German labour market policy—becoming more British in some respects*

Until recently the German structure of labour market policy has been radically different from the British set-up. This applies to the normative dominance of benefit principles, funding structure, the institutional design and governance, the orientation within labour market programmes, as well as the role of unemployment support policy within the wider German political economy (see Clasen 2005). However, within the past ten years a number of reforms have been introduced which have altered many of these characteristics. As a result, German labour market policy has indeed become more 'British' in some respects, although crucial differences remain, as will be demonstrated in the subsequent section.

Until recently labour market policy in Germany involved three distinct types of benefit support, as well as institutionally distinct provision of training and other labour market programmes. Unemployment insurance was, and remains, funded by earmarked mandatory contributions to the unemployment insurance fund operated by the Federal Employment Agency (FEA), which is not part of the government and which incorporates social partners in decision-making processes especially with regard to the structure of labour market programmes. The unemployment insurance fund provides earnings-related benefits and covers the costs of labour market programmes for contributors. For job seekers no longer entitled a secondary scheme (unemployment assistance) applied which, until 2004, was means-tested and paid for by general taxation. However, in a somewhat unorthodox fashion it granted earnings-related rather than flat-rate benefits. Finally, many of those not in receipt of either of the above benefits claimed general flat-rate and means-tested social assistance administered and funded by local authorities. Recipients of the latter rarely participated in federal labour market programmes. However, depending on local circumstances and priorities, many municipalities and local authorities offered separate employment-orientated schemes for working-age recipients (Voges et al. 2001).

In the wake of what are called the 'Hartz' reforms, the above structure was subjected to major changes implemented between 2003 and 2005 (Fleckenstein 2008). The background to and details of this reform have been discussed extensively elsewhere (e.g. Kemmerling and Bruttel 2006; Oschmiansky et al. 2007; Seeleib-Kaiser and Fleckenstein 2007; Eichhorst et al. 2008). For the purpose of this chapter I shall highlight merely those aspects which seem most relevant in a comparative perspective and which, in some respects, indicate a shift towards the British approach. These include a decline in the prominence of insurance-based transfers, a concomitant growth of means-testing, a more wide-ranging embrace of activation and a reorientation within the repertoire of active labour market programmes.

Particularly, the first two of these aspects can be linked to the Hartz reforms which have brought about no change of benefit rates for those in receipt of unemployment insurance, but significantly shortened the maximum benefit entitlement. Depending on individual contribution records, prior to 2005 some unemployed (those over the age of 45) were able to receive more than the standard (twelve months') benefit support, with a maximum of thirty-two months for those older than 57. Since then a standard period of twelve months for all claimants under the age of 55 has been introduced (and a maximum of eighteen months for older claimants). However, in 2008 the government extended the maximum entitlement (for older persons) again (to twenty-four months).

The reduced entitlement to unemployment insurance was one reason for its relative decline in recent years. An even more important cause was the merger of the previous unemployment and social assistance schemes. The new UBII scheme now provides means-tested benefits for, mainly, long-term unemployed persons outside the contributory UBI scheme. Its creation was administratively cumbersome due to the need to devise new funding and administrative structures within the multilevel German welfare state (for details see Clasen and Goerne 2012). Nevertheless, the reform has brought about a considerable degree of integration in terms of rights and obligations pertaining to benefit support and labour market programmes for persons outside of unemployment insurance. As a result, there are now considerably more claimants of assistance than insurance-based benefits. In fact, in 2008 the ratio of UBII to UBI claimants was about four to one. Thus, on the face of it, the landscape of German unemployment protection seems to have become very similar to the British due to the prevalence of assistance support and similarly sized minorities of unemployed entitled to insurance benefits in both countries. However, as will be discussed below, such an interpretation would ignore important differences in the type of benefits received as well as in administrative definitions of unemployment assistance.

As for active labour market policy there clearly has been a shift towards activation which started even before the Hartz reforms. Traditionally German labour market programmes focused on vocational qualification, retraining, and further education. In the 1980s and 1990s public job creation programmes expanded strongly and constituted up to 40 per cent of all measures (Heinelt and Weck 1998). However, the overall composition of labour market programmes shifted away from vocational training after 2002, while subsidies for self-employment and short-term training measures became more prominent. Sell (2004) characterizes this new orientation as a move towards 'faster and cheaper' programmes. After 2003 the 'Hartz' reforms led to a further decline of participant numbers in vocational training and qualification measures. By 2007 these programmes represented only 10 per cent of all measures for UBI and UBII combined, making this former core programme a 'niche product' (Oschmiansky and Ebach 2009).

In addition, long-term benefit claimants became more strongly encouraged to take up 'minor' employment through an increased use of wage subsidies in the context of some regional pilot projects (Blien et al. 2002), and later through wage subsidies to temporary employment agencies. Legislation in 2002 also introduced standardized and obligatory profiling of job seekers, as well as so-called 'integration agreements' for claimants of unemployment assistance. Similar to, and inspired by, the UK these agreements were quasi-contracts specifying claimants' rights and responsibilities, as well as actions to be taken by the public employment office. Job start-up subsidies, subsidies to low-wage jobs, and a more prevalent use of third-party providers are other measures which have expanded too over the past ten years. Since 2005 'integration agreements' have become mandatory for all UBII claimants and the service delivery for those claimants incorporates elements in accordance with the 'case management' approach which had already been applied in social assistance offices to some extent.

The Hartz reform has also introduced new rules for increasing the use of sanctions, as well as tougher criteria of job offers regarded as suitable for claimants. In principle, any legal job became defined suitable (for UBII recipients) immediately at the start of benefit receipt. This had already been the case for previous claimants of social assistance but previously public employment offices had been unable to offer jobs to claimants of unemployment assistance which paid wages not commensurate with earnings received prior to unemployment or, after six months, did not pay at least as much as the level of benefit received.

13.4 Remaining differences

As pointed out above, around one-fifth of unemployed persons in both countries receive the first-tier insurance-based unemployment benefit. While this suggests a considerable degree of convergence, differences should not be ignored both in terms of benefit generosity and recipient rates. First, unlike in the UK unemployment insurance in Germany has remained earnings-related in character. The benefit is not only higher than in the UK but has hardly declined relative to wages, compared with a steady erosion of the relative value of contributory-based JSA in the UK. In general terms, while unemployment insurance provides a replacement rate of around 65 per cent in Germany (in relation to previous individual earnings) the British flat-rate benefit is close to 10 per cent (of average earnings).

The relative size of UBII relative to UBI claimant groups suggests that recent reforms have seriously weakened the role of unemployment insurance in Germany given that in the late 1990s around half of all unemployed claimants received insurance-based support. For three reasons it can be questioned, though, whether this decline should be interpreted as evidence for the fading importance of the insurance principle in German unemployment support (see also Clasen and Goerne 2011). First, while the declining share of insurance-based support was partly the consequence of those aspects of the Hartz reforms which shortened the maximum entitlement of UBI and tightened eligibility criteria (and thus transferred some claimants from insurance to assistance support), the number (and the share) of recipients of means-tested UBII increased for other reasons too. When UBII was introduced in January

2005, the number of claimants was markedly higher than the sum of those who had received unemployment assistance and social assistance (registered as unemployed) in December 2004. This is because, in contrast to previous social assistance, under the UBII system each workless adult within a claimant household is counted as unemployed. In addition, the previous social assistance system suffered from relatively low take-up rates, possibly due to stigmatization effects which do not seem to be associated with the receipt of UBII (Bundesagentur 2005). Finally, in the past a substantial proportion of working-age social assistance claimants did not register as unemployed with the public employment service. In 1998 only about 40 per cent of all working-age claimants were registered in this way (Blien et al. 2002). By contrast, after the Hartz reform 90 per cent of previous working-age social assistance claimants became defined as being 'able to work' and thus transferred to UBII (Eichhorst et al. 2008: 47). In short, the creation of a single scheme for working-age benefit claimants increased the scope of unemployment assistance due to an administrative redefinition of 'ability to engage in paid work' as the core criterion of benefit eligibility (Konle-Seidl 2009).

However, although deemed to be employable, many UBII claimants are not actually counted as unemployed. In September 2009 this included parents with children under the age of 3 and persons older than 58 who have been in receipt of UBII for more than twelve months and were looking after relatives, claimants participating in a labour market programmes, and many UBII claimants who combined benefits with earnings (see Clasen and Goerne 2011). In other words, while UBII broadened the administrative definition of unemployment support, not all UBII claimants are actually registered as unemployed. In fact, in December 2009 less than half of all UBII claimants were unemployed in an administrative sense (Bundesagentur 2010b). In short, administrative redefinitions resulted in UBII becoming a rather broad and encompassing benefit category which, despite its terminology, is not only claimed by officially unemployed persons.

A second reason against the notion of a waning of the insurance principle in Germany similar to the UK has to do with the relative stability of the scope of contributory-based support before and after the Hartz reforms. In the early 1980s unemployment insurance was payable for a maximum of twelve months and was received by around 40 per cent of all registered unemployed in West Germany. Throughout the 1990s the ratio remained below 50 per cent and was about 40 per cent in the early 2000s (Reissert 2004). After the Hartz reform the ratio dropped to about one-third of all registered unemployed (Bundesagentur für Arbeit 2010b). In other words, there has been a relative decline of the scope of unemployment insurance, but the scale of this decline in recent years is modest rather than radical.

Finally, in the mid-1990s between 50 per cent and 60 per cent of all West Germans who entered unemployment received insurance benefits. As discussed above, many claimants of UBII are not unemployed. However, in recent years the monthly number of persons entering UBI was about equal to the number of those accessing UBII (Bundesagentur für Arbeit 2010b). This indicates the continuing relevance of insurance-based support for jobless persons. In addition, close to 90 per cent of all those who enter UBI leave the benefit receipt within twelve months, i.e. before the entitlement runs out, and only about 8 per cent of those who leave UBI actually transfer to UBII (Bundesagentur für Arbeit 2010b). In other words, the Hartz reform has certainly not strengthened the insurance principle, but it has not dented its role much either.

As for active labour market programmes in Germany, a general shift towards principles which had already become dominant in the UK (such as a focus on job search support, activation, more obligations on the part of job seekers) has been noted above. However, while there is no differentiation by benefit receipt in the UK, the type of transfer unemployed persons are entitled to remains relevant in Germany. Different regulations apply in terms of the definition of what are deemed as 'suitable jobs', i.e. employment opportunities which can be offered to, and have to be accepted by, UBI and UBII claimants, respectively. The use of case management differs between the two claimant, groups, as well as the types of labour market programmes typically offered. For example, while short-term provision and 'work first' principles figure now more strongly within the contemporary repertoire of German labour market programmes than in the past (Bundesagentur für Arbeit 2010c), this applies particularly to recipients of UBII. Job creation is a good case in point. While diminished in scope compared to the 1990s, it still accounted for around a third of all measures in 2007 and has remained prominent for UBII claimants. The Hartz reform led to the introduction of a new public employment programme which offers temporary work experience in areas of 'public interest' for claimants who are often difficult to place into unsubsidized jobs. Participants receive pay which is only slightly above their benefit level (so-called €1 jobs). While such programmes are new to previous claimants of unemployment assistance, they are fairly common for those who previously relied on social assistance. Once again this shows that recent reforms have led to a considerable degree of integration, albeit only for the long-term unemployed. It is both this sort of compartmentalization, as well as the relative scope of job creation programmes, which continues to set British and German labour market policy apart.

13.5 Conclusion

Labour market policies in the UK as well as in Germany have been considerably reformed since the mid-1990s. Similar types of reforms started earlier in the UK, which focused largely on reforming active programmes for various groups unemployed, and increasingly also other working-age people who have become obliged to be 'activated' in a process of 'perpetual reform' (Griggs et al. 2011). Somewhat belatedly but fairly rapidly in recent years Germany followed along the same route, adopting principles of activation and 'work first'-oriented employment support, as well as apparently departing from insurance principles in favour of means-tested assistance support. It can be argued that labour market policy has changed over time in both countries, and that the gap between the two countries has indeed narrowed, with Germany having become somewhat 'more British' along the way.

However, as discussed, characteristic differences should not be overlooked. Perhaps most importantly, the British model is egalitarian at a modest level while Germany maintains separate policy structures for different groups of unemployed, determined largely by the type of benefit receipt. Indeed, notwithstanding an overall change in the orientation of active labour market programmes in particular, the level of social protection provided within unemployment insurance, especially for short-term unemployed, has remained fairly high as well as relevant for a large section of job seekers.

It is thus not so much the structure of labour market policy per se but the type of unemployment protection and the level of benefit received by the long-term unemployed in Germany which has become more similar to support received by their British counterparts. This becomes apparent when labour market policy is set in a wider context of employment change in both countries. For the UK, labour market programmes and unemployment support have become integral components of a wider welfare-to-work strategy, which includes lenient employment protection legislation but also the national minimum wage as well as the extensive use of tax credits in support of a flexible and deregulated labour market, which has been portrayed as a key competitive advantage in a global economy (Cm 3968 1998).

Similarly, it can be argued that the Hartz reforms are compatible with, or even encourage, the flexibilization within the German labour market. As the chapter has shown, this applies to the long-term unemployed in particular, for whom benefit eligibility has become more strongly connected with personal work conditionality and for whom the entry into temporary and 'minor forms' of employment, e.g. low-paid and part-time work, have been made financially more attractive. The broad orientation of the Hartz reforms, i.e. a tougher sanctioning regime, incentives to enter minor employment, and generally a stronger 'work first' orientation, certainly corresponds with a considerable growth in non-standard employment since the late 1990s, and a corresponding expansion of a low-wage sector (Kalina and Weinkopf 2009) both in terms of total numbers and as share of all employees. It seems fairly safe to argue that any further convergence of labour market policy in the two countries will be influenced by, as well as contribute to, the development of this particular segment of the German labour market.

14

Conclusion: parallel paths, great similarities, remaining differences

Jochen Clasen, Steffen Mau, Traute Meyer, and Martin Seeleib-Kaiser

The idea for this concluding chapter is to revisit the four sections of the book. In addition to highlighting the main findings, we focus on signs which allow us to assess whether and where we were able to identify growing, or diminishing, similarities between British and German social policy. Moreover, in each of the four sections, we reflect on broader trends in the three domains of family policy, pensions, and employment policy in Europe more generally. As indicated in the introduction, convergence has not been applied in any strict analytical or consistent manner across all chapters. We are fully aware that convergence is a complex concept. For policies to converge they must have been different at a previous point in time. From a theoretical point of view, it is very unlikely to observe complete convergence of policies in different countries at any specific point in time due to different starting points and country-specific policy and institutional contexts. Whether one can speak of policy convergence will thus also depend on the level of abstraction. Moreover, policies can differ, diverge, or converge along various dimensions, for instance in relation to policy objectives, the choice of instruments, and the setting of instruments.[1] Finally, it is very likely that processes of convergence along certain dimensions coincide with processes of divergence (or continued difference) along other dimensions. Thus processes of divergence and convergence might coincide (Seeleib-Kaiser 1999; Katz and Darbishire 2000; Mills et al. 2008).

Rather than a strict framework of analysis, convergence has thus served as an overarching theme for the chapters of this book. Put simply, we were

---

[1] For a recent quantitative study of social policy convergence within the OECD, see Schmitt and Starke (2011).

interested in the question whether the distances between social policy structures and principles in the two countries under observation have become larger or smaller in recent years. Moreover, our focus was to look beyond public policy provision and include the role of occupational welfare at least to some extent. As discussed in the introductory chapter, not all welfare state aspects lend themselves to contrasting the two countries under investigation. However, particularly in pension and employment policy, but also in family policies (despite more common ground in some respects) British and German approaches have differed considerably during the post-WWII period. On the other hand, the contexts in which welfare states operate have changed considerably since the 1990s and, despite different 'starting points', both countries have tried to find responses to very similar challenges, such as intensified economic internationalization or demographic ageing. It seemed thus reasonable to assume that, if anything, policies might have become more, rather than less, similar. However, before we turn to this assumption in respect of the specific policy domains, we revisit the first section of the book, which investigated similarities and differences in public attitudes towards social policy, solidarity, and social justice.

14.1 Social justice, solidarity, and the European social model

Recent welfare reforms in both the UK and Germany have indicated a shift away from what is sometimes called 'passive social policy' towards emphasizing responsibility, activation, and the enhancement of human and social capital as new policy objectives (Esping-Andersen et al. 2002; Taylor-Gooby 2008). Against this background the first part of this volume focused on people's perceptions of the role of the government, private responsibilities, and notions of social justice with regard to equality of opportunity and social inequalities. The issue at stake was whether the general public approves the overall direction of reform: how are the new themes viewed and discussed by ordinary citizens? Our research rested on the assumption that the acceptance and sustainability of reforms depends, by and large, on the need to generate a corresponding sense of justice. Strong and durable solidarities arise from appealing and morally plausible principles of social justice.

Despite institutional differences in social protection arrangements, we found that people in the two countries share remarkably similar attitudes towards inequality and poverty and do not differ much in terms of the desirability of government action to address such problems either. We found that most people regard inequality as a problem, smaller majorities think governments should do something about it, and yet smaller (but still substantial) groups want their governments to redistribute to the poor. However, the results indicate stronger support for state interventions such as income redistribution in Germany than in the UK. A slight shift in attitudes is observable in both countries. Despite societies becoming more unequal, British citizens have become less likely to express concerns about poverty and inequality, while in Germany the awareness of inequality has decreased since the late 1990s. In some areas attitudes correspond closely to the respective welfare regime model (see also Mau 2003). In Germany the idea that market freedoms imply advantages for the better-off in the core areas of social provision are viewed with disapproval. By contrast, in the UK such advantages are regarded as perfectly acceptable. Whether these attitudes are now changing in the light of the current recession and the greater awareness of inequalities in society is still unclear.

In both countries there is a strong emphasis on equality of opportunity as a major objective as well as on work as the way of contributing to society. However, there are differences in the ways in which these notions are understood. British citizens tend to acknowledge and regret social inequalities in life chances, but nevertheless take a firm view that individuals are able to overcome such obstacles as long as they are sufficiently determined. In Germany, the idea of contributions to society is much more likely to be understood within the logic of social insurance, i.e. making financial contributions to a common fund based on stable employment. Correspondingly, it is emphasized that the government should take on the role of supporting more vulnerable groups in accessing employment, while in the UK the role of government is much more regarded as regulating welfare so as not to undermine individuals' commitment to take responsibility for themselves. This stronger notion of individualism and market freedom is also reflected in the social acceptability of buying better services in the core areas of education and health care, which make a substantial difference to people's opportunities in life.

In addition to the growing emphasis on individualism and the role of market-based exchanges, both the British and German welfare states are faced with the need to accommodate greater diversity (Mau and Burkhardt 2009b). As higher levels of migration resulting from globalization produce more heterogeneous populations, also in other European countries, guarantees of equal treatment and equal opportunities may be questioned and tensions between different ethnic communities may arise. A number of writers (e.g. Alesina and Glaeser 2004) have argued that greater diversity may undermine the solidarity on which the commitment to welfare is based (see Taylor-Gooby 2005 and Crepaz and Damron 2009 for counter-arguments). However, we found that many Germans do not seem to view foreigners as a major problem. Migration is not particularly embraced, but accepted as one important factor for the labour market to function. However, asked about the impact of foreigners on the overall living situation, particularly British respondents with routine occupations emphasized negative consequences, such as beliefs about high rates of illegitimate migration, cultures of benefit fraud, and a fear that migrants threaten the UK's welfare system. However, such perceptions were particularly associated with recent migrants, who were seen as overwhelming in number. In contrast, ethnic homogeneity per se was not seen as important and the integration of many different racial groups was held as a point of national pride. In Germany distributional conflicts seem to be relatively contained. In terms of conditions of inclusion into the welfare system, the payment of taxes and employment are crucial in both countries. Hardly anybody would deny access to the benefit system to migrants who have paid their 'dues'.

Overall we found both similarities as well as differences in the way citizens in both countries view the welfare state. While attitudes are broadly aligned with the respective welfare state arrangements, recent reforms may well weaken cross-national differences. For example, the notion of personal responsibility and labour market activation measures are now widely accepted, even among lower socioeconomic classes. There are indications that public understandings as to the major objectives of the welfare state are beginning to shift too. However, it would mean jumping to conclusions if these changes were to be interpreted as abandonment of the commitment to the state responsibility for social policy. In line with other studies, we found that the core principles of the western welfare states find lasting popular support. Although the many problems and challenges are clear to most people, an overall tendency towards an erosion of mass support for the welfare state is not apparent (Svallfors 2010b). Criticisms tend to be aimed at perceived inefficiencies and negative side-effects, rather than at the level of fundamental principles of redistribution and collective solidarity.

In a wider European context, Germany and the UK do not stand out. Research has demonstrated that in most European welfare states shifts in attitudes are relatively contained, more incremental than fundamental (Svallfors 2003, 2006, 2007). Issues such 'social investment' (i.e. shifting resources to education, training, and families), greater reciprocity, and accommodation to greater social diversity are topics debated across most European societies (Taylor-Gooby 2009). Nonetheless, rather than demanding a shrinking and less comprehensive welfare state, people call for social policies which are able to respond to social needs and which combine efficiency and social justice. Against this background, preferences can be demonstrated to be embedded in institutions, collective memory, and the social groups to which people belong (Rothstein 1998; Brooks and Manza 2006). There is also evidence that the national level is still an important influence on public attitudes towards welfare state policies in industrialized nations (Blekesaune and Quadagno 2003). However, despite substantial cross-country variation, it is difficult to systematically link attitudinal differences to different welfare state regimes. If any, there is mixed support for the thesis that people's preferences in terms of social justice largely reflect differences in the normative principles prevailing in different welfare systems (Arts and Gelissen 2001; Svallfors 2003; Jaeger 2006). However, recent evidence indicates that welfare regime types matter for coping with diversity. Crepaz and Damron (2009), for example, have shown that comprehensive social policies reduce welfare chauvinism and do not foster the impression that public funding is diverted to undeserving foreigners. Welfare states which facilitate the integration of 'newcomers' do not foster higher levels of social conflict. Other welfare regimes, and particularly those in which discourses about deservingness and fraud are typical, seem to be much more vulnerable to distributive conflicts between the native population and groups of immigrants.

To some extent national social policy debates are reflected also at European level. Currently there is much talk about the European Social Model as a vision of a society in which economic growth, the mitigation of social inequality, and the protection against social risks can be effectively combined. In stark contrast to market-dominated societies, the European Social Model is associated with the ability to reconcile economic and social demands. European policy makers and the European Commission often claim that both competitiveness and justice are relevant for the building of a successful Europe for the future. The idea of 'social investment' is important in this context. At first glance, this policy will not face strong public objections as more resources for education, training, and allowing parents to participate in the labour market seems to be beneficial to the whole society. However, public funds invested in stabilizing the international financial system have left most European countries with enormous burdens of debt. At the time of writing it remains unclear how governments will be able to regain fiscal capacity in order to satisfy societal needs. The public provision of pensions, health care, and unemployment protection are central aspects in this respect. Attempts to introduce substantial cuts or to divert expenditure away from these areas are just as likely to face strong opposition as they did in the past. In citizens' eyes it is the responsibility of national governments, and the European Union, not only to foster deregulation and market flexibility but also to guarantee social protection, to support people finding employment, make work pay, and mitigate social inequalities. It is clear that even greater income inequalities, higher levels of structural unemployment, and, more recently, vastly grown public debt, bear enormous social and political risks and that any major welfare reform efforts must take into account the social costs involved. Any compelling strategy needs to abstain from unduly emphasizing liberalization, activation, and flexibility, and should embrace measures which contain the growth of social inequality, facilitating labour market access and providing better support for those in need. In the face of demographic ageing in many European countries, migration will remain a major issue, but its effects and long-term repercussions will depend on the ability of welfare states to facilitate integration, enhance immigrants' human capital, and contain tensions between natives and new-comers. In other words, Europe's long-term social development will depend on the way economic growth, fiscal stability, and social cohesion can be success-fully reconciled.

14.2 Family policies: parallel trends and cross-national variation

Chapters 5 to 8 of this volume investigated one of the most dynamic policy domains in the UK and Germany. While family-orientated policies in both countries have traditionally been based on the 'strong male breadwinner model' (Lewis 1992) very distinct policy approaches have been pursued in the past. In the UK the family has widely been considered a private matter and an explicit family policy was largely non-existent. In Germany the family as an institution has been explicitly supported through a wide array of transfer programmes. Irrespective of these differences, both countries left the respon-sibility for childcare to families and, by implication, to mothers. However, during the past decade policies in both countries have undergone a transfor-mation in this respect. Have the various developments led to a policy convergence?

As the chapters have shown, family policies have developed along a number of common trajectories. Contrary to a wide range of other social policies, family policies have not been retrenched during the past decade but followed a clearly expansionist trend. At a general level commonalities can certainly be identified, including the expansion of childcare-related services, a move towards considering or conceptualizing children as a particular category of and for social policy, an increased emphasis on reconciliation of work and family life, and a closer focusing of state support on parenthood and parenting. Overall, family policies in both countries have become ever more employment-orientated and to a significant extent subordinated under economic policy. In other words, family policies have increasingly been con-ceptualized as 'policies for the market'. Thus, not very dissimilar to the other policy areas covered in this book, family policies are considered as a contribu-tion to improved economic performance, whilst at the same time fostering child well-being and a better work–life balance for parents. This dialectic function can also explain why businesses in both countries, and particularly companies which require high general skills, have expanded occupational family policies in recent years. The expansion of occupational family policies, as well as the introduction of specific statutory flexible working time arrangements have highlighted the important role played by employers and organized business in family policy during the past decade.

Despite these commonalities, a significant number of differences at the level of specific policy instruments have prevailed. Whilst in Britain family policies have focused more on the socioeconomic disadvantaged population, family policies in Germany are in principle more universal. The expansion of childcare services in England was initially and primarily aimed at children in poorer areas.[2] In contrast, policy expansion in Germany will eventually lead to a general entitlement of a place in a childcare facility. The different approach to childcare services is also reflected in the design of early childhood education and leave programmes. Whilst it can be argued that the comparatively low maternity leave entitlement in Britain primarily benefits mothers on low incomes, the earnings-related parental leave benefit in Germany is biased towards middle-and-higher income parents (Henninger et al. 2008). If we include occupational family policies, however, these differences become somewhat less pronounced, as many British companies requiring general skills offer extra-statutory leave policies. The differences in specific policy choices can to some extent be explained by institutional policy legacies and socioeconomic contexts. Many British policies were driven by the specific aim to reduce and avoid poverty and improve the situation of children from socioeconomically disadvantaged backgrounds. By contrast, in Germany, increasing the fertility rate and improving early childhood education for all were key policy aims.

Thus, no clear picture emerges regarding a convergence or continued difference in the domain of family policies. Nevertheless, in some respects there is more rather than less similarity given that an explicit family policy is now evident in both countries. Furthermore, many specific policies regarding the expansion of childcare services, the provision of leave entitlements for parents, as well as the statutory 'family-friendly' working times arrangements developed in parallel, moving both formerly strong male breadwinner countries closer towards the 'adult worker model' (Lewis 2009). Thus, at an abstract level one could argue that both countries currently pursue very similar policy goals. Nevertheless, some specific aims associated with these policies as well as the specific policy designs continue to demonstrate policy difference. Hence, it might be appropriate to characterize the development as divergent convergence.

Obviously, these developments did not occur in isolation. Throughout the EU and OECD world family policy has moved up the political agenda.

---

[2] Nevertheless, this development might eventually lead to a more universal coverage, according to the aspirations enshrined in the concept of 'progressive universalism' (see Wincott 2006).

In the 1980s and 1990s many changes focused on reforming pension and unemployment policies, as well as 'making work pay'; but recent initiatives have primarily and explicitly centred on families and family policies. Policy makers, at both national and the supra-national level, now regard the expansion of family policies as a significant contribution to the sustainability of political economies (cf. Mahon 2008; Lohmann et al. 2009). Across the OECD (and the same holds for EU-15), spending on family benefits has increased by half a percentage point of GDP since 1990 (Adema and Ladaique 2009: 24). Whereas in the past, discussions about the economic sustainability of welfare states revolved primarily around the question of the viability of existing financing structures under likely future conditions (such as rapidly ageing societies and ever more globalized 'national' economies), more recent debates have highlighted the necessity of improving child welfare and a more viable work–life balance. Such policies are said to positively contribute to future economic development and are characterized as a 'social investment', which in the long run is said to be more or less self-financing (cf. Jenson and Saint-Martin 2006; Esping-Andersen 2002a, 2009). However, as many of these policies have only developed within the past decade, largely with the exception of Scandinavian countries, it remains to be seen whether countries will indeed achieve the benefits promised by the protagonists of such an investment strategy. In particular, it can be questioned whether the gap in achievement between children with parents from socioeconomically disadvantaged backgrounds and those with privileged parents will significantly narrow through early childhood education. What happens if these aims are not achieved?

On a more normative level, it may be asked whether and to what extent these policies subordinate families and family policy under the imperatives of capitalism (Gilbert 2008). While policy is to some extent always instrumental, an approach entirely driven by economic rationality fails to grasp moral and relational considerations, which loom large in people's decision making around their family. Unless policy takes account of family as a domain of life that has its own exigencies and relations, economically determined family policies are unlikely to be ineffective in the long term.

In the short term the current economic and financial crisis may delay planned expansions of public policies, such as the extension of paid maternity leave in Britain, and lead to some cutbacks of occupational family policies. However, it seems less likely that the current situation will have a lasting negative effect on the expansionary trajectory of family policies for four reasons. First, family policies are relatively inexpensive compared with pensions and health care, for example, and cutbacks are thus unlikely to have a significant effect on stressed public finances. Second, public opinion increasingly seems to support the employment of both parents, as well as policies which facilitate this option, especially increased childcare provision. Third, in principle the main political parties in both countries support a further expansion of employment-orientated family policies. Finally, albeit for different reasons and from different perspectives (Fleckenstein and Seeleib-Kaiser 2011), employers in both countries strongly support an expansion of childcare facilities for economic reasons.

14.3 Towards German liberalism and British social democracy—transcending established pension boundaries

Chapters 9 to 11 explored the question of convergence from the perspective of the British and German pension regimes. Adopting a long-term perspective in many respects there is a good fit between the public-occupational pension mixes and conventional models of the liberal and the coordinated/conservative type of capitalism and welfare states. In liberal Britain, public pension benefits have been below the poverty line since 1945, except for a brief period during the 1970s, while occupational and personal pensions were voluntary for employers and employees. The German social insurance system and occupational pensions preserved given earnings differences in retirement and therefore fitted the 'conservative' label well between 1957 and 2001.

Nevertheless, both labels have limits. First, provided the role of the state as employer and regulator is included, the British post-war regime was less liberal than often suggested. Through nationalization in the 1950s and the expansion of the welfare state from the 1960s onwards good quality occupational pension schemes benefited most public-sector employees. As a spillover effect, all occupational schemes became more tightly regulated. Altogether, this statist dimension protected a substantial share of the population well, and we therefore labelled the British pension regime, until 2007, as liberal–statist hybrid. Second, landmark reforms in the first decade of the millennium rendered old labels inappropriate given that Britain has become more social democratic, while Germany is now more liberal than it was before. British reforms of 2008/9 increased public benefit provision and introduced employer quasi-compulsion. German reforms reduced state benefits significantly and introduced incentives for occupational and personal schemes on a voluntary basis.

Our research on the impact of these reforms on hypothetical future pensioners shows that the level of social protection in Germany has declined strongly for all citizens who exclusively accrue rights under the new system, leaving such citizens at risk of poverty if they have wages below the average, while British reforms have reduced future poverty risks substantially for young employees. Crudely put, before the reforms an employee starting a career would have been better off under the German system; thereafter he or she would be better advised to opt for the British public pension system. The rapid growth in personal pension schemes in recent years has done little, and even less than the expansion of occupational benefits, to compensate future German retirees for the shortfall in public pension entitlement. In contrast, British citizens who rely on state benefits and a personal pension scheme are projected to be better off under the reformed system than their German counterparts.

This summary suggests that in answer to the main question of the book, both countries' pension regimes have been subjected to considerable change but have not become more similar. Put differently, during the 2000s the British and German pension systems both broke with previously prevailing principles of their respective policy logic, but there was no convergence. In both countries centre-left governments decided that only significant reform could help to break free of the problems that had plagued their systems since the 1990s. In Britain this transformation was embodied by a change of the main planks of the liberal part of the regime: the very low public benefits and employer voluntarism. In Germany it was expressed by the dismantling of its conservative hallmark, status preservation. What drove such transformation? In Britain action was taken because existing policies had failed to encourage saving and when the occupational pensions sector declined rapidly in the early 2000s it was feared that without reforms too many future pensioners would become dependent on means-tested benefits, undermining a system built on voluntary savings. Such a situation appeared undesirable to all stakeholders and it led to a compromise which increased compulsion for both business and the state (see also Bridgen and Meyer 2011). In Germany the high costs of public pensions motivated reform. This focus on avoiding increased dependency on the means-test in Britain and on curbing expenditure in Germany, respectively would be seen as a response to problems which have been regarded as typical for the mature liberal and conservative, or Bismarckian, welfare state, respectively (see Esping-Andersen 1996a: 16–18, 1996b: 82; Pierson 2001: 435). It shows how pension institutions influence policy makers' view of social problems and their reform decisions (Bonoli 2003b: 399). In short, despite similar macroeconomic and social trends, we have found no evidence of either institutional convergence or convergence in terms of outcome for future retirees who accrue full pension rights under the new systems.

How do British and German pension reforms and outcomes compare with those of other European countries? In line with the argument just made, we would expect to see similar developments in countries with similar institutional configurations. This is indeed the case for conservative welfare states, i.e. for countries such as France, Italy, or Poland which, like Germany have Bismarckian, social insurance-based public systems. Bonoli (2003: 402–3) has argued that the burden of their increasing pension expenses could not be divided between public and private providers. The cost pressure caused by slow productivity growth, de-industrialization, welfare state maturation, ageing populations, household changes, and economic globalization thus focused on state pensions in these countries, leading to stronger retrenchment of public retirement benefits than in countries with multi-pillar systems. Since the 1990s governments in all Bismarckian countries have cut back state pension provision. To compensate, all countries have implemented measures aimed at fostering the growth of occupational and personal pensions which are based on voluntarism (Bonoli and Palier 2007; Ebbinghaus and Gronwald 2011). These fundamental changes are typical for conservative pension regimes in Europe, which reduces the salience of arguments which assume that coordinated political economies will preserve their high earnings-related benefits to protect the competitive advantage of their production systems (Hall and Soskice 2001: 57–8). The actual take-up of non-statutory alternatives, however, has been slow in Poland (Benio and Ratajczak-Tuchołka 2007), Italy (Raitano 2007), and France (Bonoli and Palier 2007: 566).

It is more difficult to find European systems similar to the British liberal-statist hybrid. Bonoli (2003b: 400–3) has suggested that Britain, Denmark, the Netherlands, and Switzerland represent their own 'world of pension provision' because they all have Beveridgean systems with low public pensions, supplemented by occupational and personal savings schemes. As a consequence, public pensions were both more affordable than in Bismarckian countries and increases in contributions to be made to the second and third pension pillars could not be blamed directly on the state (see also Ebbinghaus and Gronwald 2011). Looking at the trends since the 1990s, public pension entitlements in Beveridgean countries have not been cut back substantially, but occupational benefits have lost value. This is true for Britain, as we have shown in Chapter 10, and also applies to the Netherlands and Switzerland (Bannink and de Vroom 2007; Bertozzi and Bonoli 2007; Bridgen and Meyer 2009). Denmark is an exception because its multi-pillar system developed late, and occupational schemes still expanded during the 1990s and 2000s (Andersen forthcoming).

However, while the British institutional structure fits into the Beveridgean group, it differs in two respects. First, British public pensions were lower than in the other three countries mentioned above. In 2007 British public pensions offered future retirees the lowest gross replacement rates of statutory pensions within all OECD member states, much below that of other Beveridgean countries in Europe and even below levels found in other liberal welfare states such as the US, New Zealand, and Australia (for details, see OECD 2007b: 33–5).

Second, Britain relied on employer voluntarism much longer than other mature multi-pillar countries. For example, membership in occupational pension schemes was made (quasi-) compulsory during the 1980s and 1990s in the Netherlands, Switzerland, and Denmark—and at the point of introduction public pension levels had already been significantly higher and broader in scope compared with the British public pension in 2009 (see Anderson 2007; Bannink and de Vroom 2007; Bonoli 2007b; Green-Pedersen 2007). Thus, the other Beveridgean welfare states offered citizens better statutory protection against poverty than Britain, combined with additional (quasi-) compulsory employer contribution at a much earlier date, rendering the systems more resistant to fast decline. The mass closure of British defined benefit schemes to new entrants during a time of market turbulence in the early 2000s was not possible on this scale in the other, more regulated countries of this group. Indeed, as discussed above, such retrenchment is more typical for liberal regimes under cost containment pressure and where the citizens most affected are politically too weak to resist cuts (Hall and Soskice 2001: 57–8; Pierson 2001: 434–5). However, the introduction of a higher state pension and quasi-employer compulsion in Britain is not characteristic for liberal regimes. In short, considering British pensions in 2010 the features of a liberal regime have retreated and the system resembles more closely the other members of the Beveridgean group.

Not only the welfare state but also business, the other key institution able to facilitate broad risk pooling, has been under cost containment pressure for some time. Any regime reliant on voluntarism is therefore unlikely to prevent substantial poverty risks for future generations of pensioners. This does not bear well for those Bismarckian countries which have only recently made a turn towards second-pillar voluntarism. Policy makers here could learn from the British case that under conditions of voluntarism business withdrew as the costs of schemes rose, irrespective of tax incentives. The reason why occupational schemes are holding up better to the pressure in the Netherlands, Switzerland, and Denmark is legislation or collective action which has not allowed businesses to disengage from occupational welfare provision. There is also no evidence to suggest that voluntary personal savings schemes are sufficient to facilitate social inclusion. Citizens simply cannot or will not save enough voluntarily during their working lives to be protected in the future, and this is true in particular for those on lower incomes (Bridgen and Meyer 2007a).

Against this background, how likely is it that occupational pensions will become compulsory in the Bismarckian world? Two factors make such a scenario doubtful in the medium term: first, as Chapter 9 showed, the key reason for changing the Bismarckian system was to reduce non-wage labour costs for employers. Since the introduction of compulsory occupational pensions would bring those straight back in, it is unlikely that governments will embark on such a course, unless there is strong political pressure to do so. However, the build-up of such pressure is also improbable, because, as Pierson (1994) argued, retrenchment is unpopular and politicians tend to make cuts by stealth, i.e. by passing measures that become effective gradually over time (see Bonoli and Palier 2007).

Until 2020 or so the revamped British pension system will face strong retrenchment pressures. Keynesian policies adopted by the previous Labour government in response to the financial crisis of 2008 led to very high public debts which will constrain governments for many years to come. Nevertheless, the institutional transformation of 2007 and 2008 is unlikely to be reversed. After all, the structural problems of the system had become too pressing, i.e. the low level of the public pension, rapidly declining employer voluntarism, and a looming increase in reliance on means-tested benefits which reinforced the disinclination to save. It is thus more probable that governments will be tempted to make savings via a delayed phasing-in of the reforms. Moreover, politicians will seek to retrench the system's statist dimension: the welfare state as employer might shrink through job cuts, and pressure on public-sector pensions will increase; already there has been talk of reducing the generosity of unfunded public-sector pension schemes (Bridgen and Meyer 2011). We therefore expect the new pension legislation will become effective, but that policy makers will be looking to further the level of public as well as private benefits stipulated by the legislation.

14.4 Education, employment, and unemployment

The remaining two chapters discussed cross-national differences and potential trends of convergence in labour market policies, as well as in the ways education and employment structures are connected in the two countries. In both of these fields there have been considerable differences in the past. This applies to the level of spending on active labour market programmes, the role of insurance within unemployment support, as well as the type and prevalence of vocational training in Germany and the UK. Particularly, the latter has been seen as indicative of differences in the ways in which national political economies are structured (Hall and Soskice 2001). Arguably, the prevalence of vocational training and its institutionalization is associated with the demand and supply of industry-specific skills and thus manifests and underpins Germany's character as a 'coordinated market economy'. By contrast, the relatively small role played by publicly provided vocational training has been associated with the significance of the demand for general skills in the British 'liberal market economy'.

Accordingly, differences in transitions between training and employment have been prominently investigated in recent years (e.g. Shavit and Müller 1998). By contrast, despite the increase in the number of university graduates, particularly in the UK over the past two decades, the role of higher education and its impact on graduate employment have been researched to a much lesser degree. In Chapter 12 we have shown that in this field German–British differences have very long historical roots and diversity has tended to prevail to some extent until today. Although policies in the 1990s started to respond more to labour market needs, and notwithstanding considerable differences across degree programmes, British universities still tend to provide courses aimed less at conveying applied knowledge and more at personal development and raising general skills, particularly at undergraduate level. The match between the content of degree programmes and first job is thus often not very strong. By contrast, as in vocational training, within the same subjects in many universities and other higher education institutions in Germany there is a stronger emphasis on professional education and occupation-specific training. These differences underpin differences in graduate labour markets, which tend to be more segmented in Germany than in the UK. These findings indicate that attempts to harmonize higher education credentials and training, as envisaged by the EU's Bologna process, for example, might confront policy legacies and barriers which are located at the intersection between graduate training and national labour markets. In other words, while there are instances of greater cross-national similarity than in the past, for example at postgraduate level education, cross-national differences in the level of demand for occupationally specific skills and knowledge seem to prevail and are likely to remain an obstacle for convergence.

In other respects however, national labour markets have become more, rather than less, similar since the 1990s, with Germany approaching the UK rather than the other way round. This can be shown by the greater degree of flexibilization and deregulation and gradual expansion of a low-wage segment within the German labour market since the 1990s, as well as indications of a growth of income inequality (Giesecke and Verwiebe 2008) or the number of those who might be considered 'working poor' (Gießelmann 2009). The introduction and extension of subsidized so-called marginal employment (*geringfügige Beschäftigung*), partly additional to but also replacing standard forms of employment, is certainly one of the most noticeable changes in the German labour market over the past decade. Whether and to what extent this has influenced, or in turn has been fostered by, changes in labour market policy would be difficult to disentangle. There is no doubt however, that both are associated with each other.

It can thus be argued that the decline in the level of spending but even more so the composition of active labour market policy, with a shift away from training and qualification and the focus on job search and short-term 'work first' schemes in Germany, has narrowed the gap between the two countries, with Germany following the UK along a similar path. Moreover, some commentators have seen signs of convergence not only in active labour market policy but also in the field of unemployment protection (e.g. Mohr 2008). However, it is important to note that what are sometimes called 'Bismarckian' elements within social protection (Palier 2010), for example status-confirming earnings-related benefits, separate funds, and some role for social partners, still apply to German unemployment insurance, even if the role or scope of all these aspects is less pervasive now than it once was. By contrast, the notion of (a different type of) social insurance seems to have all but disappeared for persons under retirement age within the British welfare state. Thus, as far as social rights for short-term unemployed persons are concerned, there are still considerable differences between the two countries. For others, and for the overall approach within labour market policy as a whole, cross-national contrasts are now less sharp than they once were.

Germany and the UK are certainly not the only countries in which labour market policies have been subjected to significant reforms since the 1990s. Indeed, most European countries have altered both the repertoire of their active labour market programmes, and the character of unemployment protection as a social right. This has been noted in the plethora of articles on 'activation' since the late 1990s. Effectively this refers to the tighter link benefit provision on the one hand and active measures supporting the return to work on the other. Measures must be developed to ensure that unemployment policy no longer merely focuses on income security, but on enhancing employability through appropriate job search support services and by building links between benefit rights and participation in labour market programmes.

However, in addition to 'activation' two other related processes can be observed across many European countries which indicate a trend towards a post-industrial adaptation to the problem of unemployment (Clasen and Clegg 2011). In the context of the decline of full-time, often permanent, and male-dominated jobs and the growth of more varied forms of service market participation, especially in the service sector, labour market policies seem to be shifting. In many countries the aim to reintegrate job seekers in correspondence with acquired qualifications and previous labour market positions appears to be replaced with policies of awarding flexibility and adaptability on the part of job seekers. Thus, as discussed in Chapter 13, the recent reforms in Germany, as well as the secular trend in the UK, might be considered instances of benefit homogenization, making insurance benefits less status-confirming or even substituting earnings-related with flat-rate benefits.

Moreover, reversing policies of the 1980s which were aimed at reducing labour supply by facilitating temporary and permanent exit from employment, during the 1990s many countries began to extend the remit of labour market policies to persons in receipt of benefits other than unemployment transfers. Thus, unemployment as an administrative category began to be reconfigured in recent years, reflected in a blurring of boundaries between previously separate benefit arrangements, such as unemployment benefits, sickness and disability benefits, or support for single parents. This new focus not only on unemployed but on all working-age benefit recipients, and on avoiding the circulation of claimants between different forms of benefit dependency, might indicate a growing awareness of the need to tackle the 'welfare without work syndrome' (Hemerijk and Eichhorst 2010: 331). Elsewhere, we have considered these trends as processes of 'triple integration', i.e. policies which blur the boundaries between previously distinct logics of contributory and non-contributory benefit provision, connect 'active' and 'passive' forms of labour market policies more closely, and bring together programmes originally aimed at different risk categories. Having assessed the empirical evidence of these types of policy integration across twelve European countries (Clasen and Clegg 2011) it remains to be seen whether the current fiscal and economic crisis will lead to a temporary break in this trend, or even a return to what were often defeatist policies of 'labour shedding' in the past.

References

Aalberg, T. (2003). *Achieving Justice: Comparative Public Opinions on Income Distribution*. Leiden, Boston: Brill.

ABI (Association of British Insurers) (1998). *Insurance Statistics Yearbook 1987–1997*. London: ABI.

—— (2005). *State of the Nation's Saving*. London: ABI.

—— (2007). *Statistical overview of UK insurance in 2006*. —Data bulletin September. London: ABI.

—— (2008). 'Money in funded pensions 2006', Data bulletin January. London: ABI.

ACA (Association of Consulting Actuaries) (2009). 'Twilight or a new dawn for Defined Benefit Schemes?', Report 1, 2009 Pension Trends Survey. London: Association of Consulting Actuaries. Available at <http://www.aca.org.uk>, accessed 18 June 2010.

Adema, W. and Ladaique, M. (2009). 'How expensive is the welfare state? Gross and net indicators in the OECD Social Expenditure Database (SOCX)', *OECD Social, Employment and Migration Working Papers*, No. 92. Paris: OECD.

Agulnik, P. (1999). 'The proposed State Second Pension', *Fiscal Studies*, 20 (4): 409–21.

—— Barr, N., Falkingham, J., and Rake, K. (1999). *Partnership in Pensions? Responses to the Pensions Green Paper*, LSE STICERD Research Paper No. CASE 024. London: CASE.

Alemann, A. V. and Sielschott, S. (2007). 'Gleichstellung per Gesetz? Vom Gesetzentwurf zum Deal zwischen Regierung und Wirtschaftverbänden', in P. Imbusch and D. Rucht (eds.), *Profit oder Gemeinwohl? Fallstudien zur gesellschaftlichen Verantwortung von Wirtschaftseliten*. Wiesbaden: VS Verlag für Sozialwissenschaften, 161–99.

Alesina, A. and Glaeser, E. L. (2004). *Fighting Poverty in the US and Europe. A World of Difference*. Oxford: Oxford University Press.

Allen, J. and Scruggs, L. (2004). 'Political partisanship and welfare state reform in advanced industrial societies', *American Journal of Political Science*, 48 (3): 493–512.

Allison, P. D. (1984). *Event History Analysis: Regression for Longitudinal Data*, Sage University Paper series on Quantitative Applications in the Social Sciences, 46. Beverly Hills: Sage.

Allmendinger, J. (1989). 'Educational systems and labour market outcomes', *European Sociological Review*, 5 (3): 231–50.

AltEink, G. (2004). *Gesetz zur Neuordnung der einkommensteuerrechtlichen Behandlung von Altersvosorgeaufwendungen und Altersbezügen (Alterseinkünftegesetz)*. Bonn: Deutscher Bundestag.

Altersvermögensgesetz (2000). *Gesetzentwurf der Fraktionen SPD und BÜNDNIS 90/DIE GRÜNEN: Enwurf eines Gesetzes zur Reform der gesetzlichen Rentenversicherung und zur*

Förderung eines kapitalgedeckten Altersvorsorgevermögens. 14.11.2000. Bundestagsdrucksache 14/4595. Berlin: Deutscher Bundestag.

Andersen, J. G. (2011). 'Denmark: The silent revolution of the Danish pension system. Social democratic multipillarization', in B. Ebbinghaus (ed.), *Varieties of Pension Governance. The Privatization of Pensions in Europe.* Oxford: Oxford University Press, 183–209.

Anderson, K. M. (2007). 'The Netherlands: Political competition in a proportional system', in E. M. Immergut, K. M. Anderson, and I. Schulze (eds.), *The Handbook of West European Pension Politics.* Oxford: Oxford University Press, 713–57.

—— and Meyer, T. (2003). 'Social democracy, unions, and pension politics in Germany and Sweden', *Journal of Public Policy*, 23 (1): 23–55.

—— —— (2006). 'New social risks and pension reform in Germany and Sweden', in K. Armingeon and G. Bonoli (eds.), *The Politics of Pension Rights for Childcare. Post Industrial Welfare States. Politics and Policies.* London: Routledge, 171–91.

Andreß, H.-J. and Heien, T. (2001). 'Four worlds of welfare state attitudes? A comparison of Germany, Norway, and the United States', *European Sociological Review*, 17 (4): 337–56.

Arneson, R. (1997). 'Egalitarianism and the undeserving poor', *Journal of Political Philosophy*, 5 (4): 327–50.

Arts, W. and Gelissen, J. (2001). 'Welfare states, solidarity and justice principles: Does the type really matter?', *Acta Sociologica*, 44 (4): 283–300.

Atkinson, A. B. (2007). 'The distribution of earnings in OECD countries', *International Labour Review*, 146 (1–2): 41–60.

Auth, D. (2007). 'Pronatalistischer Aktionismus: von der bevölkerungspolitischen Instrumentalisierung und Ökonomisierung der Familienpolitik in Deutschland', in D. Auth and B. Holland-Cunz (eds.), *Grenzen der Bevölkerungspolitik. Strategien und Diskurse demographischer Steuerung.* Opladen & Farmingdon Hills: Verlag Barbara Budrich, 81–102.

BaFin (Bundesanstalt für Finanzdienstleistungsaufsicht) (2009). *Jahresbericht 2008.* Berlin: BaFin.

Bahle, T. (2005). 'Family policies in the enlarged European Union: Persistent diversity in "old" and transition to the periphery in the "new" Europe?'. Contribution to the conference 'Social Conditions in the Enlarged Europe', WZB, Berlin, 8–9 December 2005.

—— (2008). 'The state and social services in Britain, France and Germany since the 1980s', *European Societies*, 10 (1): 25–47.

Baldwin, P. (1990). *The Politics of Social Solidarity. Class Bases of the European Welfare State 1875–1975.* Cambridge: Cambridge University Press.

Ball, S. J. and Vincent, C. (2005). 'The "childcare champion"? New Labour, social justice and the childcare market', *British Educational Research Journal*, 31 (5): 557–70.

Bambra, C. (2007). 'Defamilisation and welfare state regimes: A cluster analysis', *International Journal of Social Welfare*, 16: 326–38.

Bannink, D. and de Vroom, B. (2007). 'The Dutch pension system and social inclusion', in T. Meyer, P. Bridgen, and B. Riedmüller (eds.), *Private Pensions versus Social Inclusion? Non-state Provision for Citizens at Risk in Europe.* Cheltenham: Edward Elgar, 79–106.

Banting, K. G. (2000). 'Looking in three directions: Migration and the European welfare state in comparative perspective', in M. Bommes and A. Geddes (eds.), *Immigration and Welfare: Challenging the Borders of the Welfare State*. London, New York: Routledge, 13–33.

—— Johnston, R., Kymlicka, W., and Soroka, S. (2006). 'Do multiculturalism policies erode the welfare state? An empirical analysis', in K. G. Banting and W. Kymlicka (eds.), *Multiculturalism and the Welfare State: Recognition and Redistribution in Contemporary Democracies*. Oxford: Oxford University Press, 49–91.

Bara, J. and Budge, I. (2001). 'Party policy and ideology: Still New Labour?', *Parliamentary Affairs*, 54 (4): 590–606.

Barclays Capital (2009). *Barclays Capital Equity Gilt Study*. Available at <http://www.barcap.com/Client+offering/Research/Global+Asset+Allocation/Equity+Gilt+Study>, accessed June 2010.

Barr, N. (1999). 'A public–private partnership in pensions: Getting the balance right', in P. Agulnik, N. Barr, J. Falkingham, and K. Rake (eds.), *Partnership in Pensions? Responses to the Pensions Green Paper*. London: CASE, 30–45.

—— and Coulter, F. (1990). 'Social security: Solution or problem?' in J. Hills (eds.), *The State of Welfare. The Welfare State in Britain since 1974*. Oxford: Clarendon Press, 274–337.

BASF (2007). BASF Report 2007. Available at <http://www.basf.com/group/investor-relations_en/index>, accessed June 2010.

Bauer, T. K. (2002). 'Migration, Sozialstaat und Zuwanderungspolitik', *DIW. Vierteljahreshefte zur Wirtschaftsforschung*, 71 (2): 249–71.

Bayer (2008). Bayer Schering Pharma Annual Report 2008. Available at <http://www.investor.bayer.com/en/>, accessed June 2010.

Beblo, M. and Wolf, E. (2004). 'Chancengleichheit und Vereinbarkeit von Familie und Beruf: Faktoren des betrieblichen Engagements', *WSI Mitteilungen*, 10: 561–7.

Beck-Gernsheim, E. (2002). *Reinventing the Family*. Cambridge: Polity Press.

Begg, I., J. Draxler, and J. Mortensen (2007). *Is Social Europe Fit for Globalisation? A Study on the Social Impact of Globalization in the European Union*. Brussels: European Communities.

Benio, M. and Ratajczak-Tuchołka, J. (2007). 'The Polish pension system and social inclusion', in T. Meyer, P. Bridgen, and B. Riedmüller (eds.), *Private Pensions versus Social Inclusion? Non-state Provision for Citizens at Risk in Europe*. Cheltenham: Edward Elgar, 193–219.

Berger, P. and Kahlert, H. (2006). 'Einführung: Das "Problem" des demographischen Wandels', in P. Berger and H. Kahlert (eds.), *Der demographische Wandel. Chancen für die Neuordnung der Geschlechterverhältnisse?* Frankfurt am Main and New York: Campus, 9–26.

Berié, H. (1978). 'Neue statistische Ergebnisse', *BetrAV*, 33 (7): 201–9.

Berner, F. (2006). *Beyond the Distinction Between Public and Private: Hybrid Welfare Production in German Old-Age Security*. Regina Working Paper no. 10. Bielefeld, University of Bielefeld. Available at <http://www.uni-bielefeld.de/soz/Forschung/Projekte/regina/pdf/Arbeitspapier10.pdf>, accessed November 2008.

—— (2009). *Der hybride Sozialstaat. Die Neuordnung von öffentlich und privat in der sozialen Sicherung*. Frankfurt and New York: Campus.

Bertozzi, F. and Bonoli, G. (2007). 'The Swiss pension system and social inclusion', in T. Meyer, P. Bridgen, and B. Riedmüller (eds.), *Private Pensions versus Social Inclusion? Non-state Provision for Citizens at Risk in Europe*. Cheltenham: Edward Elgar, 107–35.

Bertram, H. (2006). 'Nachhaltige Familienpolitik und die Zukunft der Kinder', in H. Bertram, H. Krüger, and K. Spieß (eds.), *Wem gehört die Familie der Zukunft? Expertisen zum Siebten Familienbericht der Bundesregierung*. Opladen & Farmingdon Hills: Verlag Barbara Budrich, 7–12.

—— Rösler, W., and Ehlert, N. (2005). *Nachhaltige Familienpolitik. Zukunftssicherung durch einen Dreiklang von Zeitpolitik, finanzieller Transferpolitik und Infrastruktur*. Berlin: BFSFJ.

BetrAV (Betriebliche Altersversorgung) (1957). 'Ruhegeldrückstellungen sind kein Instrument einer steuerlichen Selbstfinanzierung', *BetrAV*, 12 (8/9): 113–15.

—— (1958). 'Rückwirkungen der Rentenreform—Pensionsfonds fließen über', *BetrAV*, 13 (11): 118–19.

—— (1967). 'Umstrittene betriebliche Sozialpolitik', *BetrAV*, 22 (8): 153–7.

—— (2007). 'Entwurf eines Gesetzes zur Förderung der betrieblichen Altersversorgung', *BetrAV*, (6): 560–3.

BetrAVG (Betriebsrentengesetz) (2005). *Gesetz zur Verbesserung der Betrieblichen Altersversorgung (Betriebsrentengesetz)*. Berlin: Deutscher Bundestag.

Beyer, J. (2005). 'Pfadabhängigkeit ist nicht gleich Pfadabhängigkeit! Wider den impliziten Konservatismus eines gängigen Konzepts', *Zeitschrift für Soziologie* 34 (1): 5–21.

Bischoff, H.-A. (1965). 'Die sozialpolitische Bedeutung der betrieblichen Altersversorgung', *Betriebliche Altersversorgung*, 20 (4/5): 86–90.

Bispinck, R. (2001). *Tarifliche Altersvorsorge. Eine Analyse von tariflichen Regelungen in 57 ausgewählten Tarifbereichen*. Düsseldorf: WSI.

Black, J. and Nobles, R. (1998). 'Personal pensions misselling: The causes and lessons of regulatory failure', *The Modern Law Review*, 61 (6): 789–820.

Blair, A., Karsten, L., and Leopold, J. (2001). 'Britain and the Working Time Regulations', *Politics*, 21 (1): 40–6.

Blair, T. (1998). *The Third Way*. London: Fabian Society.

—— and Schröder, G. (1999). 'Der Weg nach vorne für Europas Sozialdemokraten', *Blätter für deutsche und internationale Politik*, 44 (7): 887–96.

Blake, D. (2003). *Pension Schemes and Pension Funds in the United Kingdom*. Oxford: Oxford University Press.

Blekesaune, M. and Quadagno, J. (2003). 'Public attitudes toward welfare state policies. A comparative analysis of 24 nations', *European Sociological Review*, 19: 415–27.

Bleses, P. and Seeleib-Kaiser, M. (2004). *The Dual Transformation of the German Welfare State*. Cheltenham: Palgrave.

Blien, U., Walwei, U., and Werner, H. (2002). *Labour Market Policy in Germany: Job Placement, Unemployment Insurance and Active Labour Market Policy in Germany*, IAB Labour Market Research Topics, 49. Nürnberg: Institut für Arbeitsmarkt- und Berufsforschung.

Blossfeld, H.-P., Klijzing, E., Mills, M., and Kurz, K. (eds.) (2005). *Globalization, Uncertainty and Youth in Society*. London: Routledge.

—— and Rohwer, G. (1995). *Techniques of Event-History Modeling. New Approaches to Causal Analysis*. Mahwah, NJ: Erlbaum.

BMAS (Bundesministerium für Arbeit und soziale Sicherung) (2009). *Entwicklung der Privaten Altersvorsorge*. Berlin: BMAS.

BMBF (Bundesministerium für Bildung und Forschung) (2002). *Hochschulrahmengesetz*. Fassung der Bekanntmachung vom 19. Januar 1999 (BGBl. I S. 18), zuletzt geändert durch Artikel 1 des Gesetzes vom 8. August 2002 (BGBl. I S. 3138). Berlin: BMBF.

—— (2004a). *Das Tagesbetreuungsausbaugesetz (TAG). Gesetz zum qualitätsorientierten und bedarfsgerechten Ausbau der Tagesbetreuung und Weiterentwicklung der Kinder- und Jugendhilfe*. Berlin: BMFSFJ.

—— (2004b). *Erwartungen an einen familienfreundlichen Betrieb*. Berlin: BMFSFJ.

—— (2005). *Familienfreundliche Regelungen in Tarifverträgen und Betriebsvereinbarungen: Praxis guter Praxis*. Berlin: BMFSFJ.

—— (2006a). *Familie zwischen Flexibilität und Verlässlichkeit. Perspektiven für eine lebenslaufbezogene Familienpolitik. Siebter Familienbericht*. Berlin: Bundesministerium für Familie, Senioren, Frauen und Jugend.

—— (2006b). *Familienfreundlichkeit im Betrieb Ergebnisse einer repräsentativen Bevölkerungsumfrage*. Berlin: BMFSFJ.

—— (2006c). *Unternehmensmonitor Familienfreundlichkeit 2006: Wie familienfreundlich ist die deutsche Wirtschaft? Stand, Fortschritte, Bilanz*. Berlin: BMFSFJ.

—— (2007). *Politik für die Zukunft. Ausbau der Tagesbetreuung für Kinder unter drei Jahren in Deutschland. Daten für die Medien*. Berlin: BMFSFJ.

—— (2009). *Elterngeld und Elternzeit*. Berlin: BMFSFJ.

BMFSFJ and Bertelsmann Stiftung (2003). *Grundlagenpapier der Impulsgruppe Allianz für die Familie. Balance von Familie und Arbeitswelt*. Berlin: BMFSFJ and Bertelsmann Stiftung.

Boeri, T., Hanson, G., and McCormick, B. (eds.) (2002). *Immigration Policy and the Welfare System*. Oxford: Oxford University Press.

Bommes, M. and Halfmann, J. (eds.) (1998). *Migration in nationalen Wohlfahrtsstaaten. Theoretische und vergleichende Untersuchungen*. Osnabrück: Universitätsverlag Rasch.

Bonoli, G. (1997). 'Classifying welfare states: A two-dimension approach', *Journal of Social Policy*, 26 (3): 351–72.

—— (2000a). 'Public social attitudes to social protection and political economy traditions in Western Europe', *European Societies*, 2 (4): 431–52.

Bonoli, G. (2000b). *The Politics of Pension Reform: Institutions and Policy Change in Western Europe*. Cambridge: Cambridge University Press.

—— (2003a). 'Social policy through labour markets. Understanding national differences in the provision of economic security to wage earners', *Comparative Political Studies*, 36: 983–1006.

—— (2003b). 'Two worlds of pension reform in Western Europe', *Comparative Politics*, 35 (4): 399–416.

—— (2005). 'The politics of the new social policies', *Policy and Politics*, 33 (3): 431–49.

—— (2007a). 'Too narrow and too wide at once: The welfare state as dependent variable in policy analysis', in J. Clasen and N. A. Siegel (eds.), *Investigating Welfare State Change. The 'Dependent Variable Problem' in Comparative Analysis*. Cheltenham: Edward Elgar, 24–42.

—— (2007b). 'Switzerland: The impact of direct democracy', in E. M. Immergut, K. M. Anderson, and I. Schulze (eds.), *The Handbook of West European Pension Politics*. Oxford: Oxford University Press, 203–47.

—— (2011). 'Active labour market policies changing economy context', in J. Clasen and D. Clegg (eds.), *Regulating the Risk of Unemployment. National Adaptations to Post-industrial Labour Markets in Europe*. Oxford: Oxford University Press (forthcoming).

Bonoli, G. and Palier, B. (2007). 'When past reforms open new opportunities: Comparing old-age insurance reforms in Bismarckian welfare systems', *Social Policy & Administration*, 41 (6): 555–73.

Börsch-Supan, A., Reil-Held, A., and Schunk, D. (2007). 'The savings behaviour of German households: First experiences with state promoted private pensions', MEA—Discussion Paper 136–2007. Mannheim: Research Institute for the Economics of Aging, Mannheim University.

Bothfeld, S. (2005). *Vom Erziehungsurlaub zur Elternzeit. Politisches Lernen im Reformprozess*. Frankfurst: Campus Verlag.

Bowles, S. and Gintis, H. (2000). 'Reciprocity, self-interest and the welfare state', *Nordic Journal of Political Economy*, 26 (4): 33–53.

Brandth, B. and Kvande, E. (2001). 'Flexible work and flexible fathers', *Work, Employment and Society*, 15 (2): 251–67.

Bridgen, P. (2000). 'The One Nation idea and state welfare: The Conservative Party and pensions in the 1950s', *Contemporary British History*, 14 (3): 83–104.

—— (2006). 'A straitjacket with wriggle room: The Beveridge Report, the Treasury and the Exchequer's pension liability 1942–1959', *Twentieth Century British History*, 17 (1): 1–25.

—— (2010). 'Towards a social democratic pension system? Assessing the significance of the 2007 and 2008 Pension Acts', *Social Policy Review 22*. Bristol: Policy Press.

—— and Lowe, R. (1998). *Welfare Policy Under the Conservatives 1951–1960. A Guide to the Documents in the Public Record Office*. London: Public Record Office.

—— and Meyer, T. (2005). 'When do benevolent capitalists change their mind? Explaining the retrenchment of Defined Benefit Pensions in Britain', *Social Policy and Administration*, 39 (4): 764–85.

—— —— (2007a). 'Private pensions versus social inclusion? Citizens at risk and the new pensions orthodoxy', in T. Meyer, P. Bridgen, and B. Riedmüller (eds.), *Private Pensions versus Social Inclusion? Non-state Provision for Citizens at Risk in Europe*. Cheltenham: Edward Elgar.

—— —— (2007b). 'The British pension system and social inclusion,' in T. Meyer, P. Bridgen, and B. Riedmüller (eds.), *Private Pensions versus Social Inclusion? Non-state Provision for Citizens at Risk in Europe*. Cheltenham: Edward Elgar, 50–78.

—— —— (2009). 'The politics of occupational pension reform in Britain and the Netherlands: The power of market discipline in liberal and corporatist regimes', *West European Politics*, 32 (3): 586–610.

—— —— (2011) 'Exhausted voluntarism—the evolution of the British liberal pension regime', in B. Ebbinghaus (ed.), *Varieties of Pension Governance. The Privatization of Pensions in Europe*. Oxford: Oxford University Press, 265–91.

Brooks, C. and Manza, J. (2006). 'Social policy responsiveness in developed democracies', *American Sociological Review*, 71 (3): 474–94.

BSA (British Social Attitudes) (2004). *Online Publishing*. Available at <http://www.data-archive.ac.uk/findingData/bsaTitles.asp>, accessed June 2010.

—— (2006). *Online Publishing*. Available at <http://www.data-archive.ac.uk/findingData/bsaTitles.asp>, accessed 20 June 2010.

BT-Pl. 14/176 (2001). Stenographischer Bericht. 176 Sitzung, Berlin, Donnerstag den 21. Juni 2001 Deutscher Bundestag. Available at <http://dipbt.bundestag.de/doc/btp/14/14176.pdf>, accessed March 2011.

Büchs, M. (2007). *New Governance in European Social Policy. The Open Method of Coordination*. London: Palgrave.

Budd, J. and Mumford, K. (2004). 'Trade unions and family-friendly policies in Britain', *Industrial and Labor Review*, 57: 204–22.

—— —— (2005). 'Family-friendly work practices in Britain: Availability and perceived accessibility', *IZA Discussion Paper*, No. 1662. Bonn: IZA.

Bundesagentur für Arbeit (2005). *Der Übergang von der Arbeitslosen- und Sozialhilfe zur Grundsicherung für Arbeitslose*. Nürnberg: Sonderbericht Statistik, Bundesagentur für Arbeit.

—— (2010a). *Arbeitsmarktdaten der Bundesanstalt für Arbeit. Arbeitslose*. Wiesbaden: Statistisches Bundesamt Deutschland.

—— (2010b). *Analytikreport der Statistik. Arbeitslosigkeit nach Rechtskreisen im Vergleich*, December 2009. Nürnberg: Bundesagentur für Arbeit.

—— (2010c). *Ausgewählte arbeitsmarktpolitische Instrumente—für Personen im Rechtskreis SGB II—mit Förderinformationen der zkT*, January 2010. Nürnberg: Bundesagentur für Arbeit.

Bundesministerium für Arbeit und Soziales (2007). *Rente—Zusätzliche Altersvorsorge—Staatliche Förderung der betrieblichen Altersversorgung*. Available at <http://www.bmas.bund.de/BMAS/Navigation/Rente/Zusaetzliche-Altersvorsorge/Betriebliche-Altersvorsorge/staatliche-foerderung.html>, accessed April 2007.

Bundesministerium für Wirtschaft und Arbeit (2003). 'Tarifvertragliche Arbeitsbedingungen im Jahr 2002', *BetrAV*, (7): 636–44.

—— (2004). *Tarifvertragliche Arbeitsbedingungen im Jahr 2004*. Available at <http://www.bmas.bund.de/BMAS/Redaktion/Pdf/tarifvertragliche-arbeitsbedingungen-2004>, accessed April 2007.

Busch, A. (1999). *The 'Neue Mitte' in Germany*. Available at <http://users.ox.ac.uk/~busch/papers/neumitte.pdf>, accessed May 2006.

Busch, A. (2005). 'Globalisation and national varieties of capitalism: The contested viability of the "German model"', *German Politics*, 14 (2): 125–39.

Bynner, J., Butler, N., Ferri, E., Shepherd, P., and Smith, K. (2001). 'The design and conduct of the 1999–2000 surveys of the national child development study and the 1970 British cohort study', *CLS Cohort Studies Working Papers*, 1: 1–303.

Castles, F. (2009). 'What welfare states do: A disaggregated expenditure approach', *Journal of Social Policy*, 38 (1): 45–62.

Cazalet Consulting (2006). *Polly Put the Kettle On. Pensions Profitability*. London: Cazalet Consulting.

Chassard, Y. and Quintin, O. (1992). 'Social protection in the European Community: Towards a convergence of policies', *International Social Security Review*, 45 (1–2): 91–108.

Chick, M. (1998). *Industrial Policy in Britain 1945-1951. Economic Planning, Nationalisation and Labour Governments*. Cambridge: Cambridge University Press.

Childcare Act (2006). Online Publishing. Available at <www.surestart.gov.uk/resources/general/childcareact/>, accessed June 2010.

The Children and Young People's Plan (England) (Amendment) Regulations (2007). Available at <http://www.legislation.gov.uk/uksi/2007/57/contents/made', accessed April 2011.

Cichowski, R. A. (2004). 'Women's rights, the European Court, and supranational constitutionalism', *Law & Society Review*, 38 (3): 489–512.

Clarke, K. (2007). 'New Labour: Family policy and gender', in C. Annesly, F. Gains, and K. Rummerey (eds.), *Women and New Labour: Engendering Politics and Policy?* Bristol: Policy Press, 155–74.

Clasen, J. (2000). 'Motives, means and opportunities. Reforming unemployment compensation in the 1990s', *West European Politics*, 23 (2): 89–112.

—— (2001). 'Social insurance and the contributory principle: A paradox in contemporary British Social Policy', *Social Policy & Administration*, 35 (6): 641–57.

—— (2005). *Reforming European Welfare States: Germany and the United Kingdom Compared*. Oxford: Oxford University Press.

—— (2009). 'The United Kingdom', in P. De Beer and T. Schils (eds.), *The Labour Market Triangle. Employment Protection, Unemployment Compensation and Activation in Europe*. Cheltenham: Edward Elgar, 70–95.

—— (2011). 'The United Kingdom—towards a single working-age benefit system', in J. Clasen and D. Clegg (eds.), *Regulating the Risk of Unemployment. National Adaptations to Post-industrial Labour Markets in Europe*. Oxford: Oxford University Press (forthcoming).

—— —— (eds.) (2011). *Regulating the Risk of Unemployment: National Adaptations to Post-industrial Labour Markets in Europe*. Oxford: Oxford University Press.

Clasen J., Davidson, J., Ganssmann H., and Mauer, A. (2006). 'Non-employment and the welfare state: the UK and Germany compared', *Journal of European Social Policy*, 16 (2): 134–54.

—— and Goerne, A. (forthcoming). 'Germany: ambivalent activation', in I. Lødemel and A. Moreira (eds.), *Workfare Revisited*. Oxford: Oxford University Press.

—— —— (2011). 'Exit Bismarck, enter dualism? Assessing contemporary German labour market policy', *Journal of Social Policy*, 40(4) (forthcoming).

Clegg, D. (2007). 'Continental drift: On unemployment policy change in Bismarckian welfare states', *Social Policy and Administration*, 41 (6): 597–617.

Clegg, H. A. (1978). *The System of Industrial Relations in Great Britain*. Oxford: Blackwell.

Cm 3959 (1998). *Meeting the Childcare Challenge: A Framework and Consultation Document*. London: The Stationary Office.

Cm 3968 (1998). *Fairness at Work*, White Paper. London: The Stationery Office.

Cm 5005 (2000). *Work and Parents: Competitiveness and Choice*, Green Paper. London: Department of Trade and Industry.

Conservative Party (2010a). Coalition agreement. Available at <http://www.conservatives. com/News/News_stories/2010/05/Coalition_Agreement_published.aspx>, accessed May 2010.

—— (2010b). *Invitation to Join the Government of Britain. The Conservative Manifesto 2010.* London: Conservative Party.

Conway, L. (2001). *The Regulatory Reform Bill (HL): Background to Red Tape Issues*, Research Paper 01/26, 14 March 2001. London: House of Commons Library.

Coppola, M. (2007). 'SAVE—Altersvorsorge in Deutschland', Conference paper, MEA-Konferenz 2007, Schwetzingen.

CRE (Conferences and the Association of European Universities) (2000). *The Bologna Declaration of 19 June 1999 on the European Space for Higher Education. Joint Declaration of the European Ministers of Education. An Explanation.* Bologna: CRE.

Crepaz, M. M. L. and Damron, R. (2009). 'Constructing tolerance: How the welfare state shapes attitudes about immigrants', *Comparative Political Studies*, 42 (2): 437–63.

Cunningham, R. (2009). *The Anglo–German Foundation 1973–2009*. London: Anglo–German Foundation.

Daimler (2008). Daimler Annual Report 2008. Available at <http://www.daimler.com/ investor-relations/en>, accessed June 2010.

Dallinger, U. (2008). 'Sozialstaatliche Umverteilung und ihre Akzeptanz im internationalen Vergleich: Eine Mehrebenenanalyse', *Zeitschrift für Soziologie*, 37 (2): 137–57.

Daly, M. (2000). 'A fine balance: Women's labour market participation in international comparison', in F. Scharpf and V. Schmidt (eds.), *Welfare and Work in the Open Economy*. Oxford: Oxford University Press, 467–510.

—— and Clavero, S. (2002). *Contemporary Family Policy. A Comparative Review of Ireland, France, Germany, Sweden and the UK*. Dublin: Institute of Public Administration.

Davis, E. P. (2001). *The Regulation of Funded Pensions: A Case Study of the United Kingdom*, Occasional Paper Series 15. London: Financial Services Authority.

De Deken, J. and Clasen, J. (2011). 'Tracking caseload—the changing composition of working-age benefit receipt in Europe', in J. Clasen and D. Clegg (eds.), *Regulating the Risk of Unemployment. National Adaptations to Post-industrial Labour Markets in Europe*. Oxford: Oxford University Press (forthcoming).

Dean, H. (2002). 'Business *versus* families: Whose side is New Labour on?', *Social Policy & Society* 1 (1): 3–10.

Dearing Report (1997). *Higher Education in the Learning Society*. The National Committee of Inquiry into Higher Education. Available at <http://www.leeds.ac.uk/educol/ ncihe/>, accessed March 2011.

Dekker, R., de Grip, A., and Heijke, H. (2002). 'The effects of training and overeducation on career mobility in a segmented labour market', *International Journal of Manpower*, 23 (2): 106–25.

Deloitte (2006). *Face to Face with the Future*. London: Deloitte.

Den Dulk, L. (2001). *Work-Family Arrangements in Organisations: A Cross-National Study in the Netherlands, Italy, the United Kingdom and Sweden*. Amsterdam: Rozenberg.

DES (Department of Education and Science) (1966). *A Plan for Polytechnics and Other Colleges. Higher Education in the Further Education System*, Cm 300b. London: DES.

Dettling, W. (2004). 'Work-Life Balance als strategisches Handlungsfeld für die Gewerkschaften', Arbeitspapier Nr. 90. Düseldorf: Hans Böckler Stiftung.

Deutscher Bundestag (2004). *Plenarprotokoll 15. WP, 123. Sitzung, Stenographischer Bericht, 09.09.2004*. Berlin: Deutscher Bundestag.

Deutscher Städtetag (2004). *Tagesbetreuungsausbaugesetz—Beschluss des Präsidium des Deutschen Städtetages vom 20.04.2004*. Available at <http://www.aus-portal.de/ aktuell/gesetze/01/index_6529.htm>, accessed May 2009.

Dex, S. and Smith, C. (2001). 'Which British employers have family-friendly policies? Analysis of the 1998 Workplace Employee Relations Survey', *Research Papers in Management Studies* 17. Cambridge: Judge Institute of Management, University of Cambridge.

DfE (Department for Education) (1985). *The Development of Higher Education into the 1990s*, Cm 9524. London: DfE.

—— (1994). *Student Numbers in Higher Education—Great Britain 1982/83 to 1992/93*. London: DfE.

DfEE (Department for Education and Employment) (1998). *Green Paper 'The Learning Age: A Renaissance for a New Britain'*. London: DfE.

DfES (Department for Education and Skills) (2003). *The Future of Higher Education. Government White Paper presented to Parliament by the Secretary of State for Education and Skills by Command of Her Majesty*. London: DfES.

—— (2004). *Higher Education, Better Regulation: Towards a New Culture of Autonomy and Accountability*. London: DfES.

—— (2006). Case Matters: Transforming the Lives of Children and Young People in Care. London: The Stationery Office.

Dickens, L. (1994). 'The business case for women's equality: Is the carrot better than the stick?' *Employee Relations*, 16: 5–18.

Diller, A. (2006). *Eltern-Kind-Zentren. Grundlagen und Recherche-Ergebnisse*. München: Deutsches Jugendinstitut. Available at <www.dji.de/bibs/4EKZ-Grundlagenbericht .pdf>, accessed March 2011.

DiMaggio, P. J. and Powell, W. P. (1983). 'The iron cage revisited: Institutional isomorphism and collective rationality in organizational fields', *American Sociological Review*, 48: 147–60.

Dingeldey, I. (2007). 'Wohlfahrtsstaatlicher Wandel zwischen Arbeitszwang und Befähigung. Eine vergleichende Analyse aktivierender Arbeitsmarktpolitik in Deutschland, Dänemark und Großbritannien', *Berliner Journal für Soziologie*, 17: 189–209.

Disney, R. and Whitehouse, E. (1992). 'The Personal Pensions stampede', IFS-Report R40. London: Institute for Fiscal Studies.

—— Emmerson, C., and Wakefield, M. (2001). 'Pension reform and saving in Britain', *Oxford Review of Economic Policy*, 17 (1): 70–94.

—— —— —— (2007). 'Tax reform and retirement saving incentives: Evidence from the introduction of Stakeholder Pensions in the UK', IFS-WP 19/07. London: Institute for Fiscal Studies.

Doern, G. B. and Phidd, R. W. (1983). *Canadian Public Policy: Ideas, Structure, Process.* New York: Methuen.

DRV (Deutsche Rentenversicherung) (2009a). *Rentenversicherung in Zeitreihen.* Berlin: Verband Deutscher Rentenversicherungsträger.

—— (2009b). *Rentenversicherung in Zeitreihen. 10—Finanzdaten.* Berlin: DRV.

—— (2009c). *Rentenversicherung in Zeitreihen. 11—Kenngrößen und Bemessungswerte.* Berlin: DRV.

—— (2007). *Flexible Working—The Right to Request and the Duty to Consider.* London: DTI.

DWP (Department for Work and Pensions) (2002). *Simplicity, Security and Choice: Working and Saving for Retirement.* London: DWP.

—— (2006). *Security in Retirement: Towards a New Pensions System,* Cm 6841. London: DWP.

DWP (Department for Work and Pensions) (2008a). *No one Written Off: Reforming Welfare to Reward Responsibility,* Public consultation, July. London: DWP.

—— (2008b). *Raising Expectations and Increasing Support: Reforming Welfare for the Future,* CM 7506. London: DWP.

—— (2009). *Pensions—Consultation on Draft Scheme Order and Rules.* London: DWP.

DWP—*SERPS Statistics,* Online publishing, available at <http://statistics.dwp.gov.uk/asd/asd1/dsu/second_tier/second_tier.asp>, accessed August 2008.

Ebbinghaus, B. (2006). 'Die sozialen Risiken der neuen Alterssicherungssysteme', in K.-S. Rehberg (eds.), *Soziale Ungleichheit, Kulturelle Unterschiede. Verhandlungen des 32. Kongresses der Deutschen Gesellschaft für Soziologie in München 2004. Teil 1.* Frankfurt am Main: Campus, 473–88.

—— and Eichhorst, W. (2009). 'Germany', in P. De Beer and T. Schils (eds.), *The Labour Market Triangle. Employment Protection, Unemployment Compensation and Activation in Europe.* Cheltenham: Edward Elgar, 119–44.

—— and Gronwald, M. (2011). 'The changing public–private pension mix in Europe: From path dependence to path departure', in B. Ebbinghaus (ed.), *Varieties of Pension Governance. The Privatization of Pensions in Europe.* Oxford: Oxford University Press, 23–56.

Education and Employment Committee (1999). *Second Report on Part-time Working,* HC 346-I, 23 March 1999. London: The Stationery Office.

Eichhorst, W., Kaiser, L., Thode, E., and Tobsch, V. (2007). *Vereinbarkeit von Familie und Beruf im internationalen Vergleich. Zwischen Paradigma und Praxis.* Gütersloh: Bertelsmann Stiftung.

—— Grienberger-Zingerle, M., and Konle-Seidl, R. (2008). 'Activation policies in Germany: From status protection to basic income support', in W. Eichhorst, O. Kaufmann, and R. Konle-Seidl (eds.), *Bringing the Jobless into Work? Experiences with Activation Schemes in Europe and the US.* Heidelberg: Springer-Verlag, 17–68.

Elias, N. and Scotson, J. L. (1965). *The Established and the Outsiders. A Sociological Enquiry into Community Problems.* London: Frank Cass & Co.

Ellis, B. (1989). *Pensions in Britain 1955–1975.* London: HMSO.

Emmenegger, P. (2009). *Regulatory Social Policy. The Politics of Job Security Regulation.* Berne: Haupt Verlag.

Emmerson, C. and Wakefield, M. (2009). *Amounts and Accounts: Reforming Private Pensions Enrolment*, Commentary C110. London: Institute for Fiscal Studies.

Employment Committee (1995). *Second Special Report in Session 1994–95. Mothers in Employment. Government Reply to the First Report of the Committee in Session 1994–95, HC 227*. London: The Stationery Office.

Erlinghagen, M. and Knuth, M. (2010). 'Unemployment as an institutional construct? Structural differences in non-employment between selected European countries and the United States', *Journal of Social Policy*, 39 (1): 71–94.

Esping-Andersen, G. (1990). *The Three Worlds of Welfare Capitalism*. Cambridge: Polity Press.

—— (1996a). 'After the Golden Age? Welfare state dilemmas in a global economy', in G. Esping-Andersen (ed.), *Wefare States in Transition: National Adaptations in Global Economies*. London: Sage, 1–31.

—— (1996b). 'Welfare states without work: The impasse of labour shedding and familialism in continental social policy', in G. Esping-Andersen (ed.), *Wefare States in Transition: National Adaptations in Global Economies*. London: Sage, 66–87.

—— (1999). *Social Foundations of Postindustrial Economies*. Oxford: Oxford University Press.

—— (2002a). 'A child-centred social investment strategy', in G. Esping-Andersen, D. Gallie, A. Hemerijck, and J. Myles (eds.), *Why We Need a New Welfare State*. Oxford: University Press, 26–67.

—— (2002b). 'Towards the Good Society, once again?', in G. Esping-Andersen, D. Gallie, A. Hemerijk, and J. Myles (eds.), *Why We Need a New Welfare State*. Oxford: Oxford University Press, 1–25.

—— with Gallie, D., Hemerijk, A., and Myles, J. (eds.) (2002). *Why We Need a New Welfare State*. Oxford: Oxford University Press.

Esping-Andersen, G. (2009). *The Incomplete Revolution: Adapting to Women's New Roles*. Cambridge: Polity Press.

Estévez-Abe, M. (2005). 'Gender bias in skills and social policies: The varieties of capitalism perspective on sex segregation', *Social Politics: International Studies in Gender, State and Society*, 12 (2): 180–215.

—— (2006). 'Gendering the varieties of capitalism a study of occupational segregation by sex in advanced industrial societies', *World Politics*, Vol. 59 (1)142–175.

—— Iversen, T., and Soskice, D. (2001). 'Social protection and the formation of skills: A reinterpretation of the welfare state', in P. A. Hall and D. Soskice (eds.), *Varieties of Capitalism: The Institutional Foundations of Comparative Advantage*. Oxford: Oxford University Press, 145–83.

European Central Bank (2004). *Statistics Pocket Book*. Available at <http//:www.ecb. europa.eu/pub/spb/html/index.en.html/pdf>, accessed January 2007.

European Commission (1997). *Employment in Europe 1997*. Luxembourg: Statistical Office of the European Communities.

—— (1998). *The 1998 Employment Guidelines*. Council Resolution of 14 December 1997 on the 1998 employment guidelines. Luxembourg: Office for Official Publications of the European Communities.

—— (2010). *Living Conditions and Social Protection; Inequality of Income Distribution.* Luxembourg: Eurostat.

European Social Survey (2002/2003). Online Publishing. European Social Survey Round 1 Data (2002). Data file edition 6.2. Norwegian Social Science Data Services Norway— Data. Archive and distributor of ESS data. Available at <http://www.data-archive.ac. uk/findingData/snDescription.asp?sn=4732>, accessed no data.

Eurostat (2010). *Expenditure on Labour Market Policies, by Type and Action (Summary Tables).* Luxembourg: Eurostat.

Eurydice (2006). *Structures of Education, Vocational Training and Adult Education Systems in Europe—2006 edition.* Brussels: Eurydice, the Information Network on Education in Europe.

Evans, G. (2006). 'Is Multiculturalism Eroding Support for Welfare Provision? The British Case', in K. Banting and W. Kymlicka (eds.), *Multiculturalism and the Welfare State: Recognition and Redistribution in Contemporary Democracies.* Oxford: Oxford University Press, 152–76.

Evans, J. M. (2001). 'Firms' contribution to the reconciliation between work and family life', *OECD Labour Market and Social Policy Occasional Papers*, No. 48. Paris: OECD.

Evers, A., Lewis, J., and Riedel, B. (2005). 'Developing childcare in England and Germany: Problems of governance', *Journal of European Social Policy*, 15 (3): 195–209.

Faist, T. (1998). 'Immigration, Integration und Wohlfahrtsstaaten. Die Bundesrepublik Deutschland in vergleichender Perspektive', in M. Bommes and J. Halfmann (eds.), *Migration in nationalen Wohlfahrtsstaaten. Theoretische und vergleichende Untersuchungen.* Osnabrück: Universitätsverlag Rasch, 147–70.

Falk, S., Sackmann, R., Struck, O., Weymann, A., Windzio, M., and Wingens, M. (2000). 'Gemeinsame Startbedingungen in Ost und West? Risiken beim Berufseinstieg und deren Folgen im weiteren Erwerbsverlauf', *Collaborative Research Center 'Status Passages and Risks in the Life Course' (Sfb 186)*, Working Paper Series, 65, Bremen: University of Bremen.

Fawcett Society (2006). *Fawcett Society Response to the Pensions White Paper 'Security in Retirement: Towards a New Pensions System'.* London: Fawcett Society.

Fawcett, H. (1996). 'The Beveridge strait-jacket: Policy formation and the problem of poverty in old age', *Contemporary British History*, 10 (1): 20–42.

Fieberg, C. (2002). 'Neue Betriebsrente im öffentlichen Dienst', *BetrAV* (3): 230–3.

Finn, D., and Schulte, B. (2008). 'Employment First': Activating the British welfare state', in W. Eichhorst, O. Kaufmann, and Konle-Seidl, R. (eds.), *Bringing the Jobless into Work? Experiences with Activation Schemes in Europe and the US.* Berlin: Springer, 297–344.

—— and Gloster, R. (2010). *Lone Parent Obligations. A Review of Recent Evidence on the Work-related Requirements within the Benefit Systems of Different Countries.* DWP research report no 632. London: DWP.

—— and Lange, J. (2010). 'Der "Wohlfahrtsmarkt" in der britischen Arbeitsmarktpolitik: Lehren für Deutschland?' *Sozialer Fortschritt*, 59 (3): 80–6.

Fitch Ratings (2008). 'Deutsche Lebensversicherer—Auf der Suche nach der verlorenen Zeit', London: Fitch Research.

References

Flecken, H.-L. (1990). 'Die geplante Erhebung des statistischen Bundesamtes zur betrieblichen Altersversorgung 1989'. *BetrAV*, 45 (4): 108–13.

Fleckenstein, T. (2008). 'Restructuring welfare for the unemployed: The Hartz legislation in Germany', *Journal of European Social Policy*, 18 (2): 177–88.

—— and Seeleib-Kaiser, M. (2011). 'Business, skills and the welfare state: the political economy of employment-oriented family policy in Britain and Germany', *Journal of European Social Policy*, 21(2).

—— Saunder, A., and Seeleib-Kaiser, M. (2011). 'The dual transformation of social protection and human capital: Comparing Britain and Germany', *Comparative Political Studies*, 44 (12) (forthcoming).

Foreman-Peck, J. and Millward, R. (1994). *Public and Private Ownership of British Industry 1820–1990*. Oxford: Clarendon Press.

Forsbach, W. (1982). 'Zur Entwicklung der betrieblichen Altersversorgung', *BetrAV*, 37 (5): 156–60.

Fresenius Medical Care (2008). *Fresenius Medical Care Annual Report 2008*. Available at <http://www.fresenius.se/internet/fag/com/faginpub.nsf/Content/Investor+Relations>, accessed March 2011.

Freud, D. (2007). *Reducing Dependency, Increasing Opportunity: Options for the Future of Welfare to Work*, independent report to the DWP. London: DWP, Corporate Document Services.

FSA (Financial Services Authority) (2000). 'In or out? Financial exclusion: A literature and research review', FSA-Consumer Research 3. London: FSA.

Furtmayr, H. and Wagner, C. (2007). 'Die Zusatzversorgung im öffentlichen Dienst— der heimliche Abschied von der Gesamtversorgung', *BetrAV* (6): 543–51.

GAD (Government Actuary Department) (2006). *Occupational Pension Schemes 2005. The Thirteenth Survey by the Government Actuary*. London: GAD.

Galinsky, E., Bond, J. T., and Sakai, K. (2008). *National Study of Employers*. New York: Families and Work Institute.

Gang, I. N., Rivera-Batiz, F. L., and Yun, M.-S. (2002). 'Economic strain, ethnic concentration and attitudes towards foreigners in the European Union'. *IZA Discussion Paper*, 578. Bonn: Forschungsinstitut zur Zukunft der Arbeit.

Gangl, M. (2001). 'European perspectives on labour market entry: A dichotomy of occupationalized versus non-occupationalized systems?', *European Societies*, 3 (4): 471–94.

—— (2002). 'Changing labour markets and early career outcomes: Labour market entry in Europe over the past decade', *Work, Employment and Society*, 16 (1): 67–90.

Ganter, S. (2003). *Soziale Netzwerke und interethnische Distanz: Theoretische und empirische Analysen zum Verhältnis von Deutschen und Ausländern*. Wiesbaden: Westdeutscher Verlag.

von Gaudecker, H.-M. and Weber, C. (2003). 'Surprises in a growing market niche: An evaluation of the German private annuities market', MEA—Working paper 2003–29. Mannheim: Mannheim Research Institute for the Economics of Aging, University of Mannheim.

———— (2006). 'Mandatory unisex policies and annuity pricing: Quasi-experimental evidence from Germany', MEA-Working paper 2006–14. Mannheim: Mannheim Research Institute for the Economics of Aging, University of Mannheim.

Gauthier, A. H. (1996). *The State and the Family: A Comparative Analysis of Family Policies in Industrialized Countries*. Oxford: Clarendon Press.

GDV (Gesamtverband der deutschen Versicherungswirtschaft) (2007). *Jahrbuch 2007. Die deutsche Versicherungswirtschaft*. Berlin: GDV.

Gelissen, J. (2000). 'Popular support for institutionalised solidarity: A comparison between European welfare states', *International Journal of Social Welfare*, 9 (4): 285–300.

Giddens, A. (1998). *The Third Way. The Renewal of Social Democracy*. Cambridge: Polity Press.

———— (1999). 'Family', *Reith Lectures*, 4, BBC Radio 4, 28 April.

Giesecke, J. and Verwiebe, R. (2008). 'Die Lohnentwicklung in Deutschland zwischen 1998 and 2005—wachsende Ungleichheit', *WSI Mitteilungen*, 61(2): 85–91.

Gießelmann, M. (2009). 'Arbeitsmarktpolitischer Wandel in Deutschland seit 1991 und das working poor-Problem: Einsteiger als Verlierer des Reformprozesses?', *Zeitschrift für Soziologie*, 38 (3): 215–38.

Gilbert, N. (2008). *A Mother's Work: How Feminism, the Market, and Policy Shape Family Life*. New Haven: Yale University Press.

Gilley, B. (2006). 'The determinants of state legitimacy: Results for 72 countries', *International Political Science Review*, 27 (1): 47–71.

Ginn, J. (2003). *Gender, Pensions and the Life Course. How Pensions need to Adapt to Changing Family Forms*. Bristol: Policy Press.

———— and Arber, S. (1993). 'Pension penalties: The gendered division of occupational welfare', *Work, Employment & Society*, 7 (1): 47–70.

———— ———— (1999). 'Changing patterns of pension inequality: The shift from state to private sources', *Ageing and Society*, 19 (3): 319–42.

———— ———— (2000). 'Personal pension take-up in the 1990s in relation to position in the labour market', *Journal of Social Policy*, 29 (2): 205–28.

Glass, J. and Fujimoto, T. (1995). 'Employer characteristics and the provision of family responsive policies', *Work and Occupation*, 22: 380–411.

Glass, N. (2005). 'Surely some mistake?', *The Guardian* (January 2005).

Goodhart, D. (2004). 'Too diverse?', *Prospect Magazine*, 95: 30–7.

Goodin, R. E. (2001). 'Work and welfare: Towards a post-productivist welfare regime', *British Journal of Political Science*, 31 (1): 13–39.

Goodstein, J. D. (1994). 'Institutional pressure and strategic responsiveness: Employer involvement in work-family issues', *Academy of Management Journal*, 37: 350–82.

Gornick, J. C. and Meyers, M. K. (2003). *Families That Work: Policies for Reconciling Parenthood and Employment*. New York: Russel Sage Foundation.

Gouldner, A. W. (1973). *For sociology. Renewal and Critique in Sociology Today*. London: Allen Lane.

Grabka, M. M. and Frick, J. R. (2008). 'Schrumpfende Mittelschicht—Anzeichen einer dauerhaften Polarisierung der verfügbaren Einkommen?', *DIW Wochenbericht*, 75(10): 101–8.

References

Green-Pedersen, C. (2007). 'Denmark: a "World Bank" pension system', in E. M. Immergut, K. M. Anderson, and I. Schulze (eds.), *The Handbook of West European Pension Politics*. Oxford: Oxford University Press, 454–98.

Griggs, J., Hammond, A., and Walker, R. (2011). 'Activation for all: Welfare reform in the UK, 1995–2009', in I. Lødemel and A. Moreira (eds.), *Workfare Revisited*. Bristol: Policy Press (forthcoming).

Groves, D. (1983). 'Members and survivors: Women and retirement-pension legislation', in J. Lewis (ed.), *Women's Welfare, Women's Rights*. London & Canberra: Croom Helm, 18–63.

Grubb, D. and Puymoyen, A. (2008). 'Long time-series for public expenditure on labour market programmes', *OECD Social, Employment and Migration Papers*, 73. Paris: OECD.

Guiraudon, V. (2002). 'Including foreigners in national welfare states: Institutional venues and rules of the game', in B. Rothstein and S. Steinmo (eds.), *Restructuring the Welfare State: Political Institutions and Policy Change*. New York: Palgrave, 129–56.

Haisken-DeNew, J. P. and Frick, J. R. (2005). *Desktop Companion to the German Socio-Economic Panel Study (SOEP)*, 8.0. Berlin: DIW.

Hall, P. A. (1993). 'Policy paradigms, social-learning, and the State—the case of economic policy-making in Britain', *Comparative Politics*, 25 (3): 275–96.

—— and Soskice, D. (2001). 'An Introduction to *Varieties of Capitalism*', in P. A. Hall and D. Soskice (eds.), *Varieties of Capitalism: The Institutional Foundations of Comparative Advantage*. Oxford: Oxford University, 1–70.

Hall, P. A. and Soskice, D. (eds.) (2001). *Varieties of Capitalism: The Institutional Foundations of Comparative Advantage*. Oxford: Oxford University Press.

Hannah, L. (1986). *Reinventing Retirement. The Development of Occupational Pensions in Britain*. Cambridge: Cambridge University Press.

Hannan, D. F., Raffe, D., Rutjes, H., Willems, E., Mansuy, M., Müller, W., and Amor, T. (1999). 'A comparative analysis of transitions from education to work in Europe (CATEWE)—a conceptual framework', *ESRI Working Paper*, 138 Available at <http://www.mzes.uni-mannheim.de/projekte/catewe/publ/publ_e.html>, accessed April 2011.

Hantrais, L. and Letablier, M. (1996). *Families and Family Policies in Europe*. Harlow: Longman.

Hayward, B., Fong, B., and Thornton, A. (2007). *The Third Work-Life Balance Employer Survey: Main Findings*. London: Department for Business, Enterprise and Regulatory Reform.

Heclo, H. (1974). *Modern Social Politics in Britain and Sweden*. New Haven and London: Yale University Press.

Heinelt, H. and Weck, M. (1998). *Arbeitsmarktpolitik. Vom Vereinigungskonsens zur Standortdebatte*. Opladen: Leske und Budrich.

Hemerijk, A. and Eichhorst, W. (2010). 'Whatever happened to the Bismarckian welfare state? From labour-shedding to employment-friendly reforms', in B. Palier (ed.), *A Long Goodbye to Bismarck? The Politics of Welfare Reform in Continental Europe*. Amsterdam: Amsterdam University Press, 301–32.

Henninger, A., Wimbauer, C., and Dombrowski, R. (2008). 'Demography as a push toward gender equality? Current reforms of German family policy', *Social Politics* 15 (3): 287–314.

Hennock, E. P. (2007). *The Origin of the Welfare State in England and Germany, 1850–1914: Social Policies Compared*. Cambridge: Cambridge University Press.

Hentschel, V. (1983). *Geschichte der deutschen Sozialpolitik (1880–1980)*. Frankfurt: Suhrkamp.

Heubeck, G. (1958). 'Die Berücksichtigung der Sozialversicherungsrenten in der betrieblichen Altersversorgung', *Betriebliche Altersversorgung*, 13 (8): 105–16.

—— (1974). 'Die Kosten der Unverfallbarkeit und der flexiblen Altersgrenze', *BetrAV*, 10 (1): 18–20.

Hillmert, S. (2001). *Ausbildungssysteme und Arbeitsmarkt: Lebensverläufe in Großbritannien und Deutschland im Kohortenvergleich [Education Systems and Labor Markets: A Cohort Comparison of Life Courses in Great Britain and Germany]*. Wiesbaden: Westdeutscher Verlag.

Hills, J. (2004). *Inequality and the State*. Oxford: Oxford University Press.

—— Ditch, J., and Glennerster, H. (1994). *Beveridge and Social Security. An International Retrospective*. Oxford: Oxford University Press.

Hills, J. Sefton, T., and Stewart, K. (eds.) (2009). *Towards a More Equal Society? Poverty, Inequality and Policy since 1997*. Bristol: Policy Press.

Hinrichs, K. (2001). 'Elephants on the move. Patterns of public pension reform in OECD countries', in S. Leibfried (ed.), *Welfare State Futures*. Cambridge: Cambridge University Press, 77–102.

—— (2003). *Between Continuity and Paradigm Shift: Pension Reforms in Germany*. Bremen: Universität Bremen.

—— (2009). 'Pensions in Europe: Convergence of old-age security systems?', in J.-K., Petersen and K. Petersen (eds.), *The Politics of Age. Basic Pension Systems in Comparative and Historical Perspective*. Frankfurt am Main: Peter Lang, 119–43.

—— and Kangas, O. (2003). 'When is a change big enough to be a system shift? Small system-shifting changes in German and Finnish pension policies', *Social Policy and Administration*, 37 (6): 573–91.

Hippe, T. (2007). 'Märkte, Wohlfahrtsstaaten oder Wohlfahrtsmärkte? Die Regulierung kapitalgedeckter Altersvorsorge zwischen individueller und kollektiver Verantwortung für die Lebensstandardsicherung im Alter'. Regina-Arbeitspapier 17. Bielefeld: Institut für Soziologie, Universität Bielefeld.

HM Government (2010). *The Coalition: Our Programme for Government*: London: Cabinet Office, May.

HMRC (HM Revenue and Customs), *Pension Statistics*. Online publishing. Available at <http://www.hmrc.gov.uk/stats/pensions/table7-4-2001-02-2008-09.xls>, accessed June 2010.

HM Treasury (2004a). *Choice for Parents, the Best Start for Children: A Ten Year Strategy for Childcare*. London: DWP.

—— (2004b). *Child Poverty Review*. London: Her Majesty's Treasury.

Hockerts, H. G. (1980). *Sozialpolitische Entscheidungen im Nachkriegsdeutschland*. Stuttgart: Klett-Contra.

Hogarth, T., Hasluck, C., and Pierre, G. (2000). *Work Life Balance 2000: Summary Report*. London: Department for Education and Employment.

—— —— Pierre, G., Winterbotham, M., and Vivian, D. (2001). *Work-Life Balance 2000: Results from the Baseline Study*. Research Report RR249. London: Department for Education and Employment, Institute for Employment Research.

Hollingsworth, J. R. and Boyer, R. (1998). 'Coordination of economic actors and social systems of production', in J. R. Hollingsworth and R. Boyer (eds.), *Contemporary Capitalism. The Embeddedness of Institutions*. Cambridge: Cambridge University Press, 1–47.

Hollis, P. (2006). 'How to address gender inequality in British pension policy', in H. Pemberton, P. Thane, and N. Whiteside (eds.), *Britain's Pension Crisis: History and Policy*. Oxford: Oxford University Press.

Holzinger, K. and Knill, C. (2005). 'Causes and conditions of cross-national policy convergence', *Journal of European Public Policy*, 12 (5): 775–96.

Home Office (1998). *Supporting Families*. A consultation document. Available at <http://www.nationalarchives.gov.uk/ERORecords/HO/421/2/acu/sfpages.pdf>, accessed April 2010.

Hood, C. (1983). *The Tools of Government*. London: Macmillan.

House of Commons (2005). *The Childcare Act*. London: The Stationary Office.

Huber, E. and Stephens, J. D. (2001). *Development and Crisis of the Welfare State*. Chicago: University of Chicago Press.

Hubrich, S. and Tivig, T. (2006). *Betriebsrenten im Alterssicherungssystem Deutschland*. Rostock: Rostocker Zentrum zur Erforschung des Demografischen Wandels.

Hudson, J., Hwang, G., and Kuhner, S. (2008). 'Between ideas, institutions and interests', *Journal of Social Policy*, 37 (2): 207–30.

Hügelschäffer, H. (2002). 'Die neue Zusatzversorgung des öffentlichen Dienstes', *BetrAV*, (3): 237–41.

IDS (Income Data Services) (2004). *Pensions after Final Salary 2003/04*. London: IDS.

—— (2006). *Pension Scheme Benchmarks: The 2006 Review of Contributions and Benefits*. London: IDS.

Infratest Burke Sozialforschung (1995). *Old Age Security in Germany in 1995 (ASID '95)*. *Summary Report*. München: IBS.

Infratest Sozialforschung (1990). *Alterssicherung in Deutschland 1986. Band III Rentner mit Zusatzsicherung*. München: IBS.

—— (1992). *Entwicklung der Alterssicherung in Deutschland 1986–1989. Fortschreibung der ASID '86 für die Jahre 1987 und 1989*. München: IBS.

ISSP (International Social Survey Programme) (2003). Online Publishing. Available at <http://www.issp.org/>, accesssed June 2010.

—— (2006). *Online Publishing*. Available at <http://www.issp.org/>, accessed June 2010.

Jæger, M. M. (2006). 'Welfare regimes and attitudes towards redistribution: The regime hypothesis revisited', *European Sociological Review*, 22 (2): 157–70.

—— (2009). 'United but divided: Welfare regimes and the level and variance in public support for redistribution', *European Sociological Review*, 25 (6): 723–37.

Jeffery, C. and Handl, V. (1999). 'Blair, Schröder and the third way', in L. Funk (ed.), *The Economics and Politics of the Third Way. Essays in Honour of Eric Owen Smith*. Münster: Lit Verlag.

Jenkins, S. P. (2004). 'Survival analysis', *Manuscript of the Essex Summer School in SSCA*. Colchester: University of Essex.

Jenson, J. (2006). 'The LEGO™ paradigm and new social risks: Consequences for children', in J. Lewis, (ed.), *Children, Changing Families and Welfare States*. Cheltenham: Edward Elgar, 27–50.

Jenson, J. and Saint-Martin, D. (2006). 'Building blocks for a new social architecture: The Lego paradigm of an active society', *Policy and Politics*, 34 (3): 429–51.

Johnson, P. and Rake, K. (1998). 'Comparative social policy research in Europe', *Social Policy Review*, 10: 257–78.

Jones, R. (2006). 'Final salary pension schemes "to be history by 2012"'. *The Guardian*, (2 August).

Jones, T. (2009). 'A pension for all: Pension reform in the United Kingdom', *Rotman International Journal of Pension Management*, 2 (2): 42–8.

Jovanovic, B. (1979). 'Job matching and the theory of turnover', *The Journal of Political Economy*, 5 (1): 972–90.

Kaase, M. and Newton, K. (1995). *Beliefs in Government*. Oxford: Oxford University Press.

Kalina, T. and Weinkopf, C. (2009). 'Niedriglohnbeschäftigung 2007 weiter gestiegen—zunehmende Bedeutung von Niedriglöhnen', *IAQ–Report*, no. 5. Duisburg: University of Duisburg: Institut für Arbeit und Qualifikation.

Kamerman, S. B. and Kahn, A. J. (1997). *Family Change and Family Policies in Great Britain, Canada, New Zealand and the United States*. Oxford: Oxford University Press.

Katz, H. C. and Darbishire, O. (2000). *Converging Divergences: Worldwide Changes in Employment Systems*. Ithaca, NY: ILR Press, Cornell University Press.

——, Lee, W. and Lee, J. (eds.) (2004). *The New Structure of Labor Relations*. Ithaca: Cornell University Press.

Kaufmann, F.-X. (2002). 'Politics and policies towards the family in Europe: A framework and an enquiry into their differences and convergences', in F.-X. Kaufmann, A. Kuijsten, H.-J. Schulze, and K. P. Strohmeier (eds.), *Family Life and Family Policies in Europe*. Oxford: Oxford University Press, 419–90.

—— (2003). *Varianten des Wohlfahrtsstaats. Der deutsche Sozialstaat im internationalen Vergleich*. Frankfurt am Main: Suhrkamp.

Keller, A. (2003). *Von Bologna nach Berlin. Perspektiven eines Europäischen Hochschulraums im Rahmen des Bologna—Prozesses am Vorabend des europäischen Hochschulgipfels 2003 in Berlin*. Berlin: Expertise im Auftrag von Feleknas Uca (MdEP).

Keller, B. (2004). 'Employment relations in Germany', in G. J. Bamber, R. D. Lansbury, and N. Wailes (eds.), *International and Comparative Employment Relations*. London: Sage, 211–53.

Kelly, E. L. (2006). 'Work-family policies: The United States in international perspective', in M. Pitt-Catsouphes, E. E. Kossek, and S. Sweet (eds.), *The Work and Family Handbook*. Mahwah: Lawrence Erlbaum, 99–123.

Kemmerling, A. and Bruttel, O. (2006). '"New Politics" in German labour market policy? The implications of the recent Hartz reforms for the German welfare state', *West European Politics*, 29 (1): 90–112.

Kenway, P. and Palmer, G. (2007). *Poverty among Ethnic Groups. How and Why does it Differ?* York: Joseph Rowntree Foundation.

Kerckhoff, A. C. (2001). 'Education and social stratification. Processes in comparative perspective', *Sociology of Education*, vol. 74, Extra Issue 2001: 3–18.

Kerschbaumer, J. (2004). 'Die Ausweitung der betrieblichen Altersversorgung über Tarifverträge: Wunschdenken oder Realität?', *BetrAV*, (2): 101–5.

Kessel, H. (1983). 'Bericht der Leitung der Fachvereinigung Direktversicherung', *Betriebliche Altersversorgung*, 38 (4): 125–7.

—— (1987). 'Bericht der Leitung der Fachvereinigung Direktversicherung', *BetrAV*, 42 (5): 163–4.

Kilpatrick, C. and Freedland, M. (2004). 'The United Kingdom: How is EU governance transformative?', in S. Sciarra, P. Davies, and M. Freedland (eds.), *Employment Policy and the Regulation of Part-time Work in the European Union. A Comparative Analysis*. Cambridge: Cambridge University Press, 299–357.

Kim, A. and Kim, K.-W. (2003). 'Returns to tertiary education in Germany and the UK: Effects of fields of study and gender', *Working Papers Mannheimer Zentrum für Sozialforschung*, 62: 1–35.

Kitschelt, H. and Streek, W. (2003). From stability to stagnation: Germany at the beginning of the Twenty-First Century, *West European Politics*, 26 (4): 1–36.

Kivinen, O. and Nurmi, J. (2003). 'Unifying higher education for different kinds of Europeans. Higher education and work: A comparison of ten countries', *Comparative Education*, 39 (1): 83–103.

Klammer, U. and Letablier, M.-T. (2007). 'Family policies in Germany and France: The role of enterprises and social partners', *Social Policy & Administration*, 41 (6): 672–92.

Klenner, C. (2005). 'Gleichstellung von Frauen und Männern und Vereinbarkeit von Familie und Beruf', in R. Bispinck (ed.), *WSI-Tarifhandbuch 2005*. Frankfurt: Bund-Verlag.

Knijn, T. and Kremer, M. (1997). 'Gender and the caring dimension of welfare states: Towards inclusive citizenship', *Soc Pol*, 4 (3): 328–61.

Kogan, I. and Müller, W. (2003). *School-to-Work Transitions in Europe: Analyses of the EU LFS 2000 Ad Hoc Module*. Mannheim: MZES.

Konle-Seidl, R. (2009). 'Erfassung von Arbeitslosigkeit im internationalen Vergleich. Notwendige Anpassung oder unzulässige Tricks?', *IAB-Kurzbericht*, 4: 1–7.

—— Eichhorst, W., and Grienberger-Zingerle, M. (2007). *Activation Policies in Germany: From Status Protection to Minimum Income Support. IAB Discussion Paper* 6/2007. Nürnberg: Institut für Arbeitsmarkt und Berufsforschung.

Korpi, W. (2006). 'Power resources and employer-centered approaches in explanations of welfare states and varieties of capitalism: Protagonists, consenters, and antagonists', *World Politics*, 58: 167–206.

Krupp, H.-J. (1983). 'Empirischer Vergleich der Alterssicherungssysteme für abhängig Beschäftigte', in S. Alterssicherungssysteme (ed.), *Darstellung der Alterssicherungssysteme und der Besteuerung von Alterseinkommen. Gutachten der Sachverständigenkommission*. Bonn: Bundesministerium für Arbeit und Sozialordnung, 114–39.

La Valle, I., Smith, R., Purdon, S., and Bell, A. (2007). *The Neighbourhood Nursery Initiative—What Impact did it Have on Families' Lives?* Research Findings IFS/NatCen. London: DfES.

Labour Party (2001). *2001 Labour Party General Election Manifesto.* Available at <www.labour-party.org.uk/manifestos/2001/2001-labour-manifesto.shtml>, accessed March 2008.

Lamping, W. and Rüb, F. W. (2004). 'From the Conservative welfare state to an "uncertain something else": German pension politics in comparative perspective', *Policy & Politics*, 32 (2): 169–91.

Land, H. (1985). 'Who still cares for the family? Recent developments in income maintenance', in C. Ungerson (ed.), *Women and Social Policy. A Reader.* Houndmills, Basingstoke: MacMillan, 50–62.

Larsen, C. A. (2006). *The Institutional Logic of Welfare Attitudes: How Welfare Regimes Influence Public Support.* Aldershot: Ashgate.

—— (2008). 'The institutional logic of welfare attitudes: How welfare regimes influence public support', *Comparative Political Studies*, 41(2): 145–68.

Lea, R. (2003). *Red Tape in the Workplace. The Re-regulation of the Labour Market II—The Sequel.* London: Institute of Directors.

Leach, R. and Percy-Smith, J. (2001). *Local Governance in Britain. Contemporary Political Studies.* Hampshire: Palgrave.

Leff, G. (1993). 'Zehntes Kapitel: Die Artes Liberales', in W. Rüegg (ed.), *Geschichte der Universität in Europa. Band 1.* München: Beck.

Leisering, L. (2007). *The Regulation of Welfare Markets: A new Avenue of Social Policy? The Case of Pension Privatisation in Europe.* Bielefeld: Universität Bielefeld.

—— (2008). 'Germany: A centrist welfare state at the cross roads', in P. Alcock and G. Craig (eds.), *International Social Policy.* Bristol: Policy Press.

Leisering, L. and Vitić, I. (2009). 'Die Evolution marktregulativer Politik. Normbildung in hybriden Bereichen sozialer Sicherung—das Beispiel der Unisex-Tarife für die Riester-Rente', *Zeitschrift für Sozialreform*, 55 (2): 97–123.

Leitner, S. (2003). 'Varieties of familialism', *European Societies*, 5 (4): 353–75.

—— (2008). 'Ökonomische Funktionalität der Familienpolitik oder familienpolitische Funktionalisierung der Ökonomie', in A. Evers and R. G. Heinze (eds.), *Sozialpolitik. Ökonomisierung und Entgrenzung.* Wiesbaden: VS Verlag für Sozialwissenschaften, 67–82.

—— Ostner, O. and Schmitt, C. (2008). 'Family policies in Germany', in I. Ostner and C. Schmitt (eds.), *Family Policies in the Context of Family Change. The Nordic Countries in Comparative Perspective.* Wiesbaden: VS Verlag für Sozialwissenschaften, 175–202.

Lenoir, R. (1991). 'Family policy in France since 1938', in J. S. Ambler (ed.), *The French Welfare State.* London: New York University Press, 144–86.

Leuze, K. (2007). 'What makes for a good start? Consequences of occupation-specific higher education for graduate career mobility', *International Journal of Sociology*, 37 (2): 29–53.

Levitas, R. (1998). *The Inclusive Society? Social Exclusion and New Labour.* London: Macmillan.

Lewis, J. (1992). 'Gender and the development of welfare states', *Journal of European Social Policy*, 2 (3): 159–73.

—— (2006). 'Gender and welfare in Modern Europe', in: R. Harris and L. Roper (eds.), *The Art of Survival Gender and History in Europe, 1450–2000*. Essays in honour of Olwen Hufton (Past and Present Supplements). Oxford: Oxford University Press 39–54.

—— (2009). *Work-Family Balance, Gender and Policy*. Cheltenham: Edward Elgar.

—— and Ostner, I. (1994). 'Gender and the evolution of European social policies', ZES Arbeitspapier Nr. 4/94. Bremen: Zentrum für Sozialpolitik.

—— and Giullari, S. (2005). 'The adult worker model family, gender equality and care: The search for new policy principles and the possibilities and problems of a capabilities approach', *Economy and Society*, 34 (1): 76–104.

—— and Campbell, M. (2007). 'Work/family balance policies in the UK since 1997', *Journal of Social Policy*, 36 (3): 365–81.

—— Knijn, T., Martin, C. and Ostner, I. (2009). 'Patterns of development in work/family reconciliation for parents in France, Germany, the Netherlands and the UK in the 2000s', *Social Politics*, 15: 261–86.

Lijphart, A. (1999). *Patterns of Democracy: Government Forms and Performance in 36 Countries*. New Haven and London: Yale University Press.

Linder, S. H. and Peters, B. G. (1989). 'Instruments of government: Perceptions and contexts', *Journal of Public Policy*, 9 (1): 35–58.

Lindsay, C. (2007). 'The United Kingdom's "work first" welfare state and activation regimes in Europe', in A. Serano and L. Magnusson (eds.), *Reshaping Welfare States and Activation Regimes in Europe*. Bern: Peter Lang, 35–70.

Linos, K. and West, M. (2003). 'Self-interest, social beliefs and attitudes to redistribution', *European Sociological Review*, 19 (4): 393–409.

Linsey, A. and McAuliffe, A.-M. (2006). 'Children at the centre? The Childcare Act 2006', *Children & Society* 20: 404–8.

Lister, R. (1998). 'From equality to social inclusion: New Labour and the welfare state', *Critical Social Policy*, 18 (2): 215–26.

Lister, R. (2003). 'Investing in the citizen-workers of the future: Transformations in citizenship and the state under New Labour', *Social Policy and Administration,* 37(5): 427–43.

—— (2006). 'Children (but not women) first: New Labour, child welfare and gender', *Critical Social Policy*, 26 (2): 315–35.

Lohmann, H. (2009). 'Welfare states, labour market institutions and the working poor: A comparative analysis of 20 European countries', *European Sociological Review*, 25 (4): 489–504.

—— Peter, F. H., Rostgaard, T., and Spiess, C. K. (2009). 'Towards a framework for assessing family policies in the EU', *OECD Social, Employment and Migration Working Papers*, No. 88. Paris: OECD.

Lynes, T. (1960). 'The National Insurance Act, 1959', *Modern Law Review*, 23 (1): 53–6.

Maarten, H. (2003). 'Job mismatches and their labour-market effects among school-leavers in Europe', *European Sociological Review*, 19 (3): 249–66.

Mackroth, P. and Ristau, M. (2002). 'Die Rückkehr der Familie', *Berliner Republik* (2). Available at <http:// b.republik.de/b-republik.php/cat/8/aid/429/title/Die_Rueckkehr_der_Familie>, accessed November 2007.

Macnicol, J. (1998). *The Politics of Retirement 1878–1948*. Cambridge: Cambridge University Press.

Mahon, R. (2008). 'Babies and bosses: Gendering the OECD's social policy discourse', in R. Mahon and S. McBride (eds.), *The OECD and Transnational Governance*. Vancouver: University of British Columbia Press.

Manow, P. (2001a). 'Comparative institutional advantages of welfare state regimes and new coalitions in welfare state reform.' in P. Pierson (ed.), *The New Politics of the Welfare State*. Oxford: Oxford University Press, 146–64.

Manow, P. (2001b). *Globalization, Corporate Finance, and Coordinated Capitalism: Pension Finance in Germany and Japan*. Cologne: Max Planck Institut für Gesellschaftsforschung.

Marchington, M., Goodman, J., and Berridge, J. (2004). 'Employment relations in Britain', in G. J. Bamber, R. D. Lansbury, and N. Wailes (eds.), *International and Comparative Employment Relations*. London: Sage, 36–66.

Marlier, E., Atkinson, A. B., Cantillon, B., and Nolan, B. (2007). *The EU and Social Inclusion: Facing the Challenges*. Bristol: Policy Press.

Marsden, D. (1990). 'Institutions and labour mobility: Occupational and internal labour markets in Britain, France, Italy and West Germany', in R. Brunetta and C. Dell'Aringa (eds.), *Labour Relations and Economic Performance*. Houndmills: Macmillan, 414–38.

Mau, S. (2003). *The Moral Economy of Welfare States. Britain and Germany Compared*. London and New York: Routledge.

—— and Burkhardt, C. (2008). 'Solidarität wird an Gegenleistung geknüpft—Zur Inklusionsbereitschaft der Deutschen gegenüber Zuwanderern', *ISI Informationsdienst Soziale Indikatoren*, 39: 12–15.

—— —— (2009a). 'Ethnische Diversität und wohlfahrtspolitische Legitimation in Europa', in H. Obinger and E. Rieger (eds.), *Wohlfahrtsstaatlichkeit in entwickelten Demokratien. Herausforderungen, Reformen, Perspektiven*. Frankfurt, New York: Campus, 191–216.

—— —— (2009b). 'Migration and welfare state solidarity in Western Europe', *Journal of European Social Policy*, 19 (3): 213–29.

—— and Veghte, B. (eds.) (2007). *Social Justice, Legitimacy and the Welfare State*. Aldershot: Ashgate.

Maurer, R. (2003). 'Institutional investors in Germany: Insurance companies and investment funds', CFS-Working Paper 2003/14, Frankfurt: Center for Fiscal Studies, Universität Frankfurt am Main.

Maurice, M., Sellier, F., and Silvestre, J.-J. (1986). *The Social Foundations of Industrial Power: A Comparison of France and Germany*. Cambridge, MA: MIT Press.

Maydell, B. v. (1983). 'Betriebliche Altersversorgung', in S. Alterssicherungssysteme (ed.), *Darstellung der Alterssicherungssysteme und der Besteuerung von Alterseinkommen. Gutachten der Sachverständigenkommission vom 19. November 1983*. Bonn: Bundesministerium für Arbeit und Sozialordnung, 243–81.

Mayntz, R. (1997). 'Politische Steuerung und gesellschaftliche Steuerungsprobleme', in R. Mayntz (ed.), Soziale Dynamik und politische Steuerung. Theoretische und methodologische Überlegunge. Frankfurt am Main: Campus, 168–208.

Mazey, S. (1998). 'The European Union and women's rights: From the Europeanization of national agendas to the nationalization of a European agenda', *Journal of European Public Policy*, 5 (1): 131–52.

Meadows, P. (2008). 'Improving the Employability of Parents', in A. Anning and M. Ball (eds.), *Improving Services for Young Children. From Sure Start to Children's Centres.* London: Sage, 123–34.

Melhuish, E. C. (2004). *A Literature Review of the Impact of Early Years Provision on Young Children, with Emphasis given to Children from Disadvantaged Backgrounds.* London: Institute for the Study of Children, Families & Social Issues.

Merkel, W. (2004). 'Soziale Gerechtigkeit, Arbeitsmarkt und Reform des Sozialstaates', in Friedrich Ebert Stiftung (ed.), *Die neue SPD. Menschen stärken—Wege öffnen.* Bonn: J. H. W. Dietz Nachf., 207–17.

Mesher, T. (1976). 'The Social Security Pensions Act 1975', *Modern Law Review*, 39: 321–26.

Meuser, M. and Nagel, U. (1991). 'Experteninterviews—vielfach erprobt, wenig bedacht', in D. Garz and K. Kraimer (eds.), *Qualitativ-empirische Sozialforschung. Konzepte, Methoden, Analysen.* Opladen: Westdeutscher Verlag, 441–71.

Meyer, T. (1997). *Ungleich besser? Die ökonomische Unabhängigkeit von Frauen im Zeichen der Expansion sozialer Dienstleistungen.* Berlin: Sigma.

—— (1998). 'Die Erosion des starken deutschen Brotverdienermodells. Sozioökonomische und institutionelle Faktoren', *Zeitschrift für Sozialreform*, 11/12: 818–38.

—— and Bridgen, P. (2008). 'Class, gender and chance: The social division of occupational pensions in the United Kingdom', *Ageing and Society*, 28 (3): 353–81.

—— Bridgen, P., and Riedmuller, B. (eds.) (2007). *Private Pensions versus Social Inclusion? Non-state Provision for Citizens at Risk in Europe.* Cheltenham: Edward Elgar.

Middlemas, K. (1979). *Politics in Industrial Society. The Experience of the British System since 1911.* London: Andre Deutsch.

Millar, J. (2008). 'Work is good for you': Lone mothers, children, work and wellbeing', *Social Security and Health Research Working Papers*, 60. Kela: Helsinki.

Miller, D. (2006). 'Multiculturalism and the welfare state: Theoretical reflections', in K. Banting and W. Kymlicka (eds.), *Multiculturalism and the Welfare State. Recognition and Redistribution in Contemporary Democracies.* Oxford: Oxford University Press, 323–38.

Milliken, F. J., Dutton, J. E. and Beyer, J. M. (1990). 'Understanding organizational adaptation to change: The case of work–family issues', *Human Resource Planning*, 13: 91–107.

Mills, M., Blossfeld, H.-P., Buchholz, S., Hofäcker, D., Bernardi, F., Hofmeister, H. (2008). 'Converging divergences? An international comparison of the impact of globalization on industrial relations and employment careers', *International Sociology*, 23 (4): 561–95.

Ministerium für Generationen, Familie, Frauen und Integration des Landes Nordrhein-Westfalen (2008). *Wege zum Familienzentrum Nordrhein-Westfalen. Eine Handreichung.* Hamm: Giebsch und Rochol.

Mohr, K. (2008). 'Creeping Convergence—Wandel der Arbeitsmarktpolitik in Großbritannien und Deutschland', *Zeitschrift für Sozialreform*, 54 (2): 187–207.

Möller, J. (2010). 'The German labor market response in the world recession—de-mystifying a miracle', *Zeitschrift für Arbeitsmarktforschung*, 42: 325–36.

Moraw, P. (1993). 'Achtes Kapitel: Der Lebensweg der Studenten', in W. Rüegg (ed.), *Geschichte der Universität in Europa. Band 1.* München: Beck.

—— (2005). 'Die Universitäten in Europa und Deutschland. Anfänge und Schritte auf einem langen Weg', in U. Sieg and D. Korsch (eds.), *Die Idee der Universität heute*. München: K. G. Saur, 25–41.

Morgan, H. and Milliken, F. J. (1992). 'Keys to action: Understanding differences in organizations' responsiveness to work-and-family issues', *Human Resource Management*, 31: 227–48.

Moss, P. (2006). 'From a childcare to a pedagogical discourse—or putting care in its place', in J. Lewis (ed.), *Children, Changing Families and Welfare States*. Cheltenham: Edward Elgar, 154–71.

Müller, W. and Gangl, M. (2003). *Transitions from Education to Work in Europe. The Integration of Youth into EU Labour Markets*. Oxford: Oxford University Press.

Müller, W. and Shavit, Y. (1998). 'The institutional embeddedness of the stratification process. A comparative study of qualifications and occupations in thirteen countries', in Y. Shavit and W. Müller (eds.), *From School to Work*. Oxford: Clarenden Press, 1–48.

Müller-Jentsch, W. (1995). 'Germany: From collective voice to co-management', in J. Rogers and W. Streeck, *Works Councils: Consultation, Representation, and Cooperation in Industrial Relations*. Cambridge, MA: NBER Books.

+ Murthi, M., Orszag, M. J., and Orszag, P. R. (2001). 'Administrative costs under a decentralized approach to individual accounts: Lessons from the United Kingdom', in R. Holzmann and J. E. Stiglitz (eds.), *New Ideas about Old Age Security*, Washington, DC: World Bank, 308–35.

Myles, J. (1998). 'How to design a "liberal" welfare state. A comparison of the USA and Canada', *Social Policy and Administration*, 32 (4): 341–64.

Nadeem, S. and Metcalf, H. (2007). 'Work-Life Policies in Great Britain: What Works, Where and How?' *Employment Relations Research Series 77*. London: Department for Business, Enterprise and Regulatory Reform.

Nesbitt, S. (1995). *British Pensions Policy Making in the 1980s. The Rise and Fall of a Policy Community*, Adlershot: Avebury.

New Labour (1997). *New Labour—Because Britain Deserves Better*. London: Labour Party.

——. (2001). 'Labour's policies to help working parents', Labour Party Press Release, 30 May 2001. London: Labour Party.

NIEER (National Institute for Early Education Research) (2008). *The State of Preschool 2008*. New Brunswick: Rutgers Graduate School of Education. Available at <http://nieer.org/yearbook/pdf/yearbook.pdf>, accessed no data.

Niemeyer, W. (1997). 'Aktueller Stand der Reform des Betriebsrentengesetzes und Auswirkungen auf die Direktversicherung', *BetrAV*, (8): 296–301.

North, D. C. (1990). *Institutions, Institutional Change and Economic Performance*. Cambridge: Cambridge University Press.

Nullmeier, F. (2001). 'Sozialpolitik als marktregulative Politik', *Zeitschrift für Sozialreform*, 47 (6): 645–68.

OECD (1994). 'The OECD Jobs Study: Evidence and explanations, Part 1: Labour market trends and underlying forces of change; Part 2: The adjustment potential of the labour market'. Paris: OECD.

—— (2001). *Starting Strong. Early Childhood Education and Care*. Paris: OECD.

References

—— (2002). *Babies and Bosses*. Reconciling Work and Family Life, Volume 1. Australia, Denmark, and the Netherlands. Paris: OECD.

—— (2003). 'Benefits and employment, friend or foe? Interaction between passive and active programmes', in *OECD Employment Outlook 2003*. Paris: OECD, 171–235.

—— (2004). *OECD Handbook for Internationally Comparative Education Statistics: Concepts, Standards, Definitions and Classifications*. Paris: OECD.

—— (2005). *Pensions at Glance, Public Policies across OECD Countries*. Paris: OECD.

—— (2006). *Starting Strong II: Early Childhood Education and Care*. Paris: OECD.

—— (2007a). *Babies and Bosses—Reconciling Work and Family Life: A Synthesis of Findings for OECD Countries*. Paris: OECD.

—— (2007b). *Pensions at a Glance. Public Policies across OECD Countries. 2007 Edition*. Paris: OECD.

—— (2008). *International Migration Outlook. Annual Report*. Paris: OECD.

—— (2009a). *Economic Outlook*. Paris: OECD.

—— (2009b). *International Migration Outlook. Annual Report*. Paris: OECD.

—— (2009c). *Statistics Portal: Harmonised Unemployment Rates*. Available at <http://stats.oecd.org/index.aspx>, accessed December 2009.

—— (2009d). *Economic Outlook*, 85. (June). Paris: OECD.

—— (2010a). 'Long time-series for public expenditure on labour market programmes'. Available at <http://stats.oecd.org/Index.aspx?DatasetCode=LMPEXP>, accessed no data.

—— (2010b). 'Benefits and wages database, gross replacement rates'. Available at <http://www.oecd.org/dataoecd/52/9/42625593.xls>, accessed no data.

Offe, C. (1991). 'Smooth consolidation in the West German welfare state: Structural change, fiscal policies, and populist politics', in F. Fox Piven (ed.), *Labour Parties in Postindustrial Societies*. Cambridge: Polity Press.

ONS (Office for National Statistics). *Employment Gazette (1955–2001)*. London: ONS.

—— (2001). *Annual Survey of Hours and Earnings*. Online Publishing. Available at <http://www.statistics.gov.uk/statbase/product.asp?vlnk=13101>, accessed August 2008.

—— (2005). *Public Sector Employment Trends*. October. London: Office for National Statistics.

—— (2008a). *Standard Occupational Classification*. Available at <http://www.ons.gov.uk/about-statistics/classifications/current/SOC2000/index.html>, accessed August 2008.

—— (2008b). *Pension Trends*. London: ONS.

—— (2008c). *Annual Survey of Hours and Earnings (ASHE)*. Available at <http://www.statistics.gov.uk/downloads/theme_labour/ASHE_2007/2007_Pensions.pdf>, accessed April 2008.

—— *Economic Trends*. (No. 10, Dec. 1962; No. 255, Jan. 1975; No. 325, Nov. 1980; No. 410, Dec. 1987; No. 422, Dec. 1988; No. 458, Dec. 1991; No. 471, Jan. 1993). London: Office for National Statistics.

OPSI (Office for Public Sector Information) (2007). 'Pensions Act 2007', in *Pensions Act 2007*. London: OPSI.

—— (2008). 'Pensions Act 2008', in *Pensions Act 2008*. London: Office for Public Sector Information.

—— (2010). *Legislation in its Original Format*. Online Publishing. Available at <http://www.opsi.gov.uk/legislation/original.htm>, accessed April 2008.

Orloff, A. S. (2006). 'From maternalism to employment for all', in J. D. Levy (ed.), *The State after Statism: New State Activities in the Age of Liberalization*. Cambridge, MA: Harvard University Press, 230–68.

Oschmiansky, Mauer, A., and Schulze Buschoff, K. (2007). 'Arbeitsmarktreformen in Deutschland. zwischen Pfadabhängigkeit und Paradigmenwechsel', *WSI Mitteilungen*, 6: 291–8.

—— and Ebach, M. (2009). 'Vom AFG 1969 zur Instrumentenreform 2009: Der Wandel des arbeitsmarktpolitischen Instrumentariums', in S. Bothfeld, W. Sesselmeier, and C. Bogedan (eds.), *Arbeitsmarktpolitik in Der Sozialen Marktwirtschaft: Vom Arbeitsförderungsgesetz zum Sozialgesetzbuch II und III*. Wiesbaden: VS, Verlag für Sozialwissenschaft, 79–93.

Osterman, P. (1995). 'Work/family programs and the employment relationship', *Administrative Science Quarterly*, 40: 681–700.

Overbye, E. (2000). 'Commitment to welfare—a question of trust'. *NOVA Skriftserie*, 4/2000. Oslo: NOVA.

Palier, B. (2005). 'Ambiguous agreement, cumulative change: French social policy in the 1990s', in W. Streeck and K. Thelen (eds.), *Beyond Continuity: Institutional Change in Advanced Economies*. New York, Oxford University Press, 127–44.

Palier, B. (ed.) (2010). *A Long Goodbye to Bismarck? The Politics of Welfare Reform in Continental Europe*. Amsterdam: Amsterdam University Press.

—— and Martin, C. (eds.) (2008). *Reforming the Bismarckian Welfare Systems*. Malden, MA, Oxford: Blackwell Publishing.

—— and Thelen, K. (2010). 'Institutionalizing dualism: Complementarities and change in France and Germany', *Politics & Society*, 38 (1): 119–48.

Pascall, G. (1986). *Social Policy. A Feminist Analysis*. London and New York: Tavistock.

Pearce, J. M. and Stockdale, J. E. (2009). 'UK responses to the asylum issue: A comparison of lay and expert views', *Journal of Community & Applied Social Psychology*, 19: 142–55.

Pensions Commission (2004). 'Pensions: Challenges and choices. The first report of the Pension Commission'. London: The Stationery Office.

—— (2005). *A New Pensions Settlement for the Twenty-first Century. The Second Report of the Pensions Commission*. London: The Stationery Office.

Pettigrew, T. F. (1998). 'Intergroup Contact Theory', *Annual Review of Psychology*, 49 (1): 65–85.

—— and Tropp, L. R. (2000). 'Does intergroup contact reduce prejudice? Recent meta-analytic findings', in S. Oskamp (ed.), *Reducing Prejudice and Discrimination*. Mahwah, NJ: Lawrence Erlbaum Associates, 93–114.

Pfau-Effinger, B. (2004). 'Historical paths of the male breadwinner family model—explanation for cross-national differences', *British Journal for Sociology*, 55 (3): 177–99.

Pierson, P. (1994). *Dismantling the Welfare State?* Cambridge: Cambridge University Press.

—— (1998). 'Irresistible forces, immovable objects: Post-industrial welfare states confront permanent austerity', *Journal of European Public Policy*, 5(S): 539–60.

—— (2000). 'Increasing returns, path dependence, and the study of politics', *The American Political Science Review*, 94 (2): 251–67.

—— (2001). 'Post-Industrial Pressures on Mature Welfare States', in P. Pierson (ed.), *The New Politics of the Welfare State*. Oxford: Oxford University Press, 80–104.

—— (ed.) (2001). *The New Politics of the Welfare State*. Oxford: Oxford University Press.

PPI (Pension Policy Institute) (2006). *An Evaluation of the White Paper State Pension Reform Proposal*. London: PPI.

Prognos AG (ed.) (2005). *Work Life Balance. Motor für wirtschaftliches Wachstum und gesellschaftliche Stabilität. Analyse der volkswirtschaftlichen Effekte*. Basel: Prognos.

Przeworski, A. and Wallerstein, M. (1988). 'Structural dependence of the State on capital', *American Political Science Review*, 82 (1): 11–30.

Puskás, G. v. (2001). 'Zukunftsperspektiven der Zusatzversorgung des öffentlichen und kirchlichen Dienstes', *BetrAV*, (4): 309–13.

—— (2002a). 'Zusatzversorgung im Umbruch', *BetrAV*, (1): 21–4.

—— (2002b). 'Die freiwillige Versicherung in der Zusatzversorgung des öffenlichen und kirchlichen Dienstes', *BetrAV*, (6): 516–19.

Ragin, C. (2000). *Fuzzy-Set Social Science*. Chicago: University of Chicago Press.

Raijman, R., Semyonov, M., and Schmidt, P. (2003). 'Do foreigners deserve rights? Determinants of public views towards foreigners in Germany and Israel', *European Sociological Review*, 19 (4): 379–92.

Raitano, M. (2007). 'The Italian pension system and social inclusion', in T. Meyer, P. Bridgen, and B. Riedmüller (eds.), *Private Pensions versus Social Inclusion? Non-state Provision for Citizens at Risk in Europe*. Cheltenham: Edward Elgar, 168–92.

Reissert, B. (2004). *Germany: A Late Reformer* (unpublished manuscript).

Rhodes, M. (2000). 'Restructuring the British welfare state: Between domestic constraints and global imperatives', in F. W. Scharpf and V. A. Schmidt (eds.), *Welfare and Work in the Open Economy*, vol. II. Oxford: Oxford University Press, 19–68.

Riedmüller, B. and Willert, M. (2007). 'The German pension system and social inclusion', in T. Meyer, P. Bridgen, and B. Riedmüller (eds.), *Private Pensions versus Social Inclusion? Non-state Provision for Citizens at Risk in Europe*. Cheltenham: Edward Elgar, 139–67.

Riphahn, R. T. (2004). 'Immigrant participation in social assistance programs: Evidence from German guestworkers', *Applied Economics Quarterly*, 50 (4): 329–62.

Ristau[-Winker], M. (2005). 'Der ökonomische Charme der Familie', *Aus Politik und Zeitgeschichte*, 23–4: 16–23.

Robbins, L. (1963). *Higher Education Report of the Committee Appointed by the Prime Minister under the Chairmanship of Lord Robbins 1961–1963*. London: HMSO.

Rose, E. (2003). 'Arbeitsrechtspolitik zwischen Re-Regulierung und Deregulierung', in A. Gohr and M. Seeleib-Kaiser (eds.), *Sozial- und Wirtschaftspolitik unter Rot-Grün*. Wiesbaden: Westdeutscher Verlag, 103–24.

Rothstein, B. (1998). *Just Institutions Matter. The Moral and Political Logic of the Universal Welfare State*. Cambridge: Cambridge University Press.

Rubery, J. and Grimshaw, D. (2003). *The Organization of Employment. An International Perspective*. Basingstoke, NY: Palgrave Macmillan, ch. 5 (Skilling the labour force).

Rüling, A. (2003). 'Einleitung: Familienpolitik = Frauenpolitik', *Femina Politica*, 12 (1): 5–14.

Rüling, A. (2008). 'Paradigmatic shifts in the political discourses on childcare for children under the age of three? A comparative study on recent political discourses in England and Germany. Sustainable growth, social inclusion and family policy—innovative ways of coping with old and new challenges'. Subproject of 'The gateway of family and education policy', intermediate report. Available at <http://www.socialpolicy.ed.ac.uk/swsg/publications>, accessed March 2009.

Ruppert, W. (1985). 'Verliert die betriebliche Altersversorgung an Bedeutung?', *Ifo Schnelldienst. Ifo Institute for Economic Research*, (9): 21–3.

—— (1997). 'Ungünstige Bedingungen für die betriebliche Altersversorgung', *Ifo Schnelldienst. Ifo Institute for Economic Research*, 50 (28): 10–19.

—— (2000a). 'Betriebliche Altersversorgung: Neue ifo Erhebung zeigt Stabilisierungstendenzen', *Ifo Schnelldienst. Ifo Institute for Economic Research*, 53 (21/7): 24–32.

—— (2000b). 'Statistik. Welchen Beitrag leistet die betriebliche Altersversorgung heute', *Betriebliche Altersversorgung*, (8): 685–7.

Rürup, B. and Gruescu, S. (2003). *Nachhaltige Familienpolitik im Interesse einer aktiven Bevölkerungsentwicklung*. Berlin: BMFSFJ.

Russell, A. (1991). *The Growth of Occupational Welfare in Britain*. Avebury: Aldershot.

Sabatier, P. A. and Jenkins-Smith, H. C. (eds). (1993). *Policy Change and Learning: An Advocacy Coalition Approach*. Boulder, San Francisco, and Oxford: Westview Press.

Sachverständigenkommission Siebter Familienbericht (2005). *Familie zwischen Flexibilität und Verlässlichkeit. Perspektiven für eine lebenslaufbezogene Familienpolitik*. Berlin: BFSFJ.

Sainsbury, R. and Stanley, K. (2007). *One for All: Active Welfare and the Single Working-age Benefit*. London: Institute for Public Policy Research.

Sattinger, M. (1993). 'Assignment models of the distribution of earnings', *Journal of Economic Literature*, 31 (2): 831–80.

Scharpf, F. and Schmidt, V. (eds.) (2001). *Welfare and Work in the Open Economy: Diverse Responses to Common Challenges*. Oxford: Oxford University Press.

Scheepers, P., Gijsberts, M., and Coenders, M. (2002). 'Ethnic exclusionism in European countries. Public opposition to civil rights for legal migrants as a response to perceived ethnic threat', *European Sociological Review*, 18 (1): 17–34.

Scherer, S. (2001). 'Early career patterns: A comparison of Great Britain and West Germany', *European Sociological Review*, 17 (2): 119–44.

—— (2005). 'Patterns of labour market entry—long wait or career instability? An empirical comparison of Italy, Great Britain and West Germany', *European Sociological Review*, 21 (5): 427–40.

Schludi, M. (2005). *The Reform of Bismarckian Pension Systems. A Comparison of Pension Politics in Austria, France, Germany, Italy and Sweden*. Amsterdam: Amsterdam University Press.

Schmähl, W. (1997). 'The public–private mix in pension provision in Germany: The role of employer-based pension arrangements and the influence of public activities', in M. Rein and E. Wadensjö (eds.), *Enterprise and the Welfare State*. Cheltenham: Edward Elgar, 99–148.

—— (2002). *The '2001 Pension Reform' in Germany—A Paradigm Shift and its Effects*. Bremen: Zentrum für Sozialpolitik.

—— (2003a). 'Dismantling the earnings-related social pension scheme', Zentrum für Sozialpolitik-ZeS-Arbeitspapier 09/2003. Bremen: Zentrum für Sozialpolitik, Universität Bremen.

—— (2003b). 'Private pensions as partial substitute for public pensions in Germany', in G. L. Clark and N. Whitehouse (eds.), *Pension Security in the 21st Century*. Oxford: Oxford University Press, 115–43.

—— (2004). 'Paradigm shift in German pension policy: Measures aiming at a new public–private mix and their effects', in M. Rein and W. Schmähl (eds.), *Rethinking the Welfare State—The Political Economy of Pension Reform*. Cheltenham: Edward Elgar, 153–204.

—— (2007). 'Dismantling an earnings-related social pension scheme: Germany's new pension policy', *Journal of Social Policy*, 36 (2): 319–40.

Schmidt, M. G. (1998). *Sozialpolitik in Deutschland*. Opladen: Leske & Budrich.

Schmidt, V. (2002). *The Future of European Capitalism*. Oxford: Oxford University Press.

Schmitt, C. and Starke, P. (2011). 'Explaining convergence of OECD welfare states: A conditional approach', *Journal of European Social Policy* (forthcoming).

Schneider, H.-P. (1983). 'Zusatzversorgung der Arbeitnehmer im öffentlichen Dienst', in S. Alterssicherungssysteme (ed.), *Darstellung der Alterssicherungssysteme und der Besteuerung von Alterseinkommen. Gutachten der Sachverständigenkommission vom 19.* Bonn: Bundesministerium für Arbeit und Sozialordnung, 211–41.

Schradin, H. A. and Reichenbach, B. (2003). 'Private Alterssicherung in der Bundesrepublik Deutschland'. IFV Mitteilungen: Institut für Versicherungswissenschaft der Universität zu Köln 1/2003, Köln.

Schulze, I. and Jochem, S. (2007). 'Germany: Beyond policy gridlock', in E. M. Immergut, K. M. Anderson, and I. Schulze (eds.), *The Handbook of West European Pension Politics*. Oxford: Oxford University Press, 660–710.

Secretary of State for Work and Pensions (2002). *Simplicity, Security and Choice. Working and Saving for Retirement*. London: The Stationery Office.

Seeleib-Kaiser, M. (1999). 'Globalisierung und Wohlfahrtssysteme: Divergenz, Konvergenz oder divergente Konvergenz?', *Zeitschrift für Sozialreform*, 45: 3–23.

—— and Fleckenstein, T. (2007). 'Discourse, learning and welfare state change: The case of German labour market reforms', *Social Policy & Administration*, 41 (5): 427–48.

—— —— (2009). 'The political economy of occupational family policy: Comparing workplaces in Britain and Germany', *British Journal of Industrial Relations* 47 (4): 741–64.

Sefton, T. (2005). 'Give and take: Public attitudes to redistribution', in A. Park, J. Curtice, K. Thomson et al. (eds.), *British Social Attitudes: The 22nd Report*. London: Sage, 1–32.

Seiter, H. (2002). 'Reform der Zusatzversorgung im öffentlichen Dienst—Altersvorsorgeplan 2001', *BetrAV*, (5): 511–13.

Sell, S. (2004). 'Die Reform der Sozialhilfe und Arbeitsförderung: Entwicklungsprozesse sozialer Unterstützungssysteme, institutionelle Schnittflächen, Synergien und Konkurrenzen'. Paper presented at the E&C-Konferenz: 'Die Chancen der

Arbeitsmarktreform für die soziale Integration von jungen Menschen in E&C-Gebieten', Leipzig, 6–7 December 2004. Available at <http://www.eundc.de/pdf/23002. pdf>, accessed March 2010.

Sevenhuijsen, S. (1998). *Citizenship and the Ethics of Care: Feminist Considerations on Justice, Morality and Politics.* London: Routledge.

Shavit, Y. and Müller, W. (1998). *From School to Work: A Comparative Study of Educational Qualifications and Occupational Destinations.* Oxford: Clarenden Press.

Smith, D. (1999). 'The changing idea of a university', in D. Smith and A. K. Langslow (eds.), *The Idea of a University.* London, PA: Jessica Kingsley, 148–74.

Smith, S. (2006). 'Persistency of pension contributions in the UK: Evidence from the British Household Panel Survey', *Journal of Pension Economics and Finance*, 5 (3): 257–74.

—— Coxon, K., Sigala, M., Sylva, K., Mathers, S., La Valle, I., Smith, R., Purdon, S., Dearden, L., Shaw, J., and Sibieta, L. (2007). *National Evaluation of the Neighbourhood Nurseries Initiative Integrated Report.* London: DfES.

Social Protection Committee (2006). 'Current and prospective theoretical pension replacement rates'. Report by the Indicators Sub-Group (ISG) of the SPC, 19 May 2006. Available at <http://ec.europa.eu/employment_social/social_protection/docs/ isg_repl_rates_en.pdf>, accessed January 2007.

Social Security Select Committee (1999). *Ninth Report 1998–99. Social Security Implications of Parental Leave, HC 543.* London: The Stationery Office.

Sommer, M. (2007). 'Fiskalische Auswirkungen einer Erweiterung des Förderrahmens von Riesterrenten', MEA-Discussion Paper 122–2007, Mannheim: Mannheim Research Institute for the Economics of Aging, Universität Mannheim.

Soskice, D. (1999). 'Divergent production regimes: Coordinated and uncoordinated market economies in the 1980s and 1990s', in H. Kitschelt et al. (eds.), *Continuity and Change in Contemporary Capitalism.* New York: Cambridge University Press, 101–34.

SPD and Bündnis'90/Die Grünen (2002). *Erneuerung—Gerechtigkeit—Nachhaltigkeit. Für ein wirtschaftlich starkes, ökologisches und soziales Deutschland. Für eine lebendige Demokratie.* Available at <http://www.boell.de/downloads/stiftung/2002_Koalitions -vertrag.pdf>. accessed April 2011.

Spence, M. (1973). 'Job market signalling', *The Quarterly Journal of Economics*, 87 (3): 355–74.

Spiegelhalter, F. (1961). 'Rentenreform und betriebliche Altersversorgung'. *Betriebliche Altersversorgung*, 16 (5): 68–74.

Spiess, K., Schupp, J., Grabka, M., Haisken-De New, J., Jakobeit, H., and Wagner, G. (2002). *Abschätzung der (Brutto-)Einnahmeneffekte öffentlicher Haushalte und der Sozialversicherungsträger bei einem Ausbau von Kindertageseinrichtungen. Gutachten des DIW im Auftrag des Bundesministeriums für Familie, Senioren, Frauen, und Jugend.* Berlin: BFSFJ.

Srinivas, P. S., Whitehouse, E., and Yermo, Y. (2000). *Regulating Private Pension Funds' Structure, Performance and Investments: Cross-country Evidence.* Washington DC: World Bank.

Stacey, J. (1996). *In the Name of the Family: Rethinking Family Values in the Postmodern Age.* Boston: Beacon Press.

Stafford, B. (1998). *National Insurance and the Contributory Principle*. London: Department for Work and Pensions.

Starke, P., Obinger, H., and Castles, F. G. (2008). 'In what ways, if any, are welfare states becoming more similar?', *Journal of European Public Policy*, 15 (7): 975–1000.

Statistisches Bundesamt (2009). *Bevölkerung und Erwerbstätigkeit. Bevölkerung mit Migrationshintergrund: Ergebnisse des Mikrozensus 2007*. Wiesbaden: Statistisches Bundesamt.

Stegmann, V. (1986). 'Zahlen über die Entwicklung der Direktversicherung seit 1975', *BetrAV*, 41 (5): 143–4.

Stewart, D., Shamdasani, P., and Rook, D. (2006). *Focus Groups Theory and Practice*. New York: Guilford Press.

Stolz, U. and Rieckhoff, C. (2005). 'Aktuelle Ergebnisse der zulagengeförderten Altersvorsorge. Erste statistische Auswertungen der Zentralen Zulagenstelle für Altersvermögen', *Deutsche Angestellten Versicherung*, 52 (9): 409–16.

Stratigaki, M. (2004). 'The cooptation of gender concepts in EU policies: The case of reconciliation of work and family', *Social Politics*, 11 (1): 30–56.

Streeck, W. (2008). *Re-forming Capitalism. Institutional Change in the German Political Economy*. Oxford: Oxford University Press.

—— and Hassel, A. (2003). 'The crumbling pillars of social partnership', *West European Politics*, 26 (4): 101–24.

Svallfors, S. (1997). 'Worlds of welfare and attitudes to redistribution: A comparison of eight western nations', *European Sociological Review*, 13 (3): 283–304.

—— (2003) 'Welfare regimes and welfare opinions: A comparison of eight western countries', *Social Indicators Research*, 64 (3): 495–520.

—— (2006). *The Moral Economy of Class. Class and Attitudes in a Comparative Perspective*. Stanford, CA: Stanford University Press.

—— (ed.) (2007). *The Political Sociology of the Welfare State: Institutions, Social Cleavages and Orientations*. Stanford, CA: Stanford University Press.

—— (2010a). 'Welfare attitudes in comparative perspective', *The Oxford Handbook of Comparative Social Policy*. Oxford: Oxford University Press (forthcoming).

—— (2010b). 'Public attitudes', in F. G. Castles, S. Leibfried, J. Lewis, H. Obinger, and C. Pierson (eds.), *The Oxford Handbook of the Welfare State*. Oxford: Oxford University Press (forthcoming).

—— and Taylor-Gooby, P. (eds.) (1999). *The End of the Welfare State? Responses to State Retrenchment*. London: Routledge.

Swank, D. (2002). *Global Capital, Political Institutions, and Policy Change in Developed Welfare States*. Cambridge University Press: Cambridge.

Sylva, K. and Pugh, G. (2005). 'Transforming the early years in England', *Oxford Review of Education*, 31 (1): 11–27.

Tapia, W. (2008). 'Comparing aggregate investment returns in privately managed pension funds: An initial assessment', OECD-Working Papers on Insurance and Private Pensions 21. Paris: OECD.

Taylor-Gooby, P. (ed.) (2004). *New Risks, New Welfare*. Oxford: Oxford University Press.

Taylor-Gooby, P. (2005). 'Is the future American? Or, can left politics preserve European welfare states from erosion through growing "racial" diversity?', *Journal of Social Policy*, 34 (4): 661–72.

—— (2008). 'The new welfare settlement in Europe', *European Societies*, 10 (1): 3–24.

—— (2009). *Reframing Social Citizenship*. Oxford: Oxford University Press.

—— Larsen, T., and Kananen, J. (2004). 'Market means and welfare ends: The UK welfare state experiment', *Journal of Social Policy*, 33 (4): 573–92.

—— and Mitton, L. (2008). 'Much noise, little progress: The UK experience of privatisation', in D. Béland and B. Gran (eds.), *Public and Private Social Policy: Health and Pension Policies in a New Era*. Basingstoke: Palgrave Macmillan, 147–68.

Thelen, K. (2003). 'How institutions evolve. Insight from comparative-historical analysis', in J. Mahoney and D. Rueschemeyer (eds.), *Comparative Historical Analysis in the Social Sciences*. Cambridge: Cambridge University Press, 208–40.

Thiel, W. (2005). 'Entwicklung und Tendenzen der Zusatzversorgung im öffentlichen Dienst', *BetrAV*, 4: 344–51.

Timmins, N. (1995). *The Five Giants: A Biography of the Welfare State*. London: Harper Collins.

—— (2009). 'Tories propose fast review of new pensions', *Financial Times* (27 September).

TNS Infratest (2005a). *Situation und Entwicklung der betrieblichen Altersversorgung in Privatwirtschaft und öffentlichem Dienst 2001–2004. Endbericht*. München: TNS Infratest.

—— (2005b). *Alterssicherung in Deutschland 2003 (ASID '03). Zusammenfassung der wichtigsten Untersuchungsergebnisse*. München: TNS Infratest.

—— (2007). *Situation und Entwicklung der betrieblichen Altersversorgung in Privatwirtschaft und öffentlichem Dienst 2001–2006. Endbericht mit Tabellen*. München: TNS Infratest.

—— (2008a). *Situation und Entwicklung der betrieblichen Altersversorgung in Privatwirtschaft und öffentlichem Dienst 2001–2007—Endbericht*. München: TNS Infratest.

—— (2008b). *Alterssicherung in Deutschland 2007 (ASID'07)*. München: TNS Infratest.

Trampusch, C. (2004). 'Vom Klassenkampf zur Riesterrente. Die Mitbestimmung und der Wandel der Interessen von Gewerkschaften und Arbeitgeberverbänden an der betrieblichen und tariflichen Sozialpolitik', *Zeitschrift für Sozialreform*, 50 (3): 223–54.

—— (2005). *Sequenzorientierte Policy-analyse: Warum die Rentenreform von Walter Riester nicht an Reformblockaden scheiterte*. Köln: Max-Planck-Institut für Gesellschaftsforschung.

Treasury (2007). *Aiming High for Children: Supporting Families*. London: HM Treasury.

Tronto, J. (1993). *Moral Boundaries: A Political Argument for an Ethic of Care*. London: Routledge.

Tsebelis, G. (2002). *Veto Players—How Political Institutions Work*. New York and Princeton: Russel Sage Foundation, Princeton University Press.

Turner, E. and Green, S. (2007). 'Understanding policy convergence in Britain and Germany', *German Politics*, 16 (1): 1–21.

Union Pension Service (2003). *UPS Pension Scheme Profiles 2003*. London: UPS.

van Oorschot, W. (2006). 'Making the difference in social Europe: Deservingness perceptions among citizens of European welfare states', *Journal of European Social Policy*, 16 (1): 23–42.

—— and Uunk, W. (2007). 'Multi-level determinants of public's informal solidarity towards immigrants in European welfare states', in S. Mau and B. Veghte (eds.), *Social Justice, Legitimacy and the Welfare State*. Aldershot: Ashgate, 217–38.

Veil, M. (2003). *Alterssicherung von Frauen in Deutschland und Frankreich. Reformperspektiven und Reformblockaden*. Berlin: Sigma.

Verger, J. (1993). 'Zweites Kapitel: Grundlagen. Die Entstehung der Universitäten', in W. Rüegg (ed.), *Geschichte der Universität in Europa. Band 1*. München: Beck, 49–80.

Vincent, C. and Ball, S. J. (2006). *Childcare, Choice and Class Practices. Middle-class Parents and their Children*. Oxon: Routledge.

Voges, W., Jacobs, H., and Trickey, H. (2001). 'Uneven development—local authorities and workfare in Germany', in I. Lødemel and H. Trickey (eds.), *'An Offer you Can't Refuse': Workfare in International Perspective*. Bristol: Policy Press, 71–104.

Wahl, A. von (2008). 'From family to reconciliation policy. How the Grand Coalition reforms the German welfare state', *German Politics and Society*, 26 (3): 25–49.

Warth, L. C. (2008). 'Contested time: Family-friendly working time policy in Germany and the United Kingdom', Ph.D. dissertation. London: London School of Economics and Political Science.

Wein, N. (2002). 'Der Altersvorsorgeplan 2001 und seine Umsetzung bei der VBL', *BetrAV*, (6): 523–5.

Weiß, A. (1955). 'Die Einrichtungen für betriebliche Altersversorgung', *BetrAV*, 10 (4/5): 30–6.

—— and Heubeck, G. (1957). 'Rentenreform und betriebliche Altersversorgung', *Betriebliche Altersversorgung*, 12 (2): 13–18.

Wennemo, I. (1994). *Sharing the Costs of Children: Studies on the Development of Family Support in the OECD Children*. Stockholm: Swedish Institute for Social Research.

Whalley, M. (2008). *Involving Parents in their Children's Learning*, 2nd edition. London: Paul Chapman.

Whitehouse, E. (2000). 'Administrative charges for funded pensions: An international comparison and assessment', *Journal of Applied Social Science Studies*, 120 (3): 311–61.

Whitehouse, G., Haynes, M., MacDonald, F., and Arts, D. (2007). 'Reassessing the "family-friendly workplace": Trends and influences, 1998–2004', *Employment Relations Research Series*, 76. London: Department for Business, Enterprise and Regulatory Reform.

Willenbacher, B. (2007). 'Nationalsozialistische Bevölkerungspolitiken', in D. Auth and B. Holland-Cunz (eds.), *Grenzen der Bevölkerungspolitik. Strategien und Diskurse demographischer Steuerung*. Opladen & Farmingdon Hills: Verlag Barbara Budrich, 37–62.

Williams, L. (2009). 'Fair rewards or just deserts? The present and future of the contributory principle in the UK', *Benefits*, 17 (2): 159–69.

Wilson, G. K. (1990). *Interest Groups*. Oxford: Basil Blackwell.

Wincott, D. (2006). 'Paradoxes of New Labour social policy', *Social Politics*, 13 (2): 286–312.

Wood, S. (2001). 'Labour market regimes under threat? Sources of continuity in Germany, Britain, and Sweden', in P. Pierson (ed.), *The New Politics of the Welfare State*. Oxford: Oxford University Press, 368–409.

Wood, S. J., de Menezes, L. M., and Lasaosa, A. (2003). 'Family-friendly management in Great Britain: Testing various perspectives', *Industrial Relations*, 42: 221–50.

Work and Parents Taskforce (2001). *About Time: Flexible Working*. Available at <http://www.dti.gov.uk/er/individual/flexworking_report.pdf>, accessed February 2005.

Index

Index

Familienzentren 8, 93, 101–6, 108
family
 -friendly policies 85, 101, 110–54
 -friendly working times 110–29, 288
family policy 6, 8–9, 21, 75–109, 114, 122–4,
 127, 130, 137, 141, 143, 282, 287–9
 employment oriented 151, 287, 290
 occupational 129–54, 287
financial markets 2–3, 225, 229, 241
firm-level family policies (see family policy)
flexibility 8, 44, 77, 82, 111, 113, 115, 118–19,
 123, 128, 137, 259, 280, 286, 295–6
flexible working time 111, 130, 136–37, 139,
 142, 145–6, 152, 288
focus group 7, 37–8, 41, 44, 53, 56–8, 60,
 62–3, 65–7, 69–70

globalization 6, 15–16, 19, 29, 32, 34, 51, 75,
 76–8, 157, 178, 180, 204, 284, 292

health (also health care) 4, 6–7, 25–6, 36–7, 42,
 46, 48, 51, 55, 64, 250, 284, 286, 289

immigration 8, 22, 29, 31, 34, 52–4, 58–9,
 60–1, 66–7, 69–71
inclusion 1, 7, 10, 29, 31, 39, 40, 51–6, 65,
 67, 69, 70, 80–1, 96, 110, 113, 119, 126,
 172, 178, 184, 186, 189, 191, 193–96, 199,
 200, 219, 238, 239–42, 285, 293
individual choice 44, 75, 218
individual opportunity 39
individual responsibility 1, 7, 20, 25, 35, 39,
 44, 51
inequality 1, 3–5, 24, 26, 35–6, 77, 84, 102,
 191, 242, 283–4, 286–7, 295
integration 1, 6, 10, 29, 52, 59, 66, 70, 87, 90,
 97, 104, 144, 247, 270, 272, 274, 276–7,
 279, 285–7, 297
International Social Survey Programme
 (ISSP) 23, 26, 30, 35
interventionist state 107, 167
investive social policy 8, 109

Justice in the Welfare State Survey 17, 23

labour market
 inactivity 1, 3, 268
 policy 4, 10, 107, 266–82, 295–6
 programmes 4, 267, 270, 274–6, 278–80,
 294, 296
laziness 39, 41, 59
legitimacy 17, 22, 28–9, 35, 46, 51–2, 82, 84,
 87, 108, 113, 134
liberalism (also liberalisation) 7, 9, 157–8, 185,
 205, 286, 290
liberal market economy 33, 160, 264, 294

liberal regime 19, 92, 159, 178, 181, 293
lone parents 4, 86, 273

making work pay 4, 83, 289
male-breadwinner model 77, 93, 100, 108, 287
maternity leave 79, 82, 115–16, 131–2, 137,
 288–9
means-tested support (also benefits) 3, 178,
 188, 219, 269, 271, 272–4, 276, 291, 294
means-testing 5, 84, 132, 159, 183
multi-pillarism (also multi-pillar system)
 176, 292

New Labour 79–80, 82–4, 110, 112, 114,
 116–19, 125–26, 147
non-state provision 6, 191, 197, 206, 207

obligation 16, 28, 37, 39, 46, 49–50, 65–6, 67,
 83, 87, 89, 122, 163, 276, 279
occupational benefits 2, 134, 145, 161, 168,
 169, 173–6, 179, 291, 292
occupational specificity 10, 245–65

parental leave 21, 82, 116–17, 120, 128–9, 132,
 142, 144, 288
parenting 80, 83, 126, 287
path-dependence 5, 109, 113, 116
pension 2, 4–5, 38, 47, 282
 means-tested 165
 occupational 9, 157–79, 182, 194, 201, 218,
 223, 225, 230, 232, 290–1, 293
 old age 2, 26–7, 46, 221
 personal (also private) 2, 10, 20–1, 34, 42,
 162–3, 165–6, 175, 180–218, 290–2
 policy 5, 6, 9, 158, 177, 181, 183–84,
 188, 192
 public (see state pension)
 reforms 20–1
 retirement 9
 state (also public) 10, 20, 27, 158–9, 161–4,
 166–9, 171–2, 174–8, 182–4, 187–90,
 193–94, 196, 198–200, 201–2, 204–5,
 207, 210, 218–19, 222–3, 225, 227–9,
 231, 237–42, 271, 291–4
 stakeholder 220, 228, 234
perceptions of the welfare state (see attitudes)
population aging 4, 6, 32, 69, 99, 166, 180,
 283, 287, 289, 292
poverty
 child 81, 84, 92, 96, 100–101, 105, 107, 110,
 118, 126
 income 55
 in-work 4
 prevention 2, 8, 101, 107, 113–14, 126
 rate 3, 55, 100, 181
 risk 164, 178, 290, 293